Muslim and British post-9/11

Identities in Reflexive Modernity

Muslim and British post-9/11

Identities in Reflexive Modernity

By
Satoshi Adachi

TRANS
PACIFIC
PRESS

First published in Japanese by Koyo Shobo in 2020 as *Saikiteki Kindai no Aidenteitei Ron: Posuto 9.11 Jidai ni okeru Igirisu no Imin Dainisedai Musurimu.*

This English edition published in 2023 by:
Trans Pacific Press Co., Ltd.
2nd Floor, Hamamatsu-cho Daiya Building
2-2-15 Hamamatsu-cho, Minato-ku,
Tokyo 105-0013, Japan
Telephone: +81-(0)50-5371-9475
Email: info@transpacificpress.com
Web: http://www.transpacificpress.com

© Satoshi Adachi 2023.
Edited by Karl Smith, Melbourne, Australia.
Designed and set by Ryo Kuroda, Tsukuba-city, Ibaraki, Japan.

Distributors

USA, Canada and India
Independent Publishers Group (IPG)
814 N. Franklin Street
Chicago, IL 60610, USA
Telephone inquiries: +1-312-337-0747
Order placement: 800-888-4741 (domestic only)
Fax: +1-312-337-5985
Email: frontdesk@ipgbook.com
Web: http://www.ipgbook.com

Europe, Oceania, Middle East and Africa
EUROSPAN
Gray's Inn House,
127 Clerkenwell Road
London, EC1R 5DB
United Kingdom
Telephone: +44-(0)20-7240-0856
Email: info@eurospan.co.uk
Web: https://www.eurospangroup.com

Japan
MHM Limited
3-2-3F, Kanda-Ogawamachi, Chiyoda-ku,
Tokyo 101-0052
Tel: +81-3-3518-9181
Fax: +81-3-3518-9523
Email: sales@mhmlimited.co.jp
Web: http://www.mhmlimited.co.jp

China
China Publishers Services Ltd.
718, 7/F., Fortune Commercial Building,
362 Sha Tsui Road, Tsuen Wan, N.T.
Hong Kong
Telephone: +852-2491-1436
Email: edwin@cps-hk.com

Southeast Asia
Alkem Company Pte Ltd.
1, Sunview Road #01-27, Eco-Tech@Sunview
Singapore 627615
Telephone: +65 6265 6666
Email: enquiry@alkem.com.sg

All rights reserved. No reproduction of any part of this book may take place without the written permission of Trans Pacific Press.

ISBN 978-1-876843-68-7 (hardback)
ISBN 978-1-920850-09-8 (paperback)
ISBN 978-1-920850-05-0 (eBook)

The publication of this book was supported by a Grant-in-Aid for the Publication of Scientific Research Results (Grant Number 21HP6002), provided by the Japan Society for the Promotion of Science.

To Emare
– my love, my hope, and my all –

From your pappy,
Satoshi, A.

Table of Contents

List of Illustrations vii

Preface to the English Edition viii

Acknowledgements xiii

Introduction xv

Part I Background and Theoretical Framework 1

   1 Muslims in the UK: Double Consciousness,
      Women and Multiculturalism 2

   2 British Muslims: Formation, Politics and Condition 32

   3 Previous Studies and Theoretical Frames 72

   4 Research Outline 102

Part II Analysis and Findings 125

   5 Discrimination, Media and Representation 126

   6 Britishness and Britain as 'Multicultural Space' 154

   7 Differentiating between Culture and Religion 182

   8 Islamic Knowledge and the Internet: The Function of *Ijtihad* 202

   9 Women and Education 230

  10 The Hijab 254

Conclusion: Towards a New Understanding of Islam 290

Appendix A. Attributes of Informants (Female) 306

Appendix B. Attributes of Informants (Male) 308

Bibliography 310

Index 349

List of Illustrations

Figures

2.1 Religious practice by religion 61
2.2 Age structure (Muslim & all population) 61
2.3 Ratios of A$^+$-C attainments in 5 or more subjects in GCSE by ethnicity 63
4.1 Informants by age and gender 116
4.2 Educational qualifications of parents of female informants (London only) 119
4.3 Educational qualifications of parents of male informants (London only) 119
4.4 Educational qualifications of informants (female) 120
4.5 Educational qualifications of informants (male) 120
6.1 Relationship between identification and commitment 157
7.1 Marriage types among informants 196

Tables

2.1 Identification with religion by ethnicity (criterion: ethnicity) 60
2.2 Identification with religion by ethnicity (criterion: religion) 60
2.3 National identity by religion (Christian, Muslim & Sikh) 62
2.4 Educational qualification by age (Muslim & All) 62
2.5 Economic activity by age in women (Muslim, All) 64
2.6 Economic activity by age in men (Muslim, All) 64
4.1 Age of informants 116
4.2 Informants by ethnicity 118
4.3 Employment status of informants (except students) 121
4.4 Marital status of informants 121

Photos

4.1 Coventry Cathedral 103
4.2 Statue of Lady Godiva in the city's central square 103
4.3 Whitechapel Road Market 106
4.4 East London Mosque 107
4.5 East London Mosque after Friday prayers (rear entrance) 107

Preface to the English Edition

The publication of this book evokes special feelings for me. Some people may wonder why a researcher from the Far East with little connection to the UK, South Asia, or Islam conducts and publishes a study of British Muslims. I shall briefly explain the background for writing this book and its theoretical perspective.

In my Ph.D. thesis, I explored post-war British policies on immigration, race relations, and social integration in the context of her historical and social backgrounds, such as the English Civil War, the multi-ethnic state, and the British Empire. Based on the results, I discussed the possibilities and limitations of post-multiculturalism, particularly liberal nationalism, as a political-philosophical theory of social integration in the global age. After completing my Ph.D., my interest shifted from theory and law to the sites and policies of social integration, and I moved on to research social integration policies in the UK, which were being implemented under the framework of community cohesion. In June 2009, I had the opportunity to undertake a research-in-residency in the Institute of Community Cohesion, which was at the forefront of the research on the UK social integration policy.

When I began my residency, Islamophobia in the UK was more intense than today, in the wake of the London terrorist bombings only four years earlier. Terrorist attacks (and attempts), the global war on terror led by the US and the UK, Muhammad cartoon controversies in European countries and other incidents were contributing to the spread of anti-Muslim sentiment. At the same time, far-right forces were gaining influence – the British National Party winning seats in the European Parliament and the formation of the English Defence League, for example. Against this background, young British Muslims' struggles on identity and integration in the UK were drawing more attention, as demonstrated by the publication of former-Islamist Ed Husain's autobiography (Husain 2007) and *Young, British and Muslim* by Philip Lewis (2007), which is a study based on research with young Muslims in North England. In this context, political discourses surrounding the community cohesion policy and shared Britishness targeting the Muslim community began to gain prominence (Adachi 2013b). However, I had a growing sense of incongruity about the discourse of conflicted Muslims as I interviewed and spent time with many young second-generation Muslims, who passionately told me of their faith in Islam while actively engaging in study, work, and interaction with non-Muslims. This experience motivated me to explore young Muslims, who were building identities and participating in society in different ways from the prevailing discourse of post-9/11 Western society.

Doubts about the prevailing discourses about Islam were commonly expressed in interview-based studies on young British Muslims published in the 2010s (Kabir 2010; Contractor 2012; Hoque 2015; Hamid ed. 2018 among others). Although this book shares interests with these preceding studies, it is not trying to gild the lily on them. A substantial proportion of recent research into young Muslims in the UK and Western society has been conducted by Muslims themselves. By utilising their skills and status as insiders, these researchers have been able to present the experiences and identities of young Muslims differently from the dominant discourses and representations. However, these studies contribute little to the theory of contemporary society, as they do not go beyond case studies of Western Muslims. With these issues in mind, this book discusses the identity and social integration of second-generation immigrant Muslims in the UK from the perspective of contemporary social theory.

Their comments and attitudes expressed in interviews were full of surprises, including their strong commitment to Islam, attachment and adaptation to British society, the meaning of wearing or not wearing a hijab, and presentation of Islam as distinct from culture. An insider-researcher might accept some of these responses as self-evident, but to this outsider, everything needed to be explained and analysed.

Social, especially sociological, theories served as projection lines for understanding the interviewees' responses: Taylor's theory of recognition, Goffman's self-presentation theory, Habermas' argument on translation in post-secular society, Giddens' reflexive modernisation theory, and Luhmann's theory of autopoietic systems were all helpful in shedding light on their situation.

Charles Taylor's theory of recognition is the starting point for my discussion (Taylor 1994). Minority groups must struggle for recognition to counter the distorted views of the host society and acquire a more positive form of cultural identity in their own community. Unfortunately, Taylor does not adequately address the environments in which struggles for recognition take place or the strategies surrounding their success or failure. Minority groups face difficulties because they must fight for positive recognition of their identity in the public sphere of the host society, the very space that stigmatises them. This is why Muslims' campaigns concerning the Rushdie Affair in the 1980s failed to gain support in Western society (Geaves 2005).

Erving Goffman investigates the identities of stigmatised groups in terms of a self-presentation strategy (Goffman 1963). He focuses on the strategic ways in which stigmatised people present their identities to maximise their self-interests within a given environment, using or ignoring the cultural values of the dominant society or outmanoeuvring the majority. It is worth noting that such self-presentation strategies are premised on the values of the host society. This is important for second-generation Muslims in the West because social values determine the conditions of recognition given to them.

Translation is a practical means to this end. Jürgen Habermas explains the importance of translation between the sacred and the secular to construct a healthy public sphere in the post-secular age (Habermas 2011). For religion to play a positive role in the modern world, religious teachings must be translated into the language of civil society. Second-generation Muslims born and raised in Western society acquire both the languages of their religion and civil society and translate between them daily. They must present their identity both by referring to Islam and by associating it with the values of civil society. Presenting their religious identity in this way increases their chance of gaining positive recognition in Western society.

Knowledge and interpretation are prerequisites for translation. Anthony Giddens' reflexive modernisation theory focuses on the ways in which expert knowledge changes the relationship between tradition and people (Giddens 1991; 1994). While tradition still forms an important part of people's identities, it is no longer accepted as self-evident as people lead increasingly diverse lifestyles spurred on by globalisation and informatisation. This pushes people to abandon the context-dependent local knowledge in favour of expert knowledge that can persuade a wider range of people. This means that people's lives are becoming more dependent on expert knowledge. Conversely, individuals with high levels of literacy seek to influence the ways of tradition by using their expert knowledge to create new interpretations. This process, which Giddens calls the 'dialectic of control', can be seen in the relationship between Islamic knowledge and today's second-generation Muslims in Britain. As demonstrated by the worldwide Islamisation of the 1970s onward, religious knowledge strengthens individuals' adherence to Islam and promotes religion-based identity formation and physical controls (e.g., scarf-wearing, beard-growing, and prayer). Nevertheless, young second-generation Muslims appear to be increasingly resistant to the practices of their own communities. They are dis-embedding Islam from its traditional understandings and re-embedding it in a form more acceptable to British society through various interpretive practices based on Islamic knowledge.

While previous studies have pointed out the importance of interpretation for young Muslims, this become more evident in the present study, which is based on research conducted in the 2010s when the world made a quantum leap towards the universalisation of information. Individuals from all walks of life gained access to Islamic knowledge according to their needs and abilities thanks to free access to the Internet, a growing number of English-language websites and subtitled video clips about Islam, and the dissemination of information through blogs and other social media provided by both academic and non-academic actors. In addition to informationalisation, increased access to higher education and community-based religious services has enabled second-generation Muslims to interpret Islam according to their individual circumstances. Flexible interpretation of religious doctrines allows them to more easily be Muslims in Western society. The informants' narratives of identity and social life in this study were well thought out and presented in a way that was understandable and acceptable to the author, as an outsider. They exuded conviction in Islam, supported by religious knowledge, and confidence that it could be recognised in democratic and liberal society by translating religious language into secular language.

Translation and interpretation can serve as important keys to resolve a paradox of second-generation Muslims in Western society: the more religious they become, the more integrated they are into society. This can be understood by using the autopoietic social systems theory of Niklas Luhmann. Luhmann explains that the 'openness' of a system to its environment is made possible by its 'closedness' (Luhmann 1984). In other words, a system (i.e., the second-generation Muslim identity) achieves openness (i.e., adaptation to Western society) through its closedness (i.e., reference to Islam).

As mentioned above, this book presents the findings from my research on Muslim identity in post-9/11 Western society and aims to position the case analysis on the front line of contemporary social theories centring on reflexive modernity.

———

News of Queen Elizabeth II's passing in September 2022 arrived while I was writing this preface to the English edition. The Queen has been a very familiar figure to many Japanese partly due to her close ties with Japan's imperial family; my mother, as a primary schoolchild, played pretend crowning with her pet cat as the queen after watching the Queen's coronation on a black and white television. Since her ascendance to the throne in 1952 following her father George VI's short reign, she has been a symbol of Britain's modernisation through the post-war transition from the British Empire to the Commonwealth (Murphy 2022). Her reign coincided with Britain's transition to a multi-ethnic and multicultural society. The ideology of 'subjects of the Queen' played a key role in accepting immigrants from the Commonwealth and the consequent cultural diversification of British society.

Zara Mohammed, Secretary General of the Muslim Council of Britain, commented upon the Queen's death that, 'the Queen was the first monarch to visit a UK mosque during her Jubilee celebrations in 2002. Audiences at events and ceremonies hosted by the royal family reflect the diversity of Britain.' The East London Mosque, one of Britain's largest, praised the Queen's contribution to religious freedom, tweeting: 'The Queen spoke of the value of all faiths, and the healing power of faith to bring together and unite communities. She will be most remembered for her sense of duty and her devotion to a life of service' (Hussein 2022).

King Charles III, who has succeeded his mother, is known to have a deep understanding of Islam and concern for the Muslim community in Britain. He, as a pious Christian, often spoke of his empathy with Islam and called on people to stop discriminating against Muslim communities, commenting that prejudice against Islam 'is a failure which stems, I think, from the straitjacket of history which we have inherited' (Al Jazeera 2022). He visited mosques amid rising Islamophobia across post-9/11 Britain to support the Muslim community and emphasised solidarity with fellow members of British society (BBC 2001; Al Jazeera 2022).

Against this backdrop, the London Central Mosque mourned the Queen's passing and celebrated the ascension of King Charles III, singing *God Save the King* (Murphy 2022). Although not all Muslims welcomed this gesture (5 Pillars 2022), it probably represented the attitude – or its ceremonial expression, at least – of many Muslims rooted in the UK (Misgar 2022).

King Charles III will have a shorter reign than his predecessor, but I hope that he and his royal household will carry out their symbolic function and practical role in making Britain 'home' for a diverse range of people, including Muslims.

27 September 2022

At home in Takarazuka, concerned about the future of my country
on the day of another state funeral

Acknowledgements

Muslim and British post-9/11: Identities in Reflexive Modernity is the English edition of my Japanese-language book published in March 2020. This publication was supported by the Japan Society for the Promotion of Science (JSPS) KAKENHI Grant Numbers JP21HP6002, as well as JP 21K01937 and JP 20H00003. I am very grateful for JSPS's support for my research over the last fifteen years, including the field studies on which this book is based. The Japanese edition of this book won the JSS Award (Book Division) of the Japan Sociological Society in 2021.

This English publication project was made possible by the support of many people. Dr Hideyuki Okano, a former colleague at Kindai University, provided information about the JSPS grant and helped me apply for it. I thank Yuko Uematsu, Managing Director of Trans Pacific Press, for understanding the significance of this book in a short time and agreeing to publish it. Minako Sato and Dr Karl Smith provided me with much support and advice during the translating and editing processes. I also thank Dr Yoshimichi Sato of Tohoku University for introducing me to the publisher. He has provided generous assistance with my research and job seeking on many occasions since I was a postgraduate student.

I had a lot of help in the research field. I conducted my first long-term study in the UK when I was a Visiting Researcher at the Institute of Community Cohesion (iCoCo). I am grateful to Professor Ted Cantle CBE, the Executive Chair of iCoCo, and Dr Harris Beider for giving me an opportunity to conduct research at the leading organisation for social integration policy in the UK. Mark Hinton, Heather Parker, Fatima Hans Mangera, Aya Takeuchi and Minoru Yoshioka of the Foleshillfields Vision Project, a community-based organisation in Coventry, welcomed me and provided many opportunities to fraternise with young Muslim members. Participation in the group's events designed for citizenship education and multicultural dialogue inspired me to undertake this study of young second-generation Muslims. The group also assisted with the first two phases of my interviews. In the London Muslim Centre, which was the main venue for the third and fourth phases of interviews, Salman Farsi, the Media and Communications Officer, was particularly helpful. He understood the significance of my study and facilitated the conduct of interviews in the Centre by negotiating with senior management and transmitting information on Facebook. I was at the Institute of Education, University College London, during the third and fourth phases and received much advice from my supervisor, Dr Hugh Starkey. At every meeting with him, I was secretly delighted to see his mannerism exuding British playfulness and generosity, including his constant smile, sarcastic sense of humour and goodbye wink.

And above all, I would like to extend my gratitude to the real stars of this book, the second-generation Muslim informants who maintain their faith and live strong lives in Western society. Some of them have become friends and discussed many topics from Islamic teachings and Asian family issues to their love stories at parties and dinners. Although most of the informants had limited contact with me, only during the interview sessions, they supported my research by genuinely answering my questions and referring me to new informants. I am not sure if this book will live up to their expectations, but nothing would make me happier as a researcher and a person who spent considerable time in Muslim communities than if they find something in this book that recompenses them for their generous cooperation.

Finally, I thank my family for their support. I learned the 'spirit of self-sufficiency' from my mother Chihoko and father Kenichi, who have run small businesses for five decades. They influenced my career choice as a researcher. In particular, my indefatigable mother, who is back to work at the age of 77 after spending six months in hospital following a stroke two years ago, is the reason for my commitment to researching (Muslim) women who are struggling to overcome difficulties and achieve in society. My older brother Takayoshi, who has fought an intractable illness with the support of his faith, changed my ideological position from an atheistic Marxist to a sociologist who appreciates the functions of religion. He encouraged my interest in Islam. I pray for the happiness of my brother, his wife Toshiko, their son Masayoshi, and daughter Renka.

I lead a nomadic life, moving from one place to another depending on the field of research or work, and am blessed to have my partner Haruna with me to share a happy time together. She also gave birth to our first child during this English publication project, doubling the happiness of my family. My daughter Emare, barely a year old, was the biggest obstacle to the project. Going to work and leaving behind the cutest girl in the whole world – I suspect that she is from the planet '*Kawaii*' – was one of the hardest things to do, and indeed I often interrupted my work for her. This book is infused with my hope that she will grow up healthy and become a globe-trotting woman one day.

I dedicate this book to the women of three generations – Chihoko, Haruna and Emare – with my deepest appreciation and love.

Introduction

In February 2019, 19-year-old British woman Shamima Begum, covered with a black full-body veil, was discovered in a Syrian refugee camp by *The Sunday Times* reporter Anthony Loyd (Loyd 2019). The former student of Bethnal Green Academy, situated in an East London Asian community, flew to Turkey from Gatwick Airport, entering Syria in February 2015 with two classmates, Kadiza Sultana and Amira Abase. Like their friend Sharmeena Begum, who had travelled to Syria before them, the girls left their home country to join the Islamic State of Iraq and the Levant (ISIL) to be 'brides of ISIL'[1]. At the Syrian refugee camp following the collapse of ISIL, Begum told reporters her story and expressed her wish to return to England with her new-born baby – her two other children had already died – while revealing her ambivalence towards both ISIL and England. However, the then Home Secretary Sajid Javid – who has a Muslim background but is not practising – informed her family of the revocation of her British citizenship (Farley 2018)[2]. She was left in the refugee camp with no prospect of repatriation while her baby died of malnutrition.

The case of the three school-girls leaving for Syria had a major impact on me as a researcher living and conducting research on the Muslim community in East London at the time. I had already interviewed many young Muslims by then and could not understand the sentiments of the 15-year-old girl who had gravitated toward extremism, left her life in a developed country, and headed for an unknown land at the risk of her own life whatever her circumstances might have been. I remember a mosque spokesperson in my research field responding with bewilderment to a BBC reporter's questions on this incident.

This book may be of limited use in elucidating the motives of young Muslims who wish to join extremist organisations. Many of the young people I met in my research seemed to be well adapted and felt attached to British society while having faith in Islam at the same time. Although there has been much debate about Muslim youth radicalisation in the political and social arenas, we have few opportunities to listen to the 'voices' of the majority of Muslims who live in British society (Gale and Hopkins 2009: 2). I believe it is more valuable to focus on the wider section of the community who has integrated with British society rather than the radicalised minority to understand Muslims in the UK and Western societies (Bozorgmehr and Kasinitz 2018).

———

In September of 2009, I spent most of my time in a sombre mood at home in the small city of Coventry. After completing my PhD, I took the opportunity to work at the Institute of Community Cohesion in Coventry to research social integration policy in the UK. However, the Institute was an 'empty box' with just administrative staff and few resident researchers. Hence, I had no reason to go there except to check my email.

Then, my life took a turn for the better after a chance meeting with a Japanese in Coventry. He introduced me to the community organisation where he worked. The organisation was well-known for promoting inter-community relations in multi-ethnic inner-city neighbourhoods and offering education on citizenship and multiculturalism for local youth. He invited me to participate in the group's events, which were good opportunities for me to get to know young people, including Muslims. These young Muslims, mostly of Asian background, impressed me[3]. They used the group's office as their gathering spot and interacted with people of their own age irrespective of sex, race and religion. They hosted charity events and engaged in conversations with older white guests. On Fridays, they attended mosque for prayers, then played football with diverse community members (sometimes including me) or went out into town for shopping, coffee or simply to enjoy themselves.

In 2009, when I lived in the UK first time, a debate was raging about immigrants and Muslims. Four years after the 2005 London bombings and one year after the 2008 Lehman Brothers collapse, there was a growing backlash against immigrants, especially Eastern European immigrants whose numbers grew along with the EU expansion, and refugees, a large number of whom the UK had accepted since the 1990s despite controversies. As xenophobia was gathering force, a public re-examination of Britain's self-image as a multicultural society was well underway.

The rise of the British National Party (BNP) symbolised this 'changing tide'. Led by Nick Griffin, the BNP gained two seats in the European Parliament in 2009, making headlines as the first far-right political party in Britain to enter the political mainstream (Adachi 2008a; 2013b: 46–47)[4]. Griffin was known for his anti-immigrant and especially anti-Islam attitude and made a strong call for their removal. For example, he told a Channel 4 interviewer:

> Western values, freedom of speech, democracy and rights for women are incompatible with Islam, which is a cancer eating away at our freedoms and our democracy and rights for our women and something needs to be done about it. (Newman 2009)

Griffin's most controversial moment occurred when he appeared on BBC's political talk show *Question Time*. Many argued that the appearance of the

xvi

leader of a far-right political party on a respected television show was tantamount to giving social approval to the party (Ellinas 2010: 32). Thousands of people gathered in front of the BBC building to protest his appearance, which turned violent and resulted in several arrests.

However, I could not help but juxtapose the youth with whom I was in daily contact with the image of Muslims portrayed in the media: political mayhem; Griffin's alarmist claims about immigration and the threat of Islam; reports of terrorism, forced marriages, honour killings; Muslim youth protesting, sometimes violently, against the British and American governments; and representatives of various Islamic organisations explicitly denying women's rights[5]. Unlike arguments in mainstream political discourse, it seemed that the young people I met in poor inner-city neighbourhoods did not feel a conflict between 'living in British society' and being Muslim despite their social and economic hardships. This observation derives from my experience as an individual living in Muslim communities rather than as a researcher.

Accordingly, the issue I decided to tackle as a researcher was not found among the questions surrounding the (im)possibility of social integration such as '*Can* Muslims fit in British society?' or '*Can* Western society and Islam coexist?' (Mori ed. 2006). Instead, my focus was on the logic or strategies used by young Muslims to integrate with British society; '*How* is being Muslim and being British compatible?' or '*What logic* do young Muslims use to make it possible?'. This simple line of questions emanating from my personal experience was the starting point of this book.

————

Muslim and British post-9/11: Identities in Reflexive Modernity is a sequel to my Japanese publication *Riberaru Nashonarizumu to Tabunka Shugi – Igirisu no Shakai Togo to Musurimu (Liberal Nationalism and Multiculturalism: Social Integration Policy and Muslims in Britain)* (Keisoshobo), published in December 2013 (Adachi 2013b). Both the earlier and current volumes shared the same research interest, social integration of Muslims in post-9/11 Britain, but the former had more emphasis on philosophy, politics and policy. In contrast, the current volume focuses on the voices of Muslims themselves, which were not fully developed in the previous work, and analyses the identities of second and later generation immigrant young Muslims in the post-9/11 era to discuss their integration into society.

Through this book, I hope to share with a broader readership the wonder I experienced in this research and offer some academic value.

Note

1 Eight school girls from Bethnal Green Academy, including Begum, travelled to Syria in 2014.

2 Although Begum is of Bangladeshi descent, she has no Bangladeshi nationality. The Bangladeshi government expressed bewilderment at Home Secretary Javid's decision by stating, 'She is a British citizen by birth and has never applied for dual nationality with Bangladesh' (John 2019). Begum was entitled to challenge the British government's decision and her situation remained uncertain at the time of writing (July 2019).

3 In the British context, 'Asian' refers to people of South Asian descent, i.e., Indian, Pakistani and Bangladeshi. While the situation is changing due to a recent increase in the Chinese population, 'Asian' in the present volume refers to people with roots in these three countries.

4 This direction was carried on into the 'UK Independence Party (UKIP) whirlwind' and led to the 2016 Referendum in favour of the movement to withdraw from the EU, so-called 'Brexit', embroiling the ruling Conservative Party.

5 One prominent image of violent Muslims was the 2006 London protest over the Danish cartoon controversy. Many young Muslims marched carrying placards with aggressive slogans criticising Western countries' responses to the cartoon. Placards with messages such as 'Massacre those who insult Islam', 'Freedom go to hell', 'Be prepared for the real holocaust' and 'Europe you will pay, your 9/11 is on the way' attracted wide media coverage. While this protest was later denounced by the leaders of some Islamic organisations, it contributed significantly to the negative images of British Muslims (Christensen 2010).

PART I

Background and Theoretical Framework

Chapter

1

Muslims in the UK: Double Consciousness, Women and Multiculturalism

The problem of the twentieth century is the problem of the color-line, – the relation of the darker to the lighter races of men in Asia and Africa, in America and the islands of the sea.

The Souls of Black Folk
by W.E.B. Du Bois (2020: 7)

Situations will continue to arise where ancient Eastern established cultural and religious ethics clash with the spirit of twenty-first century children of a new generation and Western ideas.

Lord McEwan cited in
'Forced Marriage Annulled' (BBC 2002)

Young Muslims in the UK and double consciousness

In 1903, W. E. B. Du Bois condemned widespread racism faced by African American citizens in the US, where discrimination against Black people formed part of everyday life and institutionalised racial segregation lingered long after slavery. In addition, by criticising Black leaders who yielded or made concessions to white-supremacist society, he applauded the great souls of African Americans while demanding radical inter-racial equality. In the process, Du Bois raised the problem of 'double consciousness' afflicting African Americans:

> [T]he Negro is a sort of seventh son, born with a veil, and gifted with second-sight in this American world, – a world which yields him no true self-consciousness, but only lets him see himself through the revelation of the other world. It is a peculiar sensation, this double-consciousness, this sense of always looking at one's self through the eyes of others, of measuring one's soul by the tape of a world that looks on in amused contempt and pity. One ever feels his twoness, – an American, a Negro; two souls, two thoughts, two unreconciled strivings; two warring ideals in one dark body, whose dogged strength alone keeps it from being torn asunder. (Du Bois 2020: 2)

Du Bois' insight into the 'double consciousness' of Black Americans in the early twentieth century – the act of 'always looking at one's self through the eyes of others, of measuring one's soul by the tape of a world that looks on in amused contempt and pity' – may also apply to the consciousness of Muslims living in twenty-first-century Western society.

The September 11 attacks were a series of spectacular events that implanted this double consciousness more firmly.[1] On 11 September 2001, two aircraft from Boston bound for Los Angeles crashed into the Twin Towers in New York carrying full jet fuel tanks and terrified passengers. The World Trade Center Towers caught fire and collapsed. More than 3,000 people – including many Muslims – lost their lives (Abbas 2005: 3). Two other planes were also hijacked; one crashed into the Pentagon building (Department of Defense headquarters) and the other crashed in a field near Shanksville, Pennsylvania. The events which came to be known as 9/11 happened over a period of less than ninety minutes, and given its impact in global politics, the significance of its 'simultaneity' lies in not just the short intervals between the attacks but rather the fact that people around the globe simultaneously

Chapter 1

experienced the event through the media. As a result of this simultaneity, people (Muslims and non-Muslims) came to share a unique consciousness linked with global politics, which can be called 'post-9/11 experiences'. It began when the Bush administration announced the War on Terror shortly after 9/11 and embarked on a campaign to defeat Osama bin Laden-led al Qaeda and its ally, the Taliban in Afghanistan. Since then, Western society has associated Islam with 'extremism' or 'terrorism'.

Particularly in the UK, the second-generation Muslim immigrants (hereafter called 'second-generation Muslims') and their youth are perceived as vulnerable to extremist influences (Gove 2006; Husain 2007; Blunkett 2016).[2] Since the 1990s when various statistics began to include questions about religion, it has become commonly accepted that religion is a significant force in defining young Muslim identity (Modood 1997). At the time, identification with Islam did not assume the positive meaning, such as piousness or morality. Instead, it was gradually reframed as evidence of extremism which openly sought revenge on secular and democratic society, often violently. The media plays a crucial role in creating such images of Muslims (Morey and Yaqin 2011). It serves a daily dose of media coverage on conservative tendencies among young Muslims (e.g., veil, beard, anti-democratic attitude and support for conservative gender norms), extremism ingrained in the community and young people's gravitation toward it, or people denouncing the British and US governments in the name of God (Mirza et al. 2007; Husain 2007; Channel 4 2010). Such media coverage often portrays women covering their head with a scarf or veil as victims of patriarchal marriage relations such as 'forced' or 'arranged marriage' and bearded men as dangerous fanatics who turn their back on secular law and democracy while demanding a *sharia* (Islamic law)-based social system (Dwyer 1998; Archer 2001). Consequently, young second-generation Muslims have become 'new folk devils', who evoke 'moral panics' in British society (Alexander 2004; Richardson 2010; Shain 2011).[3]

These discourses doom second-generation Muslims in the West to the shackles of double consciousness. Even though they are born and raised in Western society and enjoy its culture and lifestyle, they are constantly subjected to public doubts about their allegiance to society. Everything Muslims say and do has been watched, examined and criticised through the frames of terrorism and anti-democracy since 9/11:

> 9/11 has really put pressure on us, not because we're Pakistani, but as Muslims. Government's always questioning everything we do, these days. What goes on in mosques, in homes, in schools – everywhere. It's like

us, as Muslims, we're Public Enemy Number One. It gets to you. It's bound to get to you. You try to shrug it off but it keeps coming back at you, keeps getting worse. (Alam 2006: 211)

The above lament of a young man from Bradford, an iconic city of Britain's Asian Muslim communities, is a common reflection of what young Muslims in Western society experience in the post-9/11 era.

Despite 'othering' in the Western social and political spaces, many Muslims, especially the second-generation youth, show a strong commitment to the country in which they were born and raised (PRC 2011; MCB 2015; Bozorgmehr and Kasinitz eds. 2018). They have been participating in all domains, including education, labour, community and politics, as citizens of Western society. They enjoy their rights and fulfil their duties in society while preserving their faith, although such commitment could cause a sense of relative deprivation and contribute to their discontent.

So, what kind of relationship do young second-generation Muslims in the West form with their society of birth and upbringing, and how do they manage their complex identity – or double consciousness – in the post-9/11 environment? This book focuses on young second-generation Muslims in the UK and analyses their identity and state of social integration.

The research questions in this book are as follows. How do today's young British Muslims define 'being Muslim' in non-Islamic society and participate in such society? How do they balance 'being Muslim' and 'being British' in the face of complex, sometimes contradictory, social expectations, and what are their strategies to deal with such potential conflicts? How does the seemingly rigid and closed Islamic identity combine with the desired values of Western society? What impact will arguments regarding Muslim identity and integration have on the controversy over multiculturalism (or its failure) in Europe? What is the appropriate theory to explain the identity of second-generation Muslims in British society?

This book will approach these questions by analysing interview data collected from young second-generation Muslims in the UK, drawing upon the identity theory of reflexive modernity.

Women's bodies and politics

In considering the above questions about social integration and identity, another important theme in this book is women's 'agency'. Discourses surrounding the integration of Muslims in Western society often revolve around women's agency and the autonomy of their bodies.

Chapter 1

The slogan of second-wave feminism, 'the personal is political', applies to the female body (Hanisch [1969] 2006). A woman's body symbolises her social and cultural identity and is indivisibly linked to the ideal of good social order (Yuval-Davis and Anthias 1989; Bhimji 2009: 2). In many societies, women's bodies and identities are under the control of the community, society or government – which are often dominated by men – and their appearance and conduct manifest as objects that are socially and politically debated, defined and controlled (Rose 2001; Ali and Hopkins 2012: 144). Particularly in contemporary society, the body and identity of the 'Muslim woman' are subjected to such political debate (Khan 1995; Hermansen and Khan 2009; Dwyer and Shah 2009; Rashid 2014).

In Western society, the Muslim woman's body and identity have come to be placed at the forefront of political debate over security and citizenship (Rashid 2014). The 9/11 terrorist attacks on New York in 2001 led to the invasion of Afghanistan (2001) and Iraq (2003), spearheaded by US and UK forces. It was initially defined as 'the war on terror' before being gradually repositioned as 'the war for democracy', especially after claims of the existence of weapons of mass destruction were disproved, undermining the early justifications for the Iraq war. The media and politicians used the image of veil-covered women to justify the war (El-Wafi 2006). In short, it was claimed that undemocratic Islamic states oppressed Muslim women and it was the duty of Western nations to liberate them, even by force (Bush 2001).

Women's liberation politics are increasingly significant in discourses on multiculturalism in Western societies (Pitcher 2009). Multiculturalism was an important integration principle for increasingly multicultural and multi-ethnic societies, particularly in the Anglosphere, since the latter half of the twentieth century (Kymlicka 1995). Especially in the UK, local multiculturalism in conjunction with anti-racism was thought to (partially) guarantee the cultural needs and recognition of minority communities and contribute to their integration (Modood 2013). However, since 9/11 and the London bombings on 7 July 2005 (hereafter referred to as '7/7'), multiculturalism has been perceived and criticised as 'multi-divisionism' breaking up society (Goodhart 2004; Council of Europe 2008; Cantle 2015). This criticism has been linked to concerns over women's rights. Opponents of multiculturalism perceive some oppressive customary practices such as religious costumes, spatial or social segregation of women, circumcision and arranged marriage to be preserved under the name of multiculturalism. They argue that multiculturalism confers on community leaders, who are men in most cases, an authority for them to impose certain customs on women and legitimises women's oppression on the pretext of 'preserving culture' (Phillips 2007). The scarf and veil worn by Muslim women are often interpreted as examples of undemocratic values and symbols of 'gender apartheid' as well as symptoms of fundamentalism or extremism (Abu-Lughod 2002; Ahmed 2005; Wadud 2006). Na'ima Robert, a converted Muslim in the UK, describes this situation as follows:

> Catching sight of a Muslim woman on Western city streets, covered from head to toe, rarely fails to provoke a strong reaction. Feelings of shock, horror, repulsion or pity are not uncommon, especially upon seeing this strangest of sights for the first time. Comments range from the patronizing ('Poor woman, doesn't she know she's in England now, she doesn't have to dress like that?') and the insulting ('It makes me sick to see them dressed like that!') to the ridiculous ('I bet she looks like a dog under there!'). (Robert 2005: 13)

These perceptions have drawn many criticisms, especially from Muslim women (Mahmood 2005; Bullock 2007; Poynting 2009). Those women identify with Islam wilfully and by choice, subjectively engaging with religious teachings and practices and selectively incorporating them into their own lives. For them, identifying with Islam is a democratic process by which they take back control of their bodies from both the government and their communities (Bhimji 2009; Amer 2014).

Without understanding the reality of these Muslim women who identify with Islam, it is difficult to discuss various issues concerning integration in pluralistic society – for example, the relationship between religion and the secular world, Muslim adaptation to Western society, and the future of multiculturalism. We must remember that Muslim women are neither 'passive objects' nor 'victims' in social and political discourses about their bodies but are rather 'active subjects' who participate in these discourses through everyday practice (Bhimji 2012: 30). Second-generation Muslim women in Western society are 'political agents' who stand up against media-created images of Muslim women, resist social and cultural status imposed on them, and negotiate roles and identities in their own religious and cultural communities to participate in broader society.

Such agency is not the monopoly of women who engage in social movements or political activism (Lichter 2009). In fact, many Muslim women challenge the status and definition given to them – oppressed/subservient bodies – through their response to questions about identities and their self-presentation in public and private spaces such as school, workplace and family in Western society. In this environment, their identities are (re)considered and (re)formed.

Chapter 1

While this book deals with young second-generation Muslims including males, one of its aims is to 'demystify' the myths about Muslim women by focusing on the relations between faith and agency (Contractor 2012).

Identity politics: Ontological security, multiculturalism and hybridity

In addition to practical issues such as the integration of second-generation Muslims in the UK and politics surrounding women's bodies, this book will deal with theoretical issues around identity in a multicultural society. This section investigates the background to identity debates, and outlines the functions of identity and theoretical issues that arise in analysing and understanding second-generation Muslims in contemporary Western society.

According to Nimmi Hutnik, there are two main approaches to address identity in social sciences. One is to explain identity from the viewpoint of 'a sense of personal distinctiveness, personal continuity and personal autonomy'. The other is to examine its formation based on 'the dialectic between the individual and society' (Hutnik 1985: 298). Although these two approaches are analytically distinct, they are nevertheless inseparably linked in arguments around identity.

This point is prominent in an analysis by psychologist Erik Erikson, who made identity one of the central themes in the social sciences. Erikson was interested in the function and formation of identity. He analysed correspondence in which Sigmund Freud had written about the experiences and conflicts of the Jewish people and explained the importance of 'a *subjective sense* of an *invigorating sameness* and *continuity*' found in identity. According to Erikson, Freud described 'the safe privacy of a common mental construction' of the Jews as 'inner identity'. It is something inside the individual, stemming from a common sense deeply rooted in the culture, history and experience of the Jews as a people (Erikson 1994: 19–21). Accordingly, identity can be understood as a state in which 'an individual's link with the unique values, fostered by a unique history of [her/][4]his people' (Erikson 1956: 57) is present. Freud was somehow able to live 'the difficult course' of his life because he discovered this link (Freud 2001: 274).

Identity in Erikson's work can be understood as an anxiety-controlling mechanism, reinforcing a sense of trust, predictability and control against internal and external changes (Kinnvall and Nesbitt-Larking 2009: 310). Identity is not simply the cognitive function to comprehend 'who I am' but also provides moral guidance on 'how I should live' amid fundamental uncertainty, which originates from human's 'thrownness': the sense of being thrown into an undefined world (Heidegger 1927). Sociologist Anthony Giddens called this function of identity 'ontological security', referring to 'the confidence that most human beings have in the continuity of their self-identity and in the constancy of the surrounding social and material environments of action' (Giddens 1990: 92). Ontological security is a sense of continuity linking the future (i.e., an unknown and uncertain future) and the present (or the past), or the ground for a sense of 'fundamental trust' in the world and others. Only through this fundamental trust, one can find order and the course of life in the uncertain world and grasp opportunities for fulfilment in life (Woodward 2004: 39). Conversely, ontological insecurity through identity 'diffusion' leads to crises in one's social life.

For this reason, identity requires a social anchor in which a self is situated (Taylor 1979). Forming identity is an act of identification, and needs an object to connect the self to the world. While identity 'psychologically as well as logically, is a *reflexive* relation, a relation of myself to myself', one can 'relate to myself' only through the medium of 'interaction with others *and with the world*' (Caws 1994: 378). 'Community' is often perceived as such a medium (Delanty 2003). A community, be it local, national or global, is a social space offering 'culture' or 'values' that disclose the meaning of the world and provide codes of conduct to those who belong to it. It points to a superindividual continuity that existed before an individual was born and is expected to continue after her or his death. Culture refers to 'a body of beliefs and practices in terms of which a group of people understand themselves and the world and organize their individual and collective lives' (Parekh 2006: 2–3). One is born and raised in some kind of cultural community and acquires a (more or less) consistent framework or code of conduct for understanding the relationship between oneself and the world through one's interactions with others; this becomes crystallised as identity. Therefore, the question 'Who am I/are we?' is equivalent to the expressions 'How should I/we act?' or 'Who do I/we want to be?' (Taylor 1989).

These characteristics of identity make it easy to understand how it is 'political' (Taylor 1994). People may be able to choose identities or markers to which they can form attachments. Nevertheless, people are not free to decide what meaning their choices can have, because identity and its meanings are formulated in dialogues with others in private/public arenas (May 1999). However, dialogues are not always in relationships between equals. More often than not, they occur combatively or strategically in unequal power relations between majority and minority (Du Bois 2020; Erikson 1994; Taylor 1994). In the modern 'nation-state' based on the ideal of an 'integrated

Chapter 1

society', minorities are under constant pressure to share in national identity and conversely their own cultural identities, values and representations are deemed inferior, subjected to destruction, or excluded from public spaces as 'other'. In response, some minority groups overconform to mainstream society and others break away from it to form 'identity spaces' based on their own values and representations. Inside these spaces, people can avoid the biased recognition of mainstream society and its resultant double consciousness, and form 'identity groups to which a person could "belong"', unequivocally and beyond uncertainty and doubt' to ensure ontological security (Hobsbawm 1994: 428). This is a reason that multiculturalism as a political movement is required. If a culture or group is indispensable to healthy identity formation, its protection can be normatively justifiable.

This explains why identity is frequently deployed by elites (Gurr 1986; van Dijk 1993). As identity defines the way individuals and groups relate to the world, elites try to exploit it to manipulate people to support their particular views and actions. Symbols are used for that purpose. Symbols are 'objects, acts, relationships, or linguistic formations that stand *ambiguously* for a multiplicity of meanings, evoke emotions and impel men to action' (Cohen 1974: 23) and are often retrieved from history or constructed for political mobilisation. As Abner Cohen points out, 'political man – shrewd, calculating, utilitarian – also have to be symbolist man – idealist, altruistic, non-rational' (Cohen 1979: 88). National leaders and ethnic-community leaders attempt to evoke specific identities for the benefit of themselves or their communities by invoking symbolic tools (e.g., history, heroins/heroes and scriptures). And certain identities are formed through such mobilisation and negotiation (e.g., imagined communities and politics of recognition). These symbols are also used by opposing groups toward one another. Some groups attempt to stigmatise other groups by associating them with particular representations or symbols. These symbols infer moral attributes in many cases and are used to assert one group's superiority explicitly or implicitly by characterising the other group as amoral.

Multiculturalism has been criticised both theoretically and politically for an overly rigid and essentialist understanding of culture and culture-based identity (Sen 2006; Phillips 2007). Doubts have been expressed about the multiculturalist argument that culture is an authentic thing whose essence outlives historical changes and hence needs to be conserved. For example, 'culture' in multiculturalist demands for recognition is portrayed as being more powerful and rigid than actual everyday cultural practices. Anne Phillips describes this situation as 'the ironies of the multicultural project' (Phillips 2007: 25). The irony, for Phillips, is that 'culture' comes to have a clear outline/boundary only when it is delineated by a spokesperson and not the other way around (Phillips 2007: 82).[5] The formulation of 'culture' by minority groups (Gurr 1986; van Dijk 1993) tends to provoke fierce attacks from both cultural conservatives (Bloom 1987) and egalitarian liberals (Barry 2001; Goodhart 2004). Multiculturalism has been criticised for generating 'identity politics' in which various cultural groups wage cultural war in the name of 'political correctness' and thus bring about sectarian division.[6] Identity politics reportedly undermines the minimum moral common ground required to negotiate or reach a compromise between different groups and thus ironically preserves the actual class and racial inequalities which it set out to address (Gitlin 1995; Barry 2001).[7] Another criticism of multiculturalism is that recognition of a cultural group can lead to the oppression of individual members of that group. A typical expression of this view is Susan Okin's provocative question: 'Is multiculturalism bad for women?' (Okin 1999; Cohen et al. eds. 1999). From the perspective of a particular type of feminism, demands for the preservation of cultural practices and traditions reinforce men's authority over women (Phillips 2007: 26).

More recently, the theoretical and political currents around identity tend to emphasise its openness (Adachi 2018). From this perspective, identity is not a solid construct designed by elites or spokespeople but rather something more variable that changes according to the choices people make in a globalised diverse cultural environment. It is also porous. No socially and spatially inviolable communities exist in today's globalised world (Sen 2006). In national or global social spaces, communities are open and forced to receive different people and values. This is increasing the porosity and hybridisation of identity (Bhabha 1994). It is hybrid not only in the sense that it comprises multiple identities linked by 'hyphens' but also in the sense that 'we have to imagine the addition of hyphenated identities, with each new one qualifying the one before' (Walzer 2004: 134). Here, apart from a community elite's demands or the majority's expectations, the form or meaning of one's identity becomes more aligned with personal interests and lifestyle (Hall 1987; 1991; [1989]1996). When standing on this understanding of identity, the state should enhance people's autonomy to manage their own lives as well as promote communication to enable interpenetration and mutual understanding between different communities, instead of giving official recognition to cultural groups (Cantle 2001; Sen 2006; Council of Europe 2008).

The above discussion can be summarised as follows. First, identity serves the important function of ensuring unity of self and engagement with the world. Second, cultural communities act as 'anchors' or 'sources', which secure the consistency of identity. Third, minority groups face

Chapter 1

difficulties in forming stable and positive identities through prejudice and discrimination from mainstream society. Fourth, this gives rise to the need for multiculturalism as an identity politics. Fifth, there are concerns that the cultural essentialism perceived to be inherent to multiculturalism leads to the secession of minority communities from mainstream society and the oppression of individuals, especially women, who are disadvantaged in their communities. Hence, sixth, it is argued that identity-based multiculturalist projects should be replaced by policies that promote more flexible and open identities, such as hybridity.

This general sketch of relations between identity and politics forms a theoretical background that is crucial for examining social integration among second-generation Muslims in the UK today. The next two sections will show that multiculturalism has been under fire because it promotes closed identities and has led to calls for policies to build more plural and open identity in the debate on the social integration of British Muslims.

The discourse on the failure of multiculturalism

The 'identity and social integration of young Muslims' is an important political and social theme in the UK, and Western societies more generally (Adachi 2009; 2011d; 2013a; 2013b). In the UK, two incidents in 2001 – the 9/11 terrorist attacks in the US and a spate of riots involving Asian youth in northern England – cast doubt about the integration of Muslims in secularised contemporary society. The London bombings on 7 July 2005 deepened this doubt. The 7/7 event was particularly impactful in Britain not only because it was 'our 9/11' (Guardian 2005) but also because it was perpetrated by 'home-grown' terrorists – three of the four perpetrators were from Leeds in northern England. The terrorists were born and raised in the UK and enjoyed its culture and lifestyle (BBC 2011). Nevertheless, they hated British society and its values and tried to replace them with Islamic law and morals through violence (Watson 2017). One of the perpetrators Mohammad Sidique Khan offered the following justification for his action:

> Your democratically elected governments continuously perpetuate atrocities against my people all over the world. And your support of them makes you directly responsible, just as I am directly responsible for protecting and avenging my Muslim brothers and sisters. Until we feel security, you will be our targets. And until you stop the bombing,

gassing, imprisonment and torture of my people we will not stop this fight. (BBC 2005)

This young man, who was born, graduated from university and had family in the UK, called people living in a faraway place (e.g. Afghanistan or Iraq) 'my people' whereas he called British people with whom he had daily contact 'you', clearly not regarding them as his compatriots.

The London bombings and the fact that they were perpetrated by home-grown terrorists intensified the 'failure of multiculturalism' discourse. Multiculturalism is a political ideology, which was born of the civil rights movement in the US and gained social influences to correct inequalities and injustices based on colonial history (Minamikawa 2021).[8] As discussed in more detail in Chapter 2, it was introduced to the UK during the 1960s when racial problems were surfacing as political issues (Bleich 2003). In the 1980s, multicultural policies were implemented at the local level in many areas with Muslim communities, while assimilationism was emphasised at the national level (Adachi 2011a; 2011b; 2013b: 112–5). Multiculturalism made significant inroads especially in educational facilities, where a series of policies for Muslims were implemented: offering halal food at schools, opting out of Christian worship, offering Islamic studies and allowing headscarves as part of uniforms. However, the London bombings became a catalyst for a dramatic upsurge of doubts about multiculturalism.[9]

What followed was the discourse of the 'death' or 'failure' of multi-culturalism (Bagguley and Hussain 2008: 159). This discourse ascribes the non-integration and radicalisation of Muslims to multiculturalism.[10] For instance, an article in *The Daily Mail*, 'Whatever Happened to Free Speech Britain?', offers the following critique:

> For years, this Government has actively promoted multiculturalism, encouraged Muslim 'ghettoes' and set its face against greater integra-tion. Anyone who dared to question this new apartheid was routinely denounced as a 'racist'… [I]t became an article of faith for the ethnic minorities to celebrate their own languages, culture and traditions, at the expense of shared values. There could hardly be a more effective recipe for division. (Mail Online 2006)

This article in the conservative tabloid newspaper claims that multiculturalism has engendered 'cultural apartheid' and divided society.[11] This reaction was common across the left-right ideological spectrum (Adachi 2013b: 62–6).[12]

13

Chapter 1

Politicians, policy leaders and spokespersons from the ruling New Labour Party were vocal critics of multiculturalism at the time.[13] For example, Trevor Phillips, head of the Commission for Racial Equality, which was closely associated with New Labour and used to champion multiculturalism, argued that '"anything goes" multiculturalism... leads to deeper division and inequality' in his post-7/7 address entitled 'Sleepwalking to Segregation' (Phillips 2005).

> We've emphasised what divides us over what unites us. We have allowed tolerance of diversity to harden into the effective isolation of communities, in which some people think special separate values ought to apply... [W]e are sleepwalking our way to segregation. We are becoming strangers to each other, and we are leaving communities to be marooned outside the mainstream. (Phillips 2005)

Even more noteworthy was a comment by Ruth Kelly, the first minister for the Department for Communities and Local Government which had been established for the social integration of immigrants and minorities after 7/7. She stated that 'We have moved from a period of near uniform consensus on the value of multiculturalism' and called for an 'honest debate' 'by questioning whether it is encouraging separateness' (Guardian 2006).

The failure of multicultural discourse was pronounced more clearly by Prime Minister David Cameron of the Conservative Party who came to power in 2010.

> Under the doctrine of state multiculturalism, we have encouraged different cultures to live separate lives, apart from each other and apart from the mainstream. We've failed to provide a vision of society to which they feel they want to belong. We've even tolerated these segregated communities behaving in ways that run completely counter to our values. (Cameron 2011)

Cameron named multiculturalism as the 'deep cause' of segregated communities, oppression of women and radicalism and renounced it to the world. Criticism of multiculturalism had become common among political leaders in the West, including Angela Merkel of Germany, Nicolas Sarkozy of France, John Howard of Australia and Jose Maria Aznar of Spain (Mail Online 2011). Such critiques primarily targeted Islam and positioned Muslims at the core of insecurities about immigration, terrorism, criminality and delinquency (Wieviorka 2012: 228).

14

From multiculturalism to interculturalism and liberal nationalism

The discourse of the failure of multiculturalism declared that official recognition of diverse cultures and identities was an inappropriate integration model for a multicultural, multi-ethnic and multifaith British society. In response, the UK government proposed two complementary policy ideologies based on different identity models: 'interculturalism' and 'liberal nationalism' (Adachi 2013b; 2020a).

The concept of interculturalism developed in continental Europe and Canada during the 1990s as an alternative model to the UK/US multiculturalism. It is a philosophical principle aiming for mutual learning and understanding, acculturation and shared civic values through reciprocal exchanges between different cultures (Bouchard and Taylor 2008; Council of Europe 2008; James 2008; Meer and Modood 2012; Bouchard 2012).[14] This model emphasises 'communication' and 'shared universal values (based on human rights norms)'.

In the European context, interculturalism was laid out in the *White Paper on Intercultural Dialogue* published by the Council of Europe in 2008.[15] According to the white paper, 'diversity and tolerance' alone (as emphasised by multiculturalism) cannot promote positive relations and integration among different peoples amid growing ethnic and cultural diversity; what is crucial is the promotion of intercultural dialogue, which is 'an open and respectful exchange of views between individuals and groups with different ethnic, cultural, religious and linguistic backgrounds and heritage' (Council of Europe 2008: 17). In the absence of intercultural dialogue, there is a danger that cultural groups develop hostile prejudices against one another, leading to insecurity and tension. By contrast, intercultural dialogue reduces such prejudice and insecurity by fostering an open attitude toward other cultures and enabling people to learn 'democratic values' that bind diversified European societies together. Consequently, interculturalism calls for communication between different cultural groups with resultant acculturation, the development of mutual consideration and respect, and a common understanding of universal human rights (James 2008).

Liberal nationalism was widely embraced as a social integration principle in Western countries during the 2000s (Tamir 1993; Kymlicka 2001; Adachi 2013b). The 1990s saw increasing political and economic globalisation following the end of the Cold War and the birth of the European Union, which accelerated widespread cross-border movements of information, people, and culture. One of the policy principles that emerged to deal with

Chapter 1

unprecedented levels of diversity and emergent security crises such as 9/11 was liberal nationalism. This stance refers to 'a political rationale to achieve solidarity and equality between different ethnic groups through citizenship embodying liberal and democratic values and shared national culture and identity, while enabling the recognition of cultural diversity of individual ethnic groups based on common values and national identity' (Adachi 2009: 443; 2011d). The keystone of liberal nationalism is the democratically redefined notion of 'nationality'. Here, nationality depends on the history and culture of a specific majority group, but its meaningfulness is not limited to the majority group; rather, it is open to all ethnic groups because it more or less embodies universal values such as freedom, equality, and solidarity (e.g., the self-sufficiency and self-help values valorised in the history of pioneers in the US). It is expected that different people recognise each other as 'compatriots' through shared national characteristics (e.g., language, institutions, culture, identity) and the majority takes into account the cultural demands of their minority compatriots (Miller 1995: 139–40; Kymlicka 2002: 311). It also acknowledges that nationalities are not immutable, but change over time to become more inclusive as diverse people participate in them. However, if 'the claim of a group against its own members' (Kymlicka 1995: 35) infringes on democratic values such as individual rights and autonomy – e.g. circumcision, foot-binding and honour killings – liberal nationalist states do not hesitate to actively intervene in cultural communities.

Liberal nationalism and interculturalism indicate different policy directions but they are in fact complementary ideologies. Liberal nationalism aspires for integration from 'above' by requiring people to share identities based on democratic values while interculturalism aims for integration from 'below' through interactions between local communities. 'Citizenship' is found at the node where they intersect. Citizenship is a concept involving both 'rights' and 'duties' (Crick 2003). Nurturing the body of citizens (i.e., active citizenship) through intercommunity interactions and the sharing of democratic values and identities has been posited as the keystone of integration in European society post-7/7 – and hence, in the post-multiculturalism era (Denham 2001; Crick 2003).

In the UK, both ideologies have been incorporated in social policies, especially for Muslim integration, since 2001. They are found in 'community cohesion' policy and the politics of 'Britishness', as discussed in Chapter 2.

The concept of community cohesion appeared in the *Cantle Report* on the 2001 Bradford riots. It refers to a condition in which shared values, tolerance, security, equality, network, attachment, and identity are present among people from different communities. The policy emphasised the de-segregation of social and cultural spaces formed by isolated and insular communities that cause conflict and social unrest. To that end, it aimed to address the social and spatial segregation that prevents the sharing of British values while promoting intercultural dialogue. The government cut budgets for singular ethnic communities and implemented policies to promote interactions and mutual understanding between communities (Cantle 2001; 2008). The policy was designed to change closed and rigid cultural identities perceived in some groups − initially 'Asian', then 'Muslim' − into more open ones through interaction, while at the same time promoting the formation of identities as members of a broader society, i.e., citizenship.

The New Labour government seeking a renewal of Britain at the turn of the twenty-first century proposed 'Britishness' as a new national identity aiming for the inclusion of Muslim communities, as well as the exclusion of radical Muslims, after 7/7. In this formulation, Britishness is defined by democratic values embodied in Britain's culture and history (e.g., freedom, equality, and tolerance) rather than the 'whiteness' or 'Englishness' used by previous governments (Blair 2006; Ministry of Justice 2007; Adachi 2013b). The proponents of Britishness maintained that these values made it possible to establish a British identity without rejecting diverse cultural modalities. To achieve Britishness, people of minority groups were increasingly expected to speak English, understand British society and history, pledge their allegiance to the Queen, abide by the law and contribute to society and communities. These requirements have been robustly thrust upon the Muslim community. Many politicians have been actively intervening both politically and policy-wise in the Muslim community, demanding that they share Britishness.

The promotion of community cohesion and Britishness post-7/7 marked a shift in policy from emphasising 'celebrating cultural diversity' and 'anti-racism' to 'hybridity and shared identity'. In other words, the policy target changed from how to correct institutional racism against minorities (especially Muslims) to how to turn a rigid religious identity to a more open one and how to inculcate British values and identity in Muslims (Pitcher 2009: 64).

These ideas assume the incompatibility of Islam with democratic values, as well as a rigid and culturalist understanding of identity around Muslims. They further assume that Islamic communities contribute to a breeding ground for potential, if not actual, terrorists because of their closed and particular value system (Allen 2005: 61; Kundnani 2009). These are the discourses around the integration and inclusion of Muslims in British society that involve 'othering' Islam (Bagguley and Hussain 2005: 213).

Chapter 1

Islamo-phobia, orientalism, and gender

The othering of Muslims in Western society is commonly referred to as Islamophobia, a concept denoting hostility or enmity toward Islam as a religion. The term spread around the world after it was used in the 1997 report, *Islamophobia: A Challenge for Us All* published by the Runnymede Trust, a British independent thinktank, which defined it as follows:

> The term Islamophobia refers to unfounded hostility towards Islam. It refers also to the practical consequences of such hostility in unfair discrimination against Muslim individuals and communities, and to the exclusion of Muslims from mainstream political and social affairs. (Runnymede Trust 1997: 4)

This definition highlights the social influences of anti-Muslim prejudice through its negative expressions rather than the prejudice itself. More specifically, it has the following eight features:

1. Islam seen as a single monolithic bloc, static and unresponsive to new realities.
2. Islam seen as separate and other – (a) not having any aims or values in common with other cultures; (b) not affected by them; (c) not influencing them.
3. Islam seen as inferior to the West – barbaric, irrational, primitive and sexist.
4. Islam seen as violent, aggressive, threatening, supportive of terrorism and engaged in 'a clash of civilisations'.
5. Islam seen as a political ideology, used for political or military advantage.
6. Criticisms made by Islam of 'the West' are rejected out of hand.
7. Hostility towards Islam used to justify discriminatory practices towards Muslims and exclusion of Muslims from mainstream society.
8. Anti-Muslim hostility accepted as natural and 'normal'.

(Runnymede Trust 1997: 5)

These parameters indicate that Islamophobia is one of the discourses othering Islam in the modern West, which functions as an ideology to justify condemning Muslims and excluding them from public life. This concept, presented in 1997, has become more widespread and has come to be taken more seriously since 9/11 (Allen and Nielsen 2002). The

Runnymede Trust's follow-up report (2004) states that Islamophobia is still rampant in British society and that bias against Muslims in media reporting is particularly serious.

The othering process is not a post-9/11 or post-7/7 phenomenon although it intensified drastically after those events. It has been a rather constant presence in the historical process of European society. If anything, it has even played a vital part in the self-definition of European society. Edward Said argued that discussion of the identity of Europe (or the West) as a civilisation was possible only against the idea of Islam (or the East) as a 'non-civilisation' (Said 1978)[16]. As discussed in Chapter 2, Islam had extended its influence to northern Africa and eastern and southern Europe by the seventh century, shortly after its inception. Feeling threatened by its political, cultural and religious influences, Christian theologians attacked Islam as heretical and denounced its teachings. They called for vigilance against 'Ishmaelites' (Arabs) as apostles of the Antichrist signalling the impending end of the world. This view of Islam as 'rival' was inherited by medieval and renaissance texts and came to be accepted as common knowledge through the diffusion of colonialism and modern science in Europe (Morey and Yaqin 2011: 7–10).[17]

Notably, European understandings and critiques of Islam have been riddled with gendered discourses. For instance, *The Fount of Knowledge* by Saint John of Damascus (c. 675–749) is a significant anti-Islam text. It states how irrational and dangerous Islamic doctrines are and includes commentaries on gender:

> As has been related, this Mohammed wrote many ridiculous books, to each one of which he set a title. For example, there is the book *On Woman*, in which he plainly makes legal provision for taking four wives and, if it be possible, a thousand concubines – as many as one can maintain, besides the four wives. (John of Damascus n.d.)

Further, he argues that Mohammed established a law in the name of God to legitimise his act of dissolving the marriage of his adopted son and subsequently marrying her (John of Damascus n.d.). Commentaries of this nature criticise gender relations under Islam as being barbaric and unjust, depicting men as obscene and women as oppressed.

Colonialism packaged negative representations of Islam to promote the West's mass consumption. Alexander Macfie defines this phenomenon as 'orientalism' and explains:

Chapter 1

> It [orientalism] came to mean... also a corporate institution, designed for dealing with the Orient, a partial view of Islam, an instrument of Western imperialism, a style of thought, based on an ontological and epistemological distinction between Orient and Occident, and even an ideology, justifying and accounting for the subjugation of blacks, Palestinian Arabs, women and many other supposedly deprived groups and peoples. (Macfie 2002: 4)

Orientalism refers to those perspectives that justify Western hegemony and violence by defining the East as 'radically other' and inferior to the West (Said 1978: 3). It posits the absolute difference between the West and the Orient, represents the Orient based on textual exegesis rather than empirical observation, as unchanging and uniform, and politically positions the Orient as something to be feared or to be mastered (Sayyid 1997: 32). It is important to note that the Orient is always defined by Western orientalists (e.g., diplomats, intellectuals, adventurers and novelists), and is deprived of its right to define itself, its culture, and its identity.

The gendered representations of Muslims have been popular themes for feminist historians. They have highlighted how orientalists depicted women wearing veils and scarves as evidence of oppression, deploying such representations as a tool to justify western domination (Ahmed 1992: 144–68). For example, Katherine Bullock points out that colonialists were motivated to un-veil Muslim women because the veils denied (male) rulers the privilege of gazing at women. The popularity of pornographic postcards featuring (supposedly) Muslim women in the nineteenth century was a variation on this: orientalists drew pleasure from subordinating mysterious scarf-covered women through pornography (Bullock 2007: 9–19).

Modernisation generated further pressure for unveiling of scarves worn for religious reasons. Scholar and poet Mohja Kahf traces changes in the discourses on Muslim women through the modern era. Before the eighteenth century, Muslim women had been portrayed as 'exuberant and overbearing' noble women, dynamic actors who either fought against or aided European conquerors in the many wars between Christianity (the West) and Islam (the East). From the eighteenth century onward, however, representations of Muslim women changed to objects of (sexual) oppression by irrational and violent Muslim men. They appeared in many texts as 'odalisques' in harems whose bodies were sexualised and enslaved and eventually came to be depicted as passive subjects who longed for 'liberation' by imperialists (the West) (Kahf 1999: 1–9; Amer 2014: 77–93).

The 'colonialist desire' – defined by Gayatri Spivak as 'White men ... saving brown women from brown men' (1994: 92) – in the 'liberation' discourse has been used to justify invasions in the East (non-West) to this day (Liddle and Joshi 1985). For example, Laura Bush, America's first lady in the aftermath of 9/11, declared:

> Long before the current war began, the Taliban and its terrorist allies were making the lives of children and women in Afghanistan miserable... Women have been denied access to doctors when they're sick... Women cannot work outside the home, or even leave their homes by themselves... The plight of women and children in Afghanistan is a matter of deliberate human cruelty, carried out by those who seek to intimidate and control... The fight against terrorism is also a fight for the rights and dignity of women. (Bush 2001)

Hence, Bush justified the US military incursions by alleging that women were oppressed by Muslim extremists and in need of liberation.[18] As mentioned earlier, this frame 'liberation of Muslim women from Muslim men' became an especially important justification of the US military activities in the Middle East after the allegations that Iraq was in possession of weapons of mass destruction were refuted. Heroic-interventions to rescue and liberate oppressed women has been a standard tactic of orientalists (Pitcher 2009: 110).

The politics of liberation and intervention by Western 'moral crusaders' (Abu-Lughod 2013: 201) or the 'feminist state' (Pitcher 2009: 109–34) on the grounds of women's rights are also turned towards Muslim communities in Western countries (Ramírez 2014).[19] The Western mainstream media tend to report on Muslim women wearing scarves or veils from the perspective of gender equality. The media coverage seldom views women's scarves and veils as a voluntary expression of identity; but instead, as visible evidence of oppression and the deprivation of autonomy (Tsolidis 2017: 40–41). Muslim women appear in the Western mainstream media as victims of patriarchal family relationships at best and as a 'seedbed' for terrorists at worst (Shain 2011: 31). Western society as the self-appointed defender of democratic values such as freedom, tolerance and adherence to law has willingly imposed a 'duty to integrate' (Blair 2006) on minority communities through 'muscular liberalism' (Cameron 2011) in order to save these women.

In Western society today, women's bodies are positioned at the frontline of political debates over security and citizenship while being treated as a touchstone for the 'assimilability' of Muslims and Islam in Western society

Chapter 1

(Nagel 2005: 2–3; Rashid 2014). It is reasonable to see this as a continuation of orientalist/colonialist discourse (Brah 2006: 59).

Discourse and identity

To understand othering and its effects, we need to explain the term 'discourse'. According to Michel Foucault, discourse refers to 'ways of structuring knowledge and social practice manifested in particular ways of using language and other symbolic forms in specific institutional settings' (Simpson 1997: 198). According to Alastair Pennycook:

> Discourse... does not refer to language or uses of language, but to ways of organizing meaning that are often, though not exclusively, realized through language. Discourses are about the creation and limitation of possibilities; they are systems of power/knowledge (*pouvoir/savoir*) within which we take up subject positions. (Pennycook 1994: 128)

That is, both everyday conversations and especially texts circulated through the media have the power to construct an object or (a system of) knowledge that influences people's perceptions and behaviours around the object, defining how the object is understood and its status in social space (Featherstone 1995: 112). In other words, discourse is a social practice that constructs rather than simply represents things (Fairclough 1992: 64).

Dorothy Smith calls the workings of discourse 'the ruling apparatus':

> The ruling apparatus is that familiar complex of management, government administration, professions, and intelligentsia, as well as the textually mediated discourses that coordinate and interpenetrate it. Its special capacity is the organization of particular places, persons, and events into generalized and abstracted modes vested in categorial systems, rules, laws, and conceptual practices. The former thereby become subject to an abstracted and universalized system of ruling mediated by texts. (Smith 1987: 108)

Here, discourses are a bundle of texts mediating people and organisations composing the ruling apparatus which function to abstract, categorise and generalise a particular object. In this process, an individual or group is stripped of complex characteristics and backgrounds and diminished to a form that is desired by those with power. The diverse practices of an individual or group are understood within a limited range of possibilities and incorporated into a dominant-subordinate relationship premised on that understanding.

Discourses and representations are important for identity formation precisely because they constitute an inescapable objective environment for people. This 'inescapability' stems from the fact that discourse is not directly fact-based. Discourse refers 'to interpretation, to the imposition of meaning on phenomena in the world' (Scott 2007: 7), or a framework for an understanding of fact. That is, discourses are universal and historical practices that constitute 'reality' for people, regardless of the facts. Therefore, one cannot easily reject a given discourse by reference to facts[20]. People are compelled to refer to mainstream discourses constantly to understand themselves and the world in which they find themselves, whether they accept it or not.

In this sense, mainstream discourses on Islam have significant implications for the identity formation of young Muslims in the West. Judith Butler draws on Louis Althusser's concept of 'interpellation' to explain the action of discourse:

> [T]here is no 'I' who stands *behind* discourse and executes its volition or will *through* discourse. On the contrary, the 'I' only comes into being through being called, named, interpellated, to use the Althusserian term, and this discursive constitution takes place prior to the 'I'; it is the transitive invocation of the 'I.' Indeed, I can only say 'I' to the extent that I have first been addressed, and that address has mobilized my place in speech; paradoxically, the discursive condition of social recognition *precedes and conditions* the formation of the subject. (Butler 1993: 225–6)

This means that the individual's identity ('I') is defined and enabled through discourse (interpellation from others). From another perspective, the individual or subject is only produced in response to interpellation from others and does not exist *a priori*, that is, before discourse. Therefore an individual or group identity cannot be understood without considering the influences of political and social discourses.

As discussed above, policies such as national security, multiculturalism, social integration, and anti-terrorism are inseparable from identity politics and political discourses about Muslims in Western society (Glynn 2009). Second-generation Muslims in the UK play an important role in political debates over social integration through mainstream discourses or 'discourse representation structures'. In Islam-related incidents and resultant representation structures, Muslim identity is read as a 'moral index' rather than a mere 'cultural marker' (Morey and Yaqin 2011: 3). At the same time, the communities in which their

Chapter 1

identities are cultivated are positioned as 'a place of morality' and attract various political and social interventions (Rose 1999; Pitcher 2009).

Foucauldian sociologists observe that discourses and the social representations they construct have become a means of 'governmentality' wielded by Western countries on Muslim communities (Pitcher 2009: 63, 81–2). The representation of Muslim communities as 'other' in Western society legitimises strong pressure for Muslims to assimilate to the dominant values and attitudes of the state. When Muslims do not conform to the social values and political attitudes the government demands, their non-compliance is framed as anti-democratic. As Paul Gilroy observes, in states demanding '[a]uthoritarian modes of belonging to the national collective', 'anyone who objects to the conduct of their government is likely to be identified as an enemy within and bluntly advised to go and live elsewhere', and argues that 'our dwindling rights cannot be separated from obligations that will be defined... by an ideal of patriotic citizenship' (Gilroy 2004: 26).[21] At the same time, the supposedly rigid and inflexible Muslim 'cultured self' is subjected to unremitting pressure to become a more adaptable 'entrepreneurial self' in the neoliberal era (Vintges 2012: 285-7). The recent developments in social integration policy in the UK and Europe – the coalescence of interculturalism and liberal nationalism discussed above – need to be understood in this context (Kaya 2009). The citizenship tests and integration contracts that many European countries have introduced provide a testing ground for immigrants to prove that they are open to European civilisation.[22]

As mentioned, second-generation Muslims living in twenty-first-century Western society must live a double consciousness just as African Americans did in the early twentieth century. The two distinct senses of self derive from the disconnect between one's personal experiences and the way portrayed in mainstream society. This double consciousness is the presupposition for their identity formation and part of background rules in constructing their self-presentation strategy around identity. They are forced to construct their own identities in the midst of mainstream discourses othering Muslims. In Giddens' terms, identity construction for Muslims is a 'reflexive project' carried out in the face of mainstream discourses (Giddens 1991).

How have young second-generation Muslims responded to the issues related to reflexivity to form and present their identities in the post-9/11 world? This book aims to provide a blueprint for answering these questions.

24

The composition of this book

Finally, I would like to explain the structure of this book, which is divided into two parts. Part I covers from this chapter to Chapter 4 and discusses assumptions for analysis (background, previous studies and theoretical framework, and research outline). Part II, Chapters 5 to 10, presents a concrete analysis of interview data and analytical findings.

Chapter 2 outlines the history of Asian immigrants, who constitute a majority of Muslims in the UK, as well as an overview of the current political situation concerning young Muslims and their social and economic realities. Chapter 3 reviews various identity theories on which previous studies on the social integration and identity of British Muslims are based, and discusses problems with preceding theoretical frameworks. In this part, I classify identity models from the viewpoint of 'closedness' and 'openness'. Then I describe in detail a theoretical framework called 'identity theory in reflexive modernity', which can simultaneously explain both aspects of identities, openness and closedness. This identity theory underpins the analysis in this book. Chapter 4 explains my research and the data supporting this study. It also outlines the research field, my position as an outsider and its advantages, the cognitive framework and analytical method, and the attributes of informants.

Part II presents an analysis of the research data, focusing on identity management and self-presentation strategies used by second-generation British Muslims.

The first two chapters (5 and 6) examine how second-generation Muslims perceive the UK as a social space and feel about being Muslim in it. Chapter 5 discusses their perception of discrimination or stigmas against Muslim communities. Many informants related their experiences with various stigmas from street racism, institutional racism and discourses in the mainstream media. They deeply distrusted the Western media and expressed serious concern and anger at its daily stream of negative representations of Islam and Muslim communities. Chapter 6 discusses their understanding of the relationship between being British and being Muslim or between Islam and British culture. It reveals that the UK is defined as a 'multicultural space' facilitating their social participation as Muslims and that they positively assess this tolerant characteristic.

Chapters 7 and 8 are the most important segments of this book. Chapter 7 discusses 'differentiation between culture and religion' as the most basic self-presentation strategy around identity. Informants present Islam in a positive light by drawing a line between religion and culture, and ascribe negatively perceived events and customs to Asian cultural norms. This differentiation

Chapter 1

is an essential strategy to counter mainstream discourses such as 'Islam vs. the West' while at the same time being used to resist some customs in their communities that limit their freedom. Chapter 8 explains that differentiation between culture and religion is being achieved through the acquisition of knowledge about Islam. It sheds light on the fact that today's youth distinguish between themselves and older generations based on the level of religious knowledge. Informatisation through the Internet increases the availability of religious knowledge and reinforces the personalisation of faith, thus promoting the democratisation of faith.

The following two chapters (9 and 10) focus on the 'agency' of female informants. Chapter 9 analyses their views about education and career. They referred to Islam as an egalitarian system and a resource for empowering women. Chapter 10 explores what the hijab (e.g., scarf and veil) means to Muslim women, providing a detailed discussion of how they explain both wearing and not wearing hijab from an Islamic point of view. It examines how they utilise their knowledge of Islam for the politics surrounding their autonomy, agency and bodies.

The Conclusion summarises the analysis and findings presented in Part II and clarifies the importance of the reflexive identity model for an understanding of second-generation Muslims in Western society. It also re-examines the role multiculturalism might play in Muslim integration in Western society in the post-9/11 era and suggests the significance and challenges of this study.

Note

1 The spectacle here refers to 'a social relation between people that is mediated by images' (Debord 2009). September 11 can be called a spectacular event in that its repeated media coverage connected people and organisations throughout the world that were not directly related.

2 Second-generation Muslims in this book is a collective term that includes 'second, third and fourth generation' descendants of immigrants, as well as '1.5 generation' immigrants who were born overseas and received their primary education in the UK.

3 Moral panic is 'a sociological concept that seeks to explain a particular type of overreaction to a perceived social problem' (Rohloff and Wright 2010: 2). Folk devils refer to outsiders or deviators that the media constructs as the cause of a moral panic. There have been moral panics in response to a wide range of events, from bullying and shootouts in school, illicit drugs, child abuse, and sex and violent crimes to welfare cheats, the increase of single mothers, refugees and asylum seekers and their swamping of welfare services (Cohen 2011: vii–xxvi).

4 Throughout this book, unless noted otherwise, the words in square brackets inside quotations have been added by the present author for clarification.

5 In a similar vein, Arjun Appadurai commented on the constructiveness of (multi-) culturalism:

> We have now moved one step further, from culture as substance to culture as the dimension of difference, to culture as group identity based on difference, to culture as the process of naturalizing a subset of differences that have been mobilized to articulate group identity. (Appadurai 1996: 14–5)

He explains that culture in contemporary society has become a construct for differentiating groups rather than something with historically inherited substance.

6 For example, Paul Berman criticises multiculturalism in the following way:

> In any movement based on building up a cultural identity, sooner or later someone will step forward to declare [her/] his own identity to be truer and more authentic than everyone else's, and will announce a grave impeding threat to the collective identity, and on that basis will take into [her/] his own hands the right to make decisions for all, and to unmask traitors, and to carry out the executions. (Berman 1996: 161)

7 This type of criticism originates in the critique of an Anglo-American cultural movement known as 'cultural studies', which emerged in the 1950s. Cultural studies was to provide the left with a new weapon just when Karl Marx's impoverishment theory was losing its power. From a traditional liberal perspective, however, the cultural left appears to have undermined solidarity for a common vision and equality (Gitlin 1995; Rorty 1998).

8 Multiculturalism is a political concept that originally developed in traditional immigrant countries (e.g., Canada, Australia, and the US). It is a policy principle aiming to correct inequalities and injustices propagated in the process of

Chapter 1

colonialism and nation-state formation and to restore damaged honour and dignity for indigenous peoples subordinated by new settlers as well as people who were forced to relocate – so-called 'national minorities' (Kymlicka 1995; 2007; Modood 2013). By contrast, multiculturalism in the UK and Europe addressed post-war immigrants from European and other countries who came mainly for work – so-called 'ethnic minorities'. Hence multiculturalism in the latter aimed for 'the political accommodation of minorities formed by immigration to Western countries from outside the prosperous West' (Modood 2013: 5). In other words, multiculturalism in Britain always means 'a way of thinking and talking about identity and belonging in relation to a conception of social order' (Pitcher 2009: 23) with its main focus being the question of how to integrate the growing population of immigrants and minorities into the classic nation-state.

9 For example, a newspaper column in *The Independent* (6 October 2006) argued: 'Britain may be seen abroad as having managed the transition to a multicultural society more successfully than some, but as a nation we have not overcome the tendency to suspect, even fear, "the other"' (Uberoi et al. 2011: 218).

10 We better understand what multiculturalism represents in this discourse by looking at the adjectives attached to it. For instance, Trevor Phillips of the Commission for Racial Equality expressed criticism that 'an "anything goes" multiculturalism' was leading to 'deeper division and inequality' (Phillips 2005). Others have used terms such as 'laissez-faire' (Goodhart 2004), 'unbridled' (Blunkett 2002) and 'radical' (Kepel 2005). These adjectives portray multiculturalism as letting minority cultures, especially Islamic tenets, go unchecked (i.e., laissez-faire), allowing their demands to escalate (i.e., unbridled) and consequently creating a breeding ground for riots and terrorism (i.e., radical) (Adachi 2013b: 197).

11 In a similar vein, Satoko Fujiwara, reflecting on her own childhood experience of British education in her study of Britain's post-multicultural religious education, observed: 'Prior to the introduction of multiculturalism, immigrants tried to assimilate with… British culture and society without becoming conscious about people's religion' (Fujiwara 2017: 123). According to Fujiwara, what was important in those days was the line between English and non–English rather than differences within the latter group (Muslims, Hindus, Jamaicans etc.).

12 *The Telegraph*, a similarly conservative tabloid paper, reacted even more harshly. In an article entitled 'A Victory for Multiculti over Common Sense', it declared that 'the real suicide bomb is "multiculturalism"' (Steyn 2005). Similar reactions were also found in more respected and more liberal newspapers. Under the heading of 'A Monster of Our Own Making', *The Observer* argued that 'These British bombers are a consequence of a misguided and catastrophic pursuit of multiculturalism' (Pfaff 2005). *openDemocracy* pointed out that the bombers were 'the children of Britain's own multicultural society' (Kepel 2005) in an article entitled 'Europe's Answer to Londonistan'. In 'When Multiculturalism Is a Nonsense', *The Financial Times* stated: 'It is dangerous because it destroys political community. It is demeaning because it devalues citizenship. In this sense, at least, multiculturalism must be discarded as nonsense' (Wolf 2005) (Adachi 2013b: 195–6).

13 In this book, the term 'New Labour' refers to the Labour Party, which was in government from 1997 to 2010. It was a slogan employed by party leaders Tony Blair and Gordon Brown, who subsequently became Prime Ministers, in order to transform the faltering Labour Party of the 1990s from the 'Old Labour' advocating continental European socialism to a party adopting the new philosophy of reinvigorating civic society and opening up to the globalised economy. New Labour put forward many innovative policy ideas for education, social security, local government, human rights and the economy; social integration was one of those areas (Umekawa et al. eds. 2006; Seldon ed. 2007; Adachi 2013b).

14 Interculturalism is a policy principle first developed in French–speaking Quebec Province in Canada in resistance to the multicultural model embraced by the predominantly Anglo federal government (Bouchard and Taylor 2008). Although Quebec's French-speaking people are a minority in Canadian society, they constitute a majority in the province. Accordingly, Quebec aspired to mainstream and preserve the French language and culture rather than accepting the status of an ethnic group permitted within the multicultural model proposed by the federal government. It was, however, considered neither realistic nor desirable to require all residents to assimilate into the French-speaking culture in the context of its minority status in Canada and the increasing diversity of Quebec society from globalisation. According to Quebec–born historian and sociologist Gérard Bouchard, this ambivalence of Quebec's French residents in Anglo-Canada prompted Quebec to adopt a 'dualist' model. This dualism means the official adoption of the majority (French-speaking) history and culture as mainstream while endeavouring to construct a more open relationship with minority cultures. It aims to relax the boundary between the majority and minority cultures through 'compromise and interaction' rather than eliminating the gap between them (as under the diversity model). Interculturalism here aims to alter the cultural boundary dividing the majority and the minority – albeit to a limited extent – as well as to integrate them into one society by finding universal values among different cultural groups through ongoing dialogue while recognising mainstream society's language, culture and history (Bouchard 2012: 45–91). This way of thinking has an affinity with liberal nationalism. See Bouchard (2012) and Adachi (2020a) for more details.

15 *White Paper on Intercultural Dialogue* was drafted in consultation with the policy leaders of the EU countries and approved by the Council of Europe. The view of multiculturalism expressed in this document can be regarded as the consensus view of the participating European countries (Kymlicka 2012: 212).

16 Jean-Paul Sartre called this the 'racist humanism' of Western society: the only way 'the European could make himself man was by fabricating slaves and monsters' (Sartre 1961: lviii).

17 According to William Watt, the medieval Christian world's perceptions of Islam can be summarised in four points. First, Islam is based on false knowledge although it contains a modicum of truth. Second, Islam spreads by violence and the sword. Third, Islam is a self-indulgent religion and particularly immoral in a sexual aspect. Fourth, Muhammad is the Anti-Christ and an emissary of the devil (Watt 1991: 85–6).

Chapter 1

18 Bush, of course, did not paint terrorists and ordinary Muslims with the same brush. 'The poverty, poor health, and illiteracy that the terrorists and the Taliban have imposed on women in Afghanistan do not conform with the treatment of women in most of the Islamic world, where women make important contributions in their societies. Only the terrorists and the Taliban forbid education to women' (Bush 2001). Nevertheless, the rhetoric of 'liberation of women (from men)' contributed to a negative representation of Islam and served as an important justification for Western governments to intervene in both Islamic countries and the Muslim communities within their own countries.

19 As Naaz Rashid says, 'Everyone is a feminist when it comes to Muslim women' (Rashid 2017) in today's Western society. See also Note 22 below.

20 For example, the New Labour government introduced the Home Office Citizenship Survey to implement an 'evidence-based policy' on social integration issues. After several surveys, the government discovered that Muslims had no trouble 'being British'. Yet, key government figures continued to repeat the myths of Muslim 'segregation' and 'failure to integrate' as quoted above (Uberoi et al. 2011: 210–214). Large sections of the media continue to repeat this political discourse in portraying young Muslims.

21 The UK's counter-terrorism policy provides a glimpse of this attitude. For instance, in 2005 the Home Office released a 'List of Unacceptable Behaviours' identifying justifying, glorifying or provoking terrorist acts and fostering or promoting hatred as causes for exclusion or deportation from the UK. The Terrorism Act 2006 criminalised disseminating 'terrorist publications', i.e., those that encourage or induce terrorism. A leaked statement about the government's counter-terrorism policy, scheduled to be announced in 2009, stated those who support the establishment of a cross–border Caliphate (a state reigned by Muhammad's successor), the introduction of *sharia*, armed resistance against Israel and the criminalisation of homosexuality were to be considered 'extremist'. Later, however, the official policy statement excluded these criteria because they could potentially define a majority of Muslims as extremists (Okahisa 2009: 200). Thus, the succession of counter-terror measures alludes to the government's intention to not only detect or prevent terrorism but also exclude those who disagree with the government. The case of Shamima Begum mentioned in the Introduction is clear evidence of the government's attitude.

22 For example, in August 2018, a Muslim couple's citizenship application was rejected by the city of Lausanne in the French-speaking canton of Vaud, Switzerland. Their refusal to 'shake hands' with people of the opposite sex was the reason for the rejection. Islam tells its followers to avoid physical contact with a person of the opposite sex except for certain permitted people (see Chapter 10). This decision clearly demonstrated the municipality's intent to give priority to law – Western civilisation, in truth – over religion – specifically Islam. Deputy Mayor Pierre-Antoine Hildbrand, who had interviewed the couple, stated that 'The constitution and equality between men and women prevails over bigotry' and that he was 'very satisfied with the decision' (Guardian 2018). Another example is from a DVD produced as study materials for the Netherlands'

citizenship examination which showed an image of a topless woman sunbathing on a beach and the narrator saying, 'People do not make a fuss about nudity' with scenes on nudist beaches. The same DVD shows two men kissing in a meadow to emphasise that homosexuality is normal in the Netherlands. Some concerned parties claimed that 'This isn't education, it's provocation' because it was highly likely that these depictions would repel Muslim immigrants (Crouch 2006). In this respect, even some right-wing political parties, which had been typically critical of homosexuality, began to claim tolerance of homosexuality as a European value in order to exclude Muslim immigrants. For example, Sebastian Tynkkynen, who belongs to the Finns Party Youth, a right-wing political party, and is openly gay, sang along to ABBA's *Dancing Queen* and waved a placard saying, 'Christians, don't hate us. Islam, don't kill us'. Dutch politician Pim Fortuyn argued that Muslims were turning the Netherlands into a society intolerant of gays like himself. The Alternative for Germany party, a far-right group, has a lesbian leader in the Bundestag and has also organised the Alternative Homosexuals to reach out to the LGBT community. Florian Philippot, who was once vice-president of the National Front in France, is also openly gay. A spokesperson of the right-wing political party, the Sweden Democrats, stated that homophobes 'are not welcome in our party'. Belgium's Flemish nationalist party Vlaams Belang describes itself as the most gay-friendly party because 'All other parties are willing to import thousands of Muslims who have very violent ideas against being gay or transgender'. The exclusion of Muslims through declarations of support for gays is called 'gay–friendly Islamophobia' (Economist 2018).

Chapter

British Muslims: Formation, Politics and Condition

I was born to Pakistani parents who migrated, separately, to the United Kingdom when they were young. My father was about 11, and my mother about 16. My grandfather was born in India, in Western Punjab. He was a skilled carpenter who had served in the British Army and, when he came to England in the early 1960s, he found a job with a furniture manufacturer in Birmingham. He would make trips back to Pakistan, where my father was born in Gujar Khan, a district in Punjab, while my mother was born in a small village called Bhindia, in Azad Kashmir. It's a place that she still speaks of fondly; her family owned a farm there and she remembers climbing trees, picking fruit and playing with animals when she was a child. Then, by arrangement, she was married to my father, leaving behind her idyllic village to build a new life in impoverished, cold Glasgow, where he lived in the 1970s.

'Mahtab Hussain on the Multiple Identities
of Young British Muslim Men'
by Mahtab Hussain (2018)

They attacked Edgware Road precisely because it represented a relationship between Islam and West, a cultural and ideological abomination to those who believe in the pure interpretation of Al Qaeda's message… They were also attacking the idea that you can have a British identity but still be a part of the wider global 'nation of believers'. The belief that a western city can ever be a part of the modern story of Islam in the world is sacrilegious to the fundamentalist vision.

Only Half of Me
by Rageh Omaar (2007: 36–7)

The aim of this chapter is to provide an overview of the evolution of the Asian-Muslim community in the UK and its present conditions.[1] I have focused on Asian Muslims because they constitute a majority of the Muslim 'representation' in British society due to deep historical connections. As we will see in Chapter 4, Asian Muslims also account for the great majority of informants in the present research and analysis.

This section first provides an overview of the historical background to the formation of Muslim communities in Britain. It then discusses how the presence of Muslim communities has sparked political and social debates over social integration in the UK. In particular, I will explain the increasing levels of criticism against multiculturalism and political demands for open identity formation. Finally, with reference to various statistical data, the social and economic status of Muslims in the UK will be reviewed.

The British Empire and India

After the era of his first four successors as *khalifah* (political leaders) following the death of the Prophet Muhammad in 632, Islam rapidly spread to the world.[2] The fourth caliph Ali was assassinated in 661. His rival Mu'awiya I assumed power and founded the Umayyad Caliphate in present-day Syria, which lasted until 750. Its successor, the Abbasid Caliphate, ushered in the Islamic Golden Age, which continued into the sixteenth century. During this period its political, economic and cultural influences reached across the world, deepening both its relations and conflicts with Europe. Beginning with the Crusades, which lasted from 1096 to 1270, there were wars based on fear and opposition to Islam's political and cultural incursions into the Christian-European world, accompanied by religious and political propaganda that positioned Islam as the 'other'. Meanwhile, papermaking technology from China to the Islamic World enabled the production of books and, consequently, vast amounts of knowledge originating in Islamic civilisation were exported to Europe and translated. It is well-known that they contained ancient Greek knowledge (e.g., literature, philosophy, science etc.), that was thought lost (Abbas 2005: 5–7).

A deeper connection between Britain and the Islamic world began when the former took control of India. Muslim immigration from the Indian subcontinent was inseparable from the imperial history of Britain. It was initiated by the East India Company, an agency representing the British Empire. The company was formed in 1600 and awarded a monopoly over trade with India and the East by Queen Elizabeth I. It initially intended to pursue spice trade in the East Indies but shifted its attention to South Asia

33

Chapter 2

trade after conflict with the Dutch (cf. the Amboyna massacre) (Visram 1986: 1–2; Kotani 2004: 258–9). The East India Company beat its Spanish and Portuguese counterparts to gradually strengthen its monopoly in India by the end of the sixteenth century. By 1660, the empire was hiring local soldiers called 'Sipahis' to protect Britain's trade in India (Visram 1986: 3). Through the eighteenth and nineteenth centuries, the East India Company and – after its authority was curtailed and then abolished – Britain proceeded to extend control over the Indian sub-continent (Visram 1986: 1–5). For instance, the Muslim empire of Mughal in northern India was defeated in the Battle of Buxar and lost the diwani (the right to collect provincial land revenue) of Bengal and Bihar, practically placing the two provinces under the jurisdiction of the East India Company (Kotani 2004: 259–61). In the series of Anglo-Mysore Wars in the late eighteenth century, Britain conquered several states through battles and clever schemes to incorporate some in the princely states system through treaties while claiming others as British territories (Kotani and Karashima 2004: 280–2). One year after the Indian Rebellion of 1857 was suppressed, the passage of the Government of India Act gave birth to the British Raj in India (Nagasaki 2004: 322–5).

The colonisation of India strengthened ties between Britain and its colonial population. In the process, the people of the Indian subcontinent were constituted as 'the colonised'. Around 30 million people on the subcontinent were employed by the British Empire under its colonial rule (Appleyard 1991: 11). The main occupation for Indians was 'soldier'. In the mid-eighteenth century, Indian troops were organised by the East India Company for a series of wars against France over the Carnatic region. In the mid-nineteenth century, the British Indian Army was established and a large number of Indians were engaged in military activity. The Indian Army played a significant role in the defence and expansion of the British Empire. Although there had been some alarm about the increasing numbers of Indian soldiers following the Indian Rebellion of 1857 and the locals' growing antipathy towards the British Empire, Indian troops continued to be recruited in large numbers because they were 'cheaper' (Nagasaki 2004: 322–5). The Indian Army initially played a limited role in enforcing security within India and subjugating frontiers but was increasingly deployed beyond its borders as an 'imperial fire brigade' following the Indian Rebellion (Visram 2002: 169; Nagasaki 2004: 341).[3]

In the process of becoming deeply embedded in the empire, India become an important ground for military recruitment. The recruitment activities were concentrated on certain areas and castes. For example, the British Indian Army enlisted soldiers from among the Mogul, Jat and Rajput in Punjab whereas the Indian Navy recruited around the Attock district in Punjab (Shaw 1994: 37–8). Among the so-called 'martial races' that provided primary resources for the Indian military, the Punjabi Sikhs were hired in large numbers to serve the Queen, especially after the Indian Rebellion (Virdee 2006: 9).[4] During the two World Wars, Indians became important military and labour resources for Britain, further strengthening ties. For instance, more than one million soldiers were dispatched from India by the end of the First World War, surpassing the total number of troops from other British colonies, including 'white' countries. In the Second World War, more than 2.5 million soldiers were deployed from India, again surpassing the number of troops from other British territories and colonies (Visram 2002: 169, 341).

Additionally, the activities of the East India Company and the development of the 'imperialism of free trade' (Nadel and Perry 1964) from the nineteenth century accelerated communication in commodities and people through trade. The East India Company employed many locals – especially in Sylhet, Calcutta and Mumbai – as 'lascars' (sailors) when it built factories in South Asia to maintain its monopoly on trade with Britain during the eighteenth century (Panayi 2010: 53; Ballard 1994: 5–6). Their wages were between one-sixth and one-seventh of those for European workers. From the nineteenth century, lascars worked on steam-powered merchant vessels and formed the core workforce for the distribution of products across the empire. White European workers eschewed work on steamboats as it was 'hot, dirty and tiring' (Gilliat-Ray 2010: 29; Abbas 2011: 45). Although there were laws to limit the number of lascars, Indians were employed to cover shortages of British seamen during the wars (Visram 1986: 34).[5]

Some of the sailors shuttling between the Indian subcontinent and Britain stayed in major port cities regarded as 'imperial gateways', such as London, Liverpool and Lancaster (Robinson-Dunn 2006; Gale and Hopkins 2009: 7). It was first reported that 138 lascars visited British ports in 1760. Their numbers climbed to 1,403 in 1810, 3,000 in 1842, and 10,000–12,000 in 1855 (Ansari 2004: 35; Fisher 2006: 36). Many immigrants from Sylhet district stayed at mariners' hostels in the Pool of London (along the River Thames) for holidays or re-employment on India-bound merchant vessels. Some got off the boat and tried to settle in coastal cities, but most of them were forced to live in the harsh 'imperial spaces' such as dockyards, seaport towns and slums. These people formed the foundations for emerging Muslim communities in many cities after the World Wars, including London's East End, where I conducted this research (Kershen 2005: 13; Gilliat-Ray 2010: 24; Panayi 2010: 37–45). In Liverpool, one of the empire's greatest ports, a

Muslim community had slowly formed in the nineteenth century due to its commercial ties with India and Egypt.[6]

The population of Asian immigrants in the UK increased gradually after the turn of the twentieth century. Punjab Province was a major source of migrants. Because of the local custom for family land to be divided and inherited by children, each Punjabi family had small land incapable of generating enough income to support a (extended) family. Some families were able to start farming in more fertile 'irrigated virgin lands' under an extensive irrigation scheme but ended up burdened by large debts (Visram 2002: 255). These circumstances drove many young men to go to Britain for work. Many British expatriates who employed locals as servants and maids (ayah) in India brought them to Britain when they returned (Gilliat-Ray 2010: 24–5), whether out of personal attachment, for the servants' high skills, or as 'little pets' symbolising their master status (Visram 1986: 11–3).

Nevertheless, immigrants to Britain came mainly from Europe from the early nineteenth century until the mid-twentieth century. Immigrants from the Indian subcontinent and the rest of the New Commonwealth were relatively insignificant in terms of numbers during this time.[7] That is, these political and economic ties with the colonies did not lead to a marked increase in the population of non-white minorities in Britain.

Post-war Asian immigration

The situation changed drastically after WWII. To satisfy the growing demand for labour to support Britain's post-war recovery, the government sought to secure a workforce by importing workers from predominantly non-white New Commonwealth countries. Such workers took jobs in the declining industrial sector that white people were leaving (Abbas 2005: 9; 2011: 46–7). However, non-white immigration to post-war Britain cannot be fully explained by the demand for labour alone; its path-dependent imperialist/colonialist background exerted a strong effect (Brah 1996).

The number of 'coloured' immigrants surged in post-war Britain, spearheaded by immigrants from the West Indies. The arrival of the Empire Windrush with some 430 Jamaican men onboard in 1948 is often mentioned as the start of non-white immigration to Britain, but the number of West Indies immigrants was already growing during WWII. They were an important source of British troops and labour force in the war economy. The rapid growth was partially due to the 1952 McCarran–Walter Act in the US, which restricted immigration from the West Indies. Almost immediately, the population of West Indies immigrants in the UK jumped tenfold from 17,218 in 1951 to 173,659 in 1961, and peaked at over 300,000 in 1971. Many of them found employment in industries such as machinery manufacturing, transportation, telecommunications, construction, and health care (Castles and Kosack 1973: 76–7). Immigration from the Indian subcontinent followed, increasing rapidly through the 1950s and peaking at 115,150 in 1961. They went into the textile, steel, machinery, and electrochemical industries: Indians worked as technicians and professionals and Pakistanis engaged in weaving (Castles and Kosack 1973: 76–7). These coloured immigrants were regarded as replacement workers for jobs held by white people at the time (Peach 1968: 95).

One of the major push factors for the increasing immigration from the Indian subcontinent was Pakistan's secession from India. As part of the decolonisation move made by exhausted Britain in the aftermath of WWII, Hindu-dominated India and Muslim-dominated Pakistan were separated by Partition, becoming two independent states in 1947. This resulted in the displacement of Muslims, Hindus and Sikhs between East Punjab, Indian territory, and West Punjab, Pakistani territory. However, the separation did not easily solve the problem, as the sects were mixed in both regions. Between 10 million and 15 million people were forcibly resettled as migrants or refugees in the chaotic split. After the Pakistani government began to construct the Mangla Dam in 1960, some 250 villages were submerged and over 100,000 people were displaced. Many of these people who had lost their homes headed for Britain for resettlement (Anwar 1996: 8; Gilliat-Ray 2010: 46).

When discussing the growth of immigration from particular areas of the subcontinent, including Punjab, Gujarat, Mirpur and Sylhet, we need to consider their local cultures. Specifically, there is a 'culture of migration' in these places, according to which going overseas and achieving success is believed to be a viable path to improving the status of one's family and community (Panayi 2010: 68–70; Singh 2002: 20–1). This is underpinned by a kinship system called '*biradari*' centred on 'giving and taking of gifts' and '*izzat*' (honour; see Chapter 3). People, mostly men, were encouraged to accumulate family wealth by temporary migration through *biradari*-based relationships of obligation and cooperation. It is important to note that Britain's imperial rule nurtured this culture of migration. In some agricultural districts such as Mirpur and Attock, men were expected to find work outside their community to contribute to the family income during the off-season. The opportunities for employment by the British Empire for servants, soldiers and railway workers through the East India Company and the Indian Army strengthened the culture of migration. These experiences laid the groundwork for the

Chapter 2

subsequent mass migration from the Indian subcontinent to the faraway land of Britain (Shaw 1994: 35–9).

The British Nationality Act 1948 is an institutional factor in expanding immigration from the New Commonwealth countries. It is notable that Britain did not create a citizenship of its own 'British Citizens' under this law (Karatani 2003: 116). Instead, it established the following four citizenship categories: Citizens of the United Kingdom and Colonies, Citizens of independent Commonwealth countries, British subjects without citizenship and British protected persons. Under the act, people in the Commonwealth countries were conferred the Commonwealth citizenship status, exempted from immigration control over foreigners, and granted the right of free access to the UK. In other words, people in the Commonwealth countries were given the status and comprehensive rights of British subjects just as British citizens were (Ishida 1975a: 45–7). The generosity of this law reflected the residual effect of the imperial-era ideology that all citizens of the British Commonwealth were equal as 'subjects of the Crown' regardless of race, religion, and nationality (Freeman 1979: 46; Bleich 2003: 38–9).

Nevertheless, Britain's expanding immigration intake was not without conflicts. While the Conservative Party actively sought to restrict non-white immigrants, the more liberal Labour Party shared similar views (Layton-Henry 1984: 31–43).[8] Economic stagnation in the 1950s fuelled the opposition to accepting further immigrants (Abbas 2011: 46). A series of race riots in Nottingham in central England and Notting Hill in London in 1958 brought the movement for non-white immigration control to the surface. These riots received intense media coverage of violence committed by Black immigrants while overlooking the fact that some white groups acted violently toward Black people (Solomos 1989: 44–6). As a result, immigration control became the subject of vigorous national debate.

While 1958 marked a watershed year for immigration debate, the Conservative government's Commonwealth Immigrants Act 1962 repre-sented an institutional milestone. The act made a clear distinction between British citizens and citizens of the Commonwealth and imposed immigration control on people other than British passport holders and those who were born in Britain (Solomos 1989: 51–2). Employment vouchers were issued to the following three categories of immigrants: 'applicants who could satisfy the Ministry of Labour that they had jobs to come to' (Category A); 'those who possessed training, skills or technical qualification likely to be useful in the United Kingdom' (Category B); and 'those who fell into neither of the above categories' for whom vouchers were issued on a first-come-first-served basis (Category C) (Karatani 2003: 130). That the law was intended to restrict non-

38

white immigration can be seen in the fact that holders of British passports issued in the Republic of Ireland were not subject to these immigration controls. The intent to limit non-white immigrants became more obvious when the number of employment vouchers issued to foreigners by the Labour Ministry increased even as immigration from the New Commonwealth countries decreased noticeably.[9] The number of employment voucher holders among the New Commonwealth immigrants dropped from 28,678 in 1963 to 6,788 two years later (Harada 2015: 35–6).[10]

Further restrictions on non-white immigration were publicly discussed during the 1960s. The increasing number of its former African colonies achieving independence was a key factor. In gaining independence from Britain, many African countries adopted 'Africanisation' policies, involving assimilation of non-African residents and nationalisation of social institutions. Many Indian settlers in Africa chose not to obtain citizenship in the new nations because they were discriminated against in public service recruitment, employment and business activities as governments tried to give their native people preferential access to important state functions. These Asian residents without citizenship emigrated in droves to the UK from African countries such as Uganda, Tanzania and Kenya from 1963 onward. The number of Asian arrivals from East Africa from 1965 to 1966 reached around 6,000. When the Kenyan government introduced a law permitting only temporary residency and employment for non-Kenyan nationals in 1967, more Asian residents were driven to leave the country, with 4,000 of them entering the UK in August–September 1967 (Miles and Cleary 1992: 166).

In response, campaigns to stop Asian immigration mounted in the UK. The Labour government was pressured to introduce the Commonwealth Immigrants Act 1968 to limit the influx of non-white immigrants. The law passed through parliament in only three days and had a decisive impact on Britain's subsequent immigration policy. The dilemma was how to rescue white residents in Africa while barring non-white immigrants without appearing blatantly racist. Its solution was the creation of the 'patrial' clause. Patrials refer to 'descendants of people (parents or grandparents) born, adopted or naturalised in the UK'. This clause practically refers to white people and thus was an underhanded racist policy. Subsequently, only 1,500 Asians per year were permitted to enter Britain from Kenya, Uganda and Tanzania (Ishida 1975a: 48; Freeman 1979: 57–9).

The series of immigration control laws in the 1960s changed the pattern of immigration from the Indian subcontinent greatly. For instance, the Commonwealth Immigrants Act 1962 paradoxically brought about a rapid increase in immigration from that part of the world. Travel agencies in

Chapter 2

Pakistan spread the news of the legislation as 'the last chance' and impelled men, who otherwise would not have decided to go to the UK, to emigrate. At the same time, the voucher system designed to limit immigration worked in favour of those who had relatives already working in the UK. Earlier settlers, who had established themselves in the UK, prompted a 'chain of migration on the kinship, friendship basis', acting as sponsors or guarantors for their relatives (Anwar 1996: 7). In addition, the voucher system reinforced 'the existing pattern of migration from districts with traditions of service in the Army and Navy' by granting former military personnel preferential treatment (Shaw 1994: 40).

Female immigration and community formation

The series of immigration restriction laws shifted the leading role of migrants from the men who had hitherto paved the way as 'pioneers' to their wives, fiancées and children as the central players in immigration (Brah and Shaw 1992), due to the 'family reunion' provisions. Although the voucher system under the 1962 law restricted the number of immigrants, the entry of dependent family members of immigrants already living in the UK was not subject to these regulations. Consequently, the number of family reunions continued to rise throughout the 1960s. For example, the number of employment voucher holders from the New Commonwealth countries from July 1962 to December 1968 was 77,966 whereas the number of dependent family arrivals reached 257,200 (Anwar 1996: 8–9). This considerably improved the gender balance of the Pakistani community in the UK, with the ratio of men decreasing from 82 per cent in 1961 to 58 per cent in 1982 (Anwar 1996: 27). Women, who had been relegated to an ancillary role as male immigrants' 'baggage' (King 2002: 97), came to be the main actor in the reproduction of minority communities (Yuval-Davis 1997).

In the UK, family reunion enabled the (re-)building of the *biradari* (kinship networks among Asians) or the formation of 'quasi-*biradari*'. Women's bodies and traditional costumes contributed to building 'the boundary that marks the imagined, psychic and physical space of the "community"' (Mohammed 2004: 385). The newly arrived wives or fiancées were in many cases unable to work outside of their homes due to their inability to speak English. They developed close kinship relations among women within their extended families and nearby communities, organising family ceremonies and events, including weddings, birthdays, circumcisions, children's first Quran readings and

40

welcome or farewell parties for relatives. Women were mobilised to prepare meals, gifts, and clothes for these events, which many relatives and neighbours attended (Akhtar 2014: 234). It would have been impossible to hold these events without the women. The *biradari* was rebuilt through these ceremonies and 'give-take relationships' (*lena-dena*) in the UK. New connections in the community facilitated the development of relationships between people as members of the quasi-family system even though they did not belong to the same *biradari* in the home country (Shaw 1994: 41–8). The re-embedding of the *biradari* in the host community significantly changed the conditions of Muslim identity and community. While the extent of religious practice among single male Muslim immigrants had been generally weak before the family reunion program began in earnest, the situation changed dramatically from the 1960s onward (Lewis 1994; Ansari 2004). This was partly because the issues of child-raising and education emerged.

As the door to coloured immigration was being shut, the 'myth of return' (Anwar 1996) – the prospect of returning home after earning money in the host country, previously shared by immigrants – was gradually dismantled and many immigrants chose to settle their families in the UK (Gilliat-Ray 2010: 49; Hoque 2015: 25). It has created a new immigration pattern, bringing significant change to the Muslim community. The growing numbers of children and women in the community increased interest in preserving a cultural space and women came to be expected as main providers of community service to protect community members from the impacts of the Western lifestyle as well as to contribute to the preservation of their native culture (Shaw 1994: 48-50). For example, the hijab and ethnic costumes created a visible religious or ethnic community in their neighbourhood. Meals shared with family and relatives served as an important reminder of their cultural roots (Rayaprol 1997: 68).

The development of the Muslim community was also shaped by structural changes in the economy. Virinder Kalra depicts the transformation of the Muslim community in Oldham, North of England, in his book *From Textile Mills to Taxi Ranks*. Many older Muslim men lost their jobs due to a downturn in manufacturing, but their unemployment prompted them to become more involved in their community. They began to spend more time at local mosques or engage in community activities.[11] The mosque became an important place for men who had lost their economic roles to reclaim their authority in the community. Economic changes also led to increased community participation by young men. In the former industrial zone of Northern England, many young men had found employment in service labour such as driving taxis and self-employment. These jobs facilitated their participation in prayer

Chapter 2

and religious activities, allowing them to manage their time on their own. It strengthened their commitment to Islam and their influence within the Muslim community (Kalra 2000).

Community development centring on the mosques gathered momentum as a result. The spread of mosques in the UK was initially slow after the first registration in Woking, South East England, in 1889. In fact, there were no more than ten officially registered mosques until 1965. The number gradually rose during the 1960s, reaching 18 by 1966, 79 in 1975, 295 in 1985 and 554 in 1995. The current number ranges between 1,500 and 3,000 (Lewis 1994: 13; Ahmad 2012: 172).

Multiculturalism in the UK

The evolution of these spatial and cultural communities prepared the ground for multiculturalism as a political movement. While the origins of multiculturalism in the UK are disputed, I would like to outline its post-war development in this section.[12]

During the 1950s, many regional cities appointed public officers to deal with housing, employment and other social needs and problems of the mainly Caribbean immigrants in cooperation with support groups and self-help groups. In the 1960s, the immigration issue grew into a central agenda in politics as demonstrated by the Notting Hill Riots of 1958, the 1964 general election in the Smethwick constituency, and the 'Rivers of Blood' speech made by Enoch Powell in 1968 (FitzGerald 1998: 162; Adachi 2013b: 99). At the same time, local-level support systems for immigrants and ethnic minorities were created by a number of laws during the 1960s. For example, the Local Government Act 1966 and the Local Government Grants Act 1969 enabled financial support for impoverished communities of predominantly Caribbean immigrants (Solomos 1989: 89–93).[13]

The most important legal measures for problems arising from Britain's cultural and ethnic diversity were instituted in the 1960s and 1970s, in three versions of the Race Relations Act (1965, 1968 and 1976).[14] These acts were ground-breaking in that they prohibited racial discrimination in employment and housing as well as physical and non-physical discrimination. In particular, the Racial Relations Act 1976 obliged local authorities to actively eliminate unfair discrimination and promote equal opportunities among different racial groups. The race relations laws were important for multiculturalism because they paved the way for immigrants to practice cultural manners and customs without being disadvantaged in mainstream society. For example, the Racial Relations Act 1976 included a clause prohibiting 'indirect discrimination', which refers to discrimination arising 'where apparently neutral institutional practices, which do not directly target minority groups, nevertheless have a disproportionately adverse impact upon members of such groups' (Poulter 1997: 64). Due to this provision, various conventional practices were reviewed from a racial discrimination viewpoint and disparate treatment of individuals based on their colour, race, nationality or ethnicity became unjustifiable. Although the law did not explicitly address 'religious' discrimination, it partially covered such issues in practice. This was demonstrated by the judicial decision in *Mandla v. Dowell Lee*. In this case, a Sikh boy appealed to be allowed to wear a turban in school, and the House of Lords ruled that the school master's refusal amounted to unlawful discrimination. The plaintiffs won the case based on the court's judgment that Sikhs were considered an 'ethnic' group having a shared origin and history (Poulter 1997: 63). Unlike Sikhs and Jews, Muslims were not recognised as an ethnic group under the Racial Relations Act 1976. Interestingly, however, the rights granted to the former religious groups by the law were partially extended to the latter ones as well. For example, wearing scarves by female Muslim pupils and students was recognised as a matter of common cultural convention in schools attended by Muslims (Poulter 1997: 64).[15]

Schools were on the front lines of multiculturalism policy. As mentioned, Asian communities were established through family reunions and took great interest in their children's socialisation for community reproduction. Especially in urban areas such as Bradford and Manchester, Muslims formed religious and educational organisations to promote Islamic studies at schools and make schools more religion-oriented. Consequently, many schools introduced Islamic studies, providing halal food and permitting scarf-wearing (Singh 2002: 100–1, 120–1).

Multiculturalism began to make waves in the UK during the 1980s (Baringhorst 1992; Modood 2015: 14–5), a period marked by the end of the long-standing 'post-war consensus politics' on welfare and the country's transition to 'neoliberalism'. The Conservative government led by Margaret Thatcher pressed forward with economic liberalisation while implementing England/Christian/white-centric social policies through the British Nationality Act 1981 and the Education Reform Act 1988. In this context, migrants and minorities were not to be integrated into mainstream British society, but were positioned outside it through economic marginalisation and spatial exclusion. Meanwhile, local authorities at the coal-face of conflicts, discrimination, economic deprivation and other problems associated with cultural and ethnic diversity began to deliver social policies that were more accommodating of differences. They presumed cultural differences in the

Chapter 2

provision of education, community, welfare, employment and administrative services and introduced positive measures to correct structural disadvantages faced by minorities (Adachi 2009; 2011d; 2013b: 102). These local-level social policies to redress racial discrimination came to be vaguely referred to as 'multiculturalism', although it was rarely officially identified as such.

Britain's 'state multiculturalism' peaked during the first term of the New Labour government between 1997 and 2001 (Modood 2015). The agenda of the New Labour Party led by Tony Blair was the 'renewal of Britain' through a transition 'from an over-centralised and uniform state – the old Britain of subjects – to a pluralist and decentralised democracy – the new Britain of citizens' (Brown 1999). Dubbed 'Cool Britannia', it sought to embody freedom, creativity and diversity befitting the twenty-first-century world. As mentioned later, it included a renewal of self-image and national identity (i.e., Britishness) as well as social institutions.

In 1999, the Macpherson Report (*The Stephen Lawrence Inquiry*) on the murder of Stephen Lawrence was released. The report does not focus on the case itself but on the police investigations and organisation. According to the report, the police looked down on Lawrence's mother and treated Lawrence's non-white friend as a suspect instead of a witness and victim in the case. The investigating officers dealt with minorities in a discriminatory manner and failed to take their evidence and testimonies seriously. As a result, five suspects, all young white men, were not charged due to insufficient evidence. Macpherson Report defines the treatment of minorities by the police in the Lawrence case as 'institutional racism' and presented a detailed picture of inequalities and discrimination ingrained in the organisation (Macpherson 1999). This shocking report ensured that the notion of institutional racism came to be widely recognised, including within the central government. Consequently, the government enacted the Race Relations (Amendment) Act 2000 to eliminate the racism ingrained in Britain's social institutions and organisations and promote good race relations. The law imposed the duty to ensure racial equality and more positive race relations upon employers, policy makers and service providers and required the police and other government agencies to stamp out discrimination (Adachi 2013b: 131–2).

Under the New Labour government, Islamic and other non-traditional faith schools were given access to the funding for state schools, which was previously only accessible for mostly Christian schools. It enabled some Islamic schools, albeit in a small number, to receive government funding while developing their religious beliefs (Adachi 2013b: 286–91). In 1997, the Muslim Council of Britain (MCB) was founded as a national umbrella body with 380 member organisations to represent Muslims' interests. The

MCB was officially connected to the New Labour Party and assumed the role of representing the voices of Muslim communities to the government.[16] Lobbying by the MCB resulted in the inclusion of the 'religious affiliation' question in the 2001 Census (Abbas 2011: 149). After 9/11, the government had numerous discussions with the MCB seeking condemnation for terrorist attacks by Islamic extremist groups as well as opinions and support for the invasions of Iraq and Afghanistan.

The Rushdie Affair: Awareness and othering of Islam

Sociologist Tariq Modood states that the Rushdie Affair is 'the single most important event in the story of British Multiculturalism' (Modood 2015: 14). The Rushdie Affair refers to a series of incidents surrounding the publication of *The Satanic Verses* (1988), a novel authored by Indian-born Salman Rushdie. The book adopts the narrative technique of 'magic realism' that blends fantastical and magical extraordinary events into the real world (Hadjetian 2008). Its contents were controversial. *The Satanic Verses* is premised on the Islamic vision of the world and cleverly incorporates allegories in its narrative progression. The novel was seen by many Muslims as mocking the Quran and insulting the prophet Muhammad, sparking large protests and heated debates around the world. The affair received worldwide attention when Iranian leader Ayatollah Khomeini sentenced Rushdie to death by issuing a '*fatwa*' (legal ruling) and an Islamic organisation announced a bounty for Rushdie's execution in 1989.

When initial peaceful protests were ignored, protesters in Britain took their complaints to the legal arena. Some Muslim groups appealed to the Race Relations Act 1976 and the Public Order Act 1986. However, Islam as a religious group fell outside the scope of the legal protection under the Race Relations Act because the law only addressed race-based discrimination. The British Muslim Action Front and the Bradford Council of Mosques called for the application of the common law of blasphemy, but this was also rejected because the law was not intended for non-Christian religions (Meer 2010: 74–5). This lack of social and legal support prompted many more political protests in Muslim communities.

Among numerous events, one incident in Bradford stood out. Bradford is a mid-sized city in northern England that developed on the back of the textile and manufacturing industries. Its large Asian population and the growing influence of its Muslim community were already a cause of concern

Chapter 2

to British society (Lewis 1994: 2).[17] Bradford was of particular interest because the Bradford Council of Mosques and some other groups – thoughtlessly – staged a book-burning to protest Rushdie. Book-burning is associated with Nazism in the European context, and this incident reinforced conceptions of the intolerant side of Islam, inviting harsh criticism against the Muslim community (Geaves 2005: 69).[18]

The Rushdie Affair increased the awareness – among both Muslims and non-Muslims – of Islam as a religious identity and a vehicle for political mobilisation (Geaves 2005: 69–71; Modood 2006a: 41–2). Until then, people of subcontinental origins were defined by the attitudinally passive and politically obscure category of '(South) Asian' rather than a religious category. After the Rushdie Affair, the religious category of 'Muslim' gained prominence not only among themselves but also from politicians and the mass media. Muslims gradually became more committed to that identity. As Pnina Werbner states, the Rushdie Affair 'liberated Pakistani settler-citizens from the self-imposed burden of being a silent, well-behaved minority, whatever the provocation, and opened up the realm of activist, anti-racist and emancipatory citizenship politics' (Werbner 2002: 258). This is an ironic outcome. Just as 'the anti-Semite creates the Jew' (Sartre 1976: xi), anti-Islam created Islam. Meanwhile, mainstream society came to witness various practices – arranged marriage, polygamy, the wearing of scarves etc. – in the name of 'Islam' through the mass media. Muslims were met by an unexpectedly severe backlash from their host society, but they also discovered the global Islamic 'imagined' community (*umma*) and received support from fellow Muslims around the world (Ansari 2004: 18–9; Geaves 2005: 70).

This situation produced some ambivalence. This newly discovered identity, on one hand, highlighted previously neglected or rejected religious needs among Muslims and made possible their access to the mainstream political processes as a religious group (Geaves 2005: 69–71). In other words, Muslims were now recognised by themselves and others as an identity group with common needs. The Rushdie Affair was a catalyst for the Muslim community to learn to organise their demands by peaceful means and for mainstream society to learn why Rushdie's work provoked such intense reactions. These developments also highlighted new diversity-related needs that could not be dealt with in the existing 'race relations' framework and led to a movement to redress religion-based discrimination and misrecognition.

On the other hand, new connections with the global Islamic community linked some Muslim organisations with overseas (especially Pakistani) extremist groups in heavy-handed campaigns against Rushdie. This approach was at times associated with radical protest tactics such as book-burning and calls for Rushdie's death; it came to represent 'Islam' as a religious category in media reporting, identified with irrational fundamentalism. This reinforced the adversarial notion of the 'West-against-Islam', with Muslims seen as a threat to British law and order because they would favour the *umma* (Islamic community) as a supranational belief system over the values and rules of their host society (Mirza et al. 2007: 26).

This representation of Islam in Western society was reinforced through the Iranian Revolution led by Ayatollah Khomeini (1979), the Iran hostage crisis (1979–81), the bombing of Pan Am Flight 103 (1988), Saddam Hussain's occupation of Kuwait (1990), the World Trade Center bombing (1993) and the USS Cole attack (2000) and became definitive after the September 11 Twin Towers attacks (2001) and the 7 July London bombings (2005) (Brah 2006: 58; Kabir 2010: 17–8; Sardar and Ahmad 2012: 2–3).

Parallel lives and youth radicalisation

As discussed above, multiculturalism gathered strength in the UK during the 1980s and peaked in the first term (1997–2001) of Prime Minister Blair's New Labour government (Modood 2015: 15–7). In its second and third terms (2001–2007) following 9/11, however, the focus of social integration policy shifted from 'diversity' to 'integration' (Abbas 2011: 121). The political discourse of 'the failure of multiculturalism' formed the new backdrop, as discussed in Chapter 1.

A specific condition envisaged by the political discourse against multiculturalism is 'parallel lives'. This term was used in the official report on the 2001 race riots involving Asian (especially Muslim) youth in Northern England and became the core concept in the New Labour government's understanding of ethnic diversity from then on. It refers to a cyclic pattern by which 'the ignorance about each other's communities had been turned into fear, and even demonization' and generated 'intolerance, discrimination and, in extreme cases, violence' (Mactaggart 2004: 7; Cantle 2001: 28).[19] The perception of parallel lives was associated with multiculturalism after 7/7 and spoken of as a particular trait of the Muslim community. The idea of 'self-segregation' is the key point in this view. It reflects criticism that the Muslim community, with the support of multiculturalism, voluntarily avoided interaction with mainstream society and created its own cultural space incompatible with British society, with potential to become a hotbed of extremist ideologies.

Chapter 2

For example, the then Home Secretary David Blunkett made the following comment on young second-generation Muslims in his lecture at the University of York in 2003:

> It is a worrying trend that young, second-generation British Muslims are more likely than their parents to feel they have to choose between feeling part of the UK and feeling part of their faith – when in fact as citizens of the United Kingdom and adherents of a major faith they should feel part of wider, overlapping communities. (Blunkett 2016)

Blunkett explains that second-generation Muslims living in a segregated space are finding it difficult to adapt to British society and share in its values because they vacillate between being British and being Muslim and fail to balance them. Other mainstream politicians have also expressed this point of view. For example, Ruth Kelly, Minister for Communities and Local Government, and Liam Byrne, Minister for Borders and Immigration, in the New Labour cabinet stated that 'There is, however, a particular issue with a minority of second and third generation young Muslims' as to their ability to feel British (Kelly and Byrne 2007: 25). Michael Gove, who later became the Minister for Education in the Conservative-Liberal Democratic coalition government, expresses his concerns about the threat of Islamism in his book *Celsius 7/7*:[20]

> A rising generation has been encountered by those Muslims most prominent in public life to put their Islamic identity ahead of their citizenship... That generation will also have had its sense of grievance nurtured even as its sense of separateness has been reinforced. (Gove 2006: 106)

His argument is that the younger generation Muslims are caught up in a certain kind of rigid undemocratic ideology in a segregated space and unable to share the identity and values of British society as demonstrated by the perpetrators of 7/7.

Philip Lewis, who conducted research in Bradford, highlights and discusses conflict and problems besetting young British Muslims in his book *Young, British, and Muslim* (2007). According to his research, Britain's Muslim community chooses segregated living to maintain its cultural life but fails to understand the problems of young Muslims who were born and raised in Western culture or to give them meaningful guidelines for living as Muslims in Western society. As a result, it is unable to offer a foundation for the positive identities young people are looking for and creates a space for extremism to exploit this deficiency (Lewis 2007; Choudhury 2007).

Lewis points out a serious intergenerational conflict in Britain's Muslim community. He warns that young Muslims living in British society are shackled by the *biradari* system underpinning the Asian Muslim communities:

> Policy-makers worry about the existence of 'parallel worlds', especially in northern cities. Whatever the precise nature, extent, reasons for and significance of such social, cultural and spatial separation, it is clear that young Muslims within those spaces consider themselves British and share many aspects of popular youth culture with their non-Muslim peers. Their problem is with the many traditionally-minded parents who seek, usually unsuccessfully, to limit their access to it. (Lewis 2007: 149)

In traditional communities in South Asia, especially in the countryside, Islamic practices are deeply embedded in the *biradari* rather than in their personal relationships with God. The *biradari* is not just a kinship network but also a system of status and honour permeating every aspect of life, including religion, morals, law, politics, marriage, and financial dealings. However, it has no significant connection with the Western world and cannot function as the bedrock for British identity or the guidelines for living in British society. Lewis quotes a documentary and film maker's comment on this:

> The Pakistani community in Britain has been established here for over forty years. Now in their third generation they face a crisis which threatens to undermine their future. At the heart of the problem lies the *biradari*, the extended clan network that governs all families and gives values and a sense of identity. Invisible to the outside world, a battle is taking place between *biradari* diehards and those who believe it has no place in modern British society. The youth are the casualties. (Lewis 2007: 46)

For example, surveys show that the imams (prayer leaders) of most mosques in the UK were trained overseas, not in the UK, and deliver prayers in Urdu or Arabic rather than English (KCLEC 2007; Dyke 2009). If young second-generation Muslims do not understand languages other than English very well, these imams cannot influence them and cannot contribute to the formation of a positive British Muslim identity. As discussed in more detail below, one-half of the British Muslim population were born in the UK

Chapter 2

and a large majority of them are aged 25 or younger. The predominantly English-speaking second-generation young Muslims increasingly regard the existing religious community leaders as 'impotent' and 'unable to give any meaningful direction to young British Muslims, having never experienced the kinds of problems or challenges that they face' (Lewis 2007: 120). This is found in the following words of a young British Muslim:

> What you find is that a lot of mosques are culturally led. They are more interested in keeping ties of kinship and traditional values. This excludes the youth who follow in their footsteps. Many young Muslims in this country have a dual identity. They are Muslims, but they are also British, with the British identity being more predominant. Their issues are not being addressed by most of the mosques. (KCLEC 2007: 29–30)

Young Muslims are losing trust that religious leaders in their community can help to resolve the practical problems that they face in daily life because these leaders prioritise preserving traditional conventions rather than addressing the needs of young people and providing meaningful ideas on Islam in the context of Western society (KCLEC 2007: 31).

Extremist groups partially fill this identity gap (Meer 2010: 96). These groups are organised through global networks by young leaders who are familiar with the problems and dilemmas of Muslim youth in Western society. They use university campuses and online spaces where young people can easily participate, offering answers to the conflicts and identity issues experienced by young Muslims and framing their advice through their extremist doctrines.

Ed Husain, who joined the Islamist organisation *Hizb ut-Tahrir* (Party of Liberation) at a young age and quickly rose to its leadership during the 1990s, makes the following observation:[21]

> Britishness and the British values of democracy, tolerance, respect, compromise, and pluralism had no meaning for us. Like me, most of the students at college had no real bond with mainstream Britain. Yes, we attended a British educational institution in London, but there was nothing particularly British about it. It might as well have been in Cairo or Karachi. Cut off from Britain, isolated from the Eastern culture of our parents, Islamism provided us with a purpose and a place in life. (Husain 2007: 73)

This passage relates to the potential difficulties of living as a young Muslim in British society. Husain belonged to neither British society nor his own community. Husain and his peers faced conflict between British society and their community and chose Islamism as a new, third option. This implies that the existing Muslim community was unable to capture the hearts and minds of these young people.

These academic and social discourses are used to shore up and justify the oft-repeated political accusation of non-integration of the British Muslim community.[22] The New Labour government's Home Secretary David Blunkett criticised the self-segregation of South Asian communities and appealed to immigrants to learn English and pledge allegiance to British society in a speech referring to the *Cantle Report* on the 2001 riots in northern England. Conservative politician Norman Lamont condemned Britain's Muslim communities for engaging in forced marriage, polygamy, book-burning, supporting violent *fatwa*, and violence against the British Armed Forces. The Conservative-Liberal Democrat coalition government's Education Minister Michael Gove sent an investigator to schools when the Trojan Horse Scandal was sparked by an anonymous letter warning about the spread of Islamic radicalism in Birmingham schools. Despite numerous errors and doubtful points in the investigation, Gove drew conclusions sustaining the unproven accusation and requested that schools in Muslim communities promoted the British values of equality and tolerance (Faux 2017). Eric Pickles, the Minister for Communities and Local Government in the same coalition government, demanded in a letter to thousands of Muslim leaders in the UK to 'explain and demonstrate how faith in Islam can be part of British identity' (Hoque 2015: 33–4). These political statements endorse the mainstream discourse about parallel lives and Muslim radicalisation and serve to justify excluding discrimination and problems facing Muslim communities (e.g., poverty, racism, Islamophobia and foreign policy) from the government's agenda.

Linking identity and social integration

The post-7/7 studies and discourses created the image of 'conflict between two cultures', which will be discussed further in Chapter 3. For present purposes, it held that young second-generation Muslims were unable to find a meaningful identity in the gap between their community's culture/ religion and British society's lifestyle and values, and that this gap opened a chance for extremists to exploit them. Their culture or religion itself might not be the cause of terrorism but its closed nature prevented young Muslims' adaptation to British society and led to their inability to find their place

Chapter 2

in the broader society. In this regard, the development of new principles and practices for social integration became the most pressing issue for the government in the post-7/7 era. Next, I shall expand my brief discussion in Chapter 1 on interculturalism and liberal nationalism as new principles for integration.

Interculturalism and fluid identity

As mentioned, the philosophy of interculturalism is prominent in the 'community cohesion' policy. Community cohesion is the opposite of 'parallel lives', which create segregation and hostility between communities. The idea of community cohesion is to promote equal contact, shared values and identity, or communal life. It refers to an ideal state where members of different communities share values, tolerance, security, equality, network, attachment, and identity (Cantle 2001).[23] This formulation aims to remove cultural and spatial barriers between people and to create a sense of shared identity and belonging through reciprocal communication so that the communities do not become divided between 'us' and 'them'.

The philosophy of community cohesion is based on psychological research about intergroup bias reduction called the 'contact hypothesis' (Cantle 2008: 113–8; James 2008: 3). The theory holds that meaningful contact between members of groups from different backgrounds reduces prejudice against each other's group category (Allport 1954). From this perspective, the problem of parallel lives lies in the lack of opportunities for contact between different cultural communities, and that it has created a vicious cycle of ignorance, prejudice, hatred and violence. Community cohesion aims to break this cycle by increasing reciprocal communication, knowledge and respect between communities to build a cohesive society (Cantle 2001).[24]

Mutual contact between communities is important in dissolving prejudice and hatred against others. A parallel aim is to create a sense of unity with the broader society by opening identities that have been compartmentalised by the wall. The goal of this approach is the formation of more 'fluid identities'.

The idea of fluid identity was clearly expressed in the report entitled *Our Shared Future* (2007) by the Commission on Integration and Cohesion. The commission was established in 2006 as part of counter-terrorism measures after the 2005 London bombings (7/7) to make policy recommendations about the integration of immigrants and minorities. This report was based on research commissioned by the Ministry of Communities and Local Governments (Okahisa 2009: 199; McGhee 2010: 190) and states that the fluidity of identity is the key to the integration and coexistence of diverse

52

British Muslims: Formation, Politics and Condition

actors such as immigrants, ethnic minorities, and the white community in contemporary Britain:

> [P]eople are moving away from single identities to multiple identities not just based on race or ethnicity, but differences in values, differences in life-style, consumption, social class, differences across generations, gender etc. People now have multiple identities and adjust these to the situation they are in – and this seems particularly true for the children or grandchildren of migrants. (CIC 2007: 34)

The report proposes a desirable form of integration referring to fluid identity or 'multiple identity' as a model.

Criticisms of multiculturalism and closed cultural identity constitute the premises for this argument. The report finds that while multiculturalism allowed different communities to participate in the community in different ways, it kept them from taking an interest in concerns shared by everyone. There is anxiety that multiculturalism strengthens a sense of belonging to a particular group or community while aggravating intergroup antipathy. At the same time, people's identities are arguably fluid, multi-layered, and irreducible to any single affiliation or attribute in superdiverse British society. Fluid and multi-layered identities help to turn rigid and closed identity groups into more open ones, reduce intergroup conflict, strengthen connections with broader society and generate shared purposes and values. The Commission on Integration and Cohesion argues that integration of immigrants and minorities should be pursued via the philosophy of inter-community dialogue, which enables community cohesion and the assumption of open identities. In other words, it proposed relinquishing the essentialist understanding of culture under multiculturalism as a guiding principle for social integration and instead to promote intercommunity dialogue and the sense of mutual interdependence (CIC 2007: 46).

Liberal nationalism and Britishness

The interculturalism advocated by the Commission on Integration and Cohesion required a complementary policy philosophy because simply relinquishing multiculturalism cannot create 'shared futures' that transcend powerful particularistic cultures and religions. Hence, in addition to opening

Chapter 2

closed identities, healthy social integration requires a shared identity to bridge differences: 'Britishness'.

The question 'Who is British?' has been debated repeatedly during the formation of the modern British state, as in other countries. Institutionally, the UK was established following the union of England and Scotland in 1707 and the union of Great Britain and Ireland in 1801 – Wales had been fully annexed, including its executive power, in the sixteenth century. The UK's national identity was gradually formed through external threats such as the French Revolution, the Napoleonic Wars and the two World Wars, and the internal threat of the post-war surge of immigrants stirred up discussions anew (Colley 1992). As mentioned at the beginning of this chapter, the influx of non-white immigrants during the 1960s and 1970s was changing Britain's 'ethnoscape' (Appadurai 1996) as a white nation, and conservative politicians such as Powell and Thatcher tried to (re-)define the UK with 'whiteness' in response to this crisis (Parekh 2009: 35).

By contrast, Blair's and subsequent New Labour governments added new and more positive implications to the definition of Britishness. There was pressure in the background from globalisation symbolised by the end of the Cold War and the birth of the EU as well as localisation manifesting in devolution to Wales, Scotland and Northern Ireland (Parekh 2002). The successive New Labour governments attempted to inject positive meaning into the imperialist tradition of Britishness to displace negative connotations and construct a national identity open to democracy, internationalism and diversity. In this move, ethnic diversity was positioned as the rich cultural heritage and character of the UK. The 2012 London Olympics became a highly symbolic event for that purpose. Prime Minister Blair and London's Lord Mayor Kenneth Livingstone presented London as 'the world in one city' in their pitch for the Olympics and boasted of Britain's multi-ethnic and multicultural society (London 2012 Olympic 2005). Unlike the Conservative governments before them, Blair's New Labour government sought a renewal of Britain by giving diversity a positive role, incorporated into the new 'Cool Britain' identity.

The London bombings on 7/7 significantly shifted the social position on Britishness. The atrocity perpetrated by home-grown terrorists severely shocked British society and prompted a redefinition of Britishness to begin the journey towards an integrated society. In December 2006, Prime Minister Blair delivered an important speech on *The Duty to Integrate: Shared British Values*, which dealt with the relationship between cultural-religious diversity and (civic) integration. The evil acts of terrorism, brought about by widespread extremist ideas and ideologies among young people, were seen as evidence of a failure of shared British identity and values. The home-grown youths who committed terrorist acts had not been segregated from British society. Unlike their parents' generation, they spoke English and led a British lifestyle. The terrorists were 'integrated at one level in terms of lifestyle and work'. According to Blair, however, integration is a term associated with 'values' rather than culture or lifestyle:

> These murders were carried out by British-born suicide bombers who had lived and been brought up in this country, who had received all its many advantages and yet who ultimately took their own lives and the lives of the wholly innocent, in the name of an ideology alien to everything this country stands for. (Blair 2006)

What values characterise British identity? Blair defined them as follows:

> Obedience to the rule of law, to democratic decision-making about who governs us, to freedom from violence and discrimination are not optional for British citizens. They are what being British is about. Being British carries rights. It also carries duties. And those duties take clear precedence over any cultural or religious practice. (Blair 2006)

Blair makes clear that integration into democratic values must take priority over any cultural or religious values. He declares that what differentiates social 'division' and social 'diversity' is a set of values rather than culture, religion or lifestyle and argues that social integration needs to be achieved through sharing the right values and denying the wrong values.

Gordon Brown, who inherited the government from Blair, concretised the duty of integration by linking common values with national representations. Since the New Labour Party's ascension to power, Brown had been pushing the redefinition of Britain's national identity by frequently referring to 'Britishness'.[25] A Green Paper entitled *The Governance of Britain*, which was signed by new Prime Minister Brown and Justice Minister Jack Straw, was released in 2007. It placed Britishness at the forefront of building a national framework (Ministry of Justice 2007). For Brown, the argument about Britishness was not only about the issues of diversity and cohesion that surfaced after 2001 but also more ambitious projects such as a 'new contract' between the state and the citizen in the UK, redefinition of the UK's relationship with global society, and constitutional reform. In other words, Brown considered Britishness as a new 'social contract' concerning duties and rights between the citizen and the state, which was redefined in the context of devolution,

Chapter 2

the end of the British Empire, EU relations, domestic cultural diversity and the rise of both international terrorism and far-right activities. This changing social environment confronted the UK with questions about 'Who are we?' and 'Where should we go?' The argument about Britishness was part of the government's attempt to clarify the characteristics and principles of British society in the twenty-first century and define its future.

For Brown, British society essentially comprises 'different nations and thus plural identities' and these diverse identities could coexist with 'being British'. Muslims were no exception. However, diversity carries the risk of regressing to the more exclusionary identities prevalent in the nineteenth century such as blood, race and territory when social uncertainties rise as in today's Britain. 'Civic national identity' was conceived to counter this risk:

> We the British people should be able to gain great strength from celebrating a British identity which is bigger than the sum of its parts and a union that is strong because of the values we share and because of the way these values are expressed through our history and our institutions. (Brown 2006)

While continuing the discussion about British values initiated by Blair, Brown proposed Britishness as a national identity that embodied democratic values and nominated the sharing of such values as the guiding principle for social integration. Here, Britishness refers to 'a British identity which is bigger than the sum of its parts', which should be shared by members of diverse communities and is the prerequisite for these communities' coexistence (Adachi 2013b: 201–2).[26]

Post-7/7 social integration policy

Integration under interculturalism and liberal nationalism has been implemented through numerous policies in the UK (Glynn 2009).

The first is the use of public funds to help cultural groups maintain their identity and promote integration. This approach involves welcoming new groups such as immigrants and respecting cultural differences. Unlike previous unregulated funding provisions, however, applications from ethnic or religious groups for funds from these schemes are assessed in terms of the goal of advancing community cohesion and integration and subjected to a test if required. It is also required to curb public expenditure that benefits only a single ethnic group and fund programmes benefiting broader communities and promoting mutual understandings (CIC 2007). Second, some cultural

British Muslims: Formation, Politics and Condition

practices are regulated in the interests of equal respect and treatment for all citizens. Specific examples include forced marriage and women's exclusion from some mosques.[27] It is also proposed to raise the minimum age for entry into the UK for the purpose of marriage to 18. Third, it requires compliance with the rules imposed by law and reaffirms that it does not permit decisions to be made by religion without consent. Laws are established in parliament and interpreted by the court. Nobody could interrupt this process, which forestalls any move to apply *sharia* to Muslims in the UK. Fourth is the regulation of religious preachers coming from abroad. Preachers entering the UK are screened for their credentials and ability to use English. It was also discussed to clarify unacceptable behaviours such as propagating teachings that may promote terrorism. Fifth concerns policies for citizenship education and religious education. It is necessary to provide learning opportunities for diverse religions, including in faith schools, thereby engendering tolerance and respect for each other's religions; therefore, cooperation with schools from different faiths or backgrounds such as *madrasas* (Islamic supplementary schools) must be encouraged. Sixth, English education for immigrants is strengthened to ensure equal opportunities because English fluency is part of citizenship and one of the requirements for the acquisition of residency (Blair 2006). The seventh is prevention of terrorism. The UK adopted numerous counter-terrorism measures through the 2000s, with the Prevent Strategy receiving much attention in the aftermath of 7/7 (HMG 2008). It aims to abort terrorist attacks by identifying potential terrorists with the help of local communities. The core of the Prevent Strategy reflects the idea of community cohesion to reduce the risk of young people becoming terrorists by opening the (supposedly) 'closed' Muslim community to outside society and institutions (i.e., government): by way of 'promoting shared values', 'supporting local solutions', 'building civic capacity and leadership' and 'strengthening the role of faith institutions and leaders' (Kundnani 2009; Okahisa 2009).

As above, the UK government has been attempting to integrate the Muslim community by emphasising community cohesion and Britishness since 7/7. While these policies underscore shared values and communication between cultural communities, they tend to discount problems surrounding social-economic-political deprivation and social representations, which multiculturalism in Britain was trying to address. In addition, calling for 'the opening of intercommunity borders' risks feeding into the myth of 'the closed nature of the Muslim community'. Having 'a rigid and culturalist understanding of identity' as the premise, the government justifies othering the Muslim community and the resultant politics of interventions in the

Chapter 2

community under the pretext of border opening, as seen in its terrorism prevention policy (Bagguley and Hussain 2005: 213; Kundnani 2009).

This trait can be observed in changes to the government's relations with Islamic organisations after 7/7. As mentioned in Section 4, the government had a cooperative relationship with the umbrella Islamic interest group MCB in policymaking during the early 2000s, but the relationship was hardly stable. For instance, the government asked the MCB to support its invasions of Afghanistan and Iraq after 9/11, but the MCB withdrew its support because of backlash from anti-war factions in the Muslim community (Birt 2005). The MCB lost its special status with the government when it failed to take clear action against youth radicalisation after 7/7. The government subsequently strengthened its ties with other organisations, including the British Muslim Forum, the Sufi Muslim Council, and liberal Muslim thinktanks such as Quilliam (Abbas 2011: 149). Quilliam in particular had strong ties with the subsequent Conservative government, advising Prime Minister Cameron prior to his 'failure of multiculturalism' speech discussed in Chapter 1 (Nawaz 2012: 350–2). It is important to note that the association between Quilliam and the Conservative Party was based on the single issue of 'preventing youth radicalisation', which reflects the government's view of the Muslim community (i.e., otherness) (Ahmad 2012: 173; Sales 2012: 48).

From this perspective, it is reasonable to say that the UK's social integration policy after 7/7 switched from 'recognition of cultural diversity' accompanied by 'anti-racism' to 'sharing and blending of identities' (Thomas 2011: 77–90). In other words, its policy goal shifted from how to correct institutional racism against minorities (especially Muslims) to how to turn a rigit religious identity into a more open one and then how to inculcate Britishness into religious groups (Pitcher 2009: 64).

Muslim identity and social integration in contemporary Britain

The final section of this chapter describes the current social condition of British Muslims, based on statistics as well as data on identities and social integration.

Exact statistics on the Muslim population in the UK did not exist until recently because 'religious affiliation' was absent from official statistics until 2001. The number was roughly estimated based on immigration data such as country of origin. The estimated Muslim population ranged from approximately 700,000 to 1 million in the 1980s (Wahhab 1989; Nielsen

1992; Peach 2005) and between 1 million and 1.5 million during the 1990s (Anwar 1994; Peach 1997; Gilliat-Ray 2010: 117). Since the 'religious affiliation' question was added to the national census in 2001, the data has been more accurate. The Muslim population reached approximately 1.59 million (2.7 per cent of the total population) in 2001 and 2.79 million (4.4 per cent) in the 2011 Census. The rapid increase in recent years can be attributed to the active migrant intake by the New Labour government on the back of favourable economic conditions from the second half of the 1990s. During the 2000s, the EU enlargement caused a sharp increase in immigration from East European countries, but immigrants from the New Commonwealth countries continued to constitute a large proportion of immigration to the UK (Adachi 2013b: 30–1).

Tables 2.1 and 2.2 reveal the correlation between ethnicity and faith in England and Wales in 2011. The former cross tabulates by ethnic groups (rows) and the latter by religious groups (columns) showing per centage values. The two tables indicate the state of faiths in the UK and the characteristics of British Muslims in 2011. One notable trend is an increasing 'secularisation' (Voas and Crockett 2005). Historically, the Church of England has been and continues to be the official state church in the UK, and Christians form the largest faith group. Nevertheless, less than 60 per cent of the population now identify as Christian (Table 2.1). In contrast, the ratio of those who have no religion has reached 25 per cent. When combined with non-respondents, approximately one-third of the population does not clearly identify with religion. This trait is partially due to a relative decline in the demographic composition of white people, who tend to be Christian (91.3 per cent in 2001 to 86.0 per cent in 2011), but also to the rapid progress of secularisation in the UK. In contrast, there has been a marked increase in the Muslim population, which rose by 75 per cent over just ten years, from 1.55 million in 2001 to 2.7 million in 2011 in England and Wales. This rate of increase is second only to 82.9 per cent for the 'no religion' group (Adachi 2013b: 36–8).

A close look at Table 2.1 reveals prevalent religions for each ethnic group. Among white people, for example, Christians form the largest group (63.9 per cent), followed by people with no religion (27.3 per cent). On the contrary, the no-religion ratio is low among ethnic minorities (all below 10 per cent except the Mixed group). Christian (69.1 per cent) is the predominant religion for the Black group, and Hindu (44.0 per cent) and Sikh (22.1 per cent) are the most prominent religions among Indians. Over 90 per cent of Pakistani and Bangladeshi are Muslim, showing a remarkable level of commitment to that religion.

Chapter 2

When we look at each religion's relationship with ethnicity (Table 2.2), however, the ecumenical nature of Islam becomes apparent. Many of Britain's major religions are weighted toward particular ethnic groups. For example, Christianity is dominated by white people (92.7 per cent), Hinduism by Indians (76.2 per cent), Sikhism by Indians (74.0 per cent), and Judaism by white people (92.4 per cent). In contrast, no ethnic group holds a majority among followers of Islam, with the largest Pakistani group accounting for just

	Christian	Buddhist	Hindu	Jewish	Muslim	Sikh	Other Religion	No Religion	Religion Not Stated
All	59.3%	0.4%	1.5%	0.5%	4.8%	0.8%	0.4%	25.1%	7.2%
white	63.9%	0.2%	0.0%	0.5%	0.4%	0.0%	0.4%	27.3%	7.2%
Mixed	46.3%	0.8%	0.8%	0.3%	8.4%	0.4%	0.6%	32.3%	10.1%
Asian	10.9%	3.5%	18.5%	0.1%	43.4%	8.7%	0.9%	8.3%	5.6%
Indian	9.6%	0.3%	44.0%	0.1%	14.0%	22.1%	2.3%	3.1%	4.5%
Pakistani	1.5%	0.1%	0.3%	0.0%	91.5%	0.3%	0.1%	1.1%	5.2%
Bangladeshi	1.5%	0.1%	0.9%	0.0%	90.0%	0.2%	0.0%	1.4%	5.9%
Black	69.1%	0.2%	0.3%	0.1%	14.6%	0.1%	0.4%	7.4%	8.0%
Other	19.8%	0.6%	1.4%	2.0%	51.5%	7.2%	0.6%	9.2%	7.6%

Year: 2011, Region: England & Wales, Source: Census 2011, adapted by Author

Table 2.1 Identification with religion by ethnicity (criterion: ethnicity)

	All	Christian	Buddhist	Hindu	Jewish	Muslim	Sikh	Other Religion	No Religion	Religion Not Stated
white	86.0%	92.7%	33.8%	1.5%	92.4%	7.8%	1.8%	76.0%	93.4%	86.4%
Mixed	2.2%	1.7%	4.0%	1.2%	1.6%	3.8%	1.2%	3.1%	2.8%	3.1%
Asian	7.5%	1.4%	59.7%	95.7%	1.1%	67.6%	87.1%	16.5%	2.5%	5.8%
Indian	2.5%	0.4%	1.5%	76.2%	0.3%	7.3%	74.0%	13.7%	0.3%	1.6%
Pakistani	2.0%	0.1%	0.3%	0.5%	0.2%	38.0%	0.8%	0.2%	0.1%	1.4%
Bangladeshi	0.8%	0.0%	0.2%	0.5%	0.1%	14.9%	0.2%	0.1%	0.0%	0.7%
Black	3.3%	3.9%	1.1%	0.7%	0.6%	10.1%	0.3%	3.0%	1.0%	3.7%
Other	1.0%	0.3%	1.5%	1.0%	4.3%	10.7%	9.6%	1.5%	0.4%	1.1%

Year: 2011, Region: England & Wales, Source: Census 2011, adapted by Author

Table 2.2 Identification with religion by ethnicity (criterion: religion)

British Muslims: Formation, Politics and Condition

38.0 per cent (although the total Asian group holds a majority). Besides Asians, white (7.8 per cent) and Black (10.1 per cent) people account for significant proportions of the British Muslim population.[28]

Figure 2.1 indicates levels of participation in religious practice (i.e., practising or non-practising) in England and Wales. Among the major religions, those from the Indian subcontinent, especially Muslims, stand out for their very high rates of participation: 79.1 per cent of Muslims were actively practising their religion compared to only 33.2 per cent of Christians. Thus, Muslims were the most active group in religious practice among Britain's major religions, which contributed to Muslims becoming the target of othering in an increasingly secularised Britain.

The age distribution is another distinguishing feature of the Muslim population. Figure 2.2 compares population composition by age group

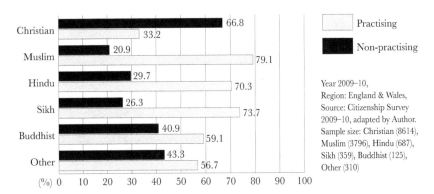

Figure 2.1 Religious practice by religion

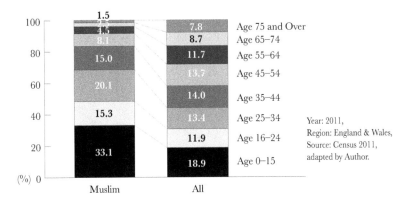

Figure 2.2 Age structure (Muslim & all population)

61

Chapter 2

between all people and Muslims in England and Wales. It indicates a high concentration of Muslims in younger age groups. People aged 24 and under account for around 31 per cent of the total population whereas they account for over 48 per cent of Muslims. When the under-35 group is added, the ratio reaches 69 per cent in Muslims against 44 per cent in the total population. The dominance of the younger age groups in Muslim population is another source of anxiety in mainstream society.

Because the main focus of this book is young second-generation Muslims, it is worth reviewing the data on the generation of immigrants. According to the 2011 Census, approximately 47 per cent or 1.28 million of 2.71 million Muslims in England and Wales were born in the UK, while 53 per cent or 1.43 million were born overseas.[29] Among other things, this point highlights the broad diversity of the group counted as 'Muslim'.

So, what is the level of integration with British society among Muslims? Let us interpret the 2011 Census data beginning with national identity. Table

	British only	British and Sub-national only	Sub-national only	Other only	Other Conbination
Christian	15.2%	9.8%	67.1%	7.2%	0.7%
Hindu	54.0%	2.4%	9.4%	31.8%	2.4%
Muslim	57.2%	2.9%	13.2%	23.7%	3.0%

Year: 2011, Region: England & Wales, Source: Census 2011, adapted by Author.
Note: 'Sub-national' means English, Welsh, Scottish and Northern Irish.

Table 2.3 National identity by religion (Christian, Muslim & Sikh)

	Muslim					All				
	16–24	25–49	50–64	65 and over	All	16–24	25–49	50–64	65 and over	All
No Qualification	11.0%	23.9%	44.7%	60.8%	25.6%	10.5%	11.2%	25.1%	52.9%	22.7%
Level 1	20.2%	13.0%	8.4%	3.7%	13.5%	17.5%	15.4%	13.1%	5.9%	13.3%
Level 2	23.2%	9.0%	5.5%	2.6%	11.4%	26.6%	16.0%	13.2%	7.7%	15.3%
Apprenticeship	1.1%	0.4%	0.8%	0.6%	0.7%	2.6%	2.1%	5.4%	5.5%	3.6%
Level 3	22.3%	7.2%	3.9%	1.8%	9.9%	25.9%	13.2%	9.5%	4.0%	12.3%
Level 4 or higher	15.2%	29.6%	18.6%	13.4%	24.0%	13.6%	36.2%	27.7%	17.6%	27.2%
Other Qualifications	7.0%	17.0%	18.1%	17.0%	14.8%	3.3%	5.9%	6.0%	6.3%	5.7%
All (Age 16 and Over)	100%	100%	100%	100%	100%	100%	100%	100%	100%	100%

Year: 2011, Region: England & Wales, Source: Census 2011, adapted by Author.
Note: Level 1: 1-4 O Levels etc., Level 2: 5+ O Levels etc., Level 3: +2 A Levels etc., Level 4: Degree etc.

Table 2.4 Educational qualification by age (Muslim & All)

62

British Muslims: Formation, Politics and Condition

2.3 charts national identity by major religion in England and Wales. A majority (67.1 per cent) of Christians chose 'Sub-national Identity only' and 15.2 per cent chose 'British only'. In contrast, over 50 per cent of people with minority religions such as Muslim and Hindu indicated their identification with British, and a large majority of them chose 'British only'. As discussed in Chapter 6, the likely cause for this is because 'sub-national identities', especially 'Englishness', are regarded as ethnic identities with racial connotations while 'Britishness' is understood as a civic identity rather than an ethnic one (ETHNOS 2005). Despite the mainstream discourse of their failed integration, more than 70 per cent of Muslims see British and/or a sub-nationality as part of their own identities in varying degrees. This percentage is surprisingly high considering that most of them are first-generation immigrants.

The next question is education. It is known that educational achievement is low among the Pakistani and Bangladesh subgroups, who account for a majority of Muslims in the UK, in comparison with Indians in the same Asian group (Joly 1995; Anwar 1996). However, this situation has improved somewhat in recent years. Table 2.4 shows the relationship between age and educational qualification among Muslims and the total population in England and Wales. According to the table, the ratio of people with no educational qualification was 11.2 per cent in the 25–49 age group and 25.1 per cent in the 50–64 age group among the total population, whereas the values almost double among Muslims (23.9 per cent and 44.7 per cent respectively). However, there is very little difference in the younger generation aged 16–24 (11.0 per cent for Muslims and 10.5 per cent for all). The ratios for the 50–64 group among the total population and the 25–49 group among

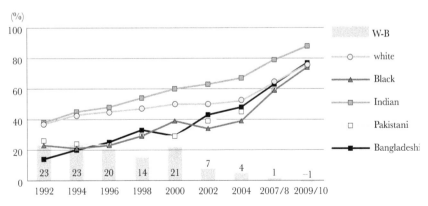

Year: 1992–2009, Region: England & Wales, Source: Youth Cohort Study (Department of Education and Skills), England & Wales in 1992-2000, and England only in 2002–2009/10. **Note:** W-B denotes a gap between white and Bangladeshi.

Figure 2.3 Ratios of A⁺-C attainments in 5 or more subjects in GCSE by ethnicity

Chapter 2

	Age 16–24		Age 25–49		Age 50 and Over		All	
	Muslim	All	Muslim	All	Muslim	All	Muslim	All
Economically Active								
Employed								
Employee: Full-time	9.1%	23.8%	16.0%	41.1%	7.3%	15.0%	12.8%	27.2%
Employee: Part-time	8.2%	11.6%	15.5%	26.1%	7.1%	14.6%	12.3%	19.0%
Self-Employed: Full-time	0.3%	0.7%	1.7%	3.5%	1.6%	2.1%	1.3%	2.5%
Self-Employed: Part-time	0.4%	0.6%	2.2%	3.6%	1.7%	2.4%	1.7%	2.7%
Full-time Students	8.5%	14.4%	1.3%	1.2%	0.2%	0.0%	2.8%	2.6%
Unemployed								
Full-time Students	6.7%	4.4%	0.5%	0.2%	0.1%	0.0%	1.8%	0.7%
Unemployed (Except Full-time Students)	6.8%	5.7%	7.2%	4.3%	2.4%	1.1%	6.2%	3.1%
Economically Inactive								
Retired	0.1%	0.1%	0.1%	0.2%	33.2%	55.0%	6.2%	24.2%
Student (Including Full-time Students)	43.6%	29.7%	4.9%	1.8%	0.7%	0.2%	13.0%	5.0%
Family Care	9.9%	5.2%	36.3%	11.5%	18.2%	3.2%	26.9%	7.0%
Long-term Illness/Disability	0.9%	1.0%	4.5%	4.0%	15.6%	4.3%	5.7%	3.7%
Other	5.5%	2.8%	9.8%	2.5%	12.0%	2.1%	9.2%	2.4%
Total	100%	100%	100%	100%	100%	100%	100%	100%

Year: 2011, Region: England & Wales, Source: Census 2011, adapted by Author.

Table 2.5 Economic activity by age in women (Muslim, All)

	Age 16–24		Age 25–49		Age 50 and Over		All	
	Muslim	All	Muslim	All	Muslim	All	Muslim	All
Economically Active								
Employed								
Employee: Full-time	10.2%	28.6%	34.6%	62.5%	17.9%	27.6%	26.1%	43.0%
Employee: Part-time	7.9%	7.7%	17.4%	5.6%	9.0%	5.1%	13.7%	5.7%
Self-Employed: Full-time	1.3%	2.7%	11.6%	13.3%	11.6%	9.6%	9.2%	10.2%
Self-Employed: Part-time	0.9%	0.8%	7.7%	2.7%	6.8%	3.4%	6.0%	2.7%
Full-time Students	10.5%	10.7%	3.3%	1.1%	0.4%	0.1%	4.4%	2.2%
Unemployed								
Full-time Students	8.0%	4.4%	0.8%	0.2%	0.1%	0.0%	2.3%	0.8%
Unemployed (Except Full-time Students)	9.1%	9.3%	8.6%	5.6%	4.9%	2.4%	8.1%	4.9%
Economically Inactive								
Retired	0.0%	0.0%	0.1%	0.2%	30.3%	44.3%	5.4%	18.3%
Student (Including Full-time Students)	46.7%	31.7%	4.7%	1.4%	0.5%	0.2%	13.5%	5.5%
Family Care	0.4%	0.3%	2.1%	1.1%	2.3%	0.6%	1.7%	0.8%
Long-term Illness/Disability	0.9%	1.3%	4.2%	4.2%	11.0%	5.1%	4.6%	4.1%
Other	4.1%	2.5%	5.0%	2.1%	5.3%	1.6%	4.8%	1.9%
Total	100%	100%	100%	100%	100%	100%	100%	100%

Year: 2011, Region: England & Wales, Source: Census 2011, adapted by Author.

Table 2.6 Economic activity by age in men (Muslim, All)

Muslims are similar (25.1 per cent and 23.9 per cent) and so are those for the over 65 group in the former and the 50–64 group in the latter (52.9 per cent and 44.7 per cent). This suggests that there is a gap of 15 to 20 years in educational achievement between the two populations and the gap is closing. Figure 2.3 shows changes in the ratios of pupils who got five GCSEs (General Certificate of Secondary Education) grades A$^+$-C.[30] According to the graph, the gap between the white group and the Bangladeshi group, the lowest cohort, was more than 20 points in the first half of the 1990s. However, the gap diminished in the 2000s and the Bangladeshi's ratio surpassed that of the white students in 2009/10, albeit by a tiny margin. In fact, the ratio of people achieving a Level 4 (higher education certificate) and more in the 16–24 group is higher among Muslims (15.2 per cent) than the total population (13.6 per cent) (Table 2.4).

However, we cannot conclude based on these findings that Muslims receive equal treatment in Britain's education system. On the contrary, there are many obstacles to academic achievement for British Muslims. For example, many of the universities attended by Muslims are former polytechnics that were promoted to university status under the Further and Higher Education Act 1992. Enrolments of South Asian students remain relatively small among elite universities in the Russell Group, such as Oxbridge.[31] Moreover, there have been allegations that these universities use racial profiling in their student selection processes (Modood 2010: 69-74; Noden et al. 2014). Various forms of institutional racism exist in classrooms. In areas with a high concentration of Asian workers in marginal employment, such as taxi drivers, there is an expectation that their children will find employment in similar jobs and hence have no aspirations for higher education. Combined with a shortage of Muslim teaching staff, there has been insufficient academic support for Muslim pupils and students at schools (Stevenson et al. 2017).

In comparison with their relative success in education, there are major constraints on Muslim participation in the labour market. Tables 2.5 and 2.6 show economic activity among women and men by age group. According to the tables, both female and male Muslims have higher unemployment rates, and the ratios of those who participate in economic activity on a full-time basis are much lower than those of the total population. Muslim men are at the bottom of Britain's labour market and many are forced to take part-time employment. Women appear to be excluded from the labour market altogether. This is partly because of community pressures inhibiting employment opportunities for women. The Asian *biradari* norms lead to women's negative attitudes toward labour. For example, 'family care' is the primary factor for the low rate of participation in the labour market among

Chapter 2

Muslim women (36.3 per cent in Muslim women to 11.5 per cent in all women). Yet, this also stems from lack of educational qualifications among Muslim women as well as unfair discrimination in the labour market due to visible religious symbols such as the hijab (Lindley et al. 2006).

Finally, we need to address the role of 'converts'. Converts have had little impact on the expansion of the Muslim population in the UK. Unlike the US, where conversions are an important factor in increasing religious affiliation, the number of converts has so far had a negligible effect on Muslim population growth in the UK, compared to factors such as immigration and reproduction. The question about religious affiliation introduced into the 2001 Census did not enquire about conversion. By comparison, the 2001 Census of Scotland had questions about conversion, and recorded 1,175 respondents converted from Islam and 1,224 people converted to Islam. The difference between these two figures, 49 converts, composes only 0.1 per cent of the net increase of the Muslim population (Brice 2014: 61). In sum, conversions do not influence the Muslim community in quantitative terms.[32]

However, converts may have an impact on the qualitative aspects of Islam (i.e., people's interpretation of or involvement with faith) (Zebiri 2008: 82) because converts tend to have a 'reflexive' consciousness of their faith that guides them in radical directions of interpretation (Eickelman and Piscatori 2004; Zebiri 2008). Converts need to have deep knowledge of and commitment to their faith to justify their decision to convert, both to themselves and to others. In other words, converts more strongly require 'objectification of faith' (Eickelman and Piscatori 2004: 37–45). Furthermore, their unfamiliarity with Arabic, the language of Islam, motivates them to go beyond the traditional sources of Islamic knowledge, such as local mosques, to access a variety of resources, especially the Internet, which in turn reinforces their reflexive relationship with Islam.[33]

However, it would be mistaken to treat any distinction between 'convert' and 'born' as absolute. In fact, a reflexive consciousness which objectifies Islam has become widespread among today's young Muslims (Ansari 2004: 17; Zebiri 2008: 38), as will be illustrated by numerous cases in this book. To clarify this point, Chapter 3 will detail the theory of reflexive identity to provide the analytical framework for this study.

Notes

1 Description in this chapter draws heavily from Adachi (2013b), which presents more details about post-war British social integration policies. For a summary of the book, refer to Adachi (2009; 2011d).

2 The word 'caliph', or *khalifah* originally means 'successor' or 'deputy'. In Islam, it refers to a person who inherited political power from Muhammad. The majority Sunni sect calls the first four caliphs the 'orthodox caliphs' (Nihon Isuramu Kyokai et al. eds. 2002: 187–8).

3 In other words, the British Empire was built and maintained with 'Indian blood' (Visram 1986: 113).

4 British bureaucrats believed at the time that various ethnic groups living in the cold and hilly areas, especially the Sikhs, were suited to become imperial soldiers because of their self–awareness as a minority following a reformist tradition and their collaboration with the British in the Indian Rebellion in addition to their physical traits and traditional discipline (Visram 1986: 114; Nagasaki 2004: 339–40; Isaka 2013: 174; Kayanoki 2013: 8).

5 The Navigation Act 1660 stipulated that at least 75 per cent of sailors on British-registered Asian trading vessels had to be British. However, many Indian lascars were employed to meet labour requirements during the American War of Independence and the Napoleonic Wars (Visram 1986: 34).

6 One effect of that was the construction of the first mosque in Liverpool by a British Muslim convert, Abdullah Quilliam (formerly William Henry Quilliam), in 1889 (Dyke 2009: 4).

7 The greatest numbers migrated from Britain's closest colony: Ireland. In mid-nineteenth century Ireland, many people were displaced from their lands by the Potato Famine and the spread of 'absentee landlords'. They emigrated to Britain and America, providing a 'labour reserve' in many developing industrial cities (Castles and Miller 1993: 55). The second largest source of migrants to Britain was the Jewish people. For example, approximately three million people left Tsarist Russia between 1880 and 1914 to escape the Pale of Settlement policy. While a large majority of them headed for the US, around 150,000 Jews migrated to the UK. Many of them settled in London's East End and worked in the apparel industry (Castles and Miller 1993: 55-6). In the early twentieth century, the raging anti-Semitism in continental Europe and oppression by Nazi Germany created massive numbers of additional Jewish migrants (Panayi 2010: 38–9). The third largest source was Germany. It has been estimated that at least 180,000 Germans (of which 120,000 were non-Jewish) migrated to Britain. Moreover, we must not forget refugees. Britain has a history of accepting political or religious refugees from continental Europe. For example, East London provided refuge to Huguenots (Calvinists) in the seventeenth and eighteenth centuries prior to a major influx of Jewish immigrants from the late nineteenth century to the early twentieth century. When Louis XIV gradually undermined the *Edict of Nantes* that guaranteed limited rights to the Protestants from 1679 and formally revoked it in 1685, about 200,000 Protestants fled France (Hayashida 2001: 168; Kershen 2005: 34–7).

Chapter 2

8   While such calls came out of concerns about social problems brought by Black immigrants such as increasing demands for housing, welfare free-riders and crime, one of the focal points was about 'Britishness'. Settlement by non–white immigrants was considered to weaken the British way of life and its identity as a white society (Harris 1988: 53).

9   Robert Miles calls this situation a 'paradox' (Miles 1989), referring to post-war Britain's preference of 'foreigners' from Poland and other East European countries over the massive numbers of 'British subjects' from her colonies as labour resources. In short, *'a demand for migrant labour continued but political and ideological factors required that the demand be met from sources other than the Caribbean and the Indian sub-continent'* (Miles and Cleary 1992: 166). This was straightforward race politics (Miles 1989; 1993). For instance, between 70,000 and 100,000 Irish people migrated to Britain between 1945 and 1951. During World War II, Britain encouraged Polish soldiers taking shelter in the country to settle there and recruited European Volunteer Workers from the continent (Solomos 1989: 41–4).

10 Although the Labour Party tried to make voucher allocations under the Commonwealth Immigrants Act 1962 more generous, it made the screening criteria for Category B more rigorous and discontinued Category C once it seized power in 1965. Further restrictions were introduced before the voucher system was abolished in 1972 (Sakuma 1998: 387; Ishida 1975b: 6–11).

11 Mosques served as sanctuaries for unemployed men who wanted to get away from their cramped and stifling 'home' controlled by women (Phillips 2009: 26).

12 Many studies refer to diverse origins of multiculturalism in the UK, including the Race Relations Act 1976 prohibiting institutional racism, the *Swann Report* (1985) promoting multicultural education, and the open-minded British Nationality Act 1948 (Goulbourne 1998; Fahrmeier 2000; Modood 2015). Historian Panikos Panayi, however, argues that its origins can be traced back to at least the end of the eighteenth century. Civil rights and religious freedoms were partially recognised for the Catholic minority during that period, and the subsequent formation of a pressure group by prominent Irish figures led to the formulation of the Roman Catholic Relief Act 1829. The act granted the Catholics equal rights to the Anglicans. This success set the 'pattern' for the cultural and political rights of Jews and other religious minorities (Panayi 2010: 259–74).

13 The Local Government Act 1966 had a provision known as 'Section 11' for funding contributions 'to local authorities who… are required to make special provision in the exercise of any of their functions in consequence of the presence within their areas of substantial numbers of immigrants from the Commonwealth whose language or customs differ from those of the community'. The government provided financial support for English language training for students whose first language was not English based on Section 11 (Dench et al. 2006: 139). It continued until the Ethnic Minority Achievement Grant was introduced in 1999.

14 The Labour Party was critical of the Conservative Party's immigration restrictionism in the early 1960s. However, the party backed away when it was faced with the surge of immigrants and public opposition. Progressives within the Labour Party tried to regain their psychological equilibrium by passing a series of race relations laws for ethnic minorities in exchange for accepting restrictive immigration policies. This ambivalence was expressed in Labour MP Roy Hattersley's aphorism: 'Without integration, limitation is inexcusable; without limitation, integration is impossible', and Home Secretary Roy Jenkins' statement, 'Together with that strong control over immigration, we must have a most determined and liberal policy of complete equality for those settled in this country. I regard these matters as two sides of the same coin' (Bleich 2003: 47; Adachi 2013b: 119).

15 This is why the headscarf controversy which happened concurrently in the UK and France in the 1980s – i.e., a debate on whether or not to legislate against the headscarf – did not become a political problem in the former. In the UK, schools were allowed to set their own rules about the scarf wearing by female students in consultation with the community. Many schools decided to accept the wearing of headscarves that matched the school colours (Adachi 2011a; 2011b).

16 However, there has been considerable debate from the very start over the extent to which the MCB genuinely represents British Muslims, stemming from the question of who and how to represent 2.8 million ethnically and denominationally diverse Muslims (Economist 2014).

17 Bradford was already the epicentre of debates on multicultural society before the Rushdie Affair. The city of Bradford announced the 12-Point Race Relations Plan, a pioneering declaration to improve race relations, with the council taking positive actions as the employer and service provider in redressing the disadvantages and injustices suffered by ethnic minorities and respecting diverse ethnic and cultural identities (Singh 2002: 196). However, this step toward a multicultural society was met with intense opposition. For instance, the Local Administrative Memorandum promoting multiculturalism in 1983 was received by school principals as bureaucratic interference by the Local Education Authority in schools' traditional authority and rights, and the Bradford branch of the National Association of Head Teachers formally opposed the memo (Tomioka 1998: 602–14). In 1984, the Honeyford Affair broke out when the headmaster of Drummond Middle School, Ray Honeyford, criticised the multiculturalist position of the Local Education Authority as well as ethnic minority pupils and their parents. The headmaster was later forced out of his job, but the nationwide multiculturalism controversy continued. It signified conflict between rising multiculturalism and traditional British values (Adachi 2009: 439).

18 There were several cases of 'thoughtlessness' on the part of Muslims. For instance, a Muslim speaker at an Islamic conference on the Rushdie Affair in Manchester called for Rushdie's death in front of the Bishop of Manchester, a Labour MP, national TV cameras and the press (Werbner 1994: 102–3).

Chapter 2

19 For example, the independent reviewers of the Bradford riots heard the following comments in interviews (Cantle 2001: 9): 'When I leave this meeting with you, I will go home and not see another white face until I come back here next week' (a Muslim of Pakistani origin); 'I never met anyone on this estate who wasn't like us from around here' (a young man from a white council estate). These comments were quoted as evidence of parallel lives where neighbouring (Asian and white) communities did not mix.

20 Gove is known for his strong anti-Islam (and pro–Israel) stance. Baroness Warsi, the first female Muslim cabinet minister in the first Conservative-Liberal Coalition led by David Cameron, later expressed her concern that the government's Muslim policy was becoming 'radicalised' by her colleague Gove, who had an outlandish anti-Islamic belief just like US President Donald Trump and his 'crazy people' (Merrick 2017).

21 *Hizb al–Tahrir* is an Islamist political organisation founded by Palestinian court judge Taqi al-Din al-Nabhani in 1953, which advocates for *sharia*-based state administration (Gilliat-Ray 2010: 77–8). Although it does not support violence to achieve its goal, the organisation has been outlawed in many countries because of its denial of democracy and advocacy for a pan-Islamic state beyond established state borders. In the UK, potential threats posed by the organisation were highlighted after 7/7, fuelling political controversy over claims that non-violent but radical beliefs could lead to violent extremism – the so-called 'conveyor belt theory' (KCLEC 2007: 31) – but the government stopped short of outlawing it (Malik 2011).

22 Husain subsequently set up an anti-extremist Islamic organisation called Quilliam together with activists including Maajid Nawaz, an ex-Islamist. However, their statements and Quilliam's activities have been criticised by many Muslims and interest groups because they function as ideologues for the government's Muslim policies, which treat the Muslim community as a potential terrorist group (Kabir 2010: 208–9; Gardham 2010).

23 According to *Cantle Report*, the idea of community cohesion comes from the concept of 'social cohesion' used by a Canadian government body called Social Cohesion Network in 1996. The concept was defined as: 'The ongoing process of developing a community of shared values, shared challenges and equal opportunity within Canada, based on a sense of trust, hope and reciprocity among all Canadians' (Cantle 2001: 69).

24 However, the contact hypothesis does not envisage that any contact can reduce prejudice. This theory assumes that interpersonal contact can reduce mutual negative biases only in the presence of appropriate contact conditions, namely, equal status, common goals, intergroup cooperation, and institutional support (Allport 1954). Community cohesion also aims to create a sense of connectedness according to the contact hypothesis (Ouseley 2001: 35). The idea had previously been expressed in policy for reconciling the Protestant and Catholic communities in the context of the long-standing Northern Ireland conflict. Based on that social experiment, the contact hypothesis was adopted to resolve inter-community racial conflicts after the Northern England riots.

British Muslims: Formation, Politics and Condition

25 Brown expressed strong feelings for Britishness, mentioning 'Britain', 'Great Britain' and 'Britishness' 59 times at the Labour Party conference in 2003, 51 times in 2004, 54 times in 2005 and 42 times in 2006 (Lee 2006: 369). In his 2005 budget speech, Brown uttered 'Britain' 44 times while mentioning his home country of Scotland only twice, drawing criticism from Scottish National Party leader Alex Salmond (Bradley 2007: 8).

26 It is no coincidence that both interculturalism and liberal nationalism reflect Durkheimian philosophy. The Commission on Integration and Cohesion envisioned a 'sense of shared futures and mutual interdependence' (CIC 2007: 46) in relation to the former while Brown stressed the importance of an 'identity which is bigger than the sum of its parts' (Brown 2006) in relation to the latter. Both principles evoke Emile Durkheim's argument about solidarity in a highly specialised and subdivided society (i.e., division of labour) (Durkheim 1893). See Walford (1998), Levitas (2005), Seida (2005), or Adachi (2007; 2013b: 78–85) for the relationship between New Labour's policies and Durkheim's theory.

27 According to Quilliam's research in 2008, 46 per cent of Britain's 501 mosques did not have a prayer room for women (Dyke 2009: 20). Many Muslim women feel that mosques are not for them.

28 This diversity is partly due to increasing numbers of refugees from Yugoslavia, Somalia, Afghanistan, Iran and Iraq (Peach 2005: 23).

29 Between 2001 and 2011, the number of 'British born' Muslims increased by around 560,000 while 'foreign born' Muslims increased by around 600,000.

30 The GCSE is a set of examinations to measure the academic attainment levels of students at the end of their compulsory education (age 16). Those who have achieved grades A^+–C in at least five subjects are qualified to advance to sixth-form colleges. The GCSE grades are the most commonly cited indicators for changes in the academic levels among British children. Students at the ages of seventeen and eighteen must pass the General Certificate of Education (GCE A-Level) examinations to gain admission to a university.

31 Oxbridge refers to Oxford and Cambridge Universities, and the Russell Group refers to Britain's twenty-four major universities, including those two.

32 Islam is regarded as an 'easy in, hard out' religion, but the 2001 Census of Scotland suggests that may be an over generalisation. Although it shows a smaller number of conversions from Islam to other religions, it is relatively easy for people to stop following their religion. According to the census data, 72 per cent of 1,175 people who left Islam no longer had any faith (Brice 2014: 60–1).

33 Some consider this to be why converts appear vulnerable to the influence of extremism. Lacking the literacy to understand Islam, including the nuanced meanings and contextual interpretations of (Arabic) words in the Quran, converts and new followers are unable to distinguish between widely-accepted interpretations and the rest and hence sometimes adopt extreme interpretations or views (Choudhury 2007: 21). Also, many converts were motivated to follow Islam by their disillusionment with Western civilisation and lifestyles, including its sexual morality, consumerism and capitalism (Zebiri 2008: 58, 144–97). Consequently, they risk idealising Islam as an anti-Western civilisation.

Chapter

Previous Studies and Theoretical Frames

> A person's act of 'seeing a thing' clearly means something different from the act of photographing it with a camera. It is no exaggeration to say that the person does not see a thing unless they can hold the image of the clear object prior to the act of seeing. To recognise something, they need to have a prepared hypothesis... Those who have no hypothesis see nothing.
>
> *Switch Back*
> by Hiroshi Mori (2001: 379)

> Terms of cultural engagement, whether antagonistic or affiliative, are produced performatively. The representation of difference must not be hastily read as the reflection of *pre-given* ethnic or cultural traits set in the fixed tablet of tradition. The social articulation of difference, from the minority perspective, is a complex, on-going negotiation that seeks to authorize cultural hybridities that emerge in moments of historical transformation. The 'right' to signify from the periphery of authorized power and privilege does not depend on the persistence of tradition; it is resourced by the power of tradition to be reinscribed through the conditions of contingency and contradictoriness that attend upon the lives of those who are 'in the minority.' The recognition that tradition bestows is a partial form of identification. In restaging the past it introduces other, incommensurable cultural temporalities into the invention of tradition. This process estranges any immediate access to an originary identity or 'received' tradition. The borderline engagements of cultural difference may as often be consensual as conflictual; they may confound our definitions of tradition and modernity; realign the customary boundaries between the private and the public, high and low; and challenge normative expectations of development and progress.
>
> *The Location of Culture*
> by Homi Bhabha (1994: 2)

Issues and challenges: closedness and openness of identity

The identities of young Muslims in the UK today have become among the most important issues in the politics of social integration, shaped by criticisms of multiculturalism.

Multiculturalism is a major political principle for integration in increasingly diversified societies (Taylor 1994; Kymlicka 1995; Modood 2013). On one hand, it seeks to redress historically cultivated injustices and inequalities against ethnic and social minority groups and gives official recognition to religions and cultures that are not represented in the secular neutral state. On the other hand, it seeks to promote the integration of minorities into mainstream society through correcting injustices and recognising cultures. With the 'super-diversity' (Vertovec 2007) generated by expanding globalisation, however, multiculturalism has been increasingly perceived as a principle leading to social division. To the extent that this is true, it is due to the effect of the cultures promoted by multiculturalism on people's identities. Multiculturalism tends to create heterogeneous cultural spaces in society by officially recognising the cultures and practices of minority communities, giving rise to identity groups that reject mainstream society's values and lifestyles. These cultural communities threaten social integration by their lack of loyalty to the state, oppressing women and youths and eroding democratic values (Goodhart 2004; Sen 2006; Council of Europe 2008; Cantle 2015).

This criticism of multiculturalism relates to the 'closedness' of identity. People feel uneasy about multiculturalism because it may create closed groups based on certain cultures or religions in such a way that it implicitly defies sharing space and values with secular civic society. Multiculturalism strengthens values and lifestyles that are sometimes incompatible with mainstream culture by asserting and actively supporting the expression of a particular group's unique culture or identity. In fact, in many European cities, Muslim diaspora communities have formed, often referred to as 'Little Dacca' and 'Little Istanbul', in which people wear religious dress such as the hijab/veil and shalwar kameez. These Muslims are seen as having developed segregated communities and reproduced their closed identities within the secularised democratic spaces of the West (Cantle 2001).

In this context, a new form of identity politics emerged in British and European societies between the 'right' calling for the exclusion of Muslims on the presumption of their closed identity and the '(centre-)left' demanding that the Muslim community open itself to 'community cohesion' and 'shared Britishness'. This 'closed-versus-open' conception is, however, insufficient to

Chapter 3

understand young second-generation Muslims in contemporary Britain and provide useful knowledge about their integration into the modern world. While the focus on the closedness of identity overemphasises the otherness of Muslims and their maladaptation to secularised space, an assertion of the openness cannot adequately explain the commitment to religious identity shown by young Muslims in Western society today (Modood 1997). It is essential to ascertain the theoretical and practical connection between the closedness and openness of identity before we can consider the social integration of second-generation Muslims in the post-9/11 era.

To that end, this chapter critically discusses previous studies on British Muslims by reference to some social theories about identity, and then explains the identity theory of reflexive modernity that links the closedness and openness of identity, which serves as the theoretical framework for this book.

From race to culture to religion

I will outline a general trend in Britain's post-war minorities research before reviewing preceding studies on Muslims in the UK.

It was not so long ago that 'Muslims' as a religious group began to draw academic interests in the UK. The study of minorities in post-war Britain was concerned with 'race', 'racial relations' or 'ethnicity' and did not treat 'religion' as socially or academically important (Banton 1967; 1977; Blackstone et al. eds. 1998; Mason 2000).

Race is a pseudo-biological concept introduced to the general public by early modern science during the eighteenth and nineteenth centuries. The race-based classification includes the perceived visibility and absoluteness of group differences and the idea of a 'natural' hierarchy between groups. Race supposedly has a biological – hence unchangeable – basis, which is identifiable by appearance; and also inevitably includes a 'natural' superior-inferior relationship (Mason 2000: 5–7). This way of thinking was highly influential in the early twentieth century, and its lexicon was widely used in post-war Britain. Non-white immigrants were called 'coloured' and named after the (specific) physical trait of skin pigmentation. The same was true in academia, where research on Black immigrants and minorities from the West Indies – who were regarded as the most contrasting to white people in terms of skin colour – was undertaken as a distinct academic field and categorised according to 'race' (Rampton 1981).

As opposed to mainstream society's interests in race, academia was interested in 'racial relations'. The term 'relations' points to the idea that 'race' is defined in the context of social structures and broader social relations rather than biologically determined (Cox 1948; Rex and Moore 1967; Barth 1969; Miles 1993). The distinctiveness, patterns and adaptation/maladaptation of the coloured and immigrant communities have been attributed to society's 'overt racism' such as hate speech and physical violence, 'institutional racism' through housing provisions, employment and education, or complex power relations such as biases among politicians and the media, conflicts with the police and capitalism rather than biological determinants.

While terms such as 'race' and 'racial relations' have remained significant, the concept 'ethnicity' came into widespread use during the 1960s. Ethnicity differs from race in that the former refers primarily to culture, whereas the latter infers a biological basis. As Michael Smith defines it, an ethnic group means 'a population whose members believe that in some sense they share common descent and a common cultural heritage or tradition, and who are so regarded by others' (Smith 1986: 192). There are three necessary characteristics in this definition: first, ethnic groups are identified by cultural elements embodied in ancestry and tradition; second, more importance is attached to belief than fact; and third, recognition by others is required.[1]

Ethnicity spread as an analytical concept partly because of a need for an alternative framework for understanding social diversity at the time (Mason 2000: 14). It involved separating 'Asian' from 'Black' in racial categories due to the rapid growth of the Asian immigrant population in the 1960s. In racial discourse, the experience of minorities was told mainly through the frame of 'Blackness'. Resistance against discrimination and racism was primarily expressed in these terms, resulting in a tendency to underrepresent the experience of Asian immigrants in academic and political arenas (Modood 1988; Hall 1991). As 'ethnic' terminology came into use instead of 'racial' terms, the realities of Asian immigrants and communities could be seen more clearly.[2] It became possible to classify diverse groups without reduction to skin colour thanks to the ethnicity concept. One of its important effects was a shift from 'racial dualism' (i.e., white or Black) to 'ethnic pluralism', more accurately reflecting a diversified reality (Modood 2015: 15).[3]

The introduction of ethnicity sparked an interest in differentiating between 'Black' (especially West Indians) and 'Asian' in the UK. For example, John Lea and Jock Young explain notable differences between West Indians and Asians in their involvement in crimes and riots (Lea and Young 1982). The cultural difference between West Indians and whites is smaller than that between Asians and whites, and especially young West Indians are more assimilated to British society and values.[4] A sense of 'relative deprivation' by structural discrimination is stronger and more serious among West Indians than Asians and pushes the former toward the path to urban riots and crimes.

Chapter 3

In contrast, Asians were regarded as 'law-abiding, docile folks' by society because they were embedded in relatively segregated communities of their own cultures that protected them from anomie despite actual deprivation and discrimination (Sarda and Ahmad 2012: 2). These contrasting accounts of West Indian and Asian cultures are commonly found in pedagogy and sociology as well. Failures of Afro-Caribbean pupils in schools were seen as evidence of lack of discipline or family bonds, whereas successes and failures of Asians were attributed to the excessive culture of their families and communities (Pugh 1991; Shain 2003; 2011; Revell 2012).

Various international political events from the late 1970s – e.g., the Iranian Revolution, the Rushdie Affair and the Iraq War – heightened interest in the 'Muslim' category as a religious identity. In academia, Muslims came to be discussed in comparison with Hindus and Sikhs; research articles with 'Muslim' in the title emerged in large numbers from the 1990s (Afshar 1989; Ali 1992; Brah and Shaw 1992; Knott and Khokher 1993; Basit 1997; Haw 1998; Dwyer 1998; 1999). What triggered this trend was the Fourth National Survey of Ethnic Minorities in Britain, provided by the Policy Studies Institute (hereafter referred to as PSI) (Modood and Berthoud eds. 1997). The PSI initiated a questionnaire survey in the 1960s to gain a broader understanding of the experiences of ethnic minorities in Britain, and conducted the fourth survey in 1993-94 in conjunction with Social and Community Planning Research. One of the features of the fourth PSI survey was the addition of questions on 'cultural identity', which included religious affiliation. The survey found that South Asians (Indians, Pakistanis and Bangladeshis) tended to reject categorisation as 'Black' while deeply identifying with their religions. Furthermore, some differences were discovered between Hindus/Sikhs and Muslims among the Asians. For example, the former were reluctant to send their children to single-sex schools, whereas a large majority of the latter were in favour. The former were positive about women wearing Western-style dresses, whereas the latter favoured more traditional clothes.

Muslims, especially the young, recognised religion as an important element in their identity formation according to empirical studies from the 1990s (Modood 1997). British Muslims generally talk about themselves from a religious rather than ethnic perspective. Islam originally meant only connectedness within the local community in which they lived but is now considered to be an essential aspect of people's identities, expressing their awareness of being members of a 'global Islamic community, or *umma*' (Kershen 2005: 48). Especially since the 2000s, studies of young people from a Pakistani or Bangladeshi background have noted the importance placed on the frame of 'Muslim' (Allen 2005; Lewis 2007; Hopkins and Gale eds. 2009;

Kabir 2010; Ahmad and Seddon eds. 2012; Bhimji 2012; Contractor 2012; Chambers and Herbert eds. 2015; Hoque 2015).

Thus, Islam as a religion has become a necessary topic for the analysis of identity and social integration in Britain. In the following sections, I review previous studies of young British Muslims, together with some leading theoretical frameworks concerning identity from the viewpoint of 'closedness' and 'openness'.

Closedness theories

Primordial identity theories

The first approach to cultural identity is 'primordialism', which is more or less premised on the idea of closed identity (Wieviorka 2005: 139).

Primordialism refers to some interpretations of culture offered by anthropologists and religious scholars such as Clifford Geertz (Geertz 1973; Grosby 2005). Geertz defines culture as follows:

> [I]t denotes an historically transmitted pattern of meanings embodied in symbols, a system of inherited conceptions expressed in symbolic forms by means of which men communicate, perpetuate, and develop their knowledge about and attitudes toward life. (Geertz 1973: 89)

Geertz understands that an ethnicity has a unique culture, a system of ideas that gives meaning to people's lives, which is passed down historically from generation to generation. He sees ethnic identity as 'given' and describes it as something that springs forth naturally based on the notion that people share blood, culture and customs. Geertz portrays these characteristics of ethnic identity as 'ineffable' (Geertz 1973: 259): they cannot be expressed or explained but precisely for this reason they exert irresistible influences on people (Eller 1999: 79).

While some anthropologists understand culture and ethnic identity as given *before* experience, this view is not supported today. The simple idea that culture has an essence that survives environmental and temporal changes relatively unscathed is not sustainable in contemporary society where spatial and social mobility has spread globally and communication and dialogue with other people or groups have become everyday practices. As discussed in Chapter 1, identity is a reflexive and political process that is constructed in interactions with others.

Chapter 3

This approach is reflected in political philosopher Charles Taylor's theory of recognition. Taylor argues that in modernity, due to the deprivation of statuses formerly given by 'social class', questions surrounding self-formation or identity, – 'What are we?' and 'Where do we come from?' – came to the fore. With the collapse of the social class system, however, it is inevitable that 'the assumption behind modern self-exploration is that we don't already know who we are' (Taylor 1989: 178). Accordingly, people are compelled to 'radically reflect' on their own identities, that is, 'Rather than objectifying our own nature and hence classing it as irrelevant to our identity, it consists in exploring what we are in order to establish this identity' (Taylor 1989: 178).

The politics of recognition is one consequence of this social/dialogical character of identity. Taylor, referring to Hegel's well-known 'the master-slave dialectic', emphasises the importance of moving out of relations of unequal recognition and towards the mutual recognition of equals. However, such recognition is not automatically achieved, and thus people's identity construction processes are sometimes painful. Identity is formed by not only 'recognition' but also 'its absence', including 'the *mis*recognition of others', and people are therefore at risk of being saddled with a 'false, distorted, and reduced mode of being' (Taylor 1994: 25). These are the conditions behind what Du Bois called 'double consciousness' (Du Bois 2020) as discussed in Chapter 1. In their double consciousness, minorities can recognise themselves and their world through the lens of 'the majority world'. Consequently, they must always grapple with images of themselves as inferior beings.

From this perspective that 'recognition creates identity', Taylor calls for correcting misrepresentations and supports struggles for recognition in the public sphere to safeguard minority groups against 'distorted recognition' by the majority. Hence identity in Taylor's theory is constructed in dialogue with society and is never monological.

Nevertheless, some have characterised Taylor as a primordialist who emphasises the closedness of identity (Templeman 1999). This is attributable to his understanding of the source of identity.

Taylor divides the domain of recognition into two parts – the 'intimate sphere' and the 'public sphere'. The former is a dialogic sphere for connection with significant others and the latter is a space where political battles are fought over positive recognition of universal equality and difference. Although both spheres are important for recognition, they play very different roles in identity formation. This point becomes clearer from the way Taylor draws on G. H. Mead. While Taylor emphasises Mead's concept of the 'significant other' in identity formation, he does not mention the 'generalized other', that is, the attitude relating to integration with society as a whole. In his theory, one's authentic identity is 'discovered' mainly in communication with significant others in the intimate sphere (Akedo 2010: 6-8). The intimate sphere is a sphere of dialogue with significant others, comprising 'love relationships' filled with 'authentic culture'. However, it is always in the public sphere that the politics of recognition, or struggles and negotiations for recognition, become an issue (Taylor 1994: 25–37). For Taylor, identity is to be discovered in intimate relationships in an authentic cultural community that is distinct from others whereas the public sphere is a place to protect the authenticity (i.e., closedness) of identity from distorted recognition (Taylor 1994: 37–44).[5]

In-between-two-cultures theories

The primordialist understanding of identity, particularly the idea of locating cultural communities as closed places where identity is acquired, is found in early studies of immigrant communities in the UK, based on the 'in-between-two-cultures' theory (Anwar 1976; Ballard and Ballard 1977; Watson ed. 1977; Stopes-Roe and Cochrane 1991; Knott and Khokher 1993; Lewis 1994; Anwar 1998). This is a theoretical framework put forward in the 1970s, mainly focusing on issues surrounding the generation gap within immigrant communities, and generated renewed interest in discussions on second-generation and younger Muslims in the post-7/7 context (Lewis 2007).

The in-between-two-cultures theory was often found in studies of Asian women. Religion was not a prominent category in post-war British minorities studies where the main analytical frame was either race or ethnicity. Most early studies, therefore, explored the framework of 'Asian descent' (i.e., Indian, Pakistani and Bangladeshi). For instance, studies on the social integration of Asian women increased significantly during the 1970s when immigrant women began settling in the UK through family reunions as discussed in Chapter 2. These studies cast a spotlight on the constraining characteristic of Asian culture. The argument was that Asian family life was organised under a strong kinship system and controlled by the concept of 'family honour' (Wilson 1978). Many ethnographic studies researched the *biradari* kinship network in Asian communities and shed light on the workings of gift-giving practices, the prestige system of honour (*izzat*) and shame (*sharam*) and the practice of endogamy through arranged or forced marriage. Discussed in this context was how far women's lives were organised through cultural systems in Asian communities (Ballard 1978; Ballard 1982; Werbner 1988). These studies (re-)produced images of 'secluded' or 'passive Asians' in portraying Asian minority communities that had previously received scant attention (Ahmad 2006: 274).

Chapter 3

The in-between-two-cultures theory is associated with a cultural pathology model for Asians, predominantly Pakistani and Bangladeshi families, which attempts to attribute low academic achievement and social maladaptation to their cultural traits. It was also used to explain the non-integration of Asian students into school culture. In contrast to Black pupils, who have been perceived as aggressive and actively maladjusted to school, Asian students, especially girls, were regarded as relatively harmless in school due to their passive attitudes. At the same time, their paternalistic culture was seen as problematic for producing attitudes that impede their autonomy and learning. The problem was attributed to families restricting their children's interaction with outside cultures (Stopes-Roe and Cochrane 1991).

As we will discuss shortly, the in-between-two-cultures theory was criticised for its view of culture as rigid and invariable, of identity as secluded and closed, and its tendency to reduce Asians' social maladaptation to their closed culture. Nevertheless, the theory does highlight a perspective worth re-examining in the post-7/7 context.

Philip Lewis, who has been conducting research in the Northern England city of Bradford for many years, makes the following comment on the problem of the British Muslim community:

> [M]any parents and religious leaders, imported into Britain's mosques from the same rural socio-cultural world, are often at a loss to help their children answer questions about Islam posed by school friends, teachers or youth workers. A new generation of Muslims are searching for expressions of Islam which can connect with their lived experience as British Muslims whose first language is English. In short, Islam has had to become self-conscious and articulate in a new and bewildering culture which owes little or nothing to it. (Lewis 2007: xvii)

Here, Lewis points to conflicts over values and social life between the first generation and their religious leaders who migrated from impoverished rural areas of the Indian subcontinent and the young generation who were born and raised in Britain. First-generation immigrants lack knowledge about British society in which second- and later-generation young people live and, therefore, cannot provide meaningful religious guidance on problems facing them. As a result, the older generation tries to impose Islamic rules on the younger generation without adequate explanations, whereas young people feel difficult to accept them as meaningful to their own lives (Lewis 1994: 189–202). This situation gives rise to anomie among some young people and

Previous Studies and Theoretical Frames

leads to family disintegration or, worse, puts them on a path to reactionary extremism in an Islamophobic environment.

The image of a Muslim as a 'post-migrant "marginal man"' (Leiken 2012: 265) torn between two cultures resonates with mainstream discourses circulated by European media and government officials (Alexander 2004). As discussed in Chapters 1 and 2, the British government's proposal for 'community cohesion' after the Northern England race riots of 2001 was premised on the concept of 'parallel lives'. It criticised self-segregation among minority (especially Asian) communities, which fostered languages, cultures and values that were irrelevant to Britain and thereby hampered young people's adaptation to British society (Cantle 2001; Ouseley 2001; Denham 2001). In this closed space, some oppressive customs (e.g., honour killing, circumcision and arranged marriage), which had previously been treated as Asian culture, came to be portrayed as characteristics of Muslim communities. Consequently, young people in those communities were asked to (partially) renounce such practices and to learn more democratic values through communication with Britain's mainstream society.

Openness theories

Interculturalism

The theoretical problem of the primordialist and in-between-two-cultures theories lie in their 'essentialist' view of culture. Defining culture and identity as 'closed, impermeable and sovereign units, completely separated from' all others, these theoretical positions perceive contacts between different cultural groups as clashing and bouncing around like billiard balls (Wolfers 1962: 19). Critics of this type of closed identity model formulated an alternative approach called 'interculturalism' which emphasise the openness of culture and identity from the 1980s.

Interculturalism is found in an identity theory in cultural studies that emphasises contingency and hybridity, criticising understandings of culture as fixed and deconstructing their representations (Gilroy 2004). Intercultural identity theorists focus on practices such as the 'translation' of culture and identity enabling contingency (Bhabha 1994), the 'positionality' of the the object (Hall 1991), and the 'third space' in which a negotiation about identities takes place (Bhabha 1994; English 2003; 2004).

At the centre of these discussions is Stuart Hall, a scholar of cultural studies, who was under the influence of post-structuralism. Hall criticised the closed 'old ethnicities/identities' underlying multiculturalism and

81

Chapter 3

endeavoured to replace them with more open 'new ethnicities/identities' from the late 1980s through the 1990s. The notion of old ethnicities refers to a kind of collective identity that is 'discovered' in 'explorations for roots' and mobilised by alienated people in racist society to protest against discrimination. Politically, this idea functions in a similar way to Taylor's multiculturalism (i.e., the politics of recognition), but theoretically, it faces the opposite direction. For Hall, identity is a 'positioning' issue and strategically emphasised or ignored according to the political situation at the time (Hall 1987: 31–4).

For example, the 'Black' category in the UK was a concept 'imported' from the US civil rights movement and politically mobilised by minority groups to protest against racism (Hall 1991: 53–6).[6] The significance of a Black identity was its inclusion of a broader population – by overcoming the divisive effect of cultural pluralism – opposing racism. Its major drawback was ignoring or suppressing the diversity within it. For instance, various Asian groups (including Muslims) were categorised as Black but their needs were rarely represented within the category. If anything, the demand for recognition of Black culture 'had a certain way of silencing the very specific experiences of Asian people' (Hall 1991: 56).

Hall notes the emergence of 'new ethnicities' from the second half of the 1980s, which means the manifestation of 'multiple identities' that can be called 'the end of innocence' (Hall [1989] 1996: 443). The model premised on the 'subject' as 'the individual in terms of a whole, centred, stable and completed Ego' (Hall 1989: 225) was dismantled to reveal the constructedness of dominant representations such as 'Blackness' and the diverse differences they contain. As demonstrated by Jacques Derrida's notion of '*différance*', partial replacement (e →a) of the existing category (*différence*) confuses people's cognition and awareness and turns it into something that generates a new image (Hall 1991: 49–50). Every category (e.g., gender, class and ethnicity) loses its traditional meanings or acquires new meanings through division, fusion and hybridisation. It is the process of changing 'roots' into 'routes', and identities in the process are constructed through each individual's positioning in the context of the history and discourses experienced by their group. These new ethnicities have a 'diasporic' nature (Hall 1997: 34).[7]

A diasporic space refers to 'the site where the native is as much a diasporian as the diasporian is the native' (Brah 1996: 209) and where 'emergent cultural identifications are articulated at the liminal edge of identity' (Bhabha 1994: 179). In this space, identities are constructed under various influences within their own communities as well as social networks extending nationally and globally.

Previous Studies and Theoretical Frames

At first glance, Hall's emphasis on the diasporic nature of identity seems to lead to divisions within a community and also undermines solidarity in the broader society through constant differentiation. Contrary to that common perception, however, the new ethnicities theory presents the possibility for solidarity through the opening of borders. For post-colonial theorist Homi Bhabha,

> the hybrid strategy or discourse opens up a space of negotiation...
> It makes possible the emergence of an 'interstitial' agency that refuses
> the binary representation of social antagonism. (Bhabha 1996: 58)

The concept of new ethnicities aims to create a rift in the 'capitalised subject' (e.g., gender, class, ethnicity) and to recognise internal diversity. Hall's new project targets not only minorities but also the majority, intending to include 'a non-coercive and a more diverse conception of ethnicity' by decoupling the 'equivalence with nationalism, imperialism, racism and the state' embedded in Britishness (or Englishness) (Hall [1989] 1996: 448). In this sense, the new ethnicities theory should be treated as a powerful tool for the 'politics of the ways of belonging' rather than the 'politics of difference'.[8] The New Labour government endeavoured to redefine national identity by distancing 'Britishness' from 'Englishness' due to the latter's racial connotations as discussed in Chapter 2 (Abbas 2011: 99). At the same time, ethnic minorities are required to fluidise their own identities to connect with Britishness. Consequently, Hall's new ethnicities theory can be understood as an identity theory for not only the openness (or decoupling) of identity but also inclusion of diversity through that opening.

Many empirical studies from the 1990s paint pictures of young people traversing multiple cultures and identities. For example, Roger Ballard, who researched Asian communities in Northern England, describes young people who enjoyed hybrid identities in the diasporic space as 'skilled cultural navigators, with a sophisticated capacity to manoeuvre their way to their own advantage both inside and outside the ethnic colony' (Ballard 1994: 31). Second-generation young people were in between the cultures of Britain and South Asia on one hand, and on the other hand felt comfortable in the diasporic space as '*desh pardesh*' or 'home from home' or 'at home abroad', where they managed and practised their multi-layered identities (Ballard 1994: 5).

Alison Shaw's study of a Pakistani community in Oxford found that while there were some conflicts over marriage and women's education between the first-generation immigrants still clinging to the myth of return and the

83

Chapter 3

home-grown second generation, the latter were trying to find a ground for 'compromise' between the generations through various logics. For example, one woman who wished to delay marriage for the sake of her career explained that the profession she aspired to would benefit her family's prestige. Similarly, many men, when choosing a career unrelated to their family's business, tried to convince their parents to approve of their choice by emphasising that it would be advantageous for their family upon return to their home country, despite not believing in the myth of return. Thus, young people in the second generation appeared as cultural navigators negotiating the borders between two cultures by finding a compromise between their personal wishes and their parents' values (Shaw 1994).

Emphasising the open aspect of identity highlights the diversity of identity strategies for minority groups to adapt to or resist mainstream society (Brah 1996). Avtar Brah and Rehana Minhas point out that Asian women leverage their cultures to fight the prejudices and bullying they experience in white-dominated spaces such as schools and workplaces. For example, they may respond in their mother tongue to unreasonable instructions from their teachers or bosses to indicate that they do not understand and to refuse compliance (Brah and Minhas 1985). In her study of secondary schools in Northern England, Farzana Shain describes the various strategies Asian schoolgirls employ. While these girls experience all sorts of discrimination and stereotyping daily, they adapt in their own ways to British schools, where they participate as minorities, by acting to deliberately reinforce their conformity or resistance to teachers' expectations or stereotypes (Shain 2003). These studies show that minority youth do not simply perform cultural practices as imported from their countries of origin; they revise or create such practices to resolve the issues they are facing in their host countries (Ballard 1979; Lewis 1994; Kalra 2000).

Intersectionality

While interculturalism focuses on the openness and linkage of identities, culture is not the only area where such linkage takes place. Various factors besides culture and ethnicity – such as class, regional characteristics, politics and gender – impact on people's social identities and influence their multi-layeredness and diversity. The intersectionality approach emphasises how various social structures and their combined effects form people's experiences and identities (Brah 1996).

Intersectionality is a concept coined by the Black feminist legal scholar Kimberlé Williams Crenshaw to discuss Black women's complex experiences of discrimination that were not captured by existing feminist frameworks (Crenshaw 1989; 1991). Intersectionality theory aims 'to observe the different areas of identity that everyone has and how people can experience multiple forms of oppression simultaneously' (Noble 2018: 7) and makes it possible to examine such complex experiences all at once (Crenshaw 1989: 14). As people's identities are determined by the social circumstances in which they find themselves from time to time, it is vital to unravel a complex web of various determining factors.

The intersectional approach is actively employed in minority feminism, descended from critical pedagogy and Black feminism (Amos and Parmar 1981) and, particularly in the UK, used in research on school maladaptation among Asian girls (Parmar 1988; Brah 1996; Basit 1997; Shain 2003). These studies view the failure of social integration of Asian women (i.e., school maladaptation, job loss and unemployment) as the product of intersectionality, which is a complex combination of various factors such as social class, gender, ethnicity, and racism, not simply a corollary of Asian culture (Dwyer 2000).

Some studies of Asian children have found that, rather than culture-based passivity, the absence of appropriate educational support by teachers and career advisors was responsible for their low achievement and maladaptation at school. For example, Asian schoolgirls were influenced by teachers' erroneous stereotypes that these girls have no life option other than marriage after graduation (Thornley and Siann 1991). It has been pointed out that lower employment rates among Pakistani and Bangladeshi women compared with Indian women reflect not only their religion but also factors such as the timing of their migration (e.g., Indian women settled earlier than Pakistani or Bangladeshi women), pre-migration social stratum, the structure of their local labour market and racism (Brah 1996). Yasmin Ali, who conducted research among Muslim communities in Northern England, points out that women's deference to traditional values is a type of defensive reaction against social discrimination and exclusion they suffer because of their diasporas (Ali 1992).

These social-structural factors do influence the religious identities of Muslims. According to Virinder Kalra, for example, the heightened level of commitment to Islam among Muslim men in Northern England during the 1980s was associated with their occupational move into taxi driving and self-employment due to the decline of manufacturing (e.g., textile) under the Thatcher government. These occupations allowed men to self-manage their time and attend mosques in their spare time (Kalra 2000). Melissa Howe argues that the spread of individualist values along with an expansion of the welfare system and a lack of available housing reduced the importance of

Chapter 3

family cohesion and kinship networks among Muslims, which in turn influence the identities of young people (Howe 2007). Pallavi Banerjee explains the strengthening of women's religious identities in New York in association with social strata. She points out that economically deprived women choose a mosque as the place for family recreation because of their tight financial positions and consequently develop Muslim identities in their relationships in the community (Banerjee 2018).

Clarifying closedness

Intercultural and intersectional approaches emphasising the openness, flexibility and porosity of identities have become the theoretical premises for research into Britain's second- and third-generation minorities since the late 1990s. Nevertheless, these positions are subject to criticism over their understanding of the openness of identity and its political consequences. The thesis that identity is open and flexible is inadequate for explaining the increasing levels of commitment to religion among young Muslims in the UK and the world. It is well documented that Muslims today manifest strong identification with Islam beyond their nations, ethnicities, and social classes (Modood 1997; Roy 2004). For them, being Muslim is not just one of many identity options; it takes precedence over all other identities. If that is the case, how can openness and flexibility be achieved within an identity?

This question is significant not only theoretically but also philosophically and politically. As discussed in Chapters 1 and 2, the political and philosophical doctrine surrounding Britain's diversity and social integration has shifted from multiculturalism to interculturalism (plus liberal nationalism). Although political interculturalism is not always identical to theoretical interculturalism in minority studies, there is no doubt that the former uses the latter theory as a reference (at least in the European context) (James 2008).

For example, it can be found in *White Paper on Intercultural Dialogue* issued by the Council of Europe in 2008. As mentioned in Chapter 1, this report aimed to provide a new principle for the coexistence of diverse cultures in European society by replacing multiculturalism (Council of Europe 2008: 9–10). It points out that multiculturalism invites cultural rigidity and conflict with mainstream society and hampers sharing cultures and values based on democracy:

> Multiculturalism is now seen by many as having fostered communal segregation and mutual incomprehension, as well as having contributed to the undermining of the rights of individuals – and, in particular,

> women – within minority communities, perceived as if these were single
> collective actors. The cultural diversity of contemporary societies has
> to be acknowledged as an empirical fact. However, a recurrent theme
> of the consultation was that multiculturalism was a policy with which
> respondents no longer felt at ease. (Council of Europe 2008: 19)

The document argues that the solidifying of cultures by multiculturalism
can undermine the 'rights of individuals' – women in particular – and that
this has been intensifying anxieties in super-diversified European society.
The Council of Europe proposes that society needs mutual understanding,
communication and respect beyond just respect for differences (Council of
Europe 2008: 17). It anticipates that minority communities can learn and
attain democratic values through communication and social mixing.

The noteworthy points in this report are as follows. First, 'cultures' in need
of dialogue are described as clashing with the rights of individuals, especially
women. Second, the implicit assumption is that such cultures originate in non-
Western societies and represent extrinsic customs and values. Third, Western
social values such as democracy and liberalism should be prioritised over
minority cultures. Fourth, it requires or even urges immigrants and minorities
to cross the boundaries of their own cultures in order to adopt mainstream
social values. These points are clearly expressed in the following passage:

> No one should be confined against their will within a particular group,
> community, thought-system, or world view, but should be free to
> renounce past choices and make new ones – as long as they are consistent
> with the universal values of human rights, democracy and the rule of
> law. Mutual openness and sharing are twin aspects of multiple cultural
> affiliation. Both are rules of coexistence applying to individuals and
> groups, who are free to practise their cultures, subject only to respect for
> others. (Council of Europe 2008: 18)

That is why multiculturism, which leads to cultural fixation, should be replaced
with intercultural dialogues enabling the crossing of cultural boundaries.

This discussion at the Council of Europe resonates with Hall's argument
on new ethnicities (Hall 1991; Bhabha 1994; Gilroy 2004). However, this
thinking runs the risk of exacerbating 'a new moral binarism' (Cohen 1999:
7) between 'good new ethnicity' underpinned by openness to diversity and
'bad old ethnicity', which is closed and causes conflict (Kawash 1997: 178–9).
In fact, multiculturalism was criticised in the post-7/7 period because of its
potential to strengthen the rigid and undemocratic old ethnicities as discussed

Chapter 3

in Chapter 2. The British government intended to use intercultural communication to open the cultural borders of some minority groups and equip them
with new ethnicities bondable to the democratically defined Britishness.

However, some scholars point out that political interculturalism is more
interested in 'securing identification' (mainly with Western social values) than
'recognition of differences' and is therefore in danger of producing more
assimilationist policies (Shannahan 2017). Moreover, seeing commitment to a
particular (religious) identity as pathological and overtly demanding compliance
with universal – and often secular – values through individualisation risks im-
posing unilateral assimilation to Western culture on minority groups. This
is called 'postmodern assimilationism' (Modood 2015: 18). New ethnicities
theory extolling hybridity could provide grounds for a justification of state
intervention in minority groups by treating the individuals and groups with a
strong commitment to religion as closed and undemocratic (McGhee 2010:
120–33).

Sociologist and political scientist Tariq Modood, an advocate for British
multiculturalism, expresses his concern that the new image of identity painted
by (liberal) scholars and political elites is merely an 'avant-garde' idea divorced
from reality. While the intercultural approach places a heavy emphasis on the
hybridity of identities – 'a litany of pollution and impurity' in Gilroy's words
(Gilroy 1993: 2) –, the strong identification with Islam among young people
today seems to be far from 'impurity'. Modood makes the following argument
on this point:

> A rejection of theories of primordial ethnic absolutism should not
> prevent us from accurately describing where most Asians are, regardless
> of whether it seems sufficiently 'new' or progressive. We must not pit
> 'new' and 'old' ethnicities against each other: we must avoid the elitism
> of cultural vanguardism that devalues and despises where the ordinary
> majority of any group or social formation is at... (Modood 1994: 873)

While acknowledging the flexibility of identity, Modood notes that some
identities take solid forms. Many studies report that Muslims in Western
society regard religion as the most important source of their identities and
see Islam as consistent and stable rather than changeable or fusible (Jacobson
1998: 118). Based on the research on British Muslims aged from 19 to 21,
Abdullah Sahin notes that even in young cohorts featuring the most flexible
identity formation, 'They did not appear to be simply code-switching or
alternating between two cultural worlds that they had reified' (Sahin 2013:
146). Similarly, Kate Zebiri's study of Muslim converts in Britain calls for

caution, observing that 'identity choices are not equally available to all people in all societies' (Zebiri 2008: 90).

Consequently, to understand Muslims in British society today, it is necessary to construct a framework that can simultaneously explain both a certain kind of closedness (i.e., identification with Islam) and openness (i.e., integration with Western culture and lifestyle) of identities. We need a third identity model that differs from the 'in-between-two-cultures' model and the 'cultural switching' (or new ethnicities) model (Sahin 2013: 48).

Agency theory

Postcolonial feminism

Before elucidating the theoretical framework used in this book to address the simultaneity of closedness and openness of identity, I explain another theoretical standpoint, post-colonial feminism, which grew in the 1980s. Postcolonial feminism is characterised by a critique of the asymmetrical colonial gaze implicitly held by privileged investigators (e.g., middle-class, white, liberal) towards Third-World women. Postcolonial feminists aim to listen to the voices of these women to find an autonomous subject in their everyday life practices. In the process, it aims to relativise the 'white and middle-class women' model (e.g., post-family, labour participation, resistance, liberation and sexual freedom) assumed by traditional Western feminism and at the same time to deconstruct negative images and myths surrounding women in the non-Western world (Knott and Khokher 1993; Werbner 1996; 1997; Dwyer 1999). It also seeks to draw attention to and bring out women's 'agency', which has been obscured within the frame of cultural difference for so long.

Many postcolonial feminist studies on Muslims examine the wearing of the hijab (e.g., scarves and veils) in both non-Islamic and Islamic societies. As mentioned in Chapter 1, the hijab has been positioned by Western mainstream discourses as a symbol of women's oppression and lack of freedom in Islam (Bowen 2008; Ali and Hopkins 2012; Amer 2014). In contrast, Muslim women's studies are asking, 'Do Muslim women need saving?' (Abu-Lughod 2013).

Through a growing body of research by Muslim women themselves in recent years, minority feminism has come to deconstruct representations of Muslim women such as 'oppressed' and 'unfree' and discuss their voluntary commitment to Islam and its values. For example, it has been found that the hijab covering Muslim women signifies such things as autonomy from

Chapter 3

men, reverence for God, resistance against Western capitalist culture com-modifying women's bodies, and desires to value inner beauty over appearance (Mahmood 2005; Bullock 2007). As discussed in Chapter 10, the hijab means 'veiling for God' rather than the result of oppression by or subordination to male counterparts, and strengthens women's autonomy (Goto 2014). Sariya Contractor views this recent change in people's attitude toward the hijab as a 'paradigm shift' in the relationship between women and Islam. The hijab is a tool for women to express their agency and choices (Contractor 2012: 92–3).

The positive implications of Islam can be found in discussions about the education of Muslim women. For instance, a study on Muslim schoolgirls and their families in the East of England by Tehmina Basit reports that they have strong aspirations for higher education while evaluating ethnicity- and religion-based values and gender roles. They perceive these values as reinforcing their career paths through education rather than contradicting them. For instance, schoolteachers tend to consider strong control of women by Muslim families as evidence of oppression, but the girls and their families recognise it as a means to protect girls from temptations outside of schoolwork (Basit 1997). These studies highlight the different meanings and values of 'freedom' between Western society and Muslim communities (Khan 1995; Stuurman 2004), expressed by a comment of a schoolgirl informant in and the title of Basit's study, 'I want more freedom, but not too much' (Basit 1997).

Anthropologist Saba Mahmood elaborates acceptance of gender roles based on Islam in her study of women engaging in the mosque movement in Egypt. Mahmood presents an idea of 'agent' that is different from the Western notion of 'subject', following Foucault's concept of *techniques de soi*. Foucault focuses on the practice of technologies (or techniques) of the self in ancient Greek and Imperial Roman societies, highlighting the way people worked on their ethical self-formation and lifestyle development as well as formulation of external rules and regulations (Foucault 1997). Such behaviours do not aim to create freedom in the narrow sense of the term but rather mean an effort to construct good relations with others in the community through various self-engaging techniques – for example, writing, contemplation and dialogue with oneself and others. Mahmood depicts women in the conservative mosque movement in Egypt, who appear far from free from the male domination structure, as 'agents' who form such ethical selves-bodies (Mahmood 2005: 29). For instance, one informant spoke of the process of learning the Islamic concept of 'shyness/modesty' (*h.ayā*) in relation to the wearing of a scarf:

> I used to think that even though shyness [al-ḥayā'] was required of us by God, if I acted shyly it would be hypocritical [*nifāq*] because I didn't actually feel it inside of me. Then one day, in reading verse 25 in Surat al-Qaṣaṣ ["The Story"] I realized that [al-ḥayā'] was among the good deeds [*huwwa min al-aʿmāl al-ṣaliḥa*], and given my natural lack of shyness [al-ḥayā'], I had to make or create it first. I realized that making [ṣanaʿ] it in yourself is not hypocrisy, and that eventually your inside learns to have al-ḥayā' too. (Mahmood 2005: 156, words in square brackets are original)

This informant explains that having 'shyness' and wearing a headscarf as an expression of shyness is not something she is forced to do by anyone – not even God! – but something she should achieve through efforts and practices that bring about the change within her.

Mahmood defines these women agents in the sense that they create the ethical body through techniques of the self, not by 'free choice' or as the 'subject' (i.e., absence of subordination) supposed by Western society (Mahmood 2005: 173). It indicates that women's autonomy becomes possible through reference to cultural norms and religious identities, not in a cultural vacuum (Modood 2013: 93).

The transition from 'subject' signifying freedom and liberation from domination to 'agent' emphasising cultural and ethical autonomy relativises a universalistic ideal of women that underpins classical feminism, and it contributes to an understanding of agency which women in non-Western societies or non-white women in the West practice in everyday life (Moore 1988; 1994; Mohanty 1984; 2003).

Culture and women, and influence of discourse

The emphasis on agency, however, can create 'the culturalization of politics' (Žižek 2008), a situation where cultural differences and different ways of life are recognised as given and unchangeable and therefore as merely tolerated. This lapses into a kind of relativism that raises concerns about conserving oppressive practices in the name of culture (Phillips 2007).

This point reflects the conflict between multiculturalism and women's rights discussed in Chapter 1. Recognising and supporting cultural and religious practices risks denying certain rights to women, a concern expressed by feminist activist Leila Hessini as follows:

Chapter 3

> When women wear the hijab, they obtain respect and freedom. In this
> sense, the hijab, which is often perceived by Westerners as a tool of male
> domination, may ultimately be a liberating force for some Moroccan
> women. However, this choice is made within a patriarchal framework.
> It is a conditioned reaction and can exist only within prescribed norms
> established by men for women. (Hessini 1994: 54)

As Althusser's concept of 'interpellation', mentioned in Chapter 1, suggests,
the subjective decision-making of religious women may merely reconfirm
a command from authority.[9] Consequently, identities committed and
presented by such women risk reinforcing stereotypes of 'foreign culture',
which may lead to their cultural groups' exclusion from mainstream politics,
economics, and education (Archer 2002; Thornley and Siann 1991). In other
words, minority feminism, contrary to its intentions, is always in danger of
reinforcing cultural relativism and thereby legitimising the cultural oppression
and exclusion of women.[10]

The question here is not whether women's deference to Islam produces
oppression. The issue lies in the ease with which women's subjective commitment to religion could legitimate Western society's mainstream discourses,
such as the religious oppression. It invites criticisms of multiculturalism
(especially from some liberals) and gives the in-between-two-cultures theory
credibility (Barry 2001; Goodhart 2004; Sen 2006).

In this light, the challenge for young second-generation Muslims in
contemporary Britain is how to build a framework bridging the gap between
their faith in Islam and their lives in Western society within the Islamic
paradigm (Geaves 2005: 66; Dassetto et al. 2007: 7). Research into the
identities and social integration of second-generation Muslims in Western
society is also required to deepen our understanding of how young Muslims
tackle these difficult challenges and how they present their identities to others.

Closed and open identities:
reflexive modernisation theory

I now recapitulate the issues surrounding these theoretical frameworks.
First, the primordialist view of identity suggests the possibility of reciprocal
communication between different groups, but it fails to develop its
interpenetration potential sufficiently, producing 'a spatial binary between
whole and partial societies, one as the principle of the other's negation'
(Bhabha 1996: 57). Accordingly, 'the "dialogic" of its hybridizing potential'

(Bhabha 1996: 57) between speakers of different languages is not expanded fully.[11] As a result, this in-between-two-cultures theory portrays Islam and Asian cultures as fixed, oppressive and conflicting with Western social institutions and values, and hence has difficulty understanding the fact that many young second-generation Muslims have integrated into British society. Second, interculturalism emphasising hybrid identities appears to be a more appropriate framework for describing realities in today's super-diverse global society (Vertovec 2007). However, this theory has been unable to adequately elucidate why an identity or culture could be recognised as a discrete category even when it seems to be open and variable. The post-structuralist approach, which emphasises the variability of identity, fails 'to capture the depth and ineluctability' of religious significations 'in the construction of identity' (McNay 2000: 90), and thus cannot provide a reasonable account for the ways that Muslims participate in a broader Western society while strongly identifying with their religion (Modood 2013: 95–105). Third, postcolonial feminist studies sought to discover minority women's 'agency' by listening to the 'voices' of those who have been silenced and undervalued as passive beings through the lens of Western liberal values. However, they ran the risk of unintentionally strengthening patriarchal authority or being represented as doing so in mainstream discourse on Islam, and in turn, contributing to reinforcing the discourse. Hence, the challenge facing young Muslims in contemporary Britain is how to participate in society as religious subjects and justify such participation from an Islamic perspective, while contending with the mainstream discourse about the conflict between Islam and Western society (Ramadan 2010; Sahin 2013).

Regarding this challenge, this book analyses the state of identity and integration among second-generation Muslims in the UK using the theory of reflexive modernisation. The concept of 'reflexive modernisation' was introduced by British sociologist Anthony Giddens (Giddens 1990; 1991). Giddens proposes this theoretical framework to explain the characteristics of contemporary society in which globalisation has become an everyday reality. Reflexive modernity refers to an age when the global mobility of commodities, money, people, capital and cultures breaks down boundaries in space and meaning that had previously separated people and forces people to live with 'a more open and problematic future' (Giddens and Pierson 1998: 116).

The hallmark of reflexive modernity can be described as 'post-traditional society', in which 'pre-existing traditions cannot avoid contact with other traditions but also with many alternative ways of life' (Giddens 1994: 97) due to globally expanded space-time (Robertson 1992). In this society, traditional social structures and norms become just some of the diverse options available

Chapter 3

for individuals, and no tradition can expect people to follow it blindly. As Giddens argues, 'traditions only persist in so far as they are made available to discursive justification and are prepared to enter into open dialogue not only with other traditions but with alternative modes of doing things' (Giddens 1994: 105) in reflexive modernity. Accordingly, a given tradition can persist and be adopted as part of someone's identity only when it keeps offering convincing meaning, history, and roles to people in contemporary society (Templeman 1999: 23–4). In other words, traditions which cannot provide convincing justifications to be sustained could be rejected.

However, 'post-traditional' does not necessarily mean that 'traditions are lost'. Rather, it refers to changing conditions under which individuals relate to traditions. Although traditions remain an important source of individuals' identities in reflexive modernity, the connection between the individual and cultural traditions is unstable, or contingent, and thus, constructing an identity has become an important 'project' that should be pursued through reflexively organised endeavours in the diversification of lifestyles (Taylor 1989; Giddens 1991: 5-9). Here, individuals find it necessary to redefine their own identities through their complex involvement with the wider society as well as community-based traditions.

One of the consequences of post-traditional society for people's identities and traditions is the deepening of 'individualisation' (Beck 1986). Individualisation refers to a condition in which the assumption of *in*-divisible identity is superseded and people are required to establish a divisible identity in terms of meaning, time and space against the backdrop of globalisation, marketisation and informatisation (Beck 1986: 127–38; Giddens 1991). People's identities are no longer self-evident and *in*-divisible; they manifest as objects to be reflexively (re-)constructed in response to an ever-changing environment (Giddens 1991).

A key in considering identity and traditions as a reflexive project is 'interpretation'. While traditions and religions usually wield influence on people's life through associated 'knowledge', which underpins Max Weber's 'legitimacy' (Weber 1956), knowledge always requires 'interpretation'. As discussed in Chapter 8, knowledge can be made available to broader people, but its legitimate interpretation has often been the sole preserve of religious and political authorities. However, in the secularised and globalised world, understandings of traditions are increasingly viewed as a matter of personal interpretation.

What is the significance of interpretation practised by the individual in contemporary society? In her comparative study of female Bangladeshi

Previous Studies and Theoretical Frames

workers in Bangladesh and the UK, Naila Kabeer points to the crucial importance of interpretation for our understanding of agency:

> [I]ndividual actors may strategise within the framework spelt out by the community's codes of conduct, but their interpretation of these codes brings into play a far more diverse range of practical outcomes than would be suggested by a formal inventory of cultural rules. An understanding of how such rules are invoked in practice and what this implies for the reconstitution or modification of the structures which generate these rules helps to illuminate 'the structuring of structures' over time. (Kabeer 2000: 45)

While Kabeer, referring to Pierre Bourdieu, acknowledges that agents are inextricably connected to structures and rules, she explains that agents do not simply carry out the 'mechanical *execution*' of rules within rigid structures, but instead influence the structures themselves through 'creative *interpretation*' (Kabeer 2000: 45). Interpretations are far more diverse than religious or holy texts, which contents are more or less limited. Moreover, this diversity of interpretations assumes an important function in understanding traditional rules in given situations and meaningfully connecting such rules to modern life. People have to construct novel relationships with their traditions through their own interpretation because traditions can no longer provide unconditional guidelines for people. That is why more positive involvement of individuals in the interpretation of religious texts and traditions is necessary.[12]

The source of interpretation enabling agency is 'discursive knowledge'. Unlike 'background knowledge', which is self-explanatory and transcribed, discursive knowledge is systematised to some extent and presentable or explainable to others (and the self). Tradition relies on background knowledge below the level of consciousness, knowledge which 'goes without saying because it comes without saying' (Bourdieu 1977: 167). Background knowledge is useful to authorities and structures because it gives rise to 'two-fold silence' (Kabeer 2000: 46), entailing 'silence of what goes without saying' on one level and 'silence of what cannot be said because the vocabulary to say it is not available' on another level (Kabeer 2000: 46). The latter is more important than the former. Even when the social environment has changed and a normative rule is no longer congruent, people have no choice but to keep following the given rule until a framework that can explain the situation well and a new rule that is more congruent with the environment is available.

Chapter 3

It should be pointed out that discursive knowledge does not 'control' people's thinking and behaviour like the 'power/knowledge' in modern society, but rather strengthens people's autonomy by enabling diverse individual interpretive practices. On one hand, Giddens – like Habermas and Foucault – argues that discursive knowledge provided by expert systems renders the local knowledge underpinning traditions redundant, thus wielding considerable influence on the masses whose community-based knowledge has been invalidated or taken away (i.e., de-skilled). On the other hand, Giddens – unlike Habermas and Foucault – argues that the expansion of discursive knowledge by expert systems involves a 'dialectic of control'. In other words, individuals can enhance their autonomy from the control of expert systems by selectively drawing on various kinds of knowledge from a vast pool of expert/discursive knowledge according to their relationship with the environment (Giddens 1990: 144–9; 1992: 28–32; 1991: 137–43). These days, expert/discursive knowledge is provided by diverse experts and practitioners – from religious authorities to bloggers – across the globe through informatisation. By utilising expert/discursive knowledge, individuals engage in the reorganisation of their cultural, religious, and ethnic traditions and identities in a form befitting complex society beyond geographical and temporal limitations (Lash and Urry 1994: 255–8).

The above discussion can be summarised as follows. Traditions can no longer expect to be accepted by people as self-evident background knowledge (i.e. local knowledge) because they are forced to relate (or compete) with different lifestyles in the context of globalisation. For its survival, a tradition needs to convince people to accept it, and discursive knowledge takes an important role for that purpose. Unlike background knowledge, discursive knowledge reaches individuals directly through informatisation as well as being transmitted collectively through a community. Individuals attempt to resolve conflicts between traditional practices and lifestyles in the globalised world by relying on a variety of discursive knowledges. The exercise of discursive knowledge injects more flexibility into the background knowledge-based tradition for a better alignment with a changing environment and revitalises it. In short, a tradition in reflexive modernity can reproduce only when it can meaningfully relate to the environment through the discursive knowledge provided by expert systems and people's interpretive practices based on the knowledge. In other words, tradition becomes capable of being open to the environment, dependent on keeping its closedness through reference to each individual's discursive knowledge (Adachi 2011c; 2015a; 2015b; 2018).

Thus, the theory of reflexive modernisation emphasises the potential for the individual's ability and practices to change traditions through reflexive interpretation and selective adoption of knowledge. It complements our understanding of the mechanisms of agency, which previous research has failed to adequately present, and provides a valuable framework for grasping the simultaneity of commitment to traditions (i.e. closedness) and their more active connection with the world outside their own communities (i.e. openness).

'European Muslims' as a social integration model

Identity's closedness and openness realised through identity management in the reflexive modernisation theory are not just abstract theoretical possibilities. In fact, this reflexivity has become an everyday practice for Muslims in Western society, especially for young people in the second and later generations. In the post-9/11 environment, they experience non-recognition daily in the form of institutional discrimination, for example, while at the same time sharing with other citizens many of hopes for the future and values through participation in social institutions and systems. Balancing being Muslim and being a citizen of Western society has become a major concern in this context.

For example, Tariq Ramadan, a Swiss-born French Islamic scholar, calls for the formation of 'European Muslims'. Ramadan talks about the state of faith and integration of Muslims in Western European societies from a Salafi reformist perspective (Ramadan 2005).[13] Ramadan's starting point is his perception that anxiety stemming from the identity crisis is pervading European societies amid growing diversity through globalisation. The Rushdie Affair, scarf/veil debates, satirical cartoon controversies, terrorism and other incidents have intensified a sense of insecurity and given rise to an anti-Islamic or Islamophobic environment. Ramadan does not criticise the situation normatively – that is, accuse such discourses as unjust – but argues that European Muslims should not turn a blind eye to such a reality. He then calls for the building of a trust relationship through rational dialogue in one another's language to deal with the psychological rejection found in European society (Ramadan 2010: 24–9).[14]

To that end, Ramadan advocates promoting a better understanding of Islam in a European context and balancing being Muslim and being a citizen of Western society (Ramadan 2010: 20–3). A key idea for this is to

Chapter 3

distinguish between 'one Islam' and 'several different interpretations and cultures'. On one hand, Islam's core beliefs, namely, 'the pillars of faith' (*aqidah*) and 'practice' (*ibadah*), 'Quranic revelation' and 'Prophetic traditions' (*sunnah*) are universal, transcending time and place. On the other hand, there are multiple interpretations that are based on different sects and traditions or made on a case-by-case basis in Islam.[15] There are also diverse local practices not directly derived from and sometimes not compatible with Islam (Ramadan 2010: 41–2). Islam has adapted to numerous local cultures through such interpretations. Muslims who migrate from non-Western society to Western society and their descendants need to re-embed Islam into the new Western cultural space out of the old cultural context whence Islam came. To that end, people – especially young people – must reconstruct their relationship with Islam through 'critical reading and reasoning' (or *ijtihad*) invoking transformation (Ramadan 2010: 47–8).

In that case, what is a reflexive Islamic interpretation described by Ramadan? Or, how does such reflexive Islamic interpretation contribute to identity formation and social integration among young second-generation Muslims? The rest of this book will examine the 'European Muslims' model proposed by Ramadan by reference to data obtained from interviews with second-generation Muslims in the UK, based on the identity theory of reflexive modernisation.

Notes

1 The first and second characteristics can be found in Max Weber's definition of ethnic groups: 'those human groups that entertain a subjective belief in their common descent because of similarities of physical type or of customs or both, or because of memories of colonization and migration'. He argued that 'this belief must be important for the propagation of group formation; conversely, it does not matter whether or not an objective blood relationship exists' (Weber 1968: 389). However, this definition lacks the third characteristic.

2 For example, the Committee for Racial Equality in Britain stopped including 'Asian' in the 'Black' category in 1988 (CRE 1988 cited in Modood 2006b: 70).

3 However, there was no assumption that all cultural groups would come under the ethnicity concept. Ethnicities referred almost exclusively to the communities of predominantly non–white immigrants from the New Commonwealth countries whereas the communities of white immigrants from Cyprus, Italy, Portugal and Ukraine were rarely discussed in terms of their ethnicities (Mason 2000: 15). In this sense, the difference between race and ethnicity is not absolute; the latter is always a 'racialised' concept (Brah 1996: 186; Malešević 2004: 1).

4 In *The Fourth National Survey of Ethnic Minorities in Britain*, 51 per cent of Pakistanis, 40 per cent of Bangladeshis and 39 per cent of Indians responded that they 'would mind a little' or 'would mind very much' about marriage between their close family members and white partners. Only 12 per cent of Caribbeans chose these answers (Modood 1997: 315).

5 Placing the public sphere outside of the authentic cultural core of people's identities poses a problem in understanding today's highly diversified society. Mainstream society's representations, institutions and cultures are as much sources of minority identities as their own family and cultural community. As Anthony Appiah points out, an identity is multifactorial and 'crucially constituted through concepts and practices made available to me by religion, society, school, and state' (Appiah 1994: 154).

6 Hall states that he had never heard of the term 'Black' before the Civil Rights movement and the de-colonisation and nationalist struggles, nor had he been called 'Black' until after he left his native land of Jamaica (Hall 1991: 53–4).

7 A diaspora refers to a community of 'immigrants who have acclimatised to their new land and "indigenised" without "assimilation" into a local culture; they selectively preserve some elements of their native culture without expecting to return to their original country' (Hashimoto 2005: 1).

8 This attempt culminated in *The Future of Multi-Ethnic Britain* report in 2000 by the Commission on the Future of Multi-Ethnic Britain, which was led by political philosopher Bhikhu Parekh and included Hall as a member. It recommended restructuring 'Britishness' into 'a community of communities' to reduce racial connotations (Parekh 2002).

Chapter 3

9   Butler offers the following argument about 'interpellation':

> 'Subjection' signifies the process of becoming subordinated by power as well as the process of becoming a subject. Whether by interpellation, in Althusser's sense, or by discursive productivity, in Foucault's, the subject is initiated through a primary submission to power. (Butler 1997: 2)

Interpellation in 'Althusser's sense' refers to the argument that one can become a subject only after one responds (i.e., subjection) to being addressed by a summoning authority (e.g., a police officer).

10 This concern can be found in recent studies of Muslim women in Malaysia, which has witnessed a rising Muslim consciousness, along with the strengthening of traditional gender roles as the result of a concerted social and political Islamisation campaign (i.e., interpellation) since the 1980s (Ong 1995; Stivens 2006; Kamogawa 2008; Frisk 2009; Osman 2013; Corman 2014). For example, Crystal Corman argues that more Malaysian Muslim women are choosing to quit their jobs despite high education qualifications to take a homemaking role and emphasise the role of men as 'breadwinners' in Islam (Corman 2014). Malia Stivens' research based on interviews with 100 households in three states reports that support for family management based on Islamic values has increased among the middle class as if in response to the political Islamisation campaign (Stivens 2006). Similarly, Sylva Frisk's participant observation-based field research of study groups in the 1990s reports that middle-class Malay women actively engaged with social Islamisation through study groups rather than simply submitting to an external authority. In the process, they increasingly stressed the importance of women's role in the family – especially in providing children's education (Frisk 2009). While these examples indicate that Islamisation has turned many women into religious subjects, they also illustrate the process of conditioning women as bodies desired by the state – 'wives and mothers' protecting the family (Adachi 2020b).

11 Taylor emphasises the importance of a 'fusion of horizons', a concept he borrows from Hans-Georg Gadamer. However, this may be a slightly misleading expression because Taylor was critical of the construction of universal values that evaluate all cultures (Taylor 1994: 70–1). It is more likely that the term means 'transformation of horizons' (Takada 2011: 87–9).

12 According to Ulrich Beck, 'Religion is the source of individualization: *Go and Pray to the God of your Choosing!* Religion is based on the decision of the individual to believe and thus ultimately on the assumption that the individual is free' (Beck 2010: 79). In other words, religion no longer defines people's lives and practices unilaterally; individual choices and practices form the very foundation of the prevailing mode of religion today.

13 'Salafism' is one of the reformist movements in Sunni Islam that advocates a return to the way of the 'predecessors' (*salaf*). It is a very conservative movement, emphasising the 'purity' of Islam and seeking its foundation strictly in the life of the early Islamic community and *sharia* (Gilliat-Ray 2010: 66–70). By contrast, what Ramadan calls Salafi reformism differs from traditional Salafist 'literalism',

Previous Studies and Theoretical Frames

permitting more flexible legal interpretation and emphasising the importance of *ijtihad* (an effort for independent legal reasoning within certain bounds) (Ameli 2002: 130–1; Ramadan 2005: 26–7). The importance of *ijtihad* – for women in particular – is discussed in Chapters 8 and 10.

14 This attitude is made possible by the practice of 'translation' discussed in Section 6 in this chapter. Habermas defines a contemporary society experiencing a return of religious influences as a 'post-secular' society and argues that religious citizens and secular citizens must translate their own language into the other's language and maintain an ongoing dialogue in order to achieve a public sphere consisting of both kinds of citizens (Habermas 2011: 23–33). However, Taylor and Butler argue that the product of translation always contains excess or deficiency and may not resolve all differences. At the same time, they maintain that considering such differences must form part of ethical foundations (Habermas et al. 2011).

15 There are some issues between Islamic teaching and its social practices (Kamada 2015: 107–8). For instance, the Quran represents absolute truth to all Muslims but it allows believers considerable leeway in deciding how they apply these teachings in various situations because its teachings are only 'guidelines'. Hence, there are many tools in Islam for textual comprehension and interpretation. *Hadith*, a collection of Muhammad's sayings and actions (*sunnah*) reported by the *sahaba* (companions of the Prophet), is one of the important sources in Islam. *Hadith* and *sunnah* are recognised as constituting a more specific code of conduct for Muslims to observe, i.e. legitimised Islamic knowledge. There is also the difficulty of applying knowledge throughout the ages. As people's living conditions vary in different times and societies, many real-life issues may not be directly dealt with in the Quran or *hadith*. The question of what is correct knowledge in different contexts is a source of frequent controversy. When this question arises in Islam, the correctness of knowledge is determined through a scholarly or community consensus called '*ijma*' or a special technique of analogical reasoning called '*qiyas*' applied by present-day *ulamas*. In *qiyas*, 'where two cases are thought to be analogous through reasoning, the rule applicable to one case is also applied to the other' (Kosugi 1994: 157). For example, the Quran prohibits the use of '*khamr*' (alcohol). The word specifically refers to grape wine, and the Quran does not explicitly prohibit other types of alcoholic drinks. However, if the reason for the prohibition is intoxication (and forgetting prayer), then other things with the same effect (alcoholic drinks in general) can be prohibited by analogical reasoning (Kosugi 1994: 1149–61).

101

Chapter

Research Outline

> Apart from whether I like it or not, I don't reject thinking about things that aren't logical. It's not like I have some deep faith in logic. I think it's important to find the point of intersection between what is logical and what is not… Well, we're speaking in hypotheticals here. If we wanted to pursue this further, we'd need some concrete examples. Like a bridge needs girders. The further you go with a hypothesis, the more slippery it gets. Any conclusions you draw from it become more fallacious.
>
> *Colorless Tsukuru Tazaki and His Years of Pilgrimage*
> by Haruki Murakami (2014: 67–8)

> If you want the sanest, most sage and also bonkers advice on love, life and religion, talk to a taxi driver. They come in all shapes and sizes: you have the kohl-eyed drivers with serbans who can tickle your funny bone, you might come across a graduate driving a taxi because it's more lucrative than a full time job… Taxi drivers are the same everywhere; they know the beat, the pulse of a city and empathise with the heart of a country.
>
> *I Am Muslim*
> by Dina Zaman (2007: 215)

This chapter outlines this research in preparation for an analysis of findings in Part II. It describes the research fields in Coventry and East London, my fieldwork process, research method, positionality, epistemological framework, analytical method, and informants' backgrounds in detail.

Research fields

I chose Foleshill, a ward of Coventry, and the London Borough of Tower Hamlets as research fields due to the presence of well-established Asian communities – Pakistani in the former and Bangladeshi in the latter. As mentioned in Chapter 2, Pakistanis and Bangladeshis account for a large majority of Britain's Muslim population and are thus central groups in this research. Let us begin by looking at each locality's characteristics.

Coventry

Coventry is a mid-sized city near Birmingham in the West Midlands of England. The Coventry Cathedral, which was destroyed in the Blitz during WWII and later rebuilt, towers symbolically in the city centre, while the legend of Lady Godiva from the eleventh century draws many tourists (Photos 4.1, 4.2).

Coventry was an industrial city known for its silk weaving and watch manufacturing in the eighteenth century. In the mid-nineteenth century, many factories were built to manufacture bicycles – which were fashionable in France at the time (Stephens 1969) – which led to the development of the automotive industry in the late nineteenth century. Coventry became the

Photo 4.1 Coventry Cathedral
Photographed by the author

Photo 4.2 Statue of Lady Godiva in the city's central square
Photographed by the author

Chapter 4

world's car manufacturing hub amid technological innovations and world-wide demand. By the 1950s, the city had production facilities for twelve car manufacturers, including Daimler, Jaguar and Alvis, and remained Britain's leading industrial city until the decline of the auto industry in the 1970s. Coventry absorbed large numbers of migrants from across the UK and overseas during its long boom (Thoms and Donnelly 2000; Portlock 2016).

Employment was the most important reason for migration to Coventry. There was an influx of 3,459 people or approximately two per cent of its population between 1921 and 1931, then a total of 42,148 people in the next eight years, accounting for 19 per cent of its total population in 1939. By 1951, it was estimated that only 30–40 per cent of its residents were born locally. Overseas immigrants, from Poland, Russia, Ukraine, the Indian subcontinent and elsewhere, had a significant impact on the city.

While there was already a substantial population of Asian immigrants before WWII, their numbers increased sharply after the war as the city accepted large numbers of immigrants for its post-war recovery. Many Asian immigrants were employed in the factories of Sterling Metals, Dunlop, and Alfred Herbert. They were compelled to work in low-skilled and low-wage jobs, even those with higher education qualifications (Virdee 2006: 39).

Asian immigrants worked long hours, saved money and sent it back to support their families at home. For example, Muhammed Ali, who arrived from East Pakistan in 1963, stated:

> I used to work for 72 hours and get £20 for doing piecework. I used to send home £30 per week so I had to borrow money from my friends and relatives. I had left my younger brothers and family behind, I had to educate them. So our earnings were for our family as well, not just for us. (Virdee 2006: 47)

Many of these migrants chose to migrate for 'management of extended family' and made a great effort to help the next generation succeed.

Most of the migrants from the Indian subcontinent came from Punjab and Gujarat along the India-Pakistan border. The smaller proportion of immigrants from Bangladesh mostly hailed from the Sylhet region. Many immigrants ended up living in Foleshill due to its low-rent housing and proximity to factories. Because non-white immigrants found it difficult to rent rooms from white property owners, they opted to purchase homes, establishing a pattern of renting them out to their fellow Asian immigrants (Virdee 2006: 1–6). The high homeownership rate became a starting point for subsequent chain migration and the formation of Asian-dominated multicultural communities in St Michael's in the city centre and Foleshill to the north. As a result, the population with an Indian background increased by 9.8 times (870 to 8,560) and those with a Pakistani background by 8.9 times (176 to 1,570) between 1951 and 1981.

More recent statistics show that the population born in the New Commonwealth countries and Pakistan reached 17,738 (6.4 per cent of the total population 274,044) in 1981. In 2001, the non-white population reached 16.1 per cent (the UK average was 7.9 per cent), making the city more multicultural and multi-ethnic. In 2011, the white British people accounted for 66.6 per cent, while the Asian population reached approximately 13 per cent (Indian 8.8 per cent, Pakistani 3.0 per cent and Bangladeshi 0.9 per cent). By religious affiliations, 53.7 per cent were Christian, followed by Muslim at 7.5 per cent and Sikh at 5.0 per cent.

The research field of Foleshill has the highest concentration of minority populations in Coventry. According to the 2011 statistics, the combined population of Pakistani (21.5 per cent) and Indian (18.7 per cent) groups surpassed the white British population (23.4 per cent), although the latter remained the single most populous ethnic group. At the same time, Foleshill is the most economically deprived of Coventry's 18 wards. For instance, the rate of children living in poverty after housing costs in Foleshill reached 49 per cent, about four times the rate in Earlsdon (12 per cent) in southern Coventry with a predominantly white population. This is reflected in the social class of the informants' parents.

London

The other field was the London Borough of Tower Hamlets, which constitutes part of what is called East London. East London has a particular resonance for the British people. As epitomised by BBC's popular drama series *EastEnders*, which has been on air since 1985, this area engendered diasporic spaces underpinned by energy, poverty and deprivation associated with ethnic diversity. It was historically the gateway linking the British Empire to the world via the Thames River. In a sense, Tower Hamlets, where a Bangladeshi community has taken hold, embodies an extreme form of this image of East London. For instance, the street market outside the Whitechapel Underground Station is called Little Dhaka, packed with street vendors with bearded men in white dress shirts and women in headscarves or veils (Photo 4.3).

Tower Hamlets has a long history of providing sanctuary for religious minorities from the European continent. Many refugees arrived here for

Chapter 4

religious, political, and economic reasons, including Huguenots (Calvinists) from France in the seventeenth–eighteenth centuries, Jews from Eastern Europe in the late nineteenth century, and Muslims from Bangladesh after WWII (Kershen 2005). Bangladeshis, most of whom were young men from Sylhet, headed to Tower Hamlets mainly for economic reasons, seeking employment as seamen. In 1795, the East India Company provided a shelter in Kingsland Road, East London, for tired Lascars – the 'wretched men' – to rest between their travels. In the mid-nineteenth century, a lodging house for seamen opened in West India Dock Road, where many young men from Sylhet stayed. This connection between Sylhet and East London facilitated mass- and chain-migration from the 1950s (Kershen 2005: 43–4). Many of these women and men ended up working under harsh conditions in 'sweatshops' – especially in the apparel industry (Castles and Miller 1993: 56; Kabeer 2000: 200–29).

In 2011, about 40 per cent of the Tower Hamlets population were Asian and a majority of them were of Bangladeshi origin (about 35 per cent of the total population). Tower Hamlets is one of the most economically deprived boroughs of London. The 2013 unemployment rate of 12.7 per cent in the borough was higher than the average London rate of 9.1 per cent. In 2011, the proportion of residents aged between 16 and 64 with no education qualification exceeded 15 per cent, the fifth highest rate in London. The educational achievement level of the Bangladeshi majority was particularly low with only 16 per cent having a degree (compared to Indian 69 per cent, white 47 per cent and Pakistani 45 per cent). In the Bangladeshi group, however, younger people had higher rates of degree-holders at 21.7 per cent in the 16–24 age bracket and 36.6 per cent in the 25–49 cohort (Schneppel 2014).

Photo 4.3
Whitechapel Road Market
Photographed by the author

Research Outline

Tower Hamlets became the centre of attention across the UK and Europe following the London bombings in July 2005. The terrorists involved were from Leeds, in Northern England, and had no association with Tower Hamlets. Yet, the neighbourhood, already renowned as a Muslim community hosting one of Europe's largest mosques (East London Mosque: hereafter ELM), came to be seen as a breeding ground for Islamic extremists after the attacks (Meer 2010: 94) (Photos 4.4 and 4.5). The fact that activists from *Jamaat-e-Islami* – a group with links with the Taliban and al-Qaeda, advocating political Islamism – frequented ELM heightened the suspicion. The connection between ELM and extremism has been reported many times through a variety of media, including former extremist activist Ed Husain's autobiographical essay *The Islamist: Why I Became an Islamic Fundamentalist, What I Saw Inside, and Why I Left* (2007), Maajid Nawaz's *Radical: My Journey from Islamist Extremism to a Democratic Awakening* (2012), and a Channel 4 documentary *Britain's Islamic Republic* (2010) by Andrew Gilligan. Consequently, ELM and Tower Hamlets came to be seen as a space ruled by retrogressive foreign cultures and a dangerous religion

Photo 4.4
East London Mosque
Photographed by the author

Photo 4.5
East London Mosque
after Friday prayers
(rear entrance)
Photographed by the author

Chapter 4

– or the wreck of multiculturalism – and became a battleground (sometimes literally) for communities, governments, media and far-right groups (e.g., The English Defence League) over Britain's social integration, security and religious freedom.

Research outline

The aim of this book is to examine the state of social integration among Britain's second-generation (including '1.5 generation') Muslims in the post-9/11 era with a focus on their identity management methods or strategies.[1] Foleshill Ward in Coventry and Tower Hamlets Borough in London were selected as fields for interview-based qualitative research.

The research was divided into four stages.

The first stage was conducted in Foleshill between September and December 2009. I worked as a visiting researcher at the Institute of Community Cohesion (hereafter iCoCo) in Coventry from June to December 2009. iCoCo is a research institute established in 2005 in a partnership between Coventry University, De Montfort University, Warwick University, and the University of Leicester with support from the Department for Communities and Local Government. It offers research and consultancy for local governments and communities about race relations, aiming 'to provide a new approach to race, diversity and multiculturalism'. Ted Cantle, who headed the review panel which produced the *Cantle Report* on the 2001 race riots in Northern England (as discussed in Chapters 1 and 2), became the first director of iCoCo. The institute is situated at Coventry University.

During my research fellowship, I participated in events organised by an NPO for racial relations, multiculturalism and inter-community solidarity in Foleshill, which enabled me to spend time with young women and men of Asian background, especially Pakistani and Indian, who worked as volunteers at these events. They were very talkative, had a sense of humour and acted as hostesses/hosts at events, welcoming guests despite their tender age of around twenty. In private conversations, they passionately told me about Islam and their faith using specific examples. Our communications deepened as we began to play football together and talk at parties. I observed that they were participating in society just as other young British people do, while expressing strong commitments to Islam. This discovery led me to focus on their identity strategies, such as 'How do they manage to balance being Muslim and British?', rather than the possibility of integration, such as 'Can Islam and Western society coexist?' or 'Can one be both Muslim and British?' (Jeldtoft 2011; Dessing et al. eds. 2013).

Based on this experience and thinking, I conducted one-on-one semi-structured interviews in the first stage to explore issues around faith and social participation while keeping identity as the central theme of the research. Informants included young volunteers at the above community organisation, their friends and family members, and others recruited through personal contacts. Interviews were conducted at either the interviewer's or informants' homes.

After analysing the data from the first stage interviews, I conducted the second stage of research in the same field from December 2012 to February 2013. I recruited participants for the survey through referrals from the NPO mentioned earlier. The organisation circulated a leaflet about my research via its mailing list, processed applicants and scheduled their interviews, which I conducted in its office or informants' homes. The format this time was a semi-structured interview with small groups, in which each member was a friend. I adopted this format because it enables young informants to be interviewed in a more familiar environment than formal one-on-one interviews with a researcher they have never met before, and as a result, they are more likely to respond to questions positively and with natural expressions. The other reason was that I recruited more Muslim women, who are considered to be a 'hard-to-reach' cohort for religious and cultural reasons. The group environment can provide peace of mind that they may not face a male interviewer in a one-on-one context.

The third stage of the research was conducted in the London Borough of Tower Hamlets from January to March 2014. I was a visiting scholar at the University of London (University College of London from December 2014) Institute of Education from April 2013 to March 2015 and lived in Tower Hamlets from September 2013. The London Muslim Centre, which adjoins ELM, helped with the research and recruited informants through a leaflet posted on the Centre's Facebook page. Interviews were conducted in the Centre's meeting room or informants' homes. I employed semi-structured small group interviews or one-on-one interviews, as appropriate. All informants were women this time because the 'subordination of women' was coming to the fore as a significant discourse on Muslim integration into Western society, and it was valuable to focus on women's voices in examining this issue.

The fourth stage was carried out in the same area from January to March 2015. While the same research as the third stage were employed, universities, workplaces and cafes were added to the interview venues and informants included both women and men. Additionally, I participated in a study group for converts at the London Muslim Centre from April 2014 to

Chapter 4

March 2015 to learn about Islam and identify the challenges facing Muslims in East London.

Each interview lasted between 80 and 140 minutes depending on the number of informants and circumstances. Throughout this research, I referred and adhered to the ethical codes of the British Sociological Association. The third and fourth stages of the research had approval from the Research Committee of the University of London Institute of Education prior to their implementation.

Outsider approach

In this section, I explain my positionality in the fields.

Unlike research on 'nature', research on 'society' is always reflexive (Nabe 2018: 272–3). In other words, the research involves social interaction between the researching and the researched, and hence the relationships can influence the quality of extracted data. In the same way that communication is generally produced through mutual choices, the interactions in social research are also established through choices strategically made by the researcher and the researched. Thus, 'rapport' and 'over-rapport' impact the validity and reliability of research (Berg 1989: 29-30; Sugino 2013: 26).

In recent years, there have been many debates about power differences and asymmetrical relationships in research (Donaldson and Pui-lan eds. 2002). As sociologists studying social minorities (e.g., LGBTQs, residents in the Global South and people with disabilities) argue, research activities reflect a social relationship and there is a certain asymmetry between the researcher and the researched (Phoenix 1994) – i.e., 'those who ask and look and those who are asked and looked at' (Geertz 1988: 131). For example, there is a notable pattern in which privileged researchers (e.g., white, heterosexual, and middle class) keep themselves in a safe place while unilaterally invading the privacy of minorities (e.g., non-white, sexual minority, and underclass). It has also been observed that categories of the vulnerable and minorities in need are created in interview processes based on this unfair relationship (Mohanty 1984: 337; Puar 1996). In this situation, informants may try to guard their privacy or deliberately present a self-image that satisfies the researchers' expectations. The problems of rapport and power tend to surface particularly in researching stigmatised minorities – such as Muslims in Western society (Jacobson 1998; Bhimji 2012; DeHanas 2013).

As mentioned, I lived in the community of the research field for a relatively long period (approximately 32 months in total). Nevertheless, I was perceived as an 'outsider' by most of the informants, largely because of my one-off relationships with each participant, but my personal attributes – non-South-Asian, non-British, and for female participants, male – were also important factors.

This so-called 'insider-outsider' problem in social research is often discussed in Muslim studies. The insider approach generally has many merits (Keval 2009). Anne Sofie Roald, who studies converts to Islam, states that insider-researchers have an advantage over outsiders in access to information because they share interests with their informants (Roald 2001: 70). For example, Bangladeshi-born Nahid Kabir reports that her background (Bangladeshi origin and experience living in Pakistan) positioned her as an insider in her research on predominantly Asian Muslims in the UK and facilitated her research (Kabir 2010: 24–6). Similarly, Fazila Bhimji states that she was able to conduct interviews with ease as a Muslim community insider who was familiar with the language (Arabic) and religious terminology (Bhimji 2012: 22). Aminul Hoque also reports that in interviews with 'third-generation' Muslims in East London, her ethnicity (Bangladeshi) played a positive role in terms of language, rapport, knowledge and familiarity with the background of the informants (Hoque 2015: 15–6).

In contrast, a researcher's outsider status presents certain difficulties. For example, Jessica Jacobson, a white British researcher who interviewed young people of Pakistani descent in Waltham Forest Borough in northeast London from 1992 to 1993, reports on the difficulty of achieving rapport with her informants' parents. Jacobson admits that her inability to communicate with the parents in their native language of Urdu or Punjabi resulted in limited access to her informants (Jacobson 1998: 54–5).

The advantages of the insider must not be overstated, though (Merriam et al. 2001). With insiders, there is an increased risk of neglecting to ask follow-up questions because they partially share in the informants' meaning world and thus view some responses as self-evident (Roald 2001: 71). Informants who are minorities within their own community – e.g., *Shiite* or gay – or embrace secular or liberal values may not reveal their circumstances or honest opinions to insider-researchers (Zebiri 2008: 12). A similar issue arises when addressing issues that are considered taboo by the community (Rabe 2003: 156–7). These issues point to the merits of an outsider-researcher; informants might feel more comfortable expressing opinions that may be unacceptable within their own community when the researcher is an outsider (Jacobson 1998: 55).

My research could not avoid issues related to rapport due to my outsider status. Some informants asked several questions about my investigation, including my background, the purpose of the interviews, and the use of the data.

Chapter 4

I dealt with this issue in the following ways. First, I contacted organisations that were trusted by informants – such as community and religious organisations – about my research and used their facilities as interview venues. Second, I prepared an 'informed consent sheet' on four A4 pages, detailing the aims, merits/demerits, data management and complaint handling procedure of the research project and explaining the outline of the interview and conditions for participation. Third, I advised the informants that they were free to leave the interview if they encountered an uncomfortable question, a problem, or for prayers. Fourth, I asked for and answered questions from informants about the research and my background, including my faith, before and after each interview.[2] Adopting this process, I did not experience any serious problem with rapport with my participants.

On the contrary, my informants exhibited an 'open-minded cosmopolitan' (Bhimji 2012: 21) attitude, responding even to unusual questions such as 'What is your identity?' in a logical manner using concrete examples and often with a touch of humour, just as Asian British Muslim participants in Fazila Bhimji's study had.[3] This open-minded attitude is partly because communicating with non-Muslims has become an everyday experience for Muslims in increasingly multicultural British society, as discussed in Chapter 6. It is also partly because the process found in interviews – being asked and answering questions about their religion – is part of the daily routine for second-generation immigrant youth. In other words, the interview process was not a unique experience for informants but to some extent reproduced their everyday communications with non-Muslims, in which they tried to clear up misconceptions about Islam and Muslims to promote better understanding of their religion.

Daniel Nilsson DeHanas identifies this as another positive benefit of being an outsider in his research on young Muslims in London's East End:

> [I]t is worth recognising that the interview situation was in itself a moment in which youth could tactically deploy their identities in reference to how they perceived me, as a white American, non-Muslim academic researcher. This does not make the exercise less valuable, but instead shows its value for studying particularly self-conscious presentations of identity. (DeHanas 2013: 75)

Informants engage in a particular type of 'self-presentation' to the interviewer. The techniques and strategies they adopt serve as valuable data for understanding identity management and social integration among second-generation Muslims in Western society.[4] As Erving Goffman observed, self-presentation through impression management is not necessarily to express a 'false self'; but rather serves stigmatised groups to counter socially ascribed negative identities and reverse the majority's values (Goffman 1959; 1963). They perceive their own identities reflexively and present them strategically to others, taking account of the social contexts in which they are involved. Thus, understanding the informants' self-presentation strategies is important in shedding light on how second-generation youth in the post-9/11 era realise social integration in Western Society as Muslims.

Policy and method for analysis

Epistemological framework

This section discusses the cognitive framework in the analysis.

There are two main types of qualitative research: the 'empirical positivist' approach and the 'interpretative' approach. The former seeks to gather and analyse 'objective facts' about individuals and society from data and narratives. The latter examines how people interpret and give meaning to 'facts', that is, 'interpreted facts' (Schütz 1973: 5), rather than the facts themselves (Bryman 2012: 28–32). Given that the main purpose of this publication is to analyse the nature of the 'identity' of second-generation immigrant Muslims, the focus is not on the objective facts surrounding their lives, but on the interpretation of their experiences. Therefore, I adopted the interpretive approach to data analysis.

The interpretive approach is founded on the idea of 'constructs' proposed by sociologist and philosopher Alfred Schütz. He commented on the inherent subject matter of social science as follows:

> Social world has a particular meaning and relevance structure for the human beings living, thinking, and acting therein. They have preselected and preinterpreted this world by a series of common-sense constructs for the reality of daily life... This world existed before our birth, experienced and interpreted by others, our predecessors, as an organized world. (Schütz 1973: 6–7)

Social science faces a world (selectively) organised through interpretation, not an objective fact or world. Such interpretation is based on 'knowledge' but it is made possible by social constructs, which provide a framework for how to understand the world (Schütz 1973: 6–7). Consequently, social scientists – especially sociologists – should aim for the elucidation of relevant knowledge and meaning constructs behind people's actions.

Chapter 4

There are different interpretive approaches. Life story researcher Atsushi Sakurai distinguishes the 'interpretive objectivism' approach and the 'interactive construction' approach. The former 'interprets a narrative based on inductive inference... illuminates social realities through repeated interviews' and 'aspires to decipher meaning structure based on "what" is told and to articulate normative and institutional realities' (Sakurai 2002: 25). The latter shines a light on both 'what is told' by the narrator as well as 'how it is told' because an interview is a 'narrative generation process' which constitutes its own social space, and thus its 'meaning structure' may change depending on the particular space or the relationship between the researcher and researched (Sakurai 2002: 28–9; Yamada 2007).

This research uses the interpretive objectivism approach, while paying heed to the interactive construction approach.[5] As discussed in the previous section, my informants understood that I was conducting this research as an outsider and related to me on that basis. As Denise Fletcher states, 'social reality is always an expression of relationship' (Fletcher 2007: 167); people's appraisals of reality and identity expressions are presented in the context of interactions with one's surroundings. This relationality applies to the specific process of interviewing. The interviewees' responses in my study should be seen as their self-presentations to a person outside their religious community (Sakurai 2002: 30–1; Fletcher 2007: 168). Hence, we need to be cautious about claiming to have identified an 'objective structure' from the collected data, as interactive constructionism reminds us. Yet, I maintain the interpretive objectivist position because, as mentioned, the exercise of explaining their identities and faith to others is a mundane everyday experience rather than a special situation for second-generation Muslims today. As discussed in Chapters 1 and 3, the relationship between Islam and British society has been continuously scrutinised in the media and everyday life since 9/11, and second-generation Muslim youth who wish to participate in mainstream society experience constant pressure to respond to such scrutiny from wider society. Conversely, an individual's response to or struggle with mainstream social discourses on Islam are the preconditions for their identity construction processes.

Accordingly, in analysing identities, this book focuses more on the interpreted facts latent in the informants' narratives embedded in particular social contexts rather than on the social 'place' or 'relationship' in which the interviews take place (Lawler 2008: 17). By focusing not only on the 'content of narratives' but also on the 'form of narrative' commonly found among informants, I analysed their integration and identity formation in Western societies, and the strategies of self-presentation practised to achieve them.

Analytical method

As mentioned, interpretive objectivism is an approach to analysing data based on inductive inference. On the assumption that social reality and a common epistemic structure exist behind each narrator, it repeats inductive reasoning by adding data for the purpose of developing a more appropriate theoretical framework to explain perceived reality (Sakurai 2002: 24–7).

Using this approach, analysis was conducted according to the following process. I transcribed the recorded interview data and analysed the resulting texts using 'thematic analysis' (Gomm 2004). Thematic analysis is a widely used method for identifying explicit/implicit ideas in the data, as well as associated themes or patterns. Virginia Braun and Victoria Clarke outline concrete steps of thematic analysis: 1) becoming familiar with the data, 2) generating initial codes, 3) searching for themes, 4) reviewing themes, 5) defining and naming themes and 6) producing the report (Braun and Clarke 2006).

As a first step, I carefully read verbatim data in comparison with the field notes taken during interviews. This step was to become familiar with the data and work up ideas for coding and classifying so that I could accurately handle data in the analytic process (Kinoshita 2016: 6). Next, drawing on my own theoretical interests, I extracted certain concepts from the interview data and categorised each case. In the process, I looked 'at data in its context adhering to the researcher's awareness of issues and carefully examining human cognition and action reflected in it and associated factors and conditions', instead of segmenting data for quantitative analysis (Kinoshita 2007: 6). In Steps 3–5, I examined the relations between concepts and extracted more general and abstract themes and categories. Individual concepts and themes were then re-examined and revised by comparing with interview data. Finally, each concept was defined, arranged and described according to the research purpose of this book. NVivo qualitative analysis software was utilised in the analysis.

The thematic analysis allows researchers to flexibly code data and relations between themes based on their interests. However, problems with the validity and reliability of interpretations can arise in some cases (Guest et al. 2012: 10–1). After receiving comments on the interpretation of data from several informants, Muslim researchers and my mentor, and reporting and discussing these findings at several conferences and workshops, I concluded that the statements in this publication are valid and reliable to a certain extent.

Chapter 4

Informants' attributes

In this final section, I outline the attributes of informants and what groups they represent (see Appendix for details).

Eighty-nine British Muslims participated in this research, including 57 women and 32 men (Table 4.1). I included a larger female sample because Western discourse tends to depict Muslim women as victims of Islam's rules, as mentioned in Chapter 1, and I wanted to examine women's reactions to such discourses for a better understanding of how Muslims integrate into Western society. To this end, Chapters 9 and 10 narrow the focus to women and discuss Islam's relationship with women's autonomy or agency. Informants' ages ranged from 16 to 40 for women and 18 to 35 for men, with an average age of 23.4 and 23.9 years respectively. A further breakdown (Figure 4.1) shows 21 women in their teens (approx. 37 per cent), 26 in their 20s (approx. 46 per cent) and 10 in their 30s or over (approx. 18 per cent). The men included 7 teens (approx. 22 per cent), 22 in their 20s (approx. 69 per cent) and 3 in their 30s (approx. 9 per cent). While young people in their teens and 20s account for over 80 per cent, participants between the ages of 30 and 40 are also included in the analysis. The latter cohort is situated in the transition period from those whose identities were formed in the early 2000s,

	No. of persons	Average Age	Youngest	Oldest
Women	57	23.4	16	40
Men	32	23.9	18	35

Table 4.1 Age of informants

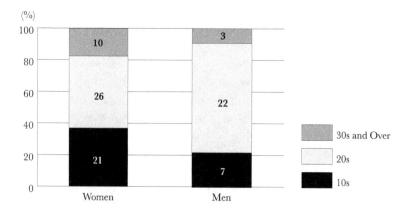

Figure 4.1 Informants by age and gender

when public discourse on Muslims changed significantly. Their inclusion can provide useful information for understanding the changes in integration and identity formation of Muslim youth since 9/11.

Religious identification is crucial for understanding second-generation Muslim immigrants in the West. Some previous studies have classified Muslims in Western society based on 'types of faith'. For example, Karen Phalet and co-authors discuss three types of religious identity – 'private', 'strict' and 'selective' Muslims – reflecting degrees of attachment to faith and observance of standards of conduct among second-generation Turkish Muslims in major cities in Germany, Belgium, the Netherlands, and Sweden. They found that while all types of Muslims demonstrated clear attachment and commitment to their faith, the degree of adherence to Islamic codes of conduct varied with 'strict' being the highest and 'private' being the lowest. Private Muslims exhibit the largest gap between consciousness and behaviour whereas strict Muslims show the most robust adherence to Islam in both consciousness and standards of conduct. Selective Muslims, in contrast, selectively and actively participate in practices involving communality (e.g., observance of Ramadhan and halal) rather than strictly adhering to all teachings. According to Phalet et al., either strict Muslims or selective Muslims formed the dominant group with the private Muslims being the smallest in all cities except in Sweden. An important finding is that those who had participated in religious activities in childhood tend to have stronger attachments to and practices of Islam (Phalet et al. 2012). It suggests that increasing opportunities in recent years for second-generation Muslims in Western society to learn about Islam and participate in religious events at a young age contributes to their strong identification with Islam.

Sahin's study of the identity of young Muslims in the UK points to a different three-part typology. First is the 'foreclosed mode' of Muslims, who interpret Islamic law non-historically and non-contextually in trying to apply it in everyday life. Consequently, foreclosed Muslims tend to see British society as morally degenerate and have no sense of belonging to it. Second is the 'diffused mode' of Muslims who, although feeling no strong personal commitment to Islam, understand themselves to be Muslim and make Islamic choices in certain aspects of their lives. This is similar to what Phalet et al. call selective Muslims. Third is the 'exploratory mode' of Muslims, who personally explore their religious teachings and try to arrange them in a manner that is meaningful to their lives and identities. According to Sahin, this is the largest category of British Muslims (Sahin 2005).

Unlike the above studies, this study does not have an explicit index for the degree of religious faith, but the following characteristics of informants were

Chapter 4

observed. From the perspective of Phalet et al.'s terminology, my informants were spread across all categories with the middle-of-the-road selective Muslims forming the largest group, followed by strict Muslims and private Muslims. There were more strict Muslims than private Muslims among the London participants, but there seemed to be more private than strict Muslims in Coventry. One possible explanation for this is the presence of stronger religious and cultural communities in London, providing an environment in which Muslims can more easily maintain their religious practices. Another possible explanation is the higher ratio of students among the Coventry informants, who are not able to maintain strict religious practices because they need more time for studying and have wider circles of friends and contacts, including non-Muslims.

In Sahin's terminology, a vast majority of informants in this research were exploratory Muslims. A small percentage were diffused Muslims, and none were of the foreclosed type. As noted by Sahin and others, a reflexive gaze toward faith found in exploratory Muslims was more prominent among women than men (Amed 2003; Sahin 2005; 2013; Contractor 2012). This may be because social expectations of men are not so different between the mainstream and Muslim communities, whereas they are markedly different for women. Hence there is greater pressure on Muslim women to reconcile the differences in role expectations between Western society and the Muslim community. This pressure reinforces women's reflexive engagement with Islam as a guideline for living. Based on these observations, I can surmise that informants in this book possess the characteristics prevalent among second-generation Muslims in Western society, especially in the UK.

Ethnicity	Women	Men
Asian (including Mixed)	52	31
Bangladeshi	(25)	(17)
Pakistani	(9)	(10)
Indian	(8)	(3)
Mixed	(10)	(1)
Black (including Mixed)	5	1
African	(4)	(0)
Caribbean	(0)	(1)
Mixed	(1)	(0)
Total	57	32

Table 4.2 Informants by ethnicity

Research Outline

Table 4.2 tabulates the informants' ethnicities, mainly Asian Muslims (Bangladeshi, Pakistani, Indian and other mixed Asian ethnicities), who form the predominant group of British Muslims and account for approximately 91 per cent (52 informants) of the women and 97 per cent (31 informants) of the men interviewed for this research.

As for their generation, a majority of participants were 'second-generation' immigrants (40 women and 27 men), followed by 'third-generation' (10 and 4) and 'fourth-generation' (2 and 1). A few of the female informants were first-generation immigrants, but five of them who received their primary education in the UK have been included in the analysis as '1.5-generation'. The 1.5-generation immigrants are deeply engaged in British lifestyles and values through the education system and media, and are thus considered to have had to deal with the questions of balancing Islam and Western culture just as the second-generation and younger Muslims have.

Figures 4.2 and 4.3 chart the educational qualifications of the parents of London informants by sex.[6] The parents' educational qualifications of both female and male informants were generally low, but the parents of female

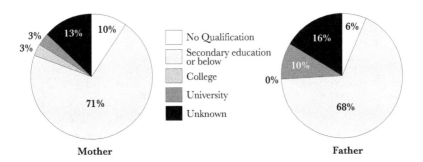

Figure 4.2 Educational qualifications of parents of female informants (London only)

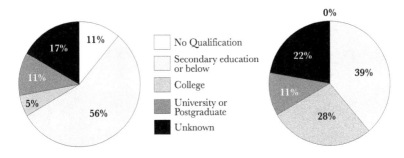

Figure 4.3 Educational qualifications of parents of male informants (London only)

119

Chapter 4

informants were lower than males. Around 70 per cent of female informants' mothers and fathers completed only secondary education or less (approx. 71 per cent and 68 per cent respectively), and together with 'none' and 'unknown', more than 90 per cent had education below 'college'. Although their fathers' education levels were slightly higher, only three (approx. 10 per cent) had 'college' or higher education. In contrast, the male informants' parents had relatively high education qualifications. The combined ratio of 'none' and 'secondary education or less' was approximately 67 per cent for their mothers and approximately 39 per cent for their fathers. Seven fathers (approx. 39 per cent) had 'college' or higher education.

Figures 4.4 and 4.5 indicate the informants' education qualifications by sex. They generally had higher educational qualifications. For example, the number of people who had some tertiary education (university and postgraduate; current, graduated or withdrew) was 38 women (approx. 67 per cent of the total) and 24 men (75 per cent). Most informants in the sixth form or college at the time of the interview expressed a desire to go to university. Thus, informants were clearly attaining much higher education

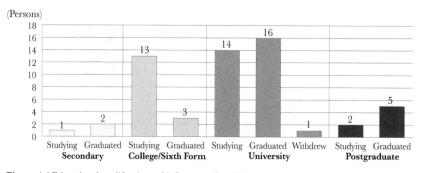

Figure 4.4 Educational qualifications of informants (female)

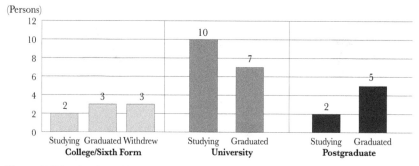

Figure 4.5 Educational qualifications of informants (male)

120

levels than their parents. It is noteworthy that women were achieving higher education qualifications regardless of the low education levels of their parents (especially mothers).

Table 4.3 depicts the informants' employment status (except students). The number of full-time workers was 22 women (approx. 67 per cent) and 13 men (approx. 68 per cent), while seven women (21 per cent) and four men (21 per cent) were employed part-time. Two women were full-time housewives, but there were no full-time househusbands. The remainder were either looking for work or on leave. The labour force participation rate among informants, especially women, was higher than the Muslim average in society, perhaps due to their high educational qualifications. Attitudes toward women's educational achievement and labour force participation are discussed in detail in Chapter 9.

Table 4.4 depicts the marital status of informants. Fifteen women (approx. 26 per cent) and eight men (25 per cent) were married at the time of the interviews, while 42 women (approx. 74 per cent, including one divorced) and 24 men (75 per cent) were single. The youngest age at marriage was 16 for women and 19 for men, and the oldest was 29 for women and 34 for men. The average age of first marriage was 21.6 for women and 24.4 for men. All

	Women	Men
Full-time	22	13
Part-time	7	4
Housewife/Househusband	2	0
On Leave	2	0
Job-Seeking	0	2
Total	33	19

Table 4.3 Employment status of informants (except students)

	Women	Men
Unmarried	42	24
Married	15	8
First Marriage Age (Youngest)	16	19
First Marriage Age (Oldest)	29	34
First Marriage Age (Average)	21.6	24.4

Table 4.4 Marital status of informants

Chapter 4

but one person of Indian descent, none of them were over 30 years old and not married. These data point to the high social expectations for marriage in their 20s in the Asian community. In fact, many of the unmarried informants, especially women, expressed a desire to marry before their mid-20s.

All informants but one belonged to the Sunni Sect or had Sunni family background. Many identified as Sunni, and some professed faith in Hanafi, which is prevalent among Asian Muslims. However, a majority of informants attached no importance to such distinctions among sects or schools and, on the contrary, took a negative view of sectarian divisions among Muslim communities, considering Islam to be 'inclusive' rather than 'divisive'. This point is discussed in Chapter 7.

In summary, informants in this research can be characterised as young second-generation (including the 1.5 and later generations) immigrants of predominantly Asian background with a strong faith in their religion, relatively high levels of participation in religious practices (albeit selective), displaying reflexive engagement with their faith, had high educational qualifications despite their parents' low education levels, participated in economic activities and were predominantly unmarried. There were more women than men at a ratio of about 2 to 1.

Part II of this book analyses the identities and social integration of second-generation young Muslims in the UK based on interview data.

Notes

1 In the following, second-generation Muslims without quotation marks refer to those who are not first-generation immigrants. A generation in quotation marks refers to a particular generation among the second and later generations, such as the 'second generation' and the 'third generation'; it also includes the '1.5 generation'.

2 The questions my informants asked most frequently were about my 'faith', especially whether I was 'Muslim or not'. A possible reason for this is a sense of caution arising from their mistrust of the way non-Muslims present Islam and the accompanying concerns that their comments might be misconstrued as discussed in Chapter 5. Nevertheless, it appeared that their suspicions were surpassed by their curiosity about a non-Muslim Japanese conducting research into Muslims in Britain. I responded to their questions by introducing my stance as 'agnostic' – distinct from 'atheist' – and explaining my ideas and history leading up to

this research.

3 If anything, the informants' open-minded attitude posed some difficulties in conducting this research. Many informants gave long detailed answers to particular questions and expressed opinions on unrelated matters within limited interview times. This raised the 'steering' problem stemming from the 'dilemma between efficiency and openness' (Flick 2009: 170–4). Christel Hopf suggests the following reasons why a researcher would deal with informants in a bureaucratic manner: 'the protective function of the interview guide', 'the interviewer's fear of being disloyal to the targets of the research', and 'the dilemma between pressure of time and the researcher's interest in information' (Hopf 1978: 101 cited in Flick 2009: 172). For these reasons, I was occasionally tempted to adopt a bureaucratic manner for interview efficiency. However, the more relaxed (non-bureaucratic) approach is more conducive to creating space for unexpected findings; a comment or insight requiring a re-examination of assumptions. I dealt with this by prioritising the discovery of fresh arguments arising from the informants' remarks by narrowing down core questions in each round of research and treating other questions as less important. It should therefore be noted that not all informants were asked the same questions that others had answered.

4 DeHanas calls Muslims' ways of self-presentation 'tactics', drawing on French philosopher Michel de Certeau, who distinguishes between 'strategy' and 'tactics' in everyday resistive practices (de Certeau 1984). A strategy refers to a calculation of power relations premised on a certain 'place' of rationality as distinct from other environments. In contrast, tactics refer to the actual practices adopted in such a place. In other words, a strategy is a set of 'official rules to mobilise language', whereas tactics refer to 'rhetoric' (i.e., parole) permitting people to use a great deal of creativity while adhering to the rules (Nakanishi 2013: 1–4). Tactics are important because they represent people's dynamism and toughness to subvert cultural impositions 'not by rejecting or altering them, but using them with respect to ends and references foreign to the system they had no choice but to accept' (de Certeau 1984: xiii). Religion as a strategy restricts and guards its sacred domain spatially and socially from the secular domain, whereas religion as tactics is capable of flexibly connecting to other secular domains through its portability – e.g., by using or not using tools signifying Islam such as prayer mats, books, the Internet and the headscarf (Woodhead 2013: 16). In this sense, the term 'strategy' in this book is closer to the 'tactics' concept used by de Certeau and DeHanas.

5 This intermediate position is proximate to 'moderate social constructionism' (Willig 2012) or 'critical realism' (Bhaskar 2008).

6 I did not ask about parents' educational qualifications in Coventry. Fragments of information gathered in interviews suggested a tendency for lower education among the parents, especially those who were first-generation immigrants, as was the case for informants in London.

PART

Analysis and Findings

Chapter

Discrimination, Media and Representation

One thing that is interesting about religion is that it is not really about what anyone might believe in terms of their religion, but about how others see you. What you believe becomes irrelevant. That religious identity defines you at certain times – and the post 9/11 era has certainly been one of these times. It is hard to be a Muslim in a post-9/11 world and not be aware of 'Muslimness'. And it has nothing to do with Islam, in a sense, or whether you believe anything in the Koran, or whether you fast or pray.

'A dark chapter in Pakistan's history'
by Kamila Shamsie (2009)

Once we were in Druids Heath, the reality of racism was thrust directly into our lives, not least because my brother and I were the only brown boys at the local Catholic school. On our very first day, we were met with racial slurs and violence. It was the first time I heard the word 'Paki' directed at me. And then the questions started: *When are you going back home?* And: *Why did you come here?* From this point on, it was made obvious to me that my identity was in question and, for the next decade, I hated being brown, a colour that sometimes brought unwanted, often violent, attention.

'Mahtab Hussain on the multiple identities
of young British Muslim men'
by Mahtab Hussain (2018)

Issues in question: Stigma and identity

Place and identity

This book aims to elucidate the reflexive identity strategies employed by Britain's second-generation Muslims in the post-9/11 social environment, but before beginning that discussion, Chapters 5 and 6 examine their perceptions of British society.

As many researchers have pointed out, identity formation does not occur solely through monologue or introspection; it is always also actuated by the presence of others (Mead 1934; Barth 1969; Tajfel 1978; Taylor 1994; Modood 2007; Kabir 2010). Your self-awareness is premised on your relationship with others and the way others see you. It is formed through both immediate and mediated communication. In other words, identity is 'a dynamic process of self-definition and ascription by others' (Ryan 2012: 109). Many studies have found that people emphasise different aspects of their identities or experience fluctuations in their religious/ethnic boundaries in response to social events (Jacobson 1998; Ameli and Merali 2004).

More recent studies of identity formation have incorporated considerations of the role of 'place' (or space) (Bhimji 2009; Mishra and Shirazi 2010; Ryan 2012). From this perspective, place includes the cultural environment, which defines the meaning and value of life, as well as the physical environment in which people live. Edward Relph states, 'To be human is to live in a world that is filled with significant places. To be human is to have and know your place' (Relph 1976: 1). Having and knowing your place is a human condition and you can understand your 'self' in it.

David Hummon aptly describes the complex relationship between place and the individual as follows:

> By *sense of place*, I mean people's subjective perceptions of their environments and their more or less conscious feelings about those environments. Sense of place is inevitably dual in nature, involving both an interpretive perspective *on* the environment and an emotional reaction *to* the environment... Sense of place involves a personal *orientation* toward place, in which ones' understanding of place and one's feelings about place become fused in the context of environmental meaning. (Hummon 1992: 262)

An individual's sense or image of place does not simply reflect the objective reality of the environment; it changes according to the individual's interpretation and emotional response to it. Accordingly, a sense of place is

Chapter 5

reflexive of place's influence and one's recognition of it. The orientation, value or identity of the individual is formed at the intersection of the individual's sense of self, sense of space, and sense of others; and in that forming, conversely, the sense of place is transformed as well.

It is therefore essential to discover how second-generation Muslims perceive and experience Britain as a social space, in addition to elucidating the current social and political situation of British society surrounding them (see Chapter 2), to understand their identities and social integration. This and the next chapters deal with this question.

Stigma and identity

Sociologist Erving Goffman defines stigma as 'an attribute that is deeply discrediting' (Goffman 1963: 13), which refers to 'the individual's condition of being disqualified from full social acceptance'. Stigma typically signifies not only a person's or group's physical traits but also their perceived moral inferiority in some respect (Göle 2003: 810). According to Goffman, stigma arises when there is a discrepancy between 'an identity assigned by others' and 'an identity the self can present'. This discrepancy activates the individual's self-consciousness and prompts people to reshape their identity through reflection. However, stigmatised individuals always find themselves in ambivalent positions and apply society's identity standards to themselves even though they cannot conform, and as a result, 'vacillates between cowering and bravado, racing from one to the other' (Goffman 1963: 18). One consequence of this is the 'double consciousness' (Du Bois 2020) discussed in Chapter 1. Evaluating one's own identity through the eyes of others can lead to the 'objectification' or 'externalisation' and ultimately 'alienation' of identity (Marx 1964).

However, the 'objectification' of identity through stigma does not always end in 'alienation'. The objectification of identity is a rather normal practice in today's globalised society (Giddens 1991; Taylor 1989). A society's double (or multiple) expectations require minority groups to take a reflexive view of their own identities by reconsidering the relationships with their traditions and selectively reconstructing such traditions as their own in new ways. This process is perhaps more pronounced for Britain's second-generation Muslims. As discussed in Chapter 1, second-generation Muslims in the post-9/11 Western society must develop identities in the face of anti-Islamic discrimination and negative discourses, which constitute an essential environment for their identity formation (Perozzo et al. 2016). Daily stigma, therefore, encourages them to become aware of their own identity, think

128

about it, and be self-loathing or defend it. Indeed, as mentioned in Chapter 2, events such as the Rushdie Affair and 9/11 have prompted Muslims in the UK and Western societies to rethink 'What Islam is' (Ramadan 2005).

This chapter analyses how second-generation British Muslims experience and perceive negative discourses and stigmas surrounding Islam.

The impact of 9/11

The 9/11 incident had a significant impact on Muslims in western societies. It reinforced anti-Muslim prejudice and phobias because the 'religious' motive for the crime seemed to be self-explanatory. Consequently, the Muslim community experienced daily 'backlash' in mainstream society, which has become an integral background for identity formation among second-generation Muslims.

According to Pakistan-born British novelist Kamila Shamsie, cited in the epigraph of this chapter, the 'post-9/11' era has made it impossible for young second-generation Muslims to be oblivious to their 'Muslimness', because the way others appraise or perceive Muslims has an overriding effect on their identities. She explains this mechanism as follows:

> You get asked, 'are you a Muslim?' Yes! And you hear all kinds of things being said about Muslims. And you start to feel yourself being Muslim in a way you never felt before. People will say: 'So what is it about Islam that makes people turn to violence?' And, on the one hand, there is the assumption that this religion is deranged, and on the other, there is the assumption that you must speak up for it. Both of these situations are uncomfortable. (Shamsie 2009)

Muslims in Western society were suddenly the focus of attention and subject to an unexpected profile by society after 9/11. They became conscious of an image of 'Muslimness' that was thrust upon them by others. This assigned image of Islam has deprived them of dignity on a daily basis.

In fact, many of my informants who were students in 2001 spoke of how 9/11 instantly changed their environment:

> September 11 happened on TV, and of course, everybody was shocked. And then the next day, we went to school, and everybody was quiet and everybody was just so shocked, including me. I was shocked as well. I was sitting at the back of the classroom. The teacher, before we started the lesson... said, 'It's very terrible'... And everybody was

Chapter 5

> nodding along, and I was nodding along as well… He said, 'The person [a bomber] is a Muslim'. Then, when he said, everybody in the class just turned around and looked at me… I was upset… 'Don't look at me'… It was just for that one minute… But even that one minute, just all these glances looking at me, I don't think I will ever forget that.
>
> (Daliya, Sudanese, 17, Coventry)

> I did remember 9/11… All my friends in my year group… were going to treat me differently because everyone knew I was a Muslim. That wasn't a hidden thing… I though, 'Oh god! They are going to treat me very differently'. That was when I was in Year 10, it happened. That's why I was a little confused.[1]
>
> (Poppy, Bangladeshi, 28, London)

Daliya, who was living in the Netherlands at the time, had not been particularly conscious of being Muslim until 9/11 even though she was the only Muslim at her school. After 9/11, however, when her teacher said that the perpetrator was a Muslim and the whole class turned and looked at her, Daliya felt shocked by her classmates' gazing at her and became highly conscious of being Muslim. Although that episode did not lead to any direct bullying or discrimination, it had a major impact on her subsequent life and her Muslim identity formation. Similarly, Poppy stated that the change in the way her friends treated her following the school assembly about 9/11 both perplexed her and motivated her to find out 'who she is'.

The impact of 9/11 was not always realised immediately. Two informants said that they recognised it one year after the event:

> I remember 9/11. I was in Year 6. I remember that as coming back from school, my sister said, 'Something happened in America', blah, blah, blah… What people saw was aeroplanes going into two buildings… then we were getting labelled about it. Going to school was completely fine because I had loads of Muslims around me because I went to like a Muslim kind of school. But we were starting school in Year 7; all that was difficult because I had a scarf and I was the only Muslim there. And Muslims were considered the cause of 9/11. That was a really big blow because you are getting labelled. I had never been labelled, 'Oh, you are a Muslim', until I got to secondary school.
>
> (Labibah, Pakistani, 22, Coventry)

Discrimination, Media and Representation

> I didn't realise the impact until I got out of that Muslim school. I was in the same school, which was very Muslim-based. There were a lot of Muslims. When I got into secondary school, I realised the impact of that incident. I realised how intense it actually was and how people felt towards it… I remember one day, I was in a lesson, and someone said, 'Oh, terrorists are all Muslims'. I was like a terrorist that is causing harm. 'You can't label it on Islam!' That's the first time I spoke, and the first and last time I spoke about it. And the whole class turned on me and said, 'No, terrorists are only Muslims'. Then I was too scared to ask anyone or even read a dictionary about it.
>
> (Majdah, Pakistani, 21, Coventry)

Both Labibah and Majdah stated that 9/11 occurred when they were attending primary school, but that it did not affect them until after they entered secondary school because of the high proportion of Muslim children in their primary schools. They both lived in a predominantly Muslim community where Muslim pupils were not stigmatised as terrorists in schools. When they progressed to a secondary school which drew pupils from a broader area and thus had more contact with non-Muslims, they routinely heard statements that associated Muslims with terrorism. They felt defenceless against these characterisations and were afraid to go to school. Their testimonies illustrate how identity or self-image is formed in communication with others. They were forced to discover the 'self' of which they had not been aware when they witnessed changes in the reaction of people around them rather than the 9/11 attacks itself.

This 'self-discovery' through the eyes of others has left some informants traumatised:

> The 9/11 attacks happened when I was 8 years old. I've grown up with this subconscious image in my brain that Muslim people are being branded as terrorists and are bad people who are violent. And this is something I've had to deal with my entire childhood growing up. This is the image that the world portrays of Islam. So it's very difficult, I think, to be Muslim.
>
> (Kashif, Bangladeshi, 22, London)

Kashif saw 9/11 and the intense social backlash at a young age and felt fearful of Islam to which he belonged. He found it difficult to be Muslim in

Chapter 5

British society and had to overcome inner conflict over his own identity as he grew up.

Second-generation Muslims have been compelled to justify their religion against prejudice and ignorance since 9/11. They have felt the need to explain to people what Islam is and is not against the overly strong association between Islam and terrorism made by the Western media.

> You almost have to answer; you have to answer because of their mistakes. Again, it's an individual who has done something wrong. Islam hasn't dictated for them to go and commit such a crime. But then the rest of us, we have to answer because of their mistake.
>
> (Tazmin, Asian mixed, 19, London)

Tazmin was frustrated by the overgeneralised assumption that terrorism was driven by the 'religion'. She argued that some terrorism was perpetuated by individuals who happen to be Muslim, but Islam did not make them do it. Nonetheless, Islam and the entire Muslim community have been severely criticised, and their integration in British society has been called into question. Second-generation Muslims have to justify their faith against this background, whether they want to or not.

At the same time, though, some informants accepted the situation, regarding it as a positive opportunity.

> I would gladly explain Islam. I don't feel that I'm being pressured to do it. If someone has a misconception about my religion, I feel like it's my duty.
>
> (Janan, Sudanese, 20, Coventry)

> It's sometimes a good thing to have non-Muslim friends because we can try to educate them.
>
> (Rizwan, Asian mixed, 19, Coventry)

> They wanted to know more. They were more interested. I would have patience… They would talk about it and say, 'Why do you wear this scarf?' 'Why do you pray?' They wanted to know more about the religion. It's nice for them to know because they are asking.
>
> (Rafima, Bangladeshi, 30, London)

These comments indicate that informants perceived people's interests in Islam, even for negative reasons, as an opportunity. They believed it was meaningful to respond directly to people's desire to find out about Islam, even if such desire initially comes from prejudice.

This attitude relates to the concept of knowledge (*ilm*) in Islam. Knowledge has normative as well as cognitive implications in Islam. Lack of knowledge does not only mean 'ignorance'; it can lead to moral deficiencies and problematic behaviours (Azram 2011: 179). Because knowledge itself is divine, transmitting correct knowledge – true Islam – is considered a 'duty' (Janan) or a laudable deed (Davids 2013: 25–6). Accordingly, these informants treated social prejudice and criticism against the Muslim community as derived from 'lack of knowledge' and saw it as their duty to correct this situation. The meaning and importance of knowledge in Islam are discussed in detail in Chapter 8.

The backlash against the Muslim community triggered by 9/11 strengthened the reflexive identity consciousness of young second-generation Muslims and provided opportunities to take a fresh look at Islam as the source of their identity:

> You have to keep on studying. Every time you listen to something, you read something and realise, 'Oh, I didn't know that'. And also, we live in a society. So I work in an office where there're very few Muslims, and [my non-Muslim co-workers are] often interested in Islamic stuff. And if I can't explain it, what I have read doesn't make sense to me. So I believe in Islam, but I should know it enough to be able to tell other people as well because they have questions and they're curious. So we want to learn as much as possible.
>
> (Malikah, Bangladeshi, 26, London)

Malikah, who worked with non-Muslims in a London office, reported that after 9/11, her colleagues began to take an interest in Islam and asked her many questions. These questions motivated her to explore Islam more deeply herself. Malikah felt that it was important to convincingly explain what she knew about Islam to non-Muslims as well as herself.

This requires the process of 'translating religious utterances into a generally accessible language' (Habermas 2011: 25–8). Habermas stresses the importance of reciprocal 'translation' between religious language and secular language for communication in the public sphere. This has become an essential micropolitical exercise in the private sphere for second-generation Muslims who cannot legitimise their participation 'as Muslims' in

Chapter 5

Britain's civic society otherwise. To translate, they need to confront and learn about their faith. As in the case of 'language', they must become sufficiently conversant with their religion to be able to translate. In this sense, young second-generation Muslims in the post-9/11 era are required to build a new relationship with their faith. This point is discussed further in Chapter 8.

Bakarah, a youth worker in her late 30s in daily contact with young people, offered the following overview of the new relationship between second-generation youth and Islam.

> I am kind of in the middle of both having older and younger. I think, since 9/11, the young people could probably jump in... When I was a younger person, my dad wasn't so religious with us. We didn't really wear a hijab... but since September 11th, younger people have been almost awakened around religion.
>
> (Bakarah, Indian, 39, Coventry)

According to Bakarah, many Muslims, including herself and her family, were not very religious before 9/11. She was impressed that many young people started to wear the hijab because she was not religious and did not wear the hijab in her youth. She attributed this to increased opportunities for today's youth to investigate their religion. Social interest in Islam prompted Muslims to re-examine their faith and deepen their understanding even if it was triggered by negative media reports (Zebiri 2008: 43).

Racism

Street racism

Since 9/11, Muslim youth in Western society have become a magnet for various acts of discrimination and racism. Racism has been commonplace in Britain's history, but it has changed in nature. Jakera spoke of her experience of the change after 9/11:

> Nowadays, discrimination is not more about the Asian aspect. At a younger age, we were called Paki because we were immigrants or we had just come here. Nowadays, it's much more towards Islam.
>
> (Jakera, Bangladeshi, 40, London)

Discrimination, Media and Representation

'Paki' is a derogatory term referring to people with a South Asian background. It is a 'racialised' discriminatory name for any dark-skinned Asian regardless of whether they are in fact Pakistani or not. Jakera, a forty-year-old Bangladeshi, pointed out that the previously common racial slur of Paki had transformed into Islam-related discrimination, or Islamophobia, since 9/11.

However, it would be incorrect to view Islamophobia as a reaction directed purely at religion. Prejudiced people do not check their target's religion or belief before acting discriminatorily. In practice, they discriminate based on the skin colour or clothing of their targets. In this sense, Islamophobia is another racialised concept.

For instance, Jakera and her best friend Syeda talked about their experience of 'street racism':

> Jakera (Bangladeshi, 40, London): There was so much backlash.
>
> Syeda (Bangladeshi, 40, London): Yeah, there are so much anger and resentment when people look at you. They look suspiciously.
>
> Jakera: Yeah, even on trains.
>
> Syeda: Especially because we dressed.

In fact, the Muslim community experienced many backlashes after 9/11, and there were frequent reports of violence targeting Muslims (French 2010). Some informants referred to discriminatory experiences such as being called 'a terrorist' (Bakarah, Indian, 39, Coventry) or 'daughters of bin Laden' (Tabassum, Indian, 26, Coventry) by passers-by on trains or in the street.

Notably, many of those who reported experiencing street racism were women. Syeda attributed this to the 'visibility' of the hijab, which is a symbol of Muslimness and thus makes the wearer a target, as will be discussed in detail in Chapter 10. Many of my informants spoke of the inherent visibility of Muslim women:

> We have experienced much discrimination yet. That comes from people's hate and misunderstanding of what we wear. And they see something in the media, and they think all Muslims have anti-Western attitudes... People don't know us. And the first thing they will see is the hijab. They will see the scarf, and they will immediately think something. It might have a negative connotation for them.
>
> (Tazmin, Asian mixed, 19, London)

Chapter 5

You probably know about the Woolwich incident last year.[2] We are actually near the place. We are not far. I actually work near Woolwich... And there are a lot of people in Woolwich, where their headscarf was being ripped off. They were being slapped because they were covering up, because obviously, people were just associating you with those two terrorists. Everyone did get worried. And, my older sister did actually ask my mom, 'When you go to Woolwich, don't wear a scarf'. Obviously, we were too upset.

(Poppy, Bangladeshi, 28, London)

My sister once was on the bus after the 9/11 attacks, the September 11th World Trade Center. After that, whenever my sister got on the bus, it would be difficult for her. The attitude towards her would be different. She actually got a lot of abuse from people because she was covered. She was wearing Muslim clothes.

(Maaz, Pakistani, 21, Coventry)

Tazmin, who lived in London's Muslim community, reported that she often experienced discrimination when she went into town. In many cases, informants referred to the hijab as the main reason Muslim women were targeted. Street racism was more likely to turn violent following the terrorist incidents. Poppy's sister felt compelled to ask their mother not to wear the hijab when she was going out. Maaz, a young man living in Coventry, reported that his scarf-wearing sisters had been 'abused' on the bus, although he had not personally experienced direct discrimination. Their testimonies show that 9/11 and subsequent terrorist attacks led to a widely held association between Muslim women's scarf/veil and extremism or anti-Western values, escalating harassment and discrimination against them (Runnymede Trust 2004).

Discriminatory treatment was not always violent. Everyday casual exchanges harbour the potential for alienation or exclusion of Muslim youth as well:

When someone asks me who I am, it kind of shocks some people. I play poker on the Internet. Obviously, people can see my face and tell I am not English but Asian. They ask me, 'Where are you from?' and I say, 'I'm from England'. They're like, 'No, you can't be'. I was like, 'I'm from England. Now, I speak English'.

(Huzaifa, Pakistani, 18, Coventry)

136

I think you get stupid questions. For example, I was on placement for a week in the hospital. It was a really hot day. I was talking to a patient, and I said like, 'Oh, it's lovely weather outside'. And he assumed, just because of my headscarf, I was not from here. He was all like, 'Oh, it must be lovely. Where are you from?' And I'm just like, 'I'm from here'. Truthfully, I have never been back to Pakistan.

(Habibah, Asian mixed, 20, Coventry)

Huzaifa's and Habibah's experiences demonstrate that as encounters and communication with non-Muslims become commonplace, Muslims routinely experience 'othering' in such exchanges. It is unavoidable because it is triggered by visible attributes such as skin colour and clothing.

Thus, second-generation Muslims are noticed for their appearance and looked at as aliens in the Western civic space. They often experience being treated as 'second-class citizens', even in the absence of malice or violence, in the sense that they are asked to justify their citizenship. Such experiences threaten their self-esteem and may inhibit their identification with Britain.

Institutional racism

The visibility of Muslim women is a factor for 'institutional racism', which is defined as:

> The collective failure of an organisation to provide an appropriate and professional service to people because of their colour, culture or ethnic origin. It can be seen or detected in processes, attitudes and behaviour which amount to discrimination through unwitting prejudice, ignorance, thoughtlessness and racist stereotyping which disadvantage minority ethnic people. (Macpherson 1999: 28)[3]

Although not always overtly, institutional racism classifies minority people in a discriminatory manner and sometimes excludes them in formal or informal relations.

Job-search is where Muslim women experience institutional racism most frequently:

> I was a *hijabi*. In terms of discrimination like racism, I think applying for work, applying for jobs. I remember, me and my friend, we had applied for a workplace. And I thought my interview went really well. I just was really chatty. And the interviewer was smiling, she gave really positive

Chapter 5

feedback. But my friend got the job and she wasn't wearing the scarf. I didn't get the job. I don't know whether it's because of my hijab. But I think it was down to the fact that a waitress is aesthetically pleasing. So if you are going around with this headscarf, some of the customers might find that offensive. So we are always not employed on that basis.

(Duha, Asian mixed, 19, Coventry)

Duha said that she responded well in the interview to become a waitress and was qualified for the position, but she did not get the job because she was wearing a headscarf. She thought that the headscarf was incompatible with the Western commercial framework in which women's bodies have monetary value, and was offensive to some consumers because of its clear expression of 'Muslimness'.

A similar situation was reported from the opposite perspective. Majdah, a non-scarf wearer in her early 20s, spoke of her interview for the same waitressing job:

I think sometimes jobs can be an issue. Me and my friend – she wears a headscarf – we went to apply for a waitressing job at a cafe. It was her idea and she was all excited. She had everything sorted. She had the answers to all the questions. She is much smarter than me and she is much more like, you would like to employ her rather than me. We did the interview, and I gave my answer and she gave her answers. I was 100 per cent sure she gave better answers than me. She is smarter than me. She knows all the right things to say. She didn't get the job, but I did. I was just thinking, 'Hmm, that's not right' because she helped me prepare for this interview... I think maybe a scarf can have an effect. She couldn't get certain jobs in certain areas.

(Majdah, Pakistani, 21, Coventry)

Majda cited the headscarf as a reason why her friend was not selected for the waitressing job despite being qualified in all respects. Like Duha, she suspected that the interviewer made the hiring decision based on the presence or absence of the scarf in the interview regardless of the applicant's ability.

Banan explained the social meaning given to the scarf in the following:

I have gone for a job interview, and I felt perhaps they thought I was not going to be compatible with the work environment, purely based on how I look... maybe more because of my visible identity as a Muslim

Discrimination, Media and Representation

woman, not so much due to my ethnicity… My gender, being a woman sometimes in a male-dominated environment, is a challenge. People perhaps think: 'It is not your place. You should just be at home'.

(Banan, Bangladeshi, 24, London)

Banan said that the scarf visually identified Muslim women as bodies unsuitable for labour. Muslim women were disadvantaged in the labour market regardless of their qualifications and skills because of perceptions that they cannot work with men or won't commit to work because they prioritise family (Dale et al. 2002: 22; Bowlby and Lloyd-Evans 2009: 45–8). Another unmarried informant stated that job interviewers' attitude toward hijab-wearing women was suggestive of their thinking: 'Oh, okay, she's a Muslim girl. She's probably going to get married young and is going to leave the company' (Yasmin, Bangladeshi, 22, London). In fact, Banan and Yasmin stopped looking for jobs in private companies and found work instead in an Islamic charity organisation. Their cases are examples of the intersectionality discussed in Chapter 3 – the intersection of gender and religion in their cases (Ali 1992; Brah 1996).

These testimonies illustrate that Muslim women tend to be portrayed as 'voiceless' in Western society (Mohanty 2003: 24–6). They are often considered faceless people who lack free will and are chained to their family, under the command of their religion or their father or husband as guardians. Nazma spoke of her experience:

People expect me not to have a voice. Even where I'm working, often I have had comments like that. They've never met an Asian woman like me because they assume, as soon as they see me, 'You should be quieter', 'You won't have a voice', or 'What would you know?'; that kind of attitude. But the thing is I have a brain. I'm not forced to wear what I'm wearing. I choose to follow my religion. I think sometimes you can be underestimated.

(Nazma, Bangladeshi, 36, London)

Nazma, who had raised three children and built her career while undertaking graduate studies, felt aggrieved by stereotypical views and lack of recognition of her abilities and efforts at work.

The experience of being regarded as 'voiceless' was common among informants over the age of thirty:

Chapter 5

> Jakera (Bangladeshi, 40, London): They will see in the media women
> in hijab and they think we are so oppressed and downtrodden, and
> this and that.
>
> Syeda (Bangladeshi, 40, London): We have no opinion, we have no value.
>
> Jakera: We have no opinion.

As we saw in Chapter 2, the labour market participation rate was generally low among Muslim women and lower in the older generation. Both the employment rate and the education continuation rate in women were lower in the over-thirty generation than in the younger generation. This feeds the perception that they lack motivation and ability. Thus, the over-thirty generation tends to be seen as victims of their oppressive community who lack the ability and will to be independent social actors (Ali and Hopkins 2012).

While there was a tendency for institutional racism to target women due to the visual symbol of the headscarf, male informants reported similar, though less frequent, experiences:

> If you're outwardly showing signs of Islam like a beard. In the Western world, it's supposed to be clean-shaven. All of the top managers, they're clean-shaven and stuff. So you kind of feel, 'Okay. You don't have a chance of going to work for one of these big Western organisations'. Everyone is clean-shaven. If you want to show your outward sign of Islam in the beard, then you kind of think there's no chance.
>
> (Sohail, Bangladeshi, 28, London)

> I think there might be slightly more racism in the big companies than on the street. He had the same sort of qualifications as a regular white person in Birmingham, but he might not get the job because he had a big beard.
>
> (Noman, Indian, 18, Coventry)

Sohail felt that having the visual male symbol of a 'beard' disadvantaged Muslim men in employment in Western society. Noman also thought that his close friend was disadvantaged when looking for a job in ordinary British companies because he maintained his religious appearance, which tended to be interpreted as excessive 'Muslimness'.

Another form of institutional racism reported by male informants was the police practice of 'stop and search'. Taimoor, a London resident, testified to his own and his friend's experiences:

140

Discrimination, Media and Representation

> I was going to play football. And this was my second year at university. So I was going to the tube station. I had a big bag with my football kit and everything... My friend, he had a little bit of a beard, he had just a rucksack. Police stopped him, they checked him, they asked for his details till he opened his bag... He's like one of the nicest, most genuine person that I have ever met. He has not a bad bone in his body. He can never hurt anybody... He was being judged for the way he looked.
>
> (Taimoor, Pakistani, 27, London)

Bearded men are sometimes watched by others on the train, subway, and bus, and stopped and searched by police on suspicion of carrying bombs.[4] Many of my informants were not wearing beards and hence were seldom subjected to stop-and-search. However, they sensed institutional racism through their friends' and family's daily experiences of religious profiling.

In comparison with women, male informants tended to report institutional discrimination based on race, in addition to religion:

> People don't know I am a Muslim because I am not like a Muslim in terms of appearance... I know someone who shows hostility toward me after knowing I am a Muslim. I have some issues because of my skin colour and religion.
>
> (Rizwan, Asian mixed, 19, Coventry)

'Forth-generation' Rizwan and his family had lived in British society for a long time and experienced less discrimination because they did not normally wear a beard or religious clothes. Still, they sometimes suffered discriminatory treatment when their Muslim faith was revealed, in addition to racial discrimination. Curiously, female informants tended to mention discrimination based on religion rather than race, whereas male informants pointed to colour-based discrimination more frequently. Women were easily identifiable as Muslim because most of them wore a headscarf, while a majority of men were identified and discriminated against based on their skin colour because they did not wear a beard signifying Islam.

The informants in my study experienced Islam-related racism in British society to varying degrees. This shared hardship must be a factor influencing second-generation Muslims' identity formation.

Chapter 5

Muslim representations in the media

It is important to examine the media when considering the relationship between discrimination and identity. The media influence both Muslims and non-Muslims beyond geographical spaces, transforming their mutual recognition and relationships, and as a result, their identities. The media have an enormous impact on the formulation of Muslim identities (especially the negative ones) (Kabir 2010: 162).

The types and situations of discrimination experienced by my informants varied depending on residence area and generation. Informants over the age of thirty tended to report discrimination at schools and workplaces. Informants in London who could easily travel outside their community tended to encounter street racism. Women were more prone than men to be victims of institutional racism. However, all informants, regardless of gender, locality, and age, expressed serious concerns about the Western media:

> The media shows like, Islam is quite a violent religion, doesn't it? If you look at it, Muslims have a bomb there... Our religion isn't like that. We will induce more peace in our religion. Islam means, basically, it means peace.
>
> (Husnain, Bangladeshi, 21, Coventry)

As Husnain noted, media reports on Muslims are typically tied to negative incidents (e.g., terrorism, sex crime and domestic violence) and very rarely shine a light on their positive aspects (e.g., charity, respect for women and valuing equality and freedom) (Said 1981).

Most informants presented antipathy against the media and accused it of having a negative influence on people. For example, Imran testified:

> The media plays a big part... The *Daily Mail* will blur it and blow it up out of proportion. They say every Muslim is a terrorist and might say these terrorists were in a mosque and they were taught terrorism. So every mosque in the world now becomes grounds for terrorism breeding... The majority and the media will pick up on and use them to represent the whole. The media can manipulate it... The media is not there for my benefit, for the Muslim benefit or the innocent persons, but for money. They'll say what they want as long as it sells. So, I think the media have no line of the truth. They are making as many sales as they can, and they write what they want.
>
> (Imran, Pakistani, 24, Coventry)

Imran claimed that *The Daily Mail* and other major media outlets discussed terrorism and the Muslim community in the same breath, and 'picked up on' one aspect of something and incorrectly attributed it to the religion. He highlighted the media's 'commercialism', regarding the media as part of a capitalist system in pursuit of economic profit instead of a means for disseminating truth or information about events as they really are. Commercialism motivates reporters and journalists to 'write what they want' and victimises the Muslim community in the process.

This is what Edward Said calls 'covering Islam'; media coverage covers up some aspects of Islam (Said 1981). As Said explains:

> In no really significant way is there a direct correspondence between the 'Islam' in common Western usage and the enormously varied life that goes on within the world of Islam, with its more than 800,000,000 people, its dozens of societies, states, histories, geographies, cultures. (Said 1981: x)

Most informants pointed to this dissociation between media representations and the actual life practices of Islam.

As noted in the quote from Imran, many informants were alarmed by media depictions of Islam because they 'make up' a reality for the masses:

> I think there is a problem also with schools and the media about the way they portray religions. It has a huge impact because that's where people are getting their information from. So people really need to be careful with the wording, what they are saying because it has a huge effect on our lives and thinking for the younger children... It can make or break you... It's not just to be discriminatory but to be stereotypical...
>
> (Majdah, Pakistani, 21, Coventry)

> Every news report will connect Islam with terrorism. Even if they're saying Islam isn't terrorism, something is mentioned side by side. It kind of reinforces the fact. It's like positive reinforcement of the notion.
>
> (Sohail, Bangladeshi, 28, London)

According to Majdah, these media reports are problematic not only because they are discriminatory but also because they plant a 'stereotype' in people's minds that generates particular perceptions and reactions toward Muslims in society. Media coverage of Muslims conveys biased expressions and views even when it seems objective. As we have already seen, Western media

Chapter 5

tend to depict scarf-wearing women as passive objects with no opinions of their own while depicting bearded men as religiose supporters of terrorism. Although it is 'only' a discourse, its repeated dissemination creates a set of discourses constituting a reality for people. It thus influences the social context surrounding Muslims, as Sohail observed, because people 'believe what the media says' (Rafima, Bangladeshi, 30, London). Moreover, the media tacitly influences people's perceptions by employing certain 'wording' in portraying something, and people are defenceless against it.

This view was prevalent, particularly among younger informants. Coventry informants in their teens and 20s observed:

> Uzma (Indian, 19, Coventry): When I think of a religion, we don't even associate it with terrorism. That's just the media's perception. We say, 'Oh, you need not to do this' and 'We are not like that'.

> Karam (Pakistani, 23, Coventry): Until 9/11 happened, I didn't even know what terrorism was. Yeah, I was young, but in terms of teaching, I never ever came across extreme views.

> Uzma: We hadn't come across it, so I don't know why they keep portraying that every Muslim is like that.

> Selikah (Indian, 17, Coventry): Yes. I think it's the language that the media uses.

> Karam: It's so derogatory, yeah.

> Uzma: I know that for some people, it's cultural things like gangs, like prostitution and stuff. They might be Muslims, but it's not Islam as a religion. It's not religion saying that to you, but they put a Muslim tag.

> Selikah: Yeah, they're picking up and blowing up. That'll become the headline, and just somebody walking will see that headline. That will automatically make Muslims negatively, automatically.

Like Imran, these women observed that the media negatively manipulated images of the Muslim community by 'picking up' and 'blowing up' a specific aspect (Ali and Hopkins 2012: 147–50). They also declared that terrorism had nothing to do with Islam, but contradicted it. They used the term 'Muslim tag' to refer to the media discourse linking their familiar everyday practices of Islam to terrorism. The Muslim tag does not simply attribute the cause of negative incidents to Islam, but is more generally what Majdah (Pakistani, 21, Coventry) called a 'stereotype' or 'wording', referring to a

144

Discrimination, Media and Representation

particular cognitive framework that associates extremism and infringement of Western democratic values to fundamental Muslim beliefs rather than an individual's personal motives (Phillips 2007).

The Muslim tag assumes a certain kind of 'double standard', exclusively targeting Islam instead of other religious-cultural groups. For example, Rehana commented on the issue of cartoons satirising Muslims:

> That's all of a sudden become acceptable. We should lighten up because it's just a joke. But when somebody does the same to a Jew about the Holocaust, that's like a big deal. I think there are a lot of hidden agendas going on.
>
> (Rehana, Bangladeshi, 26, London)

Many Muslims in Western society protest the publication of cartoons satirising the Prophet Muhammed, the founder of Islam. Defenders of the cartoons typically justify their acts on the grounds of 'freedom of expression' in secular society and reject Muslims who complain about such acts. However, Rehana referred to the Holocaust, claiming that cartoons or representations ridiculing the Jews would cause much trouble in Europe. She expressed frustration over being judged under a double standard even though both Judaism and Islam are 'Abrahamic religions'. Thus, she suspected a 'hidden agenda' behind the treatment of Muslims in European society.[5]

This criticism of the double standard extends to the media coverage of 9/11 and 7/7, and the subsequent social reaction against Muslims:

> I won't agree with what Muslims have done just like these terrorists of, you know, 7/7 and 9/11. Yeah, I don't agree with what they have done... If there was a Christian terrorist, I don't say all Christians are terrorists. Were Christians all perceived as terrorists all around the world after World War II? Have they been oppressed for the last sixty odd years, seventy odd years? No, they haven't. But somehow, one Muslim or a few Muslims, they started to plant a bomb which killed so many innocent people. I don't want to say it's a small issue; it's massive. One life is equivalent as much as anyone's life. Even if that bomb killed one person, it would have been still an issue. But does it mean that all Muslims are terrorists? That's the silliest thing I have heard. We all have radical views. We are pinpointed. You might be of no charge at all, you haven't done anything wrong, but you are questioned. When you are questioned, people look at you. And when people look at you, then you

Chapter 5

kind of start having own doubt in yourself, and, you know, things are shredded to bits.

(Zubair, Barbadian, 20, Coventry)

This young man's comment summarises a general view among my informants. He rejected terrorism committed by extremists and denied any link between such action and Islam. He complained that the media portrayed Muslims as if they were 'terrorists' regardless. He claimed that a double standard was applied to the Muslim community because terrorism committed by Christians did not stigmatise Christian society in the same way. The stigma triggers 'questioning' not only in the media but also by police on the street and reflexively reinforces the negative representations of Muslims in the minds of those who see it. Young Muslims such as Zubair fell into self-distrust or self-doubt, destabilising their identities and evoking what Du Bois called double consciousness.

Nafisa, who described herself as a 'more Westernised Muslm', was similarly frustrated:

> The only conflict is when you're not treated as British. You know, that's the only conflict. For example, if I walk down the street somewhere else, people will look at me and think I'm not from this country. They don't realise I was born here and my parents were born here. It's like that, isn't it? It's Muslims. We need to be accepted as part of this country because we do a lot of good in this country. I think that's why I'm very passionate about changing that perception because the media makes us look so bad all the time.
>
> (Nafisah, Asian mixed, 22, London)

Nafisah had no conflict between being British and being Muslim and complained that her continued treatment as a 'foreigner' or 'other' was unjust. She considered media depictions of Muslims to be the deep-rooted cause.

Durrah, a non-hijab wearer from an Asian community in London's Newham, said that she had never been subject to discrimination based on her sex, ethnicity or religion at schools and workplaces. Yet, she was anxious about media reporting. She spoke of an incident surrounding a tweet posted by Channel 4's Cathy Newman:

> This Channel 4 journalist called Cathy Newman, she went to the wrong mosque. And she sent this tweet saying, 'I've just been ushered out of the mosque, even though it's a "welcome to mosque day" and I'm dressed

146

respectfully'. Turned out that she'd gone to the wrong mosque, then they found a CCTV camera, and she hadn't been ushered out. She walked in, she spoke to some and then she walked out by herself. But the amount of vitriol [against the mosque] generated, you know, on Twitter and in the media.

(Durrah, Indian, 39, London)

Durrah felt frustrated by the fact that a journalist from a major TV station spread a false claim in the media (Twitter) and that a mosque and the Muslim community were criticised based on her disinformation. She said that this was not an isolated incident; the Muslim community experiences something like this daily.

Citizen Khan

To gain a better understanding of the media representation issue, I asked my informants about their views on *Citizen Khan*, a situation comedy first broadcast on BBC One in 2012.[6] The comedy-drama centring on the British-Pakistani Khan family was set in East Birmingham's Asian community. The series sparked controversy in the Muslim community from the start, even while gaining popularity and winning numerous TV awards. The central characters, middle-aged Mr Khan and his younger daughter Alia, drew the most criticism. For example, Khan is a 'pathological liar, racist, rude, highly irreligious' (5 Pillars 2013) man whose idiotic words and actions elicited laughs. Alia wears a hijab unlike her older sister, but she was wearing 'more make-up than a circus clown', 'constantly on her Blackberry texting her boyfriend', and 'constantly pulling the wool over her parents' eyes' (5 Pillars 2013).

Many informants expressed disapproval of the show's contents. Salimah's comment below is representative of their views:

There are a lot of things that I don't agree with. I mean, Khan does take a lot of insults in a very jokey way. He does insults with humour. He insults Islam. That's why I don't like it... For example, in the mosque, there is a ginger, a Scottish rebirth. He [Khan] always jokes [to the Scottish] like, 'You're not really a Muslim' and stuff. I don't think Islam is like that. You just need to look at *hajj*. Shoulder to shoulder, there are also so different people from all over the world. Nobody does that.

(Salimah, Bangladeshi, 33, London)

Chapter 5

Salimah found it alarming that the portrayal of Khan as narrow-minded and conservative – even though these traits generate comedy – might lead people to think that he is the archetypal Muslim. She was especially concerned by Khan calling the convert managing the mosque a 'ginger', a derogatory term (for Scots in particular). She referred to a pilgrimage to Mecca where all types of Muslims gathered from across the globe as evidence that Islam respects diversity.

Khan's mocking behaviour is the reason many informants gave for identifying *Citizen Khan* as anti-Islamic:

> The way he does is the way, you know, he is trying to mock you. I wouldn't mock anyone's religion or anyone's culture, whatever they are. I wouldn't want to do that. So I think it's trying to make fun of something that people feel important. So I don't like it.
>
> (Shoaib, Bangladeshi, 29, London)

Salimah and Shoaib shared a negative view of the portrayal of Khan making fun of non-Muslims and their cultures and religions. Their criticism emanated from Islam's spirit of 'leniency' and the idea of 'judgment', which I will discuss further in Chapters 7 and 10 respectively.

The main criticism of *Citizen Khan* was not concerned with the characters' attributes or conduct per se, but 'what they represent'. As seen above, some informants were critical of this television show on the grounds that it misrepresented Islam and Muslims:

> It is *Citizen Khan* that the husband is patriarchal and everyone is submissive to the father. And the father has a big ego problem. I think that's true within culture, but not Islamically. And that's where the two kinds of going astray happen because he has a beard, he has a mosque hat. And I think the message sometimes is taken that that is what Islam is, and that's not the case, actually.
>
> (Aflan, Pakistani, 35, London)

Aflan acknowledged that *Citizen Khan*'s portrayal might capture one aspect of Muslim family relationships rooted in their real-life 'culture', but he warned that the portrayal was mistaken as a representation of Islam.

Some informants, however, see the show as a representation of an 'Asian' family rather than an 'Islamic' one and are therefore not bothered by its depictions:

148

It's not religion. It's to do with culture, Pakistani culture, you know, Asian families, or some South East Asian families. It's not to do with religion. So it's funny. It's really well-written parts of the culture.

(Durrah, Indian, 39, London)

Unlike Aflan, Durrah perceived the show to be a comical portrayal of an 'Asian-Muslim family' and not of an 'Islamic family', that is, a representation of the 'culture' and not the 'religion'. She enjoyed watching the show because she did not think that it prejudiced Islam.

Those who had watched the show were not necessarily critical of the entire programme. For example, Salimah felt empathy with some of the characterisations:

Some of it is funny because of his second daughter. A lot of the girls do that like her… The teenage girls are out there. They're either forced to wear the hijab or wear it by choice, but they also want to look attractive. It can happen.

(Salimah, Bangladeshi, 33, London)

She expresses empathy with the portrayal of Alia, a 'teenage girl' who was 'constantly pulling the wool over her parents' eyes' (5 Pillars 2013). Salimah accepted that such behaviour 'can happen' in the real world. Jannah (Bangladeshi, 18, London) agreed. While she criticised the depictions of dominant, patriarchal men and subordinate women in the show, she professed, 'I do like Alia's character' who resorts to all sorts of measures and excuses to deny Khan's demands. Thus, some female informants related to the show's female characters through their own experiences while being generally critical of the show and Khan's character.

These points indicate some of the reasons for the show's broad support, including from Muslims, despite much criticism.[7] However, this is partly dependent on how people perceive the show. *Citizen Khan* would be rejected when it was taken as a representation of 'Islam' but might be acceptable when it was seen as depicting a 'culture'.

Chapter 5

Conclusion

This chapter has described how discriminatory practices and media representations of Islam cast shadows on second-generation Muslims' adaptation to British society. Many informants routinely experienced street or institutional racism and felt that they and the Muslim community were othered in British society and thus alienated from its civic space. The issue of post-9/11 media representations of Islam was particularly serious. The informants were strongly frustrated by the media's selective reporting of particular incidents and incorrectly ascribing their causes to Islam. They believed that the entire Muslim community had been victimised by commercially motivated sensationalism. When a crime happens, questions are raised about the perpetrators' backgrounds and motives. When the perpetrators are Muslim, however, their religion is portrayed as sufficient motivation for their actions (Phillips 2007). Informants felt that this treatment applied exclusively to Muslims and never to other religious communities.

This double standard may give second-generation Muslims a stigmatised identity and increase their sense of unfairness. As Marie Gillespie states, 'media create spaces in which identity, belonging, and security are continually questioned, negotiated, reinforced and revised' (Gillespie 2006: 908). For this reason, daily media coverage and negative description of Muslim communities might discourage second-generation Muslims from taking pride in being British or living as part of a broader society.

Importantly, the informants did not perceive the situation in a completely negative light. Many appeared to be trying to build a new relationship with their faith by studying Islam afresh through everyday questioning (Contractor 2012: 88–9). As Shamsie stated above, the situation is neither fair nor comfortable, but it has become a structural precondition for identity formation among second-generation Muslim diasporas since 9/11 (Ramadan 2010). The Islamic practice of 'seeking knowledge' is necessary to deal with this challenge. Chapter 8 focuses on this point.

A noteworthy finding from this study is the strategies employed by informants in defending Islam against media depictions. Their criticism of the media has two key questions: 'Is the media's Muslim depiction true or untrue?' and 'What does the depiction represent?' While these questions overlap to some extent, they are analytically separable. Many informants thought that media depictions of Muslims were untrue, giving false representations to society. However, as the discussion on their views of *Citizen Khan* has shown, some informants argued that media depictions more or less reflected the ways that British Muslims lived. What is problematic here is

150

that media depictions incorrectly represent the cultural life of the Muslim community as their religious life. When the programme is understood as only portraying the 'culture', it is more likely to be accepted because it is not considered as an insult to Islam.

Thus, the informants' perceptions vary greatly depending on whether a certain event or matter is attributable to (Asian) 'culture' or 'religion' (Islam). Chapter 7 examines their sensitivity to the differences between culture and religion, the reasons for their sensitivity, and the significance of the distinction for their social integration and identity formation.

Notes

1   Britain's compulsory education is categorised in two ways: Key Stages and Years. Key Stage 1 corresponds to Years 1 to 2 (5–7 years old), Key Stage 2 to Years 3 to 6 (7–11 years old), Key Stage 3 to Years 7 to 9 (11–14 years old) and Key Stage 4 to Years 10 to 11 (14–16 years old). Key Stages 1–2, called primary education, and Key Stages 3–4, called secondary education, constitute the compulsory education period.

2   The Woolwich incident refers to the murder of British army soldier Lee Rigby by two African men in Woolwich, southeast London, in May 2013. The attack was declared an act of terrorism as the perpetrators claimed after their arrests that the UK and the US were harming people in the Islamic world. Both offenders were British of Nigerian descent and considered unaffiliated 'lone wolf terrorists' (NewSphere 2013).

3   The term 'institutional racism' emerged from the US Black power movement in the late 1960s and highlights the distinction between 'individual' and 'institutional' or 'intention' and 'effect' (Singh 2002). It aims to describe discrimination that manifests as an effect of institutions rather than as an intention by an individual. Accordingly, the concept of institutional racism contributes to exposing deeply ingrained discriminatory structures that operate implicitly rather than blatantly.

4   Schedule 7 of the Terrorism Act 2000 gives examining officers at ports and airports powers to investigate travellers if they might be involved in the commission, preparation or instigation of acts of terrorism. It allows examining officers to stop, question and search individuals without any reasonable suspicion. According to the Home Office, of 85,557 people who were examined in 2009, 2,687 were held for questioning for over one hour under Schedule 7. Of 99 people who were arrested between 2004 and 2009, 48 were charged and 43 of them were found guilty by the court. Section 43 of the Act allows the stop and search of individuals on the street or in public areas if there is a 'reasonable suspicion' that they are terrorists. Section 44 authorised police officers to search

Chapter 5

individuals or vehicles for any items that might be used for a terrorist act in the area specified in the authorisation. As a result, the frequency of stop and search rose after 9/11 and increased considerably following the attempted car bombings in London's Haymarket in June 2007. However, the number of arrests under the section was very small (less than one per cent) and none of them resulted in conviction. These security crackdowns targeted particular ethnic groups in a biased manner (Choudhury and Fenwick 2011: 31). From 2001 to 2003, the rate of increase in stops and searches of Asians reached 302 per cent compared to an increase of 118 for white people (CCP 2004). This racial or religious profiling has become commonplace in the UK (Adachi 2013b: 348–9).

5   Many Muslims share the view that Western society has a 'hidden agenda' against the Islamic world. According to a survey by the Pew Global Attitudes Project, for example, a majority of the general public in Western society think that 'Muslim intolerance' is responsible for the Muhammad Cartoons Controversy, whereas an overwhelming majority of Muslims blame 'Western intolerance' (PRC 2006: 21). Similarly, many Muslims in Europe and other countries (35–75 per cent) do 'not believe' that 'Arabs carried out 9/11 attacks' (PRC 2006: 4).

6   Questions about *Citizen Khan* were asked only in the fourth round of research.

7   For example, Saira Khan, a TV presenter of Pakistani descent, rated *Citizen Khan* highly as 'a home-grown sitcom that allowed British Muslims to laugh at themselves' (Khan 2012).

Discrimination, Media and Representation

Chapter

Britishness and Britain as 'Multicultural Space'

When I telephone my mother in her family home in northern Somalia, where she returned after living in England for thirty-two years, she calls me Abdel Rahman. Why did she give me that second name and why is it so important to her? It is a question that is a fundamental part of what it is to be Muslim in the modern world – especially a Muslim living in the West. Does your Muslim identity and loyalty supersede loyalty to your nation? Do you feel Muslim first and Somali, British, French or Dutch second? Can the two identities really co-exist? My second name also says something about the often hidden aspect of Muslim lives in this post-September 11 world. Integration, at least as it is seen from the perspective of Muslims coming to and even abandoning half of ourselves... I saw that the Somalia I had believed I would return to was disappearing. Britain, formerly a place of temporary exile, would now be my home and future.

Only Half of Me
by Rageh Omaar (2007: 3–4)

I'm just as British as the next man. I have a different skin colour, wear different clothes sometimes, speak a different language, have a beard on my face, pray to a different god and eat food with my hands. So, what? I was born here, I speak English, I eat chicken and chips, have cried when England have lost a football game, I pay my taxes and I'm a pretty chilled out family-orientated guy who respects the law... I'm just as British as the next man.

British-Islamic Identity
by Aminul Hoque (2015: 166)

Issues in question: What is Britishness?

As I discussed in Chapters 1 and 2, identity is a political concept, and various group identities are constantly debated in political discourses on social integration. The prevailing discourse in the UK maintains that there is a kind of conflict between being British and being Muslim, that Muslim communities turn their backs on British society through self-segregation, and that young people live in the interstices of such society (Cantle 2001; Lewis 2007). In this context, society asks second-generation Muslims to share in a liberally defined 'British' national identity for the purpose of their integration (Goodhart 2004; Blair 2006; Cameron 2011; Adachi 2013b). However, as many researchers have pointed out, 'Britishness' is a polysemic concept and the meanings people associate with the concept differ (Ameli and Merali 2004; Parekh 2009). So, what does Britishness really mean? What is the value of being British to young second-generation Muslims? How does it connect with their faith and adaptation to society?

As mentioned in Chapter 2, the UK government attempted to subsume diverse communities by defining Britishness in terms of democratic values rather than ethnicity or race (Blair 2006; Brown 2006). In fact, most Muslims living in the UK perceive themselves as British and many believe that being Muslim is compatible with being British.

Previous studies of Britishness partly explain this perception. *Citizenship and Belonging: What is Britishness?*, published by ETHNOS, an agency special-ising in ethnic minority research, sheds light on people's understanding of 'Britishness'. This report indicates that there is no exclusive relationship between the concept of Britishness and other identities and that many ethnic minorities are actively committed to it. The important point is that non-white people tend to identify themselves as British but not English whereas white people perceive themselves as British and English. Non-white people in the UK think that the idea of 'Englishness' has a connotation of being white whereas Britishness has no such colour bias. Similarly, they believe that the idea of Britishness can be compatible with any religious identities, including Catholic, Sikh and Muslim (ETHNOS 2005).

Britishness is thus a 'civic' concept, not an 'ethnic' concept (Adachi 2008b; 2008c). This view is particularly notable among minorities. For the Scottish, the Welsh and ethnic minorities, for example, the idea or sense of Britishness has a particular connection with the passport. English people, in contrast, rarely make that connection. In other words, the white English population as the majority in the strongest sense of the word accept Britishness naturally as their embodied attribute rather than a formalised

Chapter 6

institution whereas ethnic and national minorities adopt it as an official attribute external to themselves.[1] This finding demonstrates that Britishness as a representation possesses sufficient diversity and inclusivity for people from diverse backgrounds to commit to and identify with, although it could also be perceived differently depending on an individual's historical/social position (ETHNOS 2005; Adachi 2008c; Adachi 2013b: 208–14).

Is the concept of Britishness inclusive enough to bring second-generation Muslims into society? Many preceding studies point out that 'being British' or 'Britishness' for minority groups is merely an institutional and legal right and not necessarily an object of emotional commitment (Ameli and Merali 2004; ETHNOS 2005). In fact, the issue discussed in Western political discourse is the social integration of second-generation Muslims who (allegedly) turn their back on society while enjoying this legal right – as homegrown terrorists do.

This chapter analyses how my informants perceived Britishness, understood Britain as a social space, and faced its society.

Being British

There are several ways in which an ethnic minority can identify as 'British' (Jacobson 1998; Ameli and Merali 2004; ETHNOS 2005). One way is to do so from the perspective of 'race'. A second way is by sharing a specific 'culture' – for example, affection and support for the Queen, watching BBC and liking fish and chips, while a third way is to define it as the sharing of more abstract 'values' such as freedom, equality and tolerance. The second way is measured by the degree of acclimatisation to the British lifestyle and the third way by the degree to which one accepts democratic values promoted by the British government and performs civic duties. A fourth way is to define 'being British' by 'fact of residence' and 'legal rights', i.e., nationality and citizenship.

The likelihood of second-generation immigrants identifying as British generally increases from the first to the fourth of these approaches. The first approach assumes that whiteness is the essence of Britishness, which precludes many minorities from identifying as such since race and ethnicity are the most difficult attributes to change. Identification with cultural lifestyle is easier than changing race or ethnicity, but still more difficult than identifying with shared values because it requires changing everyday behaviours.[2] The fourth approach, residence and legal rights, is the easiest condition for second-generation immigrants to identify with because of the legal fact that they have a nationality based on their birth. Conversely, the level of emotional identification is the lowest in the last case (Ameli and Merali 2004; ETHNOS 2005). As Figure 6.1 shows, the likelihood of identification with and the level of attachment to the object are expected to have an inverse relationship. So, what did my informants understand by being British?

First, none of the informants defined being British in terms of race or ethnicity. They might acknowledge that white people form a majority of the population, but none stated that whiteness was a prerequisite for being British. Aflan explained this point using the phrase 'two types of nationalism':

> There are two types of nationalism. You can say civic national if you have a passport. On the other hand, there is ethnic nationalism. So it gives you a lot of space to operate. We don't feel that you don't belong to society. You may not belong in certain places, but in all other places, you do belong, you know. I may not be English, but I am British. So there's a lot of room, a lot of scope there, and I feel like I'm a valued sort of individual in society. I don't see an issue there.
>
> (Aflan, Pakistani, 35, London)

Aflan's comment encapsulated many informants' understanding of British society. He thought that what Britain sought was 'civic nationalism' and not 'ethnic nationalism' and that what was important was an adaptation to its civic space, not an ethnic identity (Adachi 2008b; 2008c). Thus Aflan declared that he was not English (ethnicity) but British (citizen); this concurs with the ETHNOS study (2005). Aflan's reference to the existence of 'room' and 'scope' represented Britain as a 'multicultural space'; I will discuss this point in more detail below.

The most frequently mentioned reason for informants identifying as British was the 'fact of residence':

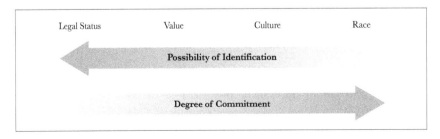

Figure 6.1 Relationship between identification and commitment

Chapter 6

Author: Do you think you're British?

Wardah (Indian, 27, Coventry): Of course we are.

Zahra (Asian mixed, 22, Coventry): I'm British, yes.

Wardah: Yes, 100 per cent British.

Zahra: Well, my parents weren't born in India to start off. So yeah, I'm British.

Wardah: Well, my dad was born here and my mom was born in India. But it makes me British because I was born here.

Zahra: I'm Fijian. My parents are Fijian. They're not Indian. My great-grandparents were Indians. It's quite a few generations. I am British.

Wardah: We're British. My kids are British. It's going to go on now. I doubt that you can have any of the Indian traditions anyways because no one tends to go back home to get married nowadays. We're Muslims. But it doesn't mean we're not British.

Wardah and Zahra, in their 20s, were 'forth-' and 'third-generation' immigrants who were deeply rooted in Britain and declared themselves British with certainty. Wardah considered herself British based on the 'fact' that she and her father were born in the UK, although her mother was born in India. Zahra identified herself as 'Fijian', referring to her diverse ethnic background, but declared that she was 'British' as her family had been living in the UK for a long time. They argued that their ethnic backgrounds had nothing to do with being British while stressing that they were British because they and their families had lived in the UK for a long time and had British nationality.

This was a common response regardless of sex and locality:

I'd definitely say I'm British. I mean, my dad was from India. My mom was born here. I was born here. My brothers were born here. But my grandparents, they were from India. Yeah, I'd say I'm definitely British.

(Ulfah, Indian, 21, Coventry)

I was born and raised here and I am nearly 30 years old. I have never had a problem with my Britishness or anything.

(Shoaib, Bangladeshi, 29, London)

Britishness and Britain as 'Multicultural Space'

> Here is the place where I live, that's it, that's all. It is the bottom line. It's got nothing to do with fish and chips.
>
> (Waqas, Pakistani, 24, Coventry)

Like Wardah and Zahra, Ulfah from Coventry had family roots in the Indian subcontinent but considered his British birth as a key element of his British identity. Shoaib, a 'second-generation' Bangladeshi immigrant, stated that he 'never had a problem' with his 'Britishness' after spending three decades living in the UK. Waqas, of Pakistani descent in his 20s from Coventry, declared that living in Britain was the 'bottom line' for being British. As far as he was concerned, it had nothing to do with race, religion or culture (fish and chips!).

Some informants offered more strongly worded explanations about their identification with Britishness through their residence:

> I think for me my main identity is Muslim. British, yes, I'm British because I'm here, I live in this country. This Britain is my land, and this is where I belong. My Lord has put me here, so I am British and I am Muslim; I am both.
>
> (Nazma, Bangladeshi, 36, London)

'Second-generation' Nazma called Britain her 'land' and expressed a strong attachment to the place because 'My Lord has put me here' and 'this is where I belong' although she also felt an affinity for her parents' country.

Atiyah, 'third-generation' Pakistani, and Hamdan, 'second-generation' Bangladeshi, expressed similar sentiments with the expression 'home':

> I always like where I am. It's just because I was born here, I was brought up here, and I like the place, you know, most. It was like, you know, let's say that you have got a boat somewhere and when you finally come back. It is a home. You are associated with home. So that is Britishness.
>
> (Atiyah, Pakistani, 20, Coventry)

> I consider myself British. And I was born here and I know everything. This is where I would call home. So, yes, I do have a certain love for the country. I do, yes.
>
> (Hamdan, Bangladeshi, 34, London)

Informants recognised their ethnicities as a biological and cultural fact and, therefore, as something inseparable from themselves. In contrast, Britain was a place they could leave temporarily but also a place they would eventually

Chapter 6

return to and live. The word 'home' suggested such a point. Britain was also an object of 'love' as informants expressed familiarity and attachment with its lifestyle and culture. Even if they encountered discrimination and hardship in daily living, they could not imagine their complete detachment from the place; it was their home (Brah and Shaw 1992: 49; Kabir 2010: 12–13).

Thus, many informants considered being Muslim and being British to be compatible with no serious conflicts:

> Britishness for most of us is that we have dual, multiple identities because our parents are from different places. You know, I have got Pakistani culture, I have got Indian culture, I have got Arab culture, and I have got British culture. So the fact that someone asks me, 'Are you British or are you Muslim?', makes me feel weird.
>
> (Bakarah, Indian, 39, Coventry)

As a 'second-generation' Indian immigrant, Bakarah pointed to what did or did not constitute a requirement for being British. She indicated that having a particular culture was not required for being British. Instead, she believed that having and recognising multiple cultural identities were more important for 'being British' or 'Britishness' (Kymlicka 1995; Miller 1995; Modood 2007). I will revisit this point in a later section.

'Way of life': Drinking and female-male relationship

Many informants defined Britain as their 'birthplace' and explained that Britishness could coexist with being Muslim. However, not all aspects of British culture were considered to be compatible with Islam. Informants strictly differentiated Islam from British culture in a few respects where they perceived conflicts between them. Most informants mentioned 'drinking' and '(free) female-male relationships' as British social practices incompatible with Islam.

It is widely known that drinking is one of the main prohibitions in Islam. The Quran states:

160

> You who believe, intoxicants and gambling, idolatrous practices, and [divining with] arrows are repugnant acts Satan's doing – shun them so that you may prosper. (5:90, square brackets in the original)[3]

> With intoxicants and gambling, Satan seeks only to incite enmity and hatred among you, and to stop you remembering God and prayer. Will you not give them up? (5:91)

In Islam, drinking is believed to distort people's faith in Allah by clouding and confusing their consciousness. Similarly, Islam decrees spatial and social distances between women and men, especially directing women to, as much as possible, avoid contact with men outside their own family. Women are also instructed not to display their 'beauty' to anyone beyond a limited group of people (24:31).[4] A famous verse called the 'command of hijab' (33:53) instructs men to stay behind the 'screen' (hijab) if they want to ask women for something.[5] These commands dictate certain limits and considerations for interactions between women and men.

However, drinking and free interaction between women and men are normal parts of socialising in Britain:

> It's just a norm to drink in this country, and all young people do it for socialising.
>
> (Yusra, Asian mixed, 17, Coventry)

> On a Friday night, they'd go out, and all the money they had was spent on alcohol and stuff… just going out every Friday night, getting drunk, coming back, sitting with girls and stuff… and they talked about it on Monday, how it was.
>
> (Sohail, Bangladeshi, 28, London)

> Everything was different when I was at uni. I was a fresher as well, and people genuinely had the philosophy that if you don't go out and don't drink, you cannot have a good night.
>
> (Karam, Pakistani, 23, Coventry)

Like Yusra, a sixth-form student in Coventry, and Sohail, working in London, most informants perceived drinking and free interactions between women and men to be normal parts of everyday life and socialising in British society. Coventry worker Karam even described the drinking culture as a British 'philosophy'.

Chapter 6

Interestingly, while informants generally had negative views of drinking, most simply descriptively referred to it as a non-Islamic custom rather than commenting on it as a moral issue. In a sense, they keep an emotional distance from drinking.

Their use of the phrase 'a way of life' is significant in considering this type of distancing. This phrase was often mentioned when they explained 'what Islam is':

> Islam is like a way of life... The Islamic answer will say, whatever the situation from any aspect of life is: whether it's marriage, how to do business, how to clean yourself and something like that. For all of these things or any aspect, Islam gives an answer and an instruction and a way to do it.
>
> (Imran, Pakistani, 24, Coventry)

> Islam is not just clothes. Islam is not just a hat. Islam is not just a book. It's a life. It's a whole way of life: eat, sleep and drink. You know, everything is Islam.
>
> (Asma, Asian mixed, 22, London)

> Actually, religion is so important to me and my family, to both of us. I'd say, it's not a religion but our way of life. I think if we were to lose that actually, we would be losing something so enormous.
>
> (Jakera, Bangladeshi, 40, London)

Imran used the phrase 'way of life' to mean the Islam-based guidelines for everyday living, including 'marriage', 'business' and 'cleanliness'. Asma explained that Islam was equivalent to a whole way of life, including 'clothes', a 'hat', the Quran, and to 'eat, sleep, drink'. Jakera stated that religion was a 'way of life' that encompassed all of the matters in people's lives, not limited to faith (*iman*). In other words, the way of life refers to concrete guidelines to judge between right and wrong, to function as codes of conduct in certain situations, and to organise people's day-to-day living.[6] As Jakera put it, it is a practical guide for living beyond 'faith in a narrow sense' of an 'inner life'.[7]

Interestingly, the term 'way of life' is also used, along with Islam, in the context of debates around alcohol and female-male relationships:

162

> There are differences in terms of Islam as a way of life. So there are certain things that we don't agree with but non-Muslims do: for example, drinking and sexual relationships outside of marriage.
>
> (Duha, Asian mixed, 19, Coventry)

> One of the problems with working and living in this country is a lot of white people just think about their way of life. They think everyone drinks. They think everyone goes out and does certain things.
>
> (Farhan, Bangladeshi, 23, London)

> The other incompatibility is obviously the way of life. The girls want to walk around nakedly in summer. They want to do that. If you are living in this land, it's difficult to surpass that.
>
> (Haris, Bangladeshi, 27, London)

Duha defined Islam as a way of life and stated that she disagreed with another way of life, i.e., drinking and sex outside marriage. Similarly, Farhan viewed drinking and pub culture as white people's way of life, which was very different from a Muslim way of life. Haris perceived women showing much flesh as an aspect of the British way of life, to which Muslims cannot conform. In this context, a way of life refers to a concrete format or guideline of behaviour; the informants perceived Islam and British culture to be incompatible on this point.

A way of life has another important connotation, too: the possibility to 'choose'. Fahad (Indian, 26, Coventry) said that 'religion is a way of life that you choose' and more generally understood a way of life to be a 'matter of choice'. While some ways of life conflict with one another, it is up to individuals to choose which lifestyle they wish to follow. Huzaifa explained this in response to a question about religious consciousness in today's youth:

> If you say to a Jewish family, 'Is your son wearing a kippah?', some will say, 'Yes, he's very religious', but some people will say, 'No'. What I'm saying is that being a Muslim is just a way of life; it's a choice. What life you live is based on your own choice.
>
> (Huzaifa, Pakistani, 18, Coventry)

Huzaifa thought it was a matter of personal choice for a Muslim to follow a particular way of life, i.e., how to organise one's own life. In other words, he acknowledged that non-Islamic ways of life were also available options, although he would not choose them.

Chapter 6

The idea of choice is important because it helps to avoid the act of 'judging' others. As discussed in more detail in Chapter 10, Islam traditionally discourages measuring the strength of others' faith. In fact, many informants reported that they would not like to be judged by others about their faith or to pass judgment on others' behaviour:

> Even though we don't mind it, it sometimes can be a bit awkward. If you are in that situation, if everyone is getting drunk and they are doing silly things but you can't participate in it, then it becomes a bit awkward. But apart from that, no. You know, I don't judge someone for their drinking because that's their own choice.
>
> (Habibah, Asian mixed, 20, Coventry)

> One of my friends, she's a Muslim and she started drinking. And I didn't like it, but I just said, 'Okay, you do whatever you want to do, but I just won't get involved'.
>
> (Arub, Bangladeshi, 18, Coventry)

Habibah and Arub both said that they avoided drinking, but they did not hate or cut off their drinking friends – even if they were Muslim. Many informants claimed to be tolerant of their friends' drinking as long as it was within certain temporal and spatial limits and not excessive. They accepted it as one lifestyle 'choice'. Although the prohibition of drinking is important to Muslims, some informants did not see it as an impediment to their friendships with non-Muslims. They perceived drinking as one's 'own choice' (Habibah), which must be respected as much as one's choice to follow Islam.

The idea of choice was reflected in the informant's comments about drinking and women-men interaction. As already mentioned, these activities are entrenched in British society as part of everyday life, and British-born/ raised Muslims are caught up in this. The informants, therefore, engaged with such a culture according to their own criteria:

> Author: Do you go out after school?
>
> Duha (Asian mixed, 19, Coventry): We could go out and go for a coffee or go for a meal. Even if you go to a bar where there is alcohol, it depends on your personal preference.

Farwah (Asian mixed, 20, Coventry): Yeah, we can basically do everything that any other person would do at the weekend with their friends, going to the cinema, going shopping, you know.

Habibah (Asian mixed, 20, Coventry): In terms of Islam, it's easygoing. For example, if we want to go dancing or go clubbing with music and stuff, we can go somewhere where it's only women. If it's only women, then we can take off our hijab, wear short clothes.

Duha and others encountered opportunities for socialising with non-Muslims at their universities and workplaces and occasionally went to venues serving alcohol but not drinking themselves. They also reported they could remove their hijab and participate in cultural activities such as dancing in women-only venues.[8]

Duha explained her socialising at university as follows:

With my Spanish group at a university, they wanted to meet up after class and go for a drink. It meant alcoholic drink, obviously. I wanted to be involved then with the people I studied with. So I thought, 'Okay, I will go out with them', but I just won't have alcoholic drinks. And there were boys, but I was also with girls and I wasn't there to flirt with boys. I thought in that way, 'It's okay if they are friends, it's innocent there'. Nothing is really there. But really, we shouldn't have so close male relationships.

(Duha, Asian mixed, 19, Coventry)

They stated that they were able to socialise with classmates after school as long as they did not drink or cross the friendship line with men. In this way, they enjoyed British social life, setting the boundaries according to their own understandings of Islam.

While most informants denied drinking alcohol, a few spoke of their drinking experiences:

All things around me, even the colours, even the colours of the room, everything has an influence. So if people are bad and the colours around me are bad, everything, my eye, my ear and my nose, is exposed to just bad breath, bad air, bad steam, and just bad hormones. Obviously, it's like a disease… I used to do all of that, including drinking.

(Haris, Bangladeshi, 27, London)

Chapter 6

> I think I did that quite a lot and it upset my parents quite a bit. I think because I was in the majority non-Muslim secondary school, so I used to have parties every weekend. And I wasn't allowed to go because of alcohol. So I used to sneak out and go.
>
> (Jannah, Bangladeshi, 18, London)

Haris admitted his experience of drinking as a university student under the pressure of British society's drinking culture. Jannah, at a rebellious age, said she had enjoyed her school's party culture, including drinking, not so long ago.

All informants expressed the belief that drinking was 'bad', including those who had experienced drinking alcohol. Nonetheless, some informants used the word 'choice' to explain such experiences:

> I'm going to be honest, I have drunk. I don't think it was because of peer pressure. It's because I want to try for myself and see what it is about… Once you become more Westernised, you adapt more. I'm not sure if pressure is the right word. I'm not sure if it's pressure, but you adapt in the way. Sometimes you don't want to do it, but you do it normally. So it's not a big issue.
>
> (Arham, Pakistani, 24, Coventry)

Arham described his reason for drinking as 'adaptation' in a more positive sense, rather than the 'pressures' of British society. He was happy with being Muslim and even expressed an intention to be a good Muslim. Nevertheless, he did not feel that drinking – in moderation – necessarily conflicted with his commitment to Islam. In other words, he thought that drinking was also an individual 'choice'. It suggests that even one's level of commitment to Islam and the performance of Islamic practices are all matters of personal choice, although renunciation of islam may be inconceivable.

The lifestyle of young Muslims is constructed through choices they make among (multiple) heritages to solve present-day issues (Giddens 1990; 1994; Bhabha 1994). There is a deep affinity between 'adaptation' and 'choice' because adaptation to the environment is implemented by choice. The informants' comments indicate that adaptation to Western culture did not necessarily threaten their Muslim identity. Rather, they selectively adapted to society by differentiating which Islamic teachings they should follow or not in a particular time and place. The idea of 'differentiation' as a basis for their choice and adaptation is crucial for young Muslims negotiating a life course in Western society, enabling them to push back against the life 'in-between

166

two worlds' imposed by society – that is, being forced to make a binary choice (Archer 2005: 68).

Britishness as 'values'

As discussed above, many informants compared and contrasted Islam and British culture in terms of a 'way of life', but they did not see their differences as an obstacle to integration with or participation in British society. On the contrary, they felt that Islam and Britishness were more congruent in another dimension – their 'values'.

Some informants talked about values in contrast to a way of life or lifestyle:

> When it comes to the same British values, for example, generally speaking, people are treated fairly and equally, there's not really too much racism now, and I think people get equal pay. And in day-to-day governance, there's no conflict between Islam and Britishness. But then, when it comes to issues like the British lifestyle, for example, a lot of people seem to live for the weekend. They work nine to five, and then on the weekends, they just get drunk and just gamble their money away. That's where there is a conflict.
>
> (Talha, Pakistani, 27, London)

Talha said that there was no serious conflict between Islam and Britishness over abstract 'values' such as equality and tolerance although he did not share in the British 'way of life' or 'lifestyle' as a set of concrete behavioural norms – for example, drinking and gambling.

Defining Britishness in terms of values was a recurring theme in these interviews:

> I think Britishness means just being a good neighbour, being a good person, paying your taxes, getting a good job, being productive for society, and stuff like that. These are Islamic values, they're British values, and I think it's compatible; I don't think it's a conflict.
>
> (Aflan, Pakistani, 35, London)

> I think being British is, as far as I understand, about being loyal; it's about being a good citizen; it's about having a certain decorum, having a certain class to the way you adapt yourself. That's what Islam teaches. Islam even teaches us to groom ourselves, to speak with good manners… I think it would clash with the current Britishness, which is a lot of alco-

Chapter 6

holism, a lot of clubbing, and a lot of football hooliganism. I don't think that's true Britishness anyway.

(Salimah, Bangladeshi, 33, London)

Aflan and Salimah, both second-generation in their 30s, defined being British as 'being a good citizen': paying taxes, having decent jobs and doing good things for society. Interestingly, they argued that Islam shared such important abstract characteristics and values (Sardar and Ahmad 2012: 7). From this perspective, Salimah suggested that some of the social and cultural practices that were considered to be typically British – excessive drinking, club culture, football hooliganism – were not really compatible with British values.

'Tolerance' was the most frequently mentioned characteristic shared between Islam and British values:

They say their values are freedom and tolerance. They don't practice it, but that's what they say. And I guess it is compatible with Islam. I think Islam is a very tolerant religion.

(Jannah, Bangladeshi, 18, London)

Being Muslim and being British are compatible because they don't go against each other. I mean the British values such as respect, tolerance and all of these values… They coincide with Islam also. Islam teaches these values.

(Daniyal, Bangladeshi, 27, London)

While mainstream social and political discourses portray Islam as intolerant of personal freedom, my informants posited tolerance as its defining characteristic. This point is discussed further in Chapter 7.

Britain as 'multicultural space'

As discussed above, many of my informants thought that drinking and interactions between women and men contradicted Islam, but they also perceived them as lifestyle options with equal selection possibility, if not equal value. What brings about this attitude? There are two possible factors. One is a way of thinking derived from Islam, and the other is linked to the characteristics of British society. I analyse the latter in this section and leave the former to Chapter 7 for further discussion.

Let us examine the informants' perceptions of British society. 'Multi-cultural space' was the most frequently mentioned characteristic of British society. Most informants appreciated that the UK was a multicultural space, within which the Islamic way of life was available as a choice:

> Husnain (Bangladeshi, 21, Coventry): We have a few Muslims in Parliament. There's a Bengali lady who is a member of the Parliament, so we have Islamic people there.
>
> Ibtisam (Bangladeshi,21, Coventry): What I am saying is controversial. Out of all the European countries, I think Britain is definitely the most tolerant towards people from different cultures, people from different backgrounds, and religions, more so than other European countries.
>
> Husnain: They know how to treat people from different countries well. They endorse rights.
>
> Ibstisam: Multiculturalism!
>
> Husnain: Yeah.

Husnain and Ibstisam rated British society highly for its diversity. Husnain expressed pride that there were minority representatives, including Muslims, in the Parliament, while Ibstisam regarded Britain's acceptance of different cultures and religions as positive, describing it as 'multiculturalism'.[9] These views reflected the fact that diversified local communities in Britain had more or less established peaceful relationships among different people.

Raniyah from East London also recognised Britain's multiculturalism, albeit to a more limited extent:

> Author: Do you think being Muslim and being British are compatible without conflicts?
>
> Raniyah (Bangladeshi, 19, London): I would say it depends on what part of Britain you're in. In East London, it's pretty easy to be a Muslim because there are so many Muslims around. Also, it's a multi-cultural society. Whereas, if I were to go to North London, where Muslims are rarely seen, people are uneducated about Islam. So it's really hard to be a Muslim there because you stand out alone, and people view you as something negative. So it just depends.

Chapter 6

Rizwan from Coventry expressed a similar view:

> If kids are brought up in a white neighbourhood and have never had a Black friend or anything, then they will give someone a weird look and they see someone as an outcast. But if you grew up nowadays, most schools have students from all mixed Asians, Caribbean, African etcetera. And when you grow up with these kinds of people, you wait a minute and think that is not so bad. They are human as well. So it really depends on people.
>
> (Rizwan, Asian mixed, 19, Coventry)

Raniyah noted that the degree of Muslim integration in British society varied depending on location, with the yardstick being whether the place is 'multicultural' or not (Ryan 2012: 107). She lived in East London, a multi-ethnic society with a sizable Muslim population and, therefore, thought that being Muslim was easier there. Rizwan pointed out that people who grew up in diverse communities tended to be more tolerant of others than those who grew up in mono-ethnic or mono-cultural communities where people were prone to prejudice.[10]

East London-born and raised Taimoor explained the positive implications of multicultural society based on his own experience at university:

> Seventy per cent of my class was from China... Some were even scared to talk to me... On TV, they see terrorists. But then it's funny when they see me eating a pizza or a burger, they just think it's not impossible. Muslims just eat curries,... Muslims don't play football, but only play cricket. They realise these are all the stereotypes built in.
>
> (Taimoor, Pakistani, 27, London)

Taimoor also said that young generations living in multicultural society could become 'more rounded' because there were more opportunities to mix with people from different backgrounds. Encounters with different people may breed misunderstandings and fears, but cumulative encounters can overcome negative discourses and stereotypes, leading to more wholesome relationships (Cantle 2001; 2008).[11]

Thus, the informants held the British characteristic of a multicultural society in high regard. For example, they often mentioned that they were 'lucky' to live in Britain:

Britishness and Britain as 'Multicultural Space'

Because even ask an Englishman about what's your culture, he wouldn't be able to say a lot. He just wouldn't because the thing with Britain is, its culture is made up of various different cultures. That's a good thing, preferably. I like Britain. It's made up of several cultures; it's made up of Indians, it's made up of Pakistani, it's made up of Iraqis, it's made of Africans, it's made up of several different cultures. That's what, personally in my eyes, makes the British culture… For example, if you'll ask an Englishman, 'What are you doing at the weekend?', he'll probably say, 'I'm going to go for a pint', but then he would also say, 'I'm going to go for a curry afterwards'. And curry is an Indian dish.

(Usama, Bangladeshi, 21, Coventry)

I think we are very lucky to live in Britain because, on the whole, it's a very multicultural society. You go to more cities and you will find a mix of Muslims, Sikhs, Hindus, Christians, and people with no faith. Personally, I don't find much of difficulty.

(Duha, Asian mixed, 19, Coventry)

I am lucky living in London, and it's still maintained, although I don't know what's going to happen 10 years down the line… At the moment, multi-faith is welcomed in England, isn't it? There is no hijab ban; there is no veil ban.

(Poppy, Bangladeshi, 28, London)

Usama declared that it was impossible to define or represent Britain by a single culture. British life comprises various cultures, and even English people rarely complete a day based solely on the English lifestyle (Parekh 2002). Usama mentioned that 'curry' had become a national dish, perceiving and appreciating that being 'multicultural' is the essence of being British.[12] Duha also expressed her understanding and definition of multicultural Britain: not simply a space where people of diverse ethnicities and religions gather and live, but also a place where differences are recognised and accepted. The provision of prayer spaces at universities and workplaces, halal foods at schools, and public support for the construction of mosques were mentioned as examples. Poppy also said that religious freedoms such as wearing the hijab had not yet been curtailed in Britain, while acknowledging that Islamophobia was a problem.

Chapter 6

The comparison of Britain's multicultural society to others was a recurring theme, with France commonly mentioned:

> Like France, at least we are not, you know, forced to take off our scarves in school and in public. And if someone chooses to wear the face veil, then they can do that. So I don't think we are too bad, whatever you think. I don't have any complaints.
>
> (Ibtisam, Bangladeshi, 21, Coventry)

Janan (Sudanese, 20, Coventry): British let us have Islamic schools.

Husnain (Bangladeshi, 21, Coventry): Our own religious schools.

Janan: Yeah! And they allow the covering of the face, niqab now.

Husnain: Unlike certain countries, they are going against, like France.

In France, with a republican tradition based on the separation of church and state, known as '*laïcité*', wearing the headscarf in schools and the veil in public spaces has become a political issue and a series of laws were enacted in the 2000s to restrict it (Bowen 2008; Joppke 2009; Adachi 2011b; 2011c; 2013b: 303–23).[13] In comparison, the informants rated Britain highly for respecting the cultural rights of diverse groups, including religious communities, and for making public funds available to them. It was common for the informants to express that they were 'lucky' to live in Britain, which respects religious freedom based on its localist tradition, while criticising France for demanding civic homogeneity to keep public spaces secular.

Both male and female informants valued the freedom of women to wear the scarf and veil in British public spaces:

> It's a benefit of living in this country. Really to say that it's acceptable to have a beard and not worry about it and to wear a headscarf and walk down the street. And obviously, we take that for granted because we are born here. But we know about other countries. It's not obviously as accepted, and there might be some people who might feel they want to grow a beard, they want to wear a headscarf, but they can't do it. I mean, we are in a very multicultural society here. So it's okay to do it.
>
> (Sufian, Pakistani, 25, Coventry)

Sufian was among the few male Muslims in Coventry who wore religious clothes. He had a beard for the same religious reason that many women wear a headscarf. He was happy that he was not judged for his religious appearance at school or on the street and considered this to be an example of multicultural Britain.[14]

The other common targets for comparison were the US and Germany:

> I would say this country is much more liberal and much more accepting. I have got friends in Germany and other countries in Europe, and they are not so tolerantly accepted.
>
> (Jakera, Bangladeshi, 40, London)

> I was actually quite shocked to realise that America is very segregated even today, where you have a Black neighbourhood, a Black doctor's society, and a Black medical society. It's very segregated between the Black person and the white person... Britain is very small. This country's folks integrate into many cultures and the society. That is good.
>
> (Usama, Bangladeshi, 21, Coventry)

Jakera believed that Britain was a more tolerant country, judging from what she had heard from Muslim friends living in other European countries. Usama, who defined Britain as a 'multicultural society', expressed his surprise at hearing from an African-American student that American society was more racially segregated while appreciating Britain for its mingling of different cultures.[15] He described the situation in Britain as an integration of multiple 'cultures' into one particular 'society'.

Many informants perceived Britain as a multicultural society in this way, with one attributing its possibility to the 'blandness' of British society or culture:

> Nazma (Bangladeshi, 36, London): We speak English.
>
> Tazmin (Asian mixed, 19, London): Yeah, we speak; that's English.
>
> Nazma: We speak English, and we're, yeah, we eat some English foods, all halal. We don't have pork at all or other things.
>
> Tazmin: British culture is very, very bland.

Nazma and Tazmin gave speaking 'English' and eating 'English foods' as the conditions of being British, suggesting that adaptation to Britain's language and food culture was evidence of being British. This points to their perception that being British has more relaxed standards than the cultural practices such as drinking and free female-male interaction discussed in a previous section. They observed that English (or British) foods could be

Chapter 6

consumed following Islamic law because halal menus were offered in many restaurants, indicating that British culture could coexist with Islam. They described British culture using the word 'bland', which suggested that British culture was tolerant enough to coexist with Islam and other cultures because it did not have a strong essence requiring the exclusion of other cultures.

Some informants refer to 'fish and chips' to explain the perceived blandness of British culture. For example, Tazmin said: 'It's just fish and chips with food. British culture isn't something strong'. Here, she referred to fish and chips as an icon of British culture and suggested that it required nothing for minorities to adapt to British society. Usama and Ahmed also used fish and chips to illustrate that British society and culture do not possess a clear enough character to exclude other cultures:

> Ahmed (Pakistani, 21, Coventry): About the British culture, they went to India, they went to Africa, they went to Europe and that kind of stuff. There is no real culture. If you look at the food, for example, Italians have their pasta, the Middle Eastern have their hummus and their meats. I don't know about America, but the French have their crepes. But Britain actually has no real food that is British or culture of British.
>
> Usama (Bangladeshi, 21, Coventry): They have fish and chips.
>
> Ahmed: Fish and chips is the only traditional thing you could say concrete 100 per cent. But apart from that, for me, it seems no culture. We are very fluid, so they could adopt anything as a culture.

Ahmed and Usama claimed that, unlike other countries, Britain did not have its own 'real' culture. Considering its imperial history, they argued that diverse cultures could take roots in Britain because it lacked its own authentic culture, except for fish and chips. They described this characteristic of British culture and identity as 'fluid' (CIC 2007).

The idea of 'choice', discussed in a previous section, comes to the fore in this space where diversity is respected. It is possible to choose Islam as a way of life in this multicultural space. Conversely, this means it is also possible for many informants to tolerate the existence of non-Islamic ways of life and cultures, such as drinking and women-men interactions, as a matter of personal choice:

> I don't drink personally even though my family does. I just see it as something like; you have brown eyes, I have green eyes and I don't drink, you drink. It's just a difference.
>
> (Yusra, Asian mixed, 17, Coventry)

> I wouldn't go out with them and go drinking. I wouldn't do that... If they ask me, 'Okay, would you come and drink with us?', I would say, 'I am sorry, no. It's against my religion. I wouldn't do that'. But... next day we can still become friends... Maybe if they want to go to a movie or something, that's fine.
>
> (Daliya, Sudanese, 17, Coventry)

Yusra's father is a white convert, and his side of the family sometimes drinks when they get together. She and her father did not participate in the drinking, but they accepted it as 'a difference'– akin to eye colour. Not all informants had non-Muslims in their families, but they reported that this attitude was important for relationships with non-Muslim friends and colleagues at schools and workplaces. As mentioned, they understood that this mutual recognition was necessary and also possible in Britain's multicultural space (Parekh 2002). Similarly, Daliya explained that declining invitations to go drinking or clubbing did not affect her friendships, pointing again to mutual respect for people with different ways of life.

British society's receptivity to diversity and freedom was a significant reason for the informants to commit to or identify with Britain:

> I'm a British Muslim. That's how I identify myself because I have chosen to live here. I don't want to go back to Pakistan, although I'd love to visit for a holiday. I don't want to go there and live there because, ultimately, it's not a developed country, and unfortunately, women don't have some of the rights that we do have here. Such rights are closer to religion than what we find there. I like the idea of freedom.
>
> (Parveen, Pakistani, 31, London)

Parveen defined herself as 'British Muslim', which meant more than simply a Muslim living in Britain (Parekh 2008; Modood 2013). She recognised and valued that there was much more freedom in Britain than in Pakistan, her family's home country. She also expressed a belief that the British value of freedom was more closely aligned with her religion than the customs and practices of Pakistani culture. The point is discussed further in Chapter 7.

Chapter 6

Conclusion

This chapter has analysed the informants' understandings of British society, which forms the context for their identity formation as second-generation Muslims. On one hand, they perceived drinking and free women-men interactions to be part of a way of life in Britain that was incompatible with an Islamic way of life. On the other hand, they recognised Britain as a 'multicultural space' and that Islam and other diverse cultural elements could coexist there (Kabir 2010: 13). Consequently, they argued that there was no conflict between being Muslim and being British. British society is 'bland' and tolerant of differences and its baseline culture is not 'strong' in demanding secularism and cultural homogeneity as requirements for 'citizenship'. Rather, it encouraged informants' tolerance of the British way of life, including drinking; they expected recognition of their Islamic way of life in return. We might say that the informants perceived Britain as a 'diasporic space', in the sense that 'the native is as much a diasporian as the diasporian is the native' (Brah 1996: 209).

This sense has been widely found in studies of Britain's second-generation immigrants. For instance, one second-generation immigrant in a study on Black immigrants put it like this:

> Well, I am British, I was born in London, but I am not the same as English people, it's like I'm a different kind of English – a different way. I mean we have different ways – a different culture. But I am still British. (Sewell 1998: 109)

Her description of 'not the same as English people... but I am still British' expressed both her claim for equal rights and her pride as a second-generation immigrant. We saw this sentiment expressed by the 'third-generation' Bangladeshi man quoted at the start of this chapter – 'I'm just as British as the next man'. Second-generation Muslims believe that being different in terms of culture and race do not conflict with being British, but rather, within such different cultures, a shared commitment to the values of British society and citizenship is possible. This, as my informants argued, is the essence of Britishness.

No doubt, this attitude is deeply embedded in the British tradition. British citizenship emphasises 'being a good member of one's local society', in contrast, for example, to France's emphasis on 'being a citizen of the state' (Crick 1998; 2000; 2003). This attitude is rooted in Britain's historical traditions, forged in its Civil Wars and the ruler-subject relationship. My

176

informants understood and enjoyed this loose British integration model in their everyday lives (Bleich 2003; Fetzer and Soper 2005; Adachi 2011b; 2011c; 2013b).[16] Moreover, they deployed their knowledge and commitment to the British tradition of tolerance to justify living as Muslims in British society.

This finding differs from previous studies, which have found that being British or Britishness is merely an institutional and legal right and does not lend itself readily to the emotional commitment of minority groups (Ameli and Merali 2004; ETHNOS 2005). On the contrary, the informants of the present study expressed a more substantial commitment to British society. Perhaps this reflects a difference in social engagement between the informants' generation and their parents' and grandparents' generations. According to a second-generation immigrant, 'what his parents called "outside world" was in fact becoming part of his "home world"' (Sahin 2013: 140). For second-generation youths, British society is the space in which they lead their lives, i.e., 'home', rather than a cold empty container that accommodates them.

In many respects, the informants' depictions of Britain's social space and values appear to reflect the New Labour government's social integration policies of the 2000s, such as community cohesion and the sharing of Britishness, as discussed in Chapter 2. Interpreting Britishness as a 'civic' concept, they identified with and committed to it. They also celebrated its values such as diversity, freedom and tolerance and seemed to enjoy 'fluid' identities in the British multicultural space (Blair 2006; Brown 2006; CIC 2007).

Then, how can Britishness and Islam be compatible? Two value systems with different traditions and histories do not synthesise automatically. Moreover, accommodating Islam in cultural interstices in British society's multicultural space has not dispelled doubts about Muslims' social integration nor silenced criticism of their perceived radicalisation, as discussed in Chapters 1 and 2. In the chapters that follow, I shift the focus to 'Islam' to analyse how second-generation Muslims define their faith, connect it to their lives in British society and accept it as a positive part of their identity.

Chapter 6

Notes

1 'Ethnic minorities' refers to minority groups formed through voluntary migration (e.g., immigrants) while 'national minorities' refers to minority groups formed through external invasion or forced migration (e.g., enslaved people and aborigines) (Kymlicka 1995). The latter category includes sub-nations in Britain (i.e., Scottish, Welsh and Northern Irish).

2 The order of the second and third conditions may be reversed in some cases. For example, 'home-grown terrorists' enjoy the lifestyle of British society but they do not share its values such as democracy and tolerance (Blair 2006).

3 In the section below, each notation of two numbers separated by a colon refers to a specific chapter and verse in the Quran. I relied on Haleem (2016) as an English-language reference.

4 'Beauty' is generally interpreted as body parts other than the face and hands (Goto 2014: 74–7). 'A limited group of people' refers to:

> '[T]heir husbands, their fathers, their husbands' fathers, their sons, their husbands' sons, their brothers, their brothers' sons, their sisters' sons, their womenfolk, their slaves, such men as attend them who have no desire, or children who are not yet aware of women's nakedness. (24:31)

5 The Quran states: 'When you ask his wives for something, do so from behind a screen: this is purer both for your hearts and for theirs' (33:53). There are various opinions about what 'theirs' means, but one of the favoured interpretations takes the view that this verse is a command for all women (their) and all men (your) (Goto 2014: 90–4).

6 Preachers who try to explain the concepts of Islam to a broader audience prefer to use terms such as 'guideline' and 'manual' for a way of life. For instance, the world-famous preacher Zakir Naik from India, a favourite of many of my informants, compares the Islamic way of life to a guideline to pass a test or a manual to operate a machine and uses it to mean 'a guide' to help people achieve their goals. He explains that it is a God-given guideline on how to get to Paradise, indicating appropriate behaviour, rules and standards of right and wrong (Naik 2014). I discuss the idea of 'test' further in Chapter 10.

7 Religious scholar Talal Asad explains that 'religion' (or *din*) 'relates more to how one lives than to what one believes' (Asad 1993: 219), referring to preacher Al Za'ayr's argument about 'advice/counsel' (*nasiha*). Among numerous words denoting religion in Islam, *din* includes broader conduct and connotes 'way of life' while '*iman*' focuses on one's inner life. As discussed in Chapter 10, faith (*iman*) was also emphasised by the informants and served an important role in their adaptation to British society.

8 I came across a wide range of interpretations about what the Islamic way of life was and how the rules should be applied. For example, when I interviewed a female informant of African descent at her home in Coventry, she removed the headscarf she normally wore outside and changed into a colourful one-piece dress. When I was invited to an Asian informant's birthday party at a restaurant,

178

Britishness and Britain as 'Multicultural Space'

I saw her enjoying mingling with non-familial men without her headscarf. In one group interview at London Muslim Centre adjoining a mosque, two informants entered the building without their scarfs – one of them was wearing a short-sleeve shirt – to attend the interview.

9 Britain has many Muslim politicians at both local and national levels. For example, London Lord Mayor Sadiq Khan was Britain's first home-grown Muslim parliamentarian, Shahid Malik was the first Muslim cabinet minister in Brown's New Labour government, and Baroness Warsi was a Minister without portfolio in Cameron's Conservative-Liberal Democrat coalition government. It is noteworthy that Muslim politicians participate in politics from across the conservative-progressive spectrum, reflecting both the size of the Muslim community and its internal diversity.

10 This is consistent with previous studies which found that place of upbringing influences people's perception of diversity (CIC 2007; Laurence and Heath 2008).

11 Immediately before this comment, Taimoor (Pakistani, 27, London) mentioned the difference between the older generations and his. 'While the older generation, they cannot socialise with others, they've just seen things on the news'. He thought that this lack of opportunities reinforced the older generation's rigid understanding of Islam. Chapters 7 and 8 discuss how and why the informants emphasised intergenerational comparisons and differences.

12 These comments evoke the famous 'chicken tikka masala' speech by Foreign Secretary Robin Cook in 1999. Cook stated that:

> Chicken Tikka Masala is now a true British national dish, not only because it is the most popular, but because it is a perfect illustration of the way Britain absorbs and adapts external influences. Chicken Tikka is an Indian dish. The Masala sauce was added to satisfy the desire of British people to have their meat served in gravy. (Condor 2011: 110)

As discussed in Chapter 2, the New Labour government had a more positive vision for diversity, at least, until 9/11 and publicised diversity as the essence of Britain even after 7/7 – even if it was merely political lip service – as it did in the London Olympics (2012) (Adachi 2013b: Allen 2015).

13 The word *laïcité* generally means 'non-cleric, non-religious', but it came to mean 'a religiously neutral state that is tolerant to all faiths', i.e., separation of church and state (Costa-Lascoux 1996: 9–10). This principle was central to the modern French state's taking control of education from the Catholic church (Bendix 1977: 105–12). However, it is not a monolithic concept, and there have been many conflicts and compromises about this type of secularism (Hayashi 2001). Despite considerable debate, Muslim headscarves in schools were left to individual schools to decide on a case-by-case basis until the French government banned the wearing of headscarves in public education institutions during the 2000s (Adachi 2011b).

14 Although not part of the present research, a young second-generation French Muslim man I interviewed in London stated:

> People here, I think, they [British people] don't mind. Even if they don't like your religion, for instance, they won't comment on it. You're free to

179

Chapter 6

do what you want, and they don't mind; they simply don't mind. My boss is amazing. She's a lady, she's not Muslim at all, but when I explained to her that I was a Muslim, she said, 'Whenever you need to leave to go to your prayer on Friday, feel free'. I mean, she knew I lived close by so that I could pray. She said, 'We can organise to have a calm corner for you to pray'. So she's really understanding. And it's not just for Muslims, it's also for Hindu people, Sikh, the same for everyone. We have a guy with a turban in my company; I had a colleague with a hijab. So, I think that, I think England has understood what the freedom of belief is... In France, they think *laïcité*... They don't make the point... because they reject all other beliefs... It's a bad time for Muslims in France, believe me. Really bad time.

His comment illustrates the extent to which Britain is a multicultural space, especially compared to France.

15 The perception that the US is a segregated dystopia is widely shared in Britain, as illustrated in the head of the Commission for Racial Equality, Trevor Phillips' observations about New Orleans (Adachi 2013b: 196–7):

It showed us a society in which the average black child still attends a black majority school. A society in which the average white person returns home at the day's end to all-white suburbs, where they won't see a non-white face until they go back to the city the next day. A democracy in which black politicians, with a few notable exceptions, represent black districts, gerrymandered in order to provide the minimum of black representation. An economy in which black businessmen sell their wares largely to a black middle class. And an education system in which most black academics are teaching at all-black colleges or in urban institutions disproportionately packed with ethnic minority students. (Phillips 2005)

16 According to many historians, Britain is not a nation-state in a classical sense. For example, its civil wars were merely part of the gradual evolutionary process (i.e., democratic accommodation) rather than a 'fundamental moment' giving birth to a modern state such as the French Revolution. The French 'civil revolution was a radical shift from the *ancien regime*, involving a great change of self-definition as a state/society by establishing the first constitution – which enshrined *laïcité* and republicanism (Tanigawa and Uegaki 2006: 52–6). By contrast, English civil wars – from Magna Carta to the Glorious Revolution – comprised the aristocracy and bourgeoisie demanding the king's recognition of their autonomy, rather than denying the king's authority (Imai 1993: 122). What British civil wars sought was 'civic liberties'. Hence, Britain retained the relationship between the monarch and his/her (liberty-seeking) subjects rather than creating a modern state and its citizenry as in France. This process did not produce a codified constitution that embodied the nation's ideal and resulted in sluggish development of the state bureaucracy. These developments had a significant influence on British attitudes to social integration, as political scientist David Marquand explains:

> [T]hanks in particular to the victory of the English landed classes over the Stuart kings – one cannot speak of a 'British state' in the way that one speaks of a 'French state'... The UK isn't a state in the continental sense. It is a bundle of islands (including such exotica as the Channel Islands and the Isle of Man which are not even represented at Westminster), acquired at different times by the English crown, and governed in different ways. Its inhabitants are not citizens of a state, with defined rights of citizenship. They are subjects of a monarch, enjoying 'liberties' which their ancestors won from previous monarchs. (Marquand 1988: 152)

French-style loyalty to the nation and the state thus did not develop in the UK (Adachi 2013b: 204–8).

Chapter

Differentiating between Culture and Religion

[T]he existence of a nation is not proved by culture, but in the people's struggle against the forces of occupation.

The Wretched of the Earth
by Frantz Fanon (2004: 159)

[A] black counter-culture is constituted on either side of the Atlantic… This transnational community is characterised by its great artistic creativity, by the expressiveness of its most visible actors, by a relationship to the body, to sexuality, to dance and to music which reflects a formidable demand for subjectification. The diaspora is built here by those who identify with it, it is not an inheritance… It produces its codes, its economy, its culture, more than it reproduces them. And by combining cultural imagination and inventiveness it employs a critique of the exclusion and racism suffered by its members.

La Différence
by Michel Wieviorka (2005: 50)

Issues in question: British society from an Islam perspective

Social integration of young Muslims is one of the key political and social themes in Britain. Two major events in 2001 – the 9/11 attacks and the Asian youth riots in Northern England cities – raised doubts about Muslim integration with contemporary Western society. Then, the London bombings in July 2005 reinforced such doubts. This incident shocked Britain not only because it was 'our 9/11' but also because it was perpetrated by 'homegrown' terrorists. British society's interest in Muslims subsequently intensified with the media highlighting various issues surrounding Islam, including scarf/veil-wearing women, bearded men in religious clothes defending terrorism, families forcing marriage on their children, and the oppression of women.

The media coverage of these incidents is based on the assumption of intrinsic conflict between modern values and religious beliefs or traditions. The underlying assumption is that irrational and undemocratic religious traditions may infringe on the civilised principles of secularised modern society. Islam, in particular, tends to be considered particularly problematic because – unlike Christian and Jewish scriptures – its religious text the Quran is read as the record of the direct words of God, which makes it difficult for Muslims to differentiate between the spatial domains of the sacred and profane (Matsuyama 2018a: 21–2; Déroche 2005: i). Consequently, Islam predicates a correspondence between secular and divine law, requiring adherence to its teachings in all domains of life (Naito and Sakaguchi ed. 2007; Shimomura 2014: 14). Moreover, the fact that many young Muslims in Britain and Europe have become more explicitly religious has deepened public doubts about Muslims' ability to integrate into secular society. They have begun wearing the scarf/veil and presenting religious symbols such as religious outfits and beards, which their parents had not worn.

Does the heightened commitment to Islam among young people really mean a rejection of secularised society or a failure of integration? Chapters 5 and 6 analysed how the informants perceived their environment and how they connected being British with being Muslim. We found that they defined British society as a multicultural space where they could participate as Muslims and indicate a strong attachment, while experiencing various kinds of discrimination and distrusting the media. But how can the situation be portrayed from the perspective of their relations to Islam? In other words, how do young second-generation Muslims perceive and define Islam to balance their religion with British society's lifestyle and values?

Chapter 7

To answer these questions, this chapter examines the differentiation between 'culture' and 'religion', which, as we will see, is the dominant self-presentation strategy for second-generation Muslims concerning their identities (Goffman 1959).

Differentiating culture and religion, and its functions

People – both Muslim and non-Muslim – have common or different images of what Islam is. Some see it as the devotion to God or the pursuit of a strict religious way of life. Others believe that it is an anti-modern rebellion against civilisation. Still, others appreciate it as the resurrection of a moral compass which represents peace and decency lost in secularised society (Bradley 2007). And some perceive it as a cheerful and open religion which is compatible with contemporary Western culture – *Happy British Muslims*, for instance.[1]

Nevertheless, a common thread discernible in the informants' narratives about 'what Islam is' was a strong tendency to explain Islam by presenting 'what it is not' or in terms of concepts contrasting with Islam, rather than offering positive statements of what it is. The most important counter-concept in this case is '(Asian) culture' (Knott and Khokher 1993; Sanghera and Thapar-Björkert 2007; Ryan 2012).

Almost all the informants in my study, regardless of locality, age or sex, referred to their own (or Asian) ethnic culture or tradition and differentiated it from Islam when explaining what Islam was. They implemented it in the following manner:

> Personally, I don't think it has something to do with Islam. I think it's more of a cultural thing.
>
> (Ibtisam, Bangladeshi, 21, Coventry)

> Islam is different from culture. It can accommodate culture as long as they don't contradict Islam, but there's a certain culture which is in conflict with it.
>
> (Talha, Pakistani, London, Pakistani, 27, London)

These brief comments indicate that the informants clearly and intentionally differentiated Islam from ethnic cultures.

Why does the differentiation between culture and religion matter to second-generation Muslims in Britain, and in what context can it be found?[2]

In analysing this point, it is necessary to revisit the issues surrounding the identity and social integration of young Muslims explored in Chapters 1 and 2. To date, the diaspora of second-generation Muslims has been discussed primarily within the frame of 'in-between-two-cultures'. According to this frame, second-generation Muslims lead their lives under multiple social expectations, including the Islam-based virtuous life, family honour and prosperity in kinship systems, personal success, and commitment to youth culture. As these expectations sometimes conflict with British society's cultural expectations, young Muslims cannot achieve and maintain healthy identities and integration into society without resolving this conflict. Accordingly, they have difficulty blending into British society while maintaining a Muslim identity.

The most pointed example of this theory is marriage and the control of women. As discussed in Chapter 2, the Asian community in Britain is based on the *biradari* kinship network with its unique prestige system of 'honour and shame'. The system assumes women are the family's face, representing its morals and prestige. For this reason, the family asserts its right to control women's bodies and lives; thus, women tend to be more tightly managed than men. Women are sometimes expected to marry a partner arranged by the family.[3] However, British-born-and-raised second-generation Muslim women want to pursue education and career just as other British people do. Does this mean that today's young Muslims are torn between two cultures?

In considering this question, it is necessary to examine their differentiation between culture and religion as an identity presentation strategy; it has three significant implications for young Muslims, especially women.

First, this differentiation enables them to positively position religion as a constructive part of their identities by ascribing oppressive practices to their cultures:

> I think disrespect for women is to do with culture rather than religion...
> I think it's more cultural in where we come from. That's something that doesn't give women their rights fully.
>
> (Zahra, Asian mixed, 22, Coventry)

> I think the culture, not the religion, doesn't give rights to women. The culture doesn't give rights to women. I mean, women are really looked down upon culturally rather than religiously. Religiously, women are, they're queens, really. That's the value religion gives to them.
>
> (Tazmin, Asian mixed, 19, London)

Chapter 7

He tried to settle down and get married, find a job... He returned back to Bangladesh and he married his cousin, who is my mom. My mom, she was told that she couldn't continue with her education. She stopped when she was about 15 years old... It has nothing to do with Islam. It's just the culture. They don't value women as highly as Islam does. Women are seen as baby machines, maids, and just the kind of doormat.

(Rukshana, Bangladeshi, 25, London)

Zahra and Tazmin stated that the harmful practices against women originated in the culture rather than the religion. Rukshana also stated that such practices were associated with the society and culture of 'Bangladesh', her family's place of origin, and not Islam. She accused the culture of treating women like 'doormats' in contradiction to what Islam teaches. By attributing oppressive practices and values to the culture, the informants emphasised that Islam did not deny women's rights as misrepresented by mainstream society and media. This differentiation thus makes it easier for second-generation Muslims to defend Islam against claims that it is anti-democratic, and thus to positively identify with Islam inside Britain's liberal space.

Second, such differentiation allows young Muslims to present Islam as a religious code, the highest standards they should commit to, while discounting their culture as 'optional' or 'not necessary to conform'. Using this differentiation, they negotiated with their families about some of the practices in their communities that threaten to obstruct their future paths and careers (Parekh 2008: 111; Ryan 2012: 112):

In Asian society, they believe that a good Islamic marriage would be if marriage is strictly arranged and it's arranged by the parents. But that's actually culture... That's from our culture. We have to be arranged marriages. Parents decide who their daughters or sons should marry and shouldn't marry, and stuff like that. But in reality, it's not what my religion says.

(Ibtisam, Bangladeshi,21, Coventry)

I always say to my mom like, 'I can't do arranged marriage' only because I'm one of those people that believe in love marriages. If I do find a girl, it's only because I chose her for myself. I love her, kind of thing. It's not religion, by the way; It's culture.

(Huzaifa, Pakistani, 18, Coventry)

Ibtisam indicated that some of their family or community practices were cultural rather than religious (Sahin 2013: 142). She identified arranged marriage as cultural and as separate from Islam. Huzaifa, a 'second-generation' Pakistani, had a mother who had constantly made suggestions for arranged marriage. He enjoyed freedom as a teenager in society and consequently hoped for a 'love marriage'. He was negotiating with his mother and family about choosing his spouse and the timing of marriage for himself, pointing out that arranged marriage was a cultural custom unrelated to Islam (Shain 2003; Bagguley and Hussain 2005; Tyrer and Ahmad 2006; Sanghera and Thapar-Björkert 2007).

Third, young Muslims employ the differentiation between religion and culture to maintain the compatibility of Islam with Western democratic society. As discussed in Chapter 6, most of the informants did not report any major obstacles to living as Muslims in British society (Maxwell 2006). For example, Nazma stated:

> Men are providers, and women should not work... Nowadays, people don't really go by that standard anymore. There are so many women who are company owners and so many women who are lawyers and doctors. That's what I think about it. People change and things change. I don't think it's a bad thing. I don't think that Islam will say: 'No, you shouldn't do that'.
>
> (Nazma, Bangladeshi, 36, London)

Nazma, a part-time post-graduate student who worked as a community worker, differentiated Islam from cultural practices, criticising the latter for subordinating women. She saw Islam as compatible with contemporary British values such as educational achievement and career building.

The key point of the explanations above was the relationship between Islam, (Asian) culture, and British values. On one hand, the informants perceived some conflict between British values and ethnic-cultural ways of life, as well as between Islam and ethnic cultures. On the other hand, they argued that British social values and Islam could coexist as there was no serious conflict between them (Haddad et al. 2006: 17). This point was clearly expressed in the following comment by Farhan from London:

> You can't identify a Muslim by race or colour, or nationality. It's a religion. It's a major world religion; one billion people are Muslim. So it doesn't really contradict being British. Because I see myself as British. I don't see myself as Bengali. I've never been to Bangladesh; I don't

Chapter 7

want to go to Bangladesh. I have no interest in Bengali culture. So I am British. But I feel there is a contradiction between being British and being Asian. I don't think there's a contradiction between being British and Muslim. I believe there's a contradiction between being British and Asian.

(Farhan, Bangladeshi, 23, London)

Farhan defined Islam as a 'world religion' of all nationalities and races. Accordingly, he perceived conflict between 'being British' and 'being Bengali', but not being Muslim. In this sense, identifying with Islam through differentiating culture and religion was a strategy for facilitating and justifying their participation in British society (Adachi 2013a; 2015b).

Contrast between culture and religion

'Restriction' and 'leniency'

Differentiating culture and religion is part of a self-presentation strategy which facilitates identification with Islam by defining it as distinct from ethnic cultures (Goffman 1959). This strategy can also be rephrased as 'self-definition by decoupling religion from culture' (Ryan 2012). It is a self-presentation strategy that positions Islam as acceptable to British society and as an essential source of identity by 'sacrificing' culture. Let's look now at how informants described Islam through 'the negation of the negation' and perceived the negative aspects of 'culture'.

Informants often used the words 'strict' or 'restriction' when talking about culture:

There are so many opportunities for women in Islam. That's pointed out and that's written in the Quran too. However, if you take an Islamic country, the restrictions that the women have are horrible... For example, a woman is beaten on the street, beaten by the police, and beaten for everyone to watch. But that's not religion. Whereas this woman is a Muslim and she is living in a Muslim country, that's culture, that's not religion.

(Karam, Pakistani, 23, Coventry)

I think, in traditional societies like Pakistan and India and places in Africa, it's different to the Western perspective. So, whereas we might

188

think that they are oppressed or they are restricted, it might be normal for them.

(Duha, Asian mixed, 19, Coventry)

The older people obviously follow not just Islam. But it is also from traditional culture… To be honest, they don't believe for a woman to be all the time outside, going everywhere and seeing everything because first, they believe it is not safe, and secondly, they believe that maybe it's not a job for women.

(Abaan, Bangladeshi, 25, London)

Karam pointed out that severe 'restrictions' on women's rights in many predominantly Islamic countries derived from the local cultures rather than their religion. Similarly, Duha attributed the oppression of women in India and her maternal home country of Pakistan to 'their society' or cultural environment, not their religion. Abaan stated that the older generation was more strongly influenced by culture than Islam and that their traditional culture did not envision women's freedom of movement and social participation. Thus, they used the words 'restriction' and 'strict' exclusively when referring to culture, not Islam.

Another noteworthy point is that the informants frequently mentioned non-Western societies – Asia, Africa and the Middle East – when they spoke about culture. In other words, they pointed to conflicts between Islam and non-Western cultures, but not between Islam and the values and practices of the Western society in which they lived. Accordingly, the differentiation between culture and religion was a strategy to position Islam as compatible with Western society.

The informants emphasised Islam's open nature and compatibility with British society as opposed to the coercive tendency of cultural customs and traditions:

In Islam, culture was a big thing, and I think it was just mainly culture. We're more open at this age. We're more open because we've lived in this country with this all different types of people and all different religions. You're taught in uni and school to question things, and Islam tells you to question things anyway. It's like all the combination of all these things, it's like, we're more open in interpretations of Islam, and also ideas and life in general… Asian culture is not all negative. But it has negative aspects. It's like chains around you. They restrict you from doing what you want, from marrying the person you want, from doing

Chapter 7

the job that you want, and from living in the place that you want. It's so restrictive. We're not cultural because we've been brought up in this country and we don't have much connection to our homeland. We're freer to do what we want to do.

(Nafisah, Asian mixed, 22, London)

Nafisah said that in the past people understood Islam as cultural, and it restricted people like 'chains around' them. In contrast, her generation could escape the influences of a closed cultural space and engage in a free interpretation of Islam, which broadened their options for social participation, thanks to Britain's open space (i.e., institutions and values). This point is developed further in Chapter 8.

Thus, many informants depict Islam as a flexible religion open to the outside world:

People have this idea that Islam is restricting. But Islam went to every country in the world, for example, Japan. Even if you are Muslim, you will wear your own clothes, you will have your own name, and you will still eat sushi.

(Shoaib, Bangladeshi, 29, London)

Shoaib's statement implies that Islam could not have spread to the world if it were 'restricting'. On the contrary, Islam is flexible enough to fit into the lifestyle of any society. He did not believe that Islam prevented people from adapting to their society.

One of the typical restrictions for people is marriage. Arranged marriage has been practised widely in Muslim communities. The informants perceived it as belonging to the cultural domain rather than Islam:

I have friends... They're from Pakistan, they're Muslim, they don't wear the hijab, and they can even wear like slightly short things to weddings and stuff like that. But they are only allowed to marry someone from this – not city, sometimes village. That is, to me, a cultural thing... I feel like that's an example of a cultural Muslim.

(Harir, Pakistani, 27, London)

Harir called marriage with a person designated by the family or relatives in the Asian community 'a cultural thing' and a person who engages in this practice in the name of Islam 'a cultural Muslim'. Ibtisam mentioned, as quoted earlier, that the older generation believed that a 'strictly arranged' marriage was a religious practice, but it was actually a cultural practice. Through such reasoning, she and others rejected some forms of marriage and asserted their autonomy in partner selection.

Wardah described the nature of Islam as 'lenient' as distinct from 'oppressive' culture:

> Her husband can't ask her... We can ask him for money. That's something he has to provide for us. Islam is lenient where you have to be with women. People make out to be, 'Oh no, they're so strict', but it is not.
>
> (Wardah, Indian, 27, Coventry)

Wardah explained that, in Islam, the husband was responsible for the family's livelihood and the wife was not, therefore, what she earned belongs to her.[4] On this basis, she argued that Islam was a 'lenient' religion encouraging women's economic autonomy as opposed to the view that Islam was 'strict' towards women. With this in mind, Tazmin stated in the previous section that 'women are queens' in Islam.

This 'lenient' nature of Islam extends to sexuality as well. For example, homosexuality is considered to be a grave taboo in Islam.

> If any two of you commit a lewd act, punish them both (4:16)

> 'How can you practise this outrage?' (7:80)

> 'You lust after men rather than women! You transgress all bounds!' (7:81)

These passages in the Quran are known as prohibitions against homosexuality. In fact, many Muslims have expressed opposition to the legal protection of homosexuality and Islam is regarded as a factor contributing to a person's intolerance of homosexuality (Mirza et al. 2007; Fish 2011: 89–92). Britain's mainstream media consider Muslims to be a homophobic group, and some Muslim organisations do, in fact, demonstrate this attitude.

However, Jannah offered the following qualifications about the controversial position on homosexuality:

> I think actually Islam is a very tolerant religion. I think you can't choose your sexuality, so it can't be forbidden. But I think most Muslims interpret the Quran in such a way, 'Having different sexuality is the worst

Chapter 7

thing'. But it's not. I know a lot of gay Muslims now. So it made me more interested in it.

(Jannah, Bangladeshi, 18, London)

She said that Islam did not punish 'homosexuality' because it is unchangeable. By referring to other Islamic traditions and values, she disagreed with the dismissive view of homosexuality and asserted Islam's compatibility with British societal values. Although Jannah's opinion was an outlier among the informants, it illustrates the potential for a more liberal interpretation of Islam. Engaged knowledge of Islam makes such interpretations possible, as will be discussed further in Chapter 8.

'Division' and 'border crossing'

The informants spoke of the differentiation between culture and religion also from the viewpoint of 'division' versus 'border crossing':

> They mainly segregate themselves by their ethnicities. There is always a Bengalis mosque, and then there is a Gujarati mosque and a Pakistani mosque.
>
> (Janan, Sudanese, 20, Coventry)

> You still have the cultural aspect… There are so many Muslims across the world. They all have different cultures, but one religion brings them together.
>
> (Nasha, Bangladeshi, 17, Coventry)

Janan and Nasha observed that many communities in the area (or the world) were divided by ethnicity and culture. Conversely, they understood Islam as 'crossing' those divisions and bringing people together (Massey 1994).

They applied this border-crossing logic not only to geographical borders but to all differences dividing people:

> In Islam, anyone can be a Muslim. You see people from different colours and different races, and just unity in a way. It's really united.
>
> (Nasira, Bangladeshi, 18, London)

192

Islam is different from culture. It can accommodate culture as long as they don't contradict Islam. But there's a certain culture which is in conflict with it... Another example is... marriage. People don't like to get married outside their ethnicities. But Islam, it doesn't treat people on racial boundaries.

(Talha, Pakistani, 27, London)

He is British Bengali and I am British Pakistani. We both have very different cultures when it comes to weddings and sort of baby birth... But, on religion, we are kind of brothers. I accept that he is my brother in religion.

(Ahmed, Pakistani, 21, Coventry)

Nasira observed that Islam was open to 'anyone'; not only people of different races and cultures but also different 'social classes' and 'castes'. Caste is a traditional South Asian system that strongly influences marriage and family relations, sometimes forcing people, especially women, to make particular choices. However, such social differences disappear and different people are equally accepted in the ideal Islamic community or *umma*. In other words, people can transcend their ethnic differences and unite in one community through their devotion to God.[5] Similarly, Talha and Ahmed referred to culture and ethnicity as signifiers of 'differences' and perceived Islam as a vehicle enabling people to overcome such differences and unite as 'brothers' (Ryan 2012: 111–13).

This view manifested in the informants' relative indifference to or denial of Islamic 'schools'. There are two main denominations in Islam from a doctrine point of view – Sunni and Shia.[6] There are four official schools within Sunni Islam – namely Hanafi, Maliki, Shafii and Hanbali (Gordon 2001). While this is a theology-based grouping, country of origin and ethnicity are major factors in the real-world grouping. For example, the Sunnis, especially the Hanafi, form the majority in the South Asian community (Kabir 2010: 60).[7] However, many informants did not believe that this school-based grouping was important.[8] For example, Ibtisam (Bangladeshi, 21, Coventry) stated: 'I don't want to think of myself as I am with this group or I am with that group' because the divisions were created by culture:

Husnain (Bangladeshi, 21, Coventry): There's a bit of history going on here. There are four scholars in Islam basically. And they have written and they interpreted Islam differently, in different ways. And there are Hanafi, the Sufis and all that stuff.

Chapter 7

Janan (Sudanese, 20, Coventry): Salafis.

Husnain: We are known as Sunnis.

Janan: But I don't follow any other teaching. I just follow what's in the Quran. I don't like being called a group name like Sunni. I think all Muslims should be the same.

Ibtisam (Bangladeshi,21, Coventry): Yeah, that isn't what the Prophet said as well. You shouldn't divide.

Janan: You shouldn't divide yourself.

Husnain: The division was done by culture.

Uzma (Indian, 19, Coventry): There are a lot of things that do overlap in some ways. And there're some things in culture, which we definitely wouldn't do in our religion. So, it's that kind of thing.

Karam (Pakistani, 23, Coventry): Yeah.

Uzma: I think the caste stuff.

Karam: Yeah, it does.

Uzma: But that's more culture and that is not religion.

Karam: That is definitely culture, yeah. Because in religion, everyone is equal, we are all equal.

Rahmah (Indian, 18, Coventry): And we have different Muslims. We have different Muslims, and then they follow one thing.

Husnain and others acknowledged the various schools of thought in Islam but declined to align themselves to any particular school or way of thinking. Ibtisam claimed that it was important to see Islam as singular, as it was at the time of the Prophet. Husnain attributed sectarian divisions to cultural rather than theological differences. Uzma and her friends presented India's caste system as an example of a cultural tradition that divides people, explaining that Islam transcends divisive institutions and unifies people on an equal footing (Meer 2010: 113–4).

In this way, many of the informants portrayed culture as something 'that divides and holds back people' while presenting Islam as something 'that transcends boundaries and unifies different peoples through leniency'.

Differentiation between 'forced' and 'arranged' marriage

The above analysis shows that the informants have a generally negative view of '(Asian) culture'. However, we must recognise that it is predicated on negative discourses about Islam. In one sense, they used culture as a scapegoat to rescue Islam from the negative characterisations that dominate in Western societies. At the same time, they were ready to offer a logic allowing the coexistence of culture and religion from an Islamic point of view. Their definition of Islam as 'autonomous' (i.e., absence of coercion) is significant for this point. In other words, cultural customs were acceptable provided they met the 'coercion–autonomy' criteria.

Perhaps the most important cultural practice to consider in this light is 'marriage'. 'Arranged marriage' is a prominent focal point in debates about Muslim social integration in Britain. Arranged marriage is a cultural matchmaking system in which, typically, parents find a marriage partner for their children, arrange their meeting and guide them to marriage. This custom is often criticised in Western society, where marriage is idealised as a union freely formed between two people. Nevertheless, arranged marriage continues to be widely practised in the South Asian communities in Britain.

Figure 7.1 shows the actual and desired types of marriage (i.e., arranged or not) among married and unmarried informants. Approximately half of the married or divorced informants had arranged marriages (nine women and four men). Of the unmarried, 15 women and 14 men expressed a desire for an arranged marriage, while 18 women and five men declared that they did not want an arranged marriage. There were seven women and five men who reported no preference. This result shows that more than half of women and men either desired or accepted arranged marriage. The number of people desiring arranged marriage is relatively higher among men.[9]

Many informants supported arranged marriage even though Western mainstream discourses regard it as problematic, signifying a denial of individual autonomy. Arranged marriage plays a significant role in the *biradari* system of the Asian community and continues to be widely practised. However, as the previous section clarified, most of the informants were critical of Asian cultures for their closed and restrictive nature, which raises a question about why many of them expressed positive attitudes toward arranged marriage.

Differentiating 'forced' and 'arranged' marriage is important to understand their attitude toward Asian cultural practices. While it is customary for parents or relatives to be involved in the selection of a child's marriage

Chapter 7

partner in Asian cultures, the informants clearly differentiated the two types of marriage:

> What needs to be said is the arranged marriage and forced marriage are two completely different things, and they shouldn't be confused.
> (Banan, Bangladeshi, 24, London)

> I think it's fine to have a love marriage. It's fine to have an arranged marriage. And whichever way you choose and as long as it's a halal [lawful] relationship, there is nothing wrong with that. But, of course, forced marriages are haram [forbidden] in Islam and a lot of people associate Muslims with forced marriages. But it's not right, really.
> (Farwah, Asian mixed, 20, Coventry)

Banan and Farwah criticised forced marriage from an Islamic point of view. Yet, they exhibited a more favourable attitude toward arranged marriage because it does not involve coercion. An arranged marriage is ultimately decided by an agreement between the partners and thus does not infringe on Islam's respect for autonomy. One informant (Tabassum, Indian, 26, Coventry) pointed to the cultural difficulties of rejecting an arranged marriage in some cases, but many others said that 'there is no pressure' (Saba, Pakistani, 25, Coventry) to decline an arranged marriage because the situation surrounding young people was changing.

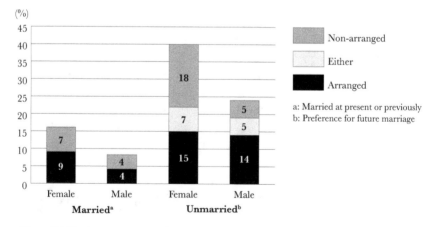

Figure 7.1 Marriage types among informants

This justification through Islam can help to make it compatible with some cultural practices. Caste-based kinship ties are important in the South Asian community, and marriages are often arranged through such networks. However, almost all informants declared that Islamic marriages had no such ethnic-based or caste-based conditions and that one chose (or could choose) a marriage partner 'if he is a good person, if he is a good Muslim' (Rafima, Bangladeshi, 30, London). This criterion for partner selection characterises 'Islam' as a religion transcending differences. In fact, some informants and their siblings have married a partner of a different race or ethnicity from themselves through the arranged marriage process.

Some of my informants favoured arranged marriage by their parents over love marriage. This indicates their identification with Asian family norms. They used religious criteria such as 'free will' and 'respect for parents' (especially mother's) wishes' to justify their positions.[10] The informants' attitudes and narratives about arranged marriage illustrate that they have formulated a logic for reconciling culture and Islam. Relying on this logic enabled the informants to avoid radically departing from their ethnic communities and protect themselves from an identity crisis.

The failure of the 'culture–religion' differentiation

The discussion above has found that second-generation Muslims differentiate between 'culture' and 'religion' as a strategy for balancing being Muslim and being British, resolving perceived conflicts between these identities. Many of them managed to assign more positive values to Islam by subverting criticisms of the religion – by ascribing negatively perceived practices and traits to culture – thanks to this differentiation. This enabled them to present Islam as compatible rather than in conflict with democratic values and thus to claim their right to participate in British society as citizens.

The importance of this strategy becomes clearer by examining cases in which the differentiation failed. Let us consider the cases of Rabab (Bangladeshi, 17, Coventry) and Nasha (Bangladeshi, 17, Coventry). The two teenage women of Bangladeshi descent lived in Coventry and were the most Westernised informants in terms of their dress and appearance.[11] They preferred to dress in Western-style clothes such as jeans and a skirt with accessories and did not wear a headscarf.

They identified as Muslim and were proud of their faith. However, they found it difficult to 'be Muslim' in British society: 'There is a huge conflict

Chapter 7

because the British way of living is completely different to Islam. Everything is different' (Nasha). They expressed frustration that the British society's way of life to which they were committed – dress, gender roles and relationships – was perceived negatively in their community:

> If other Muslim people saw us, they would feel like, 'What are you doing? Why are you showing other people?' Obviously, for white people, it's allowed... I don't want people to see us, 'Why are you representing us in a bad way? You are a Muslim. You are not supposed to do so'.
>
> (Rabab)

> Probably other Muslims are looking down on you just because you don't wear a scarf and don't dress properly.
>
> (Nasha)

Other informants also felt pressure from the Asian community about their conduct and dress. However, these two women were different in attributing this pressure and control to 'Islam' rather than 'culture'.

These two informants appear to have not managed to clearly distinguish Islam from ethnic cultures. For instance, they referred to the restrictions imposed on women by the community as 'Islam-based' and stated that they were not compatible with British social values and practices:

> Rabab: In Islam, you wear a scarf, hijab and burkha, and you stay separate. Whereas here... men can drive and so can women. If boys go to school, so can girls. If boys want, so girls can. It's not like that. Because you are girls, you have to stay at home whereas boys do something. It's nothing like that... If you go to Bangladesh or Pakistan, it will be the same; girls are covered up. But... because you are in Britain, it's completely different.
>
> Nasha: I think the British way of life is completely different to Islam in the way of women's lives, our lives.
>
> Rabab: There is written in Islam, men and women and men and women. But in Islam, you are more separate. It's more men, men, men and women.

Rabab and Nasha described the practices of Saudi Arabia and Asian countries as 'Islamic' and credited its patriarchal characteristic with depriving women of their freedom. Accordingly, they expressed unhappiness about certain Islamic teachings and community norms even while they identified as Muslim. Other informants presented Islam as impeccable by ascribing their community's oppressive practices and beliefs to ethnic cultures. By contrast, Rabab and Nasha did not differentiate culture and religion clearly, leading to their ambivalence toward Islamic teachings. Such ambivalent attitudes made it difficult to incorporate Islam as a positive part of their identities. While they wished to be Muslim, they were unable to integrate Islam with their lives in British society or to accept it as the guidelines for their own lives.

Conclusion

In Chapter 6, I have demonstrated that the informants recognised Britain as a diasporic space where many cultures and identities coexist and inter-connect. However, multicultural space does not automatically produce peaceful coexistence. Each identity develops its own connections by reflexively dealing with the tradition or culture as its source (Giddens 1990). Such reflexive re-interpretation makes a tradition more open and thus more compatible with the environment and other traditions.

Young second-generation Muslims realise such open and flexible ways of Islam primarily by distinguishing religion from culture. They defend Islam by attributing the factors targeted by social discourses in the West that are critical of Muslims – such as forced marriage and the denial of women's autonomy – to (Asian) culture. Through such reflexive interpretation of their religion, they also render Islam compatible with British values and lifestyles. To this end, they assign negative attributes such as 'restrictive' and 'divisive' to culture while associating Islam with more positive characteristics such as 'lenience' and 'border-crossing' (Zebiri 2008: 25; Ryan 2012: 108–13).

This was particularly true for women, as they were more closely associated with family honour in the *biradari* system and therefore had to negotiate their marriage and career in order to participate in mainstream society. This point will be discussed further in Chapter 9.

Chapter 7

Notes

1 *Happy British Muslims* is a video clip on YouTube showing a crowd of mostly young Muslims dancing in London to the tune of American singer Pharrell Williams' *Happy*. This video, produced and released by the Honest Policy, was praised by British society for brilliantly smashing stereotypes of Muslims. It was followed by numerous spinoffs produced by Muslims across the world, including in Germany, Malaysia and the US. At the same time, scenes of dancing and interactions between women and men drew strong criticisms from some Muslim groups and individuals (Hellyer 2014). They also spawned polemical videos such as *Honest Response to Happy British Muslim Video* and *Happy British Muslims #Sunnah Version*.

2 The differentiation between 'culture' and 'religion' can also appear as the differentiation between 'village Islam' and 'universalist Islam' (Bagguley and Hussain 2005: 218).

3 According to Tehmina Basit, who conducted a study of female students in East London, women's freedom is realised by 'marriage', not 'age' as in Western society. Women are under their father's control prior to marriage and achieve more autonomy with marriage (Basit 1997). Phillips (2009: 28) offers similar observations.

4 This idea reflects the Islamic view of family roles. Islam supposes that the family is managed and operates as a complementary relationship between spouses as to their responsibilities (Khan 2008: 10–2). Both the woman and the man are assumed to take on their respective gender roles. The husband is required to act as his wife's 'guardian' and be the breadwinner for her and the family. The wife is expected to be the husband's 'follower' who raises their children (Khan 2008: 6–8). While men are responsible for household finances, women are entitled to use their own earnings freely.

5 The 'oneness' of Islam or the Quran does not necessarily mean the 'oneness' of people's faiths. If anything, the informants accept diverse forms of people's religious practices. This is relevant to the 'individualisation of faith', which is discussed in Chapter 8.

6 The word Sunni derives from the Arabic expression 'ahl as-Sunnah wa'l-jamaah' (people of the *sunnah* and the community) to adherents of the traditions of Muhammad and his companions (Kabir 2010: 59; Matsuyama 2018b: 286). By comparison, Shia is short for the Arabic '*Shiah Ali*' (followers of Ali) and refers to people who believe that Muhammad designated his cousin Ali as his successor (Kabir 2010: 59; Hirano 2018a: 317). Sunni Muslims recognise Ali as the fourth caliph after Abu Bakr, Umar and Uthman. Shia Muslims see these three caliphs as apostates who usurped Ali's caliphate (Matsuyama 2018b: 288). However, Ali reportedly had close relationships with Abu Bakr, Umar and Uthman (Kabir 2010: 59). See Matsuyama (2018c) and Hirano (2018b) for details of their respective doctrines.

7 A majority of Hanafi followers on the Indian subcontinent belong to the Barelvi sect, and the next largest group follow the Deobandi movement. Both groups are reformist movements which arose after the British conquest of India in 1858 and

200

were traced back to Shah Waliullah Dehlawi's ideas. The Barelvi, established by Ahmed Raza (1856–1921), is characterised by its emphasis on the spirits of the Prophet and holy men, which mediate between believers and God. The Barelvi is associated with mystic traditions such as Sufism and strongly reflects indigenous cultural influences which other Muslims may reject – e.g., celebrating the Prophet's birthday. Antipathy toward British rule and doctrinal adherence were not very strong among its followers. The Deobandi is a reformist movement conceived at the Darul Uloom seminary in Deoband, northern India, in the context of resistance to British rule over India. Deobandis sought to distance themselves from British rule and culture and to revive lost faith through 'Islamic knowledge'. The Deobandi are highly critical of the Barelvi over these differences. In the British Muslim community, the influence of more conservative Wahhabism and Salafism from the Arabian Peninsula has been growing with backing from the Saudi royal family, although the number is smaller than the Barelvi and the Deobandi (Modood 2010: 20–2; Kabir 2010: 60).

8 A study of young Muslims in London published by Saied Ameli in the early 2000s also reports indifference to distinctions between Sunni and Shia among young people. Ameli discusses their orientation to unified Islam across national borders as a 'new phenomenon' (Ameli 2002: 143), but this attitude appeared to be rather common among my informants.

9 The most frequently mentioned reason for their support for arranged marriage is its 'safety net' function. For example, Rizwan (Asian mixed, 19, Coventry) stated:

> I think sometimes arranged marriages could be good because, you know, we have *rishtas* [suitable matches in marriage]. So the parents will say, 'We think this person is good for you'. But the guy will say, 'No, I don't want her'. And next time, you know, two years go by, they are 30–35 years old. And they have left it too late.

They supported this type of marriage as a safety net to reduce the risk of missing the marriageable age.

10 'Free will' as a religious value is discussed in detail in Chapter 10.

11 These two girls were among a small handful of informants who belonged to the category of 'private Muslim' (Phalet et al. 2012) or 'diffused Muslim' (Sahin 2005) discussed in Chapter 4.

Chapter

8 Islamic Knowledge and the Internet: The Function of *Ijtihad*

Reply, O Prophet, 'Show me your proof if what you say is true'.

(The Quran, 2:111)

Seeking knowledge is a duty upon every Muslim…

(*Sunan Ibn Majah*, 224)

Whoever takes a path upon which to obtain knowledge, Allah makes the path to Paradise easy for him.

(*Sahih at-Tirmidhi*, 2640)

Issues in question: Islamic knowledge and social integration

In sociology, religion has been understood as a kind of 'knowledge'. Knowledge refers to a set of concepts through which people in a social group recognise reality and which prescribes their behaviours, perceptions and relationships. Knowledge takes diverse forms, including religion, customs, traditions, magic and science (McCarthy 1996: 16).

Religion has historically played a significant role as a source of knowledge that provides common premises and communality for society. For example, Emile Durkheim theorised the principle of knowledge formation in society, or moral reality shared by people, through the analysis of primitive religious concept (Durkheim 1912). The sociology of knowledge also emphasises the importance of religion in underpinning reality, highlighting a vertical dualistic relationship between the profane world (*nomos*) and the sacred world (*cosmos*). In this schema, the latter protects the former from crises by precenting society from anomie and stabilises social order (i.e., people's reality and moral consciousness) (Berger 1967: 26–33). Historically, these two worlds had a systematic connection as elucidated in Max Weber's concept of *hierokratisch* (hierocracy) (Weber 1956), in which religious knowledge was positioned as a mechanism that validated worldly power and compelled people to accept it (Turner 2012: 127–9). In other words, religion (or religious knowledge) was seen as the linchpin of political and social integration.

In the ongoing process of modernisation, however, the status and role of religion have undergone major transformations. Two significant changes are relevant to my discussion here. First, the establishment of modern states replaced the vertical relationship between the sacred world (religion) and the profane world (society) with the horizontal relationship between the 'private' and 'public' spheres. The sacred was confined to the private sphere, substantially reducing its influence in the public sphere, at least in principle (especially in the West). Today, the 'boundary' differentiating the sacred from the profane, rather than the sacred in itself, has assumed a religious meaning underpinning society.[1] When the horizontal secularisation principle is violated, modern society experiences severe disturbances that trigger collective effervescence. Islam has recently been perceived as the greatest boundary breacher. Events such as the Rushdie Affair, 9/11, and the satirical cartoon incidents, and the 'deference to God' signified by a headscarf or a veil, are viewed as evidence that Islam breaches the secularisation principle and thus clashes with the modern social system (de Vries and Sullivan eds. 2006).

Chapter 8

Is this an appropriate framework for understanding second-generation Muslims in Western society? The second change in the status of religion as knowledge is important for examining this question. It involves the relationship between religious knowledge and people. In the past, the connection between the sacred and the profane was institutionalised by the ruling class and theological elites – *ulemas*, priests and rabbis – who dominated the production, supply and consumption of religious knowledge. This monopoly was partly because religious knowledge was inscribed in holy languages – Arabic, Greek and Hebrew – which only clerics could understand (Turner 2012: 118–9). It does not mean that lay people had no impact on religious practices, but they were not expected to interpret scriptures for themselves. While religious knowledge has a special place in Islam, it has long been accepted that 'the knowledge of the Quran and other religious fields was the reserve of the *ulema*' (Haw 1998: 60).[2] This resulted in the exclusion of many, especially women, from direct access to Islamic knowledge and thus their incorporation into traditional power relations.

However, the development of the Internet and other communication media in recent years has undermined traditional restrictions on access to religious knowledge and enabled the 'democratisation of the systems of religious communication' in the Islamic world (Turner 2012: 130). Print media, radio, television and the Internet have enabled everyone to acquire, research and interpret Islamic knowledge, which was previously reserved for the religious elite and not publicly recognised for the lay (Larsson 2011). Individuals are now able to access various sources of information to examine and determine what is and isn't an Islamic view on potentially controversial issues. This process has been described as the 'individualisation' (Roy 2004: 175–200) or 'protestantisation' (Goldberg 1991; Aslan 2005) of Islam. This reorganisation of religious knowledge has had a significant impact on young Muslims' relationship with secular society, i.e., their social integration.

How do young Muslims use religious knowledge to serve their participation in broader society? How do they understand their own generation as Muslims in terms of their relationship with knowledge? '*How* is knowledge being produced, *who* is producing it, and for *whose* consumption?' (Nagel 2005: 6). This chapter will explore answers to these questions about religion as knowledge to examine social integration among second-generation Muslims in Britain.

Distinction through knowledge

The previous chapter illustrated the importance of differentiating religion from culture for my informants. As we have seen, this involved ascribing negative cultural practices reported in the mainstream media to 'ethnic culture' and presenting 'Islam' as a positive identity that can coexist with democratic and liberal values. Why did the differentiation between culture and religion become widespread among contemporary youth?

Bakarah, in her late thirties, responded to this question as follows:

> Since September 11th, there has been almost an awakening around re-ligion for younger people. So they have done it in a way which is very distinct between religion and culture. So, I was brought up with just culture mainly, and the religion we learnt is how to read the Quran and some stuff and *namaz* [prayer], and that was it. I think that that's probably where the clash is a little bit because we are used to having the cultural thing.
>
> (Bakarah, Indian, 39, Coventry)

As discussed in Chapter 5, 9/11 had a tremendous impact on many infor-mants' identity formation. Following that 'spectacular event', the Muslim community experienced serious backlash and increasing discrimination in both lived experience and media discourse. For many young Muslims, it was a traumatic event that came out of the blue, which heightened their level of reflexive consciousness about their identity. As Bakarah explained, the older generation understood and followed their religion as cultural or ritual (i.e., how to read or pray). By contrast, the post-9/11 social scrutiny of Islam presented the younger generation with a felt need to justify their faith in the Western society in which they were born and raised. In the process, they dif-ferentiate religion from culture, i.e., defining what Islam is and isn't. Bakarah, who was already an adult before 9/11, pointed to this shift.

What factors enable the differentiation between culture and religion and distinguish the younger from the older generation? Informants often used the term 'foundation' or 'fundamentals' in their explanations:

> First, you have to get the fundamentals, which are the five pillars of Islam. After that, these smaller things come. A lot of people want to talk about the smaller things. But when they talk about the main things, they don't have a clue.
>
> (Umair, Bangladeshi, 21, London)

Chapter 8

> I think younger people become religious. It's because of, obviously, the way the older people were taught. They weren't much religious. There was religion, but it's not as strong a foundation as it is now.
>
> (Wardah, Indian, 27, Coventry)

> I think young people become religious because they have a firmer foundation. My parent's generation is more cultural; it is Asian culture. They understand Islam culturally.
>
> (Ulfah, Indian, 21, Coventry)

Umair referred to 'the five pillars of Islam' as 'the fundamentals' – 'the main things' that 'Islam is' rather than minor rules. Similarly, Wardah claimed that the older generation lacked religious 'foundations'. The key word used by Ulfah and Bakarah in discussing the foundation of their faith is 'understand'. They mentioned that the older generation understood Islam 'culturally', implying that the older generation failed to understand Islam religiously.

So, what is the meaning and function of 'foundations/fundamentals' when they use these words?:

> At the moment, the foundation is getting very strong. There are a lot of people that, obviously, start to have all these classes where they teach us what's right, what's wrong in Islam.
>
> (Wardah, Indian, 27, Coventry)

> Young Muslims nowadays know… 'Is this really a rule that we need to follow?' or 'Is this really authentic Islamically?'
>
> (Tabassum, Indian, 26, Coventry)

Wardah pointed out that the stronger religious foundations gave people a better understanding of 'what's right, what's wrong in Islam'. Tabassum said that the younger generation knew if something was 'really a rule that we need to follow… Islamically', i.e., an 'authentic' rule. Knowing authentic rules implies being equipped with religious knowledge. In other words, religious foundations mean knowledge of authentically Islamic rules. Conversely, the informants perceived that what older people believed to be Islam was based on the traditions and customs of their original ethnic community and was not authentically Islamic (Ameli 2002: 136).

The knowledge of Islam becomes a key resource or tool for young Muslims' adaptation to British society, as discussed in Chapter 7. As Tabassum observed, knowledge forms the basis for distinguishing between Islamic teachings, or 'rules one needs to follow' (i.e., religion), and the rest, or 'rules one does not need to follow' (i.e., culture). Accordingly, the acquisition of Islamic knowledge helps young second-generation Muslims to free themselves from some customary practices (which were understood as) not based on Islam and to broaden their options for lifestyles and life plans in Western society.

Salimah was born to a strict mother and a liberal father who were poles apart in their ways of thinking. She spoke of her mother forcing her to wear a scarf:

> My mum has always been quite a very practising Muslim. She observes the proper burqa. She covers her face, so you can only see her eyes. She has the face covered as well... I uncovered my face until I got caught. My mum was furious. She said, 'You are abusing the hijab, this, that and everything'. Then my dad went to her and asked, 'But why do you think she is abusing the hijab?' She didn't understand why I needed to wear the hijab. All she knows is that: 'You have to wear it. You have to wear it'. Force isn't the right way to teach somebody religion.
>
> (Salimah, Bangladeshi, 33, London)

Salimah's mother tried to make her wear a hijab without knowing its meaning. In other words, her mother's desire for her to wear the hijab was based on a cultural practice, and lacked understanding of its religious significance. This lack of appropriate Islamic knowledge leads to the closed and strict culture-based understanding of Islam discussed in Chapter 7.

The emphasis on religious knowledge and foundations was an expression of the younger generation's pride:

> My parents follow quite an old school and that they just followed, like you said, the school of thought. They followed like a strict school of thought. Whereas, me personally, I'm kind of more liberal in that I take from different schools of thought. So I'm not necessarily Hanafi all the time. My dad would place his hand below his navel. I'd place it on my chest. Because I believe the other schools, I have more compelling evidence to place the hand on the chest. But that's just like a small issue.
>
> (Sohail, Bangladeshi, 28, London)

Sohail stated that his parents 'just followed' the teachings of an 'old school' whereas he followed 'different schools of thought'. While the example he cited may be a 'small issue', it suggests his sense of pride in following his

Chapter 8

faith independently from his parents. To do so, 'compelling evidence', i.e., knowledge of Islam, is the key. In other words, the younger generation makes a *distinction* (Bourdieu 1979) between themselves and the older generation, like their parents, through religious knowledge.

Similarly, Ahmed distinguished different reasons for wearing a scarf:

> My mother still wears a headscarf, but not for religious purposes, but more so for cultural, whereas my wife, she wears the headscarf for religious purposes. There is a difference in that. But I think young people have taken interest in religion a lot more.
>
> (Ahmed, Pakistani, 21, Coventry)

According to Ahmed, both his mother and wife wore headscarfs but for different reasons, 'cultural purposes' for one and 'religious purposes' for the other. He was proud that the younger generation, like his wife, was correct in wearing the scarf for a religious purpose and meaning.

Many of the informants' remarked that religious foundations were based on the tradition of knowledge in Islam. It is well known that Islam confers great significance to knowledge. The Arabic word for knowledge is '*ilm*'. This term appears in the Quran twenty-seven times, with its derivatives and synonyms appearing more than 700 times (Akhtar 1997: 102). Multiple books of *hadith* (the collected sayings and actions of the Prophet), the second most important source of Islamic law and conduct, have dedicated chapters on knowledge, indicating its significance. Islamic jurisprudence is called *ilm fiqh* in Arabic, where *ilm* refers to an 'academic discipline' (i.e., a system of knowledge) (Nakata 2015: 252). Islamic legal scholars with religious authority are generally called '*ulama*', which literally means 'men of knowledge' (Esposito 2003: 325).

Importantly, this Islamic concept of knowledge differs from the standard English concept of 'knowledge' in both scope and meaning. Knowledge generally means retained information about something, be it sacred or profane. Islamic knowledge, however, is a more comprehensive concept that includes theory, codes of conduct and education, as well as specific information about things (Azram 2011: 179; Davids 2013: 25).[3] This conception of knowledge is understood to have originated in the words of Allah (Déroche 2005: 3; Gordon 2001; Kamada 2015: 69–70). In Islam, knowledge is related to the concept of the '*nur*', a light which is illuminating the path to Paradise – ignorance is characterised as 'unenlightened' (*jahiliyyah*) – and questing for knowledge is both a God-given duty and a necessary condition for attaining happiness (Akhtar 1997: 105).[4]

Thus Islamic knowledge refers to understanding the world created by God, which by extension means knowing God's will (Kamada 2000: 17). Knowledge is both a guide for living as a Muslim and a source of wisdom (*hikmah*) bestowing various benefits to people. Knowledge covers scientific knowledge, life knowledge, practical wisdom and a code of conduct which illuminates the path to living well and rightly (Khattab 1994: 32–3; Davids 2013: 25–6). Accordingly, the acquisition of knowledge is a vital duty for Muslim women and men. Nonetheless, as discussed in Section 1, it has not always been common in the Muslim world for lay believers, especially women, to actively pursue this knowledge. However, the environment surrounding knowledge has changed dramatically in recent years.

Changes in the environment for knowledge

Many informants spoke about differences between the religious environment of contemporary Britain, where they lived, and the religious environment their parents' and grandparents' generations had experienced either in Britain or their home countries:

> Older people are saying that, you know, 'We didn't have the chance to study and we didn't get that knowledge, when we were little, from our parents'. At that time, people didn't have money to have an education. A lot of grandparents and parents were illiterate because they didn't have an education, on their religious side as well… The religion wasn't followed properly. It was a lot of traditions that were passed down to the generations. The younger generations who were born and brought up in this country have more understanding of their religion because they go out and have an education. They are able to research their religion and have a better understanding of it.
>
> (Zahra, Asian mixed, 22, Coventry)

> I think sometimes the older generation is a bit more traditional. They follow culture rather than religion. I think the younger generation, they are starting to learn things about their religion. So, they have more knowledge probably because they have been going to school and have been educated more.
>
> (Janan, Sudanese, 20, Coventry)

> Our experiences are so different from our parents. We are more inclined to research the religion. So maybe we are more curious than the previous

Chapter 8

generation. So that could make you more religious. If you don't mind,
it makes you less religious. But you do find cases where kids are more
religious than their parents. I wouldn't say it's uncommon.

(Ibtisam, Bangladeshi,21, Coventry)

Many of informants' families lived in impoverished households or communities in their home countries. Their religious infrastructure was also
underdeveloped, and their lives and faith were governed by cultural traditions
blended with Islam rather than Islam itself (Haw 1998: 60). According
to Zahra, the older generation lacked 'the chance to study' and followed
'traditions that were passed down' because 'In villages, there weren't many
religious people. There weren't scholars. So people just believed what they
were taught and they heard. A lot of people couldn't read the Quran as well'
(Zahra).

That people 'couldn't read the Quran' is noteworthy because the
Quran, written in Arabic, is the source of all knowledge and one needs to
refer to it all the time in one's research. The parents' and grandparents'
generations did not have the right conditions (e.g., high levels of literacy,
Arabic language education, mosques for women, Islam study courses
and religious texts) for knowledge acquisition in their home countries
(Turner 2012):

I think the older generation is just more like word of mouth. Somebody
else is doing it, 'Oh, we should do it as well', rather than actually
researching and getting the knowledge and where it comes from.

(Saba, Pakistani, 25, Coventry)

Because a lot of what they know is not from reading and independent
research, it's just about what their peers are doing and what their parents
taught them. Do you understand? So, when you pass down knowledge
like this, it's not authentic and things get lost and missed in translation,
you know. My grandmother, my mother's mother, she was illiterate, she
couldn't even read and write. You understand? So, when you're passing
knowledge in this way, it's not good. Whereas I have done courses and
studied and read books myself, you know, that were written by people
that were around 600 years ago, 1400 years ago, you understand?

(Durrah, Indian, 39, London)

As these informants stated, Islam for the older generation was based on cultural traditions passed down by 'word of mouth' (Meer 2010: 95). By contrast, Durrah noted that she could learn Arabic, read a text from '1,400 years ago' (i.e., the Quran), and she understood and interpreted it. In this way, many informants perceived the traditional understanding of Islam as passive, lacking reflexive engagement with its teachings, and presented their own faith as more authentic (Parekh 2008: 124; Bhimji 2009).

Kashif expressed a similar view:

> Islam itself encourages people to study. It isn't because your father or your forefather is a Muslim. You have to become a Muslim. Whether parents are Muslims or not is not so important. As an individual, my belief is, I wouldn't say, different from my parents'. But certain things that my parents do as Muslim, they've done it because of the culture. A lot of cultures are involved. I don't do the same thing because I was born in the West. I've studied myself; hence the reason I do certain things is different. And it is primarily because of education, because I was able to go into that field, research that field and find out truly what Islam is about. So, it's just because of education. Education plays a very important vital role in everyday life.
>
> (Kashif, Bangladeshi, 22, London)

Kashif, of Bangladeshi descent in his twenties, declared that one must 'become a Muslim' by one's own choice and learning, not by inheritance – not 'because your father or your forefather is a Muslim'. He presented his faith as acquired through 'research' whereas his parents' faith was derived from their culture. His belief was founded on the knowledge he acquired through education; thus he believed he could access 'true Islam' and become a true Muslim. Conversely, an understanding of true Islam cannot be attained through cultural inheritance. It is interesting to note that, in Kashif's view, he could do so because he lived in 'Western society'. While there are numerous Islamic facilities and educational institutions in Western society, especially in London, where he lived, that kind of environment was hard to find in his family's country of origin, Bangladesh.

The young people's attitude to knowledge was also a consequence of their social environment or pressure, which related to the difference between 'being Muslim in Islamic society' and 'being Muslim in non-Islamic society':

Chapter 8

> If you are living in a Muslim country, you kind of become lazy in a sense, and you feel like you don't really have to learn more about your religion.
>
> (Janan, Sudanese, 20, Coventry)

The Islamic societies where their parents and grandparents lived had nothing to motivate them to reflect or think about their religious teachings and lives because being Muslim was self-evident. In contrast, young Muslims in non-Islamic societies are compelled to reflexively re-examine and reconstruct their identities in a world premised on different value systems along with new technologies. Selikah spoke about this desire among young people:

> Like a teenager, I would constantly question, you know, 'Why have I got to do this and why I got to do that?' So, you want to know what's actually part of your culture and religion.
>
> (Selikah, Indian, 17, Coventry)

This comment expressed a common desire by young Muslims who were born and raised in Western society and shared culture and values with other British people.

Another factor contributing to a generational gap stems from the differences in challenges faced by the first and second generations. While living in British society was an assumption for the second generation, it had been a goal to be achieved at great cost for the first generation:

> If you look back, our parents or grandparents came here for work. And now the issue isn't working, but it's life. They have established work and foundations for family. And now we have a bit more freedom to think. I think that has led to young people actually understanding the religion more.
>
> (Ahmed, Pakistani, 21, Coventry)

Ahmed was 'third-generation' with a first-generation father and a second-generation mother. He said that his late father worked long hours at a factory to establish his family in the UK and that the first-generation's inability to rethink Islam was in a sense beyond their control. He pointed out that the younger generation had the luxury of thinking about their faith and conducting their own research on Islam, as well as being exposed to and influenced by Western culture.

Another informant stated that living in a multicultural society encouraged people to deepen their knowledge (Sahin 2013: 135). Taimoor, who was quoted in Chapter 6 regarding the positive value of a multicultural society, responded to a question about whether 'the younger generation has more knowledge' as follows:

> We're more open, we've mixed with people from [different religious] schools. In mosques, I have seen people who pray in many different ways. And there are prayers done ten different ways by ten different people. But my family, my mother only knows one way because she has not been in the environment, and she's not been with other people. She just thinks there is one way to pray.
>
> (Taimoor, Pakistani, 27, London)

Taimoor pointed to an important difference between the younger generation and the parents' generation: the former participated in Britain's multicultural space whereas the latter lived within their own small community. The younger generation is exposed to different cultures and, therefore, different types of Islam. They reflect on their family's tradition, compare it with other traditions, and conduct their own research to find an interpretation of Islam that suits them best. The informants perceived research into Islam as a necessary process not only for resistance to negative social discourse but also for adapting to the realities of a multicultural society.

Thus, many informants used the term 'research' to describe their processes of deepening Islamic knowledge. This process was based on the notion of *ijtihad*, or 'independent reasoning', introduced in Chapter 3. *Ijtihad* refers to the effort to find solutions to issues uncovered by Islamic law through reasoning (Nihon Isuramu Kyokai et al. eds. 2002: 91).[5] Many informants reported conducting research into Islam in their efforts to deal with and resolve questions that are not explicitly addressed in religious books or traditions.

Ijtihad is important for second-generation Muslims who practise Islamic teachings in Europe, where Islam has no historical roots (Ramadan 2005; 2010). In societies where Islam is entrenched, discrepancies between social norms and Islamic rules rarely surface because the culture and religion have bonded organically, i.e., the distinction between them is obscure. In non-Islamic or rapidly modernising societies, however, the conflict between the code of socially acceptable behaviour and the culturally and religiously approved rules is a recurring problem. This situation can potentially trigger feelings of conflict between 'being a Muslim' and 'being a citizen'

Chapter 8

in young people. *Ijtihad*, or independent interpretation of religious texts, is important for avoiding such situations (Zebiri 2008; Ramadan 2010; Caeiro 2011; Davids 2013). Individuals must use their own judgment in dealing with unanswered questions arising in the gap between Islam and modern life. In other words, young second-generation Muslims' adaptation to British society has to be achieved through their own judgment based on religious knowledge, and not through renouncing Islam or crossing Islamic boundaries.

Likewise, a wide assortment of Muslims live in multicultural Britain with its imperial history. It is impossible for a single tradition to represent the whole of Islam in this environment. Encounters between different Islamic traditions from different regions or cultures can generate confusion about what Islam is and is not. This confusion may lead to real conflict between people belonging to different schools. The (re-)introduction of the *ijtihad* tradition has helped to alleviate the friction between schools and ethnicities by increasingly locating the onus of religious interpretation on individuals.

Dissatisfaction with traditional education and authority

Almost all informants received Islamic education at an early age from their parents and family, which were the bedrock of Islamic learning for them. Many also learned to recite chapters (*surah*) from the Quran or to read Arabic in *madrasas* (schools of Islamic instruction) or from private tutors. These collective experiences were significant in the formation of their Muslim identities. However, it did not lead to a simple transfer of knowledge or an uncritical reproduction of Muslim identity.

The early Islamic education experienced by many informants revolved around chanting passages of the Quran and learning to read (e.g., the Arabic alphabet). While this formed an essential part of their Islamic education, some informants felt that such education lacked 'meaning':

> Our siblings were just learning one-to-one. We were doing it as a group first and then became one-to-one. And my mom recited all the *surahs*. We had lessons of the Quran. But obviously, I do not know the meaning of it and God willing. I hope that I do learn the meaning of it because, obviously, you are reading it, but you don't exactly know what is said in it.
>
> (Zaheda, Bangladeshi, 25, London)

Islamic Knowledge and the Internet: The Function of *Ijtihad*

I didn't know what I was saying. The imam was just saying 'blah-blah-blah'; so I was just saying 'blah-blah-blah'. And we learned so much, all of that. But we didn't know what it was... Again, there was no meaning. We just learned ABCDEFG, and went there, we learned how to say it, but we didn't know the meaning of it. So, it's weird... I thought nothing of it until I grew a little older. I was thinking, 'Why aren't we getting the meaning of this? Why are we just saying it?'

(Haris, Bangladeshi, 27, London)

In my childhood period, every day, 5 days a week, we came back home at 4 o'clock, and then from 5 to 7, we went to an Islamic school which was in the mosque... That was basically to do Quranic studies. I don't think it was much of a benefit now. When I look back, I was taught how to read the Quran, I was taught how to read the Arabic alphabet and so on, but I was never taught the meaning. I did not understand Islam. I wasn't told. We were reading for the sake of reading. We were learning things off by heart because you're a Muslim and that's what you do. And no one said the paragraph that you just read in Arabic means, 'This is what God says' or 'This is what Islam is'. Nobody told us that.

(Tasrin, Bangladeshi, 31, London)

These informants went to *madrasas* in their communities to learn the Arabic alphabet and the Quran from an early age. Others were taught as children how to pray and other basic Islamic rules, and have followed these codes of behaviour since. However, the education they received involved, by and large, recitation in a 'parrot fashion' (Ahmad 2012: 179). They were not taught the 'meaning' of Quranic passages or 'why Islam has this rule and Muslims have to follow it'. Many informants expressed dissatisfaction with this style of education, which required blind obedience to traditions in their community (Sahin 2013: 147).[6]

Their dissatisfaction with traditional education was inseparable from their distrust of the authorities who provided it (McLoughlin 2005). Contemporary young Muslims more and more mistrust traditional authorities such as imams in community mosques and *madrasas*, as mentioned in Chapter 2 (Phillips 2007). For example, Farhan made the following comment about imams:

Especially at my mosque, I feel that imams, some imams are out of touch with how life is for a British Muslim. A lot of imams migrated here; they're not born here, and they don't know what life is. And I feel

Chapter 8

> if I went to ask them any concerns, they would be very judgmental, very condescending. So, I feel actually imam would probably be the last person I would go to for Islamic advice.
>
> (Farhan, Bangladeshi, 23, London)

Farhan said that imams in his mosque were from rural areas in other countries and had no real connection with British society. They could not give advice from the viewpoint of young British Muslims, but despite their lack of understanding, they tended to discount, criticise or look down on anyone who challenged their views. Many informants expressed the belief that mosques and imams did not provide adequate support for their young followers' deep worries and religious questions (Sahin 2013: 141). Thus, for Farhan, the mosque was merely a place for prayer, not for the furtherance of knowledge, and the imam was 'the last person' he would go to for religious advice (Bhimji 2009: 375). This problem may be more acute among those mosques controlled by the older generation who recruit their imams from their home countries through their *biradaris*. Such mosques typically do not offer support to young people in their discovery of 'true Islam' through their own research (Ahmad 2012: 174; Sahin 2013).

Jannah, for example, had attended a mosque when she was younger and had many arguments with female scholars over differences of opinion:

> I just had a very different view of Islam from imams in the mosque… I feel there're too many don'ts; 'Don't do this, don't do that'… Really, I see Islam as a very tolerant religion, I see women in Islam very high up, and I see stuff like that. But I think people with different interpretations always get in the way. So, I can't always talk to, I don't really talk to women scholars because I'm scared about what they would think if I asked. Because some stuff is very taboo to ask, isn't it?
>
> (Jannah, Bangladeshi, 18, London)

Jannah saw Islam as a tolerant religion and distrusted the mosque scholars' who attempted to use Islam to restrict women according to cultural traditions – 'Don't do this, don't do that'. She expressed reluctance to talk to imams because she perceived them as 'judgmental' toward young people (Ahmad 2012: 182–4). She also complained that they refused to deal with sexual taboos – e.g., gays and homosexuality – and did not embrace diversity.

Other informants also noted that sexual issues were taboo in mosques (Zebiri 2008: 22):

> There are Islamic online forums now; so you can find out about various taboo topics that wouldn't have been discussed in madrassa class. You'd have a hard time talking to your imam about that. Taboo subjects like sex and adolescence, these're never discussed in an Asian family household; these're never discussed in an Islamic context. It is very important, I believe, for a young Muslim man or woman to know as they're growing from a child into a teenager and into a man.
>
> (Farhan, Bangladeshi, 23, London)

The traditional authorities' silence on sexual issues may increase the difficulties experienced by young second-generation Muslims in adapting to non-Islamic society. This point supports the argument presented in Chapter 2 about the diminishing value of traditional authorities in the Muslim community (Lewis 2007; KCLEC 2007; Larsson 2011).

That kind of frustration among the young is frequently expressed in Britain's Muslim community. For example, British Islamic educator Abdullah Sahin finds it problematic that mosque-linked supplementary schools emphasise rigid top-down inculcation. He argues that this approach has resulted in poor reflective and dialogic text comprehension of Islam and the Quran that is not congruent with life in contemporary Western society (Sahin 2013: 13–7). To position Islam as a guide for people in a society where Islam is not the mainstream institution, it must be 'dis-embedded' from its original context and 're-embedded' in a new context (Giddens 1990); in other words, it must transform the meaning circulated in previous societies in a way acceptable to the second generations in their new environment. This process can be achieved through individual efforts. As we have seen, young second-generation Muslims have been bypassing the older generation's traditional comprehension to engage with Islam critically and creatively in their own living environment.

The Internet and knowledge consumption

While expressing dissatisfaction about the absence of meaning in traditional Islamic education, the informants, especially those in their teens and twenties, perceived British society as a favourable environment for pursuing knowledge: 'I think we have the opportunity to learn more because there are a lot of things here' (Nasira, Bangladeshi, 18, London). 'Here' means Britain

Chapter 8

and 'a lot of things' refers to facilities and resources available to increase their knowledge.[7]

The Internet is a particularly important tool for their research as there are numerous websites providing information and knowledge about Islam (Bunt 2003). They include online archives containing texts from the Quran and *hadith*, question and answer sites, lectures and debates on YouTube as well as opinions and tweets on blogs and Twitter (Bunt 2003; Mishra and Shirazi 2010; Larsson 2011). One informant referred to '*sheikh* Google' (Kesvani 2019: 55–62):[8]

> There are Muslim scholars called *sheikh* Google. So, if you have problems, you just type into Google and get a response. And it's good because it's accessible information.
>
> (Banan, Bangladeshi, 24, London)

Banan said that she could easily access religious texts and images from renowned scholars and lay preachers via Google and other search engines for listening or deeper learning relating to her area of interest.

Knowledge acquired on the Internet played an important role in the formation of young people's Islamic identities, helping to inject substantive meaning into the perfunctory forms of Islam that they had learned at home and in the community. For example, Abaan was unhappy about traditional learning in the community and noted the advantages of the Internet:

> The Internet has a lot of information in one place; you cannot discount it. You can find out about anything on Internet… I found out about many prayers. There are prayers for everything: for when you go to sleep, for when you wake up, for when you're having difficulties in life, for when you're heartbroken. Whatever it is, your reason in life is to find prayer. Maybe there is no concise book that you can find, which has every single prayer. But on the Internet, you just type into something like on Google; very easily you can find something.
>
> (Abaan, Bangladeshi, 25, London)

As Abaan observed, the Internet has made it possible for Muslims to acquire extensive knowledge on every conceivable subject with minimal time and effort. By actively learning what Muslims should do or the meaning of each action or teaching, today's young second-generation Muslims can develop a deeper understanding of Islam than what is available from reciting the

218

Quran and blindly following traditional rules. This deeper understanding serves to connect Islam with their identities in a positive way.

One of the most popular tools was YouTube, where many speeches and lectures on Islam were available in English:

> Author: Do you have some interesting sites or favourite sites on Islam?
>
> Parveen (Pakistani, 31, London): Well, there are a few people I'd like to add to that list, actually… He's American. He's very good. He's American.
>
> Nasira (Bangladeshi, 18, London): This one, I think, is American and he's Indian.
>
> Author: Do they provide Islamic knowledge in English?
>
> Nasira: Yeah, in English.

> We go on YouTube a lot, and we go on and talk to gain our knowledge. When we started the first steps of the Quran, we basically went on YouTube. We find the *surahs* up on YouTube, the recitation up. It was in Arabic, and then at the bottom, it was in English. So we know what it means. And then, me and my sister, when we were looking at it, then we saw what it says in English. We got really emotional because we didn't know the meaning of it. So when we were looking at that, we gained knowledge. When we read it, we know what it means.
>
> (Zaheda, Bangladeshi, 25, London)

Many informants reported accessing the Internet daily and actively using it to pursue knowledge. They utilised it in many ways, including searching for particular passages of the Quran or *hadith*, looking into Q & A sites by Islamic scholars, and studying the teachings of their favourite scholars on YouTube. They relied on the Internet to answers to their questions – e.g., prayer methods, photographs and music, marriage, sexual relationships and loans – from various sources ranging from prominent overseas scholars to younger 'native' (i.e., American or British) preachers in their familiar language.

'English' is an important medium for their knowledge acquisition. In Islam, only the Arabic-language editions of the Quran are recognised as sacred scripture, and all translations are treated as just commentaries (Shimomura 2014: 19–20). Hence, Arabic is fundamental to religious interpretation in Islam. Some of the informants reported they attended religious schools or

Chapter 8

taken Arabic courses and could directly access and understand the religious texts. However, most of my informants stated that they could recite the Quran but could not decipher the complex Arabic texts or fully understand their meaning:

> I learned Arabic, but I did not necessarily know the meaning. That is quite common, yes, quite common in our community because for teachers you have, English is not their first language. And that was the challenge because English was my first language.
>
> (Banan, Bangladeshi, 24, London)

While learning Arabic is necessary for reading the original text, accessing Islam in their native English is also important for those who seek a deeper understanding of Islam and its religious texts in relation to their daily lives in Western society. The Internet has thus become a vital tool for second-generation Muslims.

Triangulation and *ijtihad*

While recognising the benefits of the Internet for their research, the informants were also cautious about the information that they found there. In fact, the advent of new technology has always stirred up debate among religious elites in history, because Islamic knowledge and religious guidelines have been supposed to be transmitted to people through *ulamas*, who have enough religious knowledge to examine the validity of the holy text (Larsson 2011). However, new media (e.g., radio, telephone, television and the Internet) can supply anonymous information to people without examination by traditional authorities in the community. Peter Mandaville commented as follows about the problem of anonymity on the Internet:

> Due to the largely anonymous nature of the Internet, one can also never be sure whether the 'authoritative' advice received via these services is coming from a classically trained religious scholar or a hydraulic engineer moonlighting as an amateur religious scholar. (Mandaville 2001: 183)

My informants were well aware of these issues. While a large majority of them routinely utilised the Internet to access Islamic sites and programmes, many also stated that they did not rely too much on the Internet in their search for knowledge. During these interviews, informants provided many arguments about the pros and cons of the Internet:

220

Islamic Knowledge and the Internet: The Function of Ijtihad

> If you have problems, people just type into Google and get a response. It's good because it's accessible information. But it's also bad because anybody can go up and post information. It can be right; it can be wrong. There're always two sides to the Internet. It can be used in a really good way, but it can also be used... to manipulate, exploit and abuse.
>
> (Banan, Bangladeshi, 24, London)

'The Internet is good, but...' was a common sentiment expressed by the informants. They had certain reservations about relying on the Internet for their research of religious knowkedge. In fact, they utilised diverse resources, including books, parents and relatives, siblings, imams and knowledgeable friends (Bhimji 2009; Mishra and Shirazi 2010):

> There's an Islamic society at my university. And there are people, there are people who have good knowledge of Islam. And they're quite easeful to ask if any questions, or you know, there're lots of answers they prepare... If they don't know, then they can help me out. And also, I can call up people in mosques at home... We also sometimes watch TV from preachers, Peace TV, for example... I try to, you know, go through reliable stuff online. But there are always those websites which are not reliable. They'd give you the wrong information... There are always those, there're dodgy websites, there're bad websites, you know. They try to do bad things, stuff like that. And you have to be careful not to fall into trouble... They say something without having the evidence, or without quoting stuff from the Quran or from those main sources and the main books, just like *Sahih al-Bukhari* and *Sahih Muslim*, and a few others.
>
> (Jacob, Bangladeshi, 19, London)

Jacob was a university student and a member of an Islamic student group. He named the group's senior and former members and its regular lectures by scholars as his main sources of knowledge. When he wanted to learn more, he sought correct knowledge by asking imams or preachers through telephone or satellite TV. Jacob considered the Internet an important source of information but remained vigilant against misinformation. He reported constantly cross-checking with recognised Islamic texts such as the Quran and *hadith* books by eminent scholars to verify the accuracy of information.[9]

Salimah (Bangladeshi, 33, London), a school teacher in London, sought an Islamic perspective on a given matter by searching the Internet and comparing different views. First, she found a site that 'matches my school of

Chapter 8

thought' online and searched for knowledge on particular issues, and then accessed other sources 'from books, from live scholars, from all of that' to confirm whether the information online was right or wrong. For Salimah, 'the Internet is just a small part of your knowledge'. Similarly, a large majority of informants reported having utilised the Internet for particular purposes such as finding prayer procedures and rules, Quran phrases, *hadith* contents, halal foods, or lectures and courses on the Quran and Arabic online or in mosques. When they searched for controversial themes – e.g., marriage, women's role at home, the wearing of the headscarf and the correct way to pray – they cross-checked with multiple resources such as books, imams and other people in the manner of 'triangulation'. This illustrates that they derived informatisation from a broader religious infrastructure than just the Internet. Depending on multiple resources for knowledge, they might reduce the risks of exposure to radicalised ideas and biased doctrinal interpretations, which were rampant in the online space.

The Internet and individualisation

The Internet promotes the 'individualisation' of faith (Roy 2004). Fahad commented on the young generation's increased freedoms in their engagement with their faith:

> We are in an information age. Young people are more inclined to do their own research. So obviously, when they have got access to all of that information, they can make their own choices and they are free to do so.
>
> (Fahad, Indian, 26, Coventry)

In the information age, access to information is inexpensive and no longer monitored by family or community members. Informants could access any information on the Internet at any time to deepen the understanding of their religion. They sometimes used religious knowledge to reject certain customs and to increase their ability to participate in British society as Muslims. Through the Internet – especially English-language materials – they could individually participate in the interpretive process, which was formerly the exclusive domain of scholars proficient in Arabic. Young second-generation Muslims are developing a personal Islam, called 'my Islam' (Bokhari 2013: 62), underpinned by knowledge acquired from diverse sources.

The individualisation of faith is in many cases achieved through 'shopping around' for knowledge in the free online 'religious market' (Matsuyama 2017: 230–3; Piela 2013):

> The Internet is a huge advantage because there are a lot of *sheiks*. And that's our teachers, Muslim teachers. They write blogs and Facebook messages about our religion, what to follow and what not to. On Google, if I ask a question, I usually do. Like, if I'm a bit insecure about one topic in our religion, I'd research it. And I'd like to gain more knowledge by reading up on these *sheiks*. Some *sheikhs* have different opinions, so I'll just like the one that I'm most comfortable with, I would follow that, actually.
>
> (Toslima, Bangladeshi, 18, London)

Like Toslima and Fahad, many informants searched for subjects of interest among the *fatwas* (legal rulings) issued by Islamic scholars and comments of preachers, seeking interpretations that were compatible with their values and leanings. By discovering knowledge which does not seriously contradict Western social values, they made it possible to live their lives as Muslims in Britain.

Shopping around for religious knowledge using diverse resources, including the Internet, facilitates *ijtihad* or 'own reasoning' (Mandaville 2002; Bunt 2003; Jones 2012: 144–5).

> If I am curious about something, I will research it. And if I've got a question, I would search whatever websites. And then, if it's the website which I trust, then I would take it. If I am doubtful, then I would still not take it. And I would ask someone, WhatsApp someone and ask the question, and I will take it.
>
> (Shoaib, Bangladeshi, 29, London)

When Shoaib had a question about a religious interpretation or understanding of life, he searched for an answer on trustworthy websites, checking their FAQs or posting his question directly. If he was not fully satisfied with what he found, he used his mobile phone app to text message friends and others. He sorted through their responses and accepted what he felt to be the most convincing explanation. In contrast to the traditional way of determining the authenticity of knowledge by authority, through such reflexive inquiries, the individual takes personal responsibility for adopting a certain interpretation and using it to deal with challenges in everyday life.

Chapter 8

The Internet also offers young people, especially women, autonomy. As mentioned, controlling 'legitimate knowledge' has long been a powerful means of making people conform (Weber 1956). Such knowledge has historically been produced, consumed and supplied unilaterally by male religious authorities and patriarchs (el Saadawi 1980). Today, young people and women can access religious knowledge on the Internet and interpret it by themselves (i.e., *ijtihad*), unmediated by authorities or communities. This has greatly enhanced women's autonomy regarding both their faith and their faith-based daily life. For instance, Habibah commented:

> Personally, the Internet is good. But I actually prefer going to my dad and asking what my dad believes. I have a lot of faith in my dad. So, if this is what my dad says, then generally I do believe it. But there is sometimes like, I don't believe in my dad. When I don't agree with what dad says, I go on the Internet.
>
> (Habibah, Asian mixed, 20, Coventry)

Habibah's family followed Sufism, a mystical form of Islam. Her father was a white convert with a wealth of knowledge as a *sheikh* (head of a group) trained in Morocco. She respected her father and treated him as her primary source of knowledge. However, she did not follow everything he said. As a second-generation Muslim, she had 'different interests' from her mother, an immigrant from Bangladesh, and did not always agree with her father's teachings. She described the management of her life as a Muslim in Britain as her 'own responsibility' and therefore emphasised that she ultimately based her interpretation of Islam on her own judgement.

Other informants expressed similar views:

> I sometimes just talk to my spouse about it because he might be a bit more knowledgeable than I am. If we get into a bit of a dispute, we will take it towards the Internet to have a look at these trusted websites, which will offer questions and answers and advice.
>
> (Tabassum, Indian, 26, Coventry)

Tabassum described her husband as more knowledgeable, but when they disagreed about an interpretation in everyday life, they went to the Internet for further information. By consulting websites and reasoning together, she and her husband developed a shared understanding of Islam. They took the initiative in managing their married life in this way. The Internet enables women to directly engage with knowledge and participate as

224

active actors in society and family through the autonomous acquisition of religious knowledge.

Conclusion

The production of Islamic knowledge through various media has been viewed as a major challenge to community-based traditional authorities (e.g., imams, *ulemas* and *sheikhs*). 'The new information and communication technology could be described as an agent that started a process in which the authority and hegemony of the "old" *"ulama"* came to be questioned' (Larsson 2011: 44). Although the traditional authorities put up fierce resistance to the new media and technology, the development of radio, television and the Internet have boosted the popularity of non-expert lay preachers (Yagi 2010; 2011). Although they do not all possess formal religious qualifications, the interpretations they offer for addressing the times and places of young Muslims in their local languages satisfy diverse needs in contemporary society which cannot be met by traditional authorities.

Of course, traditional experts are not standing by quietly. Across the spectrum, from local mosques to global religious organisations, various Islamic actors transmit religious knowledge and decisions about *fatwas* daily. Many communities have organised courses on Islam and Arabic at mosques and in voluntary study groups. Online opinion pieces, legal rulings and propaganda called 'cyber *fatwa*' and 'e-Jihad' are regularly cited, exerting a potent influence on thinking about and engagement with Islam (Bunt 2003; Caeiro 2011; Mariani 2011).

The equalisation of religious knowledge through informatisation has brought about a democratisation of faith. Print media, television and the Internet have greatly enhanced people's ability to acquire, research and interpret religious knowledge, which was previously the exclusive domain of intellectual and political elites. People in the information age use various sources to personally examine controversial issues and make their own determinations on what is and is not Islam. As Mandaville states, the new information and communication technology has enabled 'greater numbers of people to take Islam into their own hands, opening new spaces for debate and critical dialogue' (Mandaville 2002: 88).

The increased knowledge and interpretation practices (*ijtihad*) among young people have brought about the democratisation of faith. New information and communications technology may transform the meaning of Islam itself by dramatically changing the relationship between Islam and its followers. Because God's words are 'ineffable' (too sacred to be uttered)

Chapter 8

(Geertz 1973: 259) – to borrow Geertz's expression cited in Chapter 3 – people needed an 'intermediary' to access and interpret his messages. However, informatisation and improved literacy have expanded opportunities for the general public to access holy texts and interpretations, and consequently, the 'ineffably' sacred has been rendered 'effable', redefined as personally appropriate for each individual's life through the practice of interpretation (Turner 2012: 127–30). This conversion of 'background knowledge' into 'discursive knowledge' can be regarded as a process of 'humanizing the sacred' (Basarudin 2016).

The individualisation of faith permits a paradoxical relationship between collective identity and the subject. French sociologist Michel Wieviorka remarks about the subject's action in identity formation as follows:

> [T]he subject, in order to construct itself, may need to refer to a collective identity; but on the other hand, it can only do so on the condition of having the possibility of deviating from it, on the condition of not being obligated to identify with it to the point of getting lost or dissolved in it. The subject implies the reflexivity of the person, including in relation to oneself. It, therefore, presupposes a capacity to distance itself from its own choices… The subject cannot be conceived without a certain mastery of its own existence. (Wieviorka 2005: 156)

The 'subject' cannot manifest entirely independently of the collective identity which provides the foundation for individuals. In this sense, the subject of making choices is premised on the collective identity (Taylor 1985). At the same time, the subject must distance itself from the collective identity to secure its ability to make its own choices. The availability of this 'capacity to distance from religious prescription' is built into religious knowledge itself. Through acquiring religious knowledge, second-generation Muslims define their relationship with their faith for themselves. Informatisation available on the Internet provides some insulation against pressure from traditional authorities and thus enhances autonomy in religious interpretation. Thanks to this informatisation, young people can escape control by authorities and their communities and engage in 'fresh reading' of religious texts. In the process, they relativise the roles and norms imposed by the older generation and negotiate their participation and life course in British society (Modood 2013: 13–1).

What is important here is the dialectic relationship between the collective identity and the subject. While the collective identity is a necessary precondition for the subject, the capacity to relativise this condition is required for the subject to emerge. A logic that makes this possible is inherent to the collective identity, Islam in this instance. Informants have become subjects capable of such distancing by conforming to Islam. *Ijtihad* can be regarded as the tangible practice of this kind of connection between the collective identity and the subject, or 'agency', so to speak. They acquire a body as an agent through their access to Islam, through which they achieve distancing (i.e. selective adoption) with Islam (Adachi 2022).

It is worth noting, as many studies have pointed out, that *ijtihad* is a particularly important activity for Muslim women living in modern society (Ameli 2002; Badran 2009; Davids 2013; Basarudin 2016). The women, who were traditionally controlled by way of exclusion from (production, distribution and consumption of) religious knowledge, have begun to resist that dominance relationship by researching and interpreting knowledge for themselves (Amed 2003: 55; Parekh 2008: 111). This issue is closely linked with their social participation and identification with Islam.

This function of religious knowledge is discussed with a focus on women in Chapters 9 and 10 next.

Chapter 8

Note

1 France's *laïcité* is a typical example. However, religious sociologist Jean Baubérot notes that *laïcité* does not exclude religion from the public sphere as completely as is generally perceived and that arguments made in the name of *laïcité* are quite diverse (Baubérot 2007: 105–24).

2 *Ulamas* in Islamic countries have expressed deep suspicions about the use of new media (e.g., print, radio, TV or the Internet) for disseminating teachings, which is no doubt an expression of their anxiety about the distribution of religious knowledge independently of their interpretations (Larsson 2011).

3 This concept of knowledge seems to be similar to knowledge in the sociological sense. In both cases, knowledge is understood as an essential resource regulating social behaviours and relationships and motivating people to behave in particular ways. In this respect, sociological analysis of Islamic knowledge presents a kind of inversion. Sociology usually analyses how the religious worldview, usually operating tacitly, influences people's social reality (Berger and Luckmann 1966; Berger 1967). In studies of Islam, however, the analytical focus is on how expressed knowledge is adapted to non-Islamic or contemporary societies (Giddens 1991).

4 In Islam, Arabian society prior to Muhammad's illumination is called '*jahiliyyah*' (Nihon Isuramu Kyokai et al. eds. 2002: 265).

5 *Ijtihad* is defined as 'a legal term for the independent "effort" to discover a legal opinion about a problem (*mujtahadat*) not precisely covered by the Quran, the *sunnah*, and *ijma* through reasoning within the permitted bounds of the *sharia*' (Nihon Isuramu Kyokai et al. eds. 2002: 91; Hallaq 1984: 3). *Ijtihad* has an important function in the flexible adaptation of the Quran and Islamic teachings from the sixth century to various contexts in different times and places. *Ijtihad* includes the creation of law through interpretation and is normally reserved for experts (*mujtahids*). However, in the contemporary globalised world, vastly different from the traditional cultural and social environments, *ijtihad* has been becoming an important practice for many Muslims (Ramadan 2010: 47–8).

6 Criticism of blind obedience to traditions and the older generation's uncritical acceptance of doctrines, as discussed in Section 3 above, is directed at the notion of '*taqlid*'. In Islamic jurisprudence, this Arabic word meaning 'imitation' refers to 'one's conformity to the independent interpretation of a legal question made by a qualified jurist (*mujtahid*) without one's own intellectual effort' (Nihon Isuramu Kyokai et al. eds. 2002: 319). While *taqlid* contributes to legal and social stability, it risks diminishing legal and social flexibility (Matsuyama 2017: 205–7). Some second-generation young Muslims feel that *taqlid* leads to rigid interpretations and strict understandings of Islam that restrict people, as discussed in Chapter 7, and makes flexible adaptation to Western social life difficult. Therefore, the practice of *ijtihad* (the opposing concept to *taqlid*) is required (Matsuyama 2017: 207–24).

7 This remark explains one of the central reasons the informants define Britain as a multicultural space where due consideration is given to religious freedom, as discussed in Chapter 6.

228

Islamic Knowledge and the Internet: The Function of *Ijtihad*

8   *Sheikh* is an Arabic word meaning 'venerable person' or 'elder' and is used as an honorific for a person of excellent faith, character and scholarship, an *ulama* or a *Sufi* (mystic) (Nihon Isuramu Kyokai et al. eds. 2002: 260–1).

9   See Chapter 3 Note 15 for ways to derive legitimate knowledge.

Chapter

Women and Education

> A Muslim education is very different from a secular one. First off, no coeducation. And women would only be allowed to study certain things. What the Muslim Brotherhood really want is for most women to study home ec, once they finish grade school, then get married as soon as possible – with small minority studying art or literature first. That's their vision of an ideal society.
>
> *Submission*
> by Michel Houellebecq (2015: 64)
>
> Men are still leading the US and, most of Europe and Africa... and Japan remained in a state of national anxiety for forty years over the prospect of a woman ascending to the Chrysanthemum Throne (until Princess Kiko, the wife of the second in line, gave birth in September 2006 to a boy, a potential successor to Emperor Akihito) ... and Muslims have readily entrusted their affairs to women. Indonesia, the largest Muslim nation, has had a woman leader. So has the second largest, Pakistan, and the third largest, Bangladesh. And the fourth largest, Turkey.
>
> *Being Muslim*
> by Haroon Siddiqui (2006: 97)

Issues in question: School adaptation and education consciousness among Muslim women in Britain

Chapters 9 and 10 focus on women and examine how they have integrated with British society as Muslims. In this chapter, we discuss education and career based on data gathered in the third- and fourth-round interviews with female informants in London.

As discussed, the integration of Muslims is one of Britain's most acute social and political issues. Its schools-based education system stands on the frontline of social integration and has thus been subjected to various policy interventions. In particular, Muslim women's integration into the education system has been a matter of public debate. For example, the headscarf/ veil controversies in the UK and other Western countries raised concerns that Islamic traditions that deny women's autonomy were causing conflict at schools which sought to nurture democratic values in students (Fetzer and Soper 2005; Bowen 2008; Joppke 2009; Adachi 2011b; 2011c). Critics viewed the scarf/veil as a symbol of patriarchal authority controlling women's bodies. Islamic extremist influence on women is also a serious problem. As mentioned in the Introduction, this issue has been debated especially since the media reported that three schoolgirls from Bethnal Green Academy in East London's Muslim community had travelled to Syria to join ISIL in February 2015. There is a widely shared perception that these British-born-and-educated girls failed to share their country's democratic values and were radicalised in the segregated space of their Muslim community.

Schools and other education settings are certainly spaces in which Western and Islamic values meet and conflict. At the same time, they are places where Muslim women learn and acquire an agency, or ability to manage their own lives and achieve their goals, while resisting social prejudices and community restrictions (Adachi 2012).[1]

As mentioned in Chapter 2, education levels among Britain's Muslim students have improved considerably in recent years. In England and Wales, the proportion of people with a degree or a higher qualification among white people reached 13 per cent in 1991, 19 per cent in 2001 and 26 per cent in 2011. The numbers have been rising also among people of Pakistani descent – 7 per cent, 18 per cent and 25 per cent – and among people of Bangladeshi descent – 5 per cent, 14 per cent and 20 per cent. The gaps between them and white people have narrowed. The data from the Higher Education Statistics Agency (HESA) show that Muslims' university enrolment ratio is higher than their population ratio.[2]

Chapter 9

The main driver of this rise in education attainment among Muslims has been women (Malik and Wykes 2018: 16). Among white British students in England, 59 per cent of girls and 52 per cent of boys passed a minimum of five GCSE subjects in 2009. Bangladeshi and Pakistani students recorded comparable figures at 58 per cent of girls and 50 per cent of boys in the former and 53 per cent of girls and 46 per cent of boys in the latter. Between 1994/5 and 2012/3, the number of full-time students studying first degrees increased by 56 per cent in white women (98,125 to 152,750), 284 per cent (1,527 to 5,865) in Pakistani women, and 467 per cent (388 to 2,235) in Bangladeshi women (Calculated from HESA's data). These increases were greater than those in men, and the number of female enrolments exceeded male enrolments for both ethnicities in 2012/3.

The improved educational circumstances are changing Muslim women's consciousness about labour force participation. As discussed in Chapter 2, the labour force participation rates are relatively low among Asian women aged twenty-five years or older, especially Muslim women, at 23 per cent for the Pakistani group and 17 per cent for the Bangladeshi group in 2001. These are the two lowest numbers among all ethnicities, in sharp contrast to 71 per cent in white British women and 62 per cent in Indian women. However, the expectation structure regarding the labour market for young women of Pakistani and Bangladeshi descent has changed in recent years (Dale et al. 2002). National census data from 2001 and 2011 show a rise in the labour force participation rate for the 16–24 age group as well as a large increase in the number of students among the non-participants, suggesting a greater career orientation among them (Gavron 2005).

Previous studies support these data. I mentioned in Chapter 3 that issues surrounding Muslim women's education in post-war Britain were dealt with in the 'Asian' frame as a minor subgenre in 'Black studies'. This led to the portrayal of Muslim women's education consciousness and experience under the 'cultural pathology model', arguing that Asian patriarchal cultures hindered female students' academic achievement. This cultural pathology model was critiqued in the 1980s, and their low achievements came to be explained by more structural factors (e.g., social strata, racism and discrimination, stereotyping by teachers and the timing of migration) (Choudhury 2002; Shain 2003).

The improved academic performance among Asian students, including Muslims, during the 2000s spurred interest in women's consciousness about 'post-16' (i.e., post-compulsory) education. There was much research on various factors impacting Asian school girls' decisions on further education and university choices. For example, Yasmin Hussain and Paul Bagguley, as

232

well as Kalwant Bhopal, examined Asian women's education consciousness and the means and resources they used for furthering their education and participating in tertiary education based on interviews (Hussain and Bagguley 2007; Bhopal 2010). These studies have found that despite their low social strata, many Asian families, including Muslims, are generally keen on their daughters' education and provide support for their further education. At the same time, there are reported cases in which cultural values and excessive expectations from their families negatively affect academic choices, and their families' (e.g., parents, husband and husband's family) lack of understanding makes it difficult for women to access education. It has become clear that Muslim women have been accessing higher education under these conditions by reconciling their own aspirations with family expectations through negotiating and compromising with their parents.

The statistics and preceding studies indicate that British Muslim women and their families have placed high value on education and participation in the education system despite some constraints. Nevertheless, past studies have failed to adequately consider Islam as a religion, which plays a crucial part in Muslim women's social and educational integration. Minority studies in Britain did not place much emphasis on a religious factor partly because the field's focus was historically on a 'racial frame' (Banton 1967; 1977; Blackstone et al. eds. 1998; Mason 2000). Similarly, the post-colonial gaze ingrained in British society left little room for portrayals of the positive relationship between Islam and the Western education system. If we fail to consider the rise of 'Islam' as the foundation for Muslim women's identities since the 1980s, especially in the post-9/11 context, however, we will not fully understand Muslim women's situation in today's Western society and education system, nor the 'agency' they exercise in these environments.

For this reason, this chapter will describe second-generation Muslim women's integration into the education system and their educational strategies, focusing on the relationship between their education consciousness and understanding of Islam. More specifically, I will analyse their thoughts about education and how family and faith influence their consciousness, based on interview data from East London's Bangladeshi community.

Education consciousness

First, I will describe the informants' comments about education. Preceding studies report that British Muslim women's interest in education has been growing in recent years (Hussain and Bagguley 2007; Bhopal 2010). The informants in my research similarly emphasised the importance of education.

Chapter 9

First, they value education in relation to careers and the labour market. They clearly characterise education as a way to gain skills and qualifications for entering the workforce. Parveen, a legal professional, expressed this attitude in a typical way:

> Just try and study as far as you can, really. Just because the more you study, the best chances you have of getting a job. Especially if you want to go into a particular career like law, accounting, or medicine, there's a set path that you have to take.
>
> (Parveen, Pakistani, 31, London)

Based on her own experience of pursuing legal studies and a career, Parveen stated that education and qualifications were essential for success in the job market and career advancement.

The importance of education and access to university, however, was not limited to those who aspired to highly specialised professions. Many informants shared a kind of siege mentality about gaining a 'degree' in order to enter the labour market. This was paradoxically highlighted by their expression that 'a degree has no value':

> These days degrees are helpful in the sense that you just tick off the box. For example, when you are applying for a job, 'Do you have a degree?' and 'Yes'. When you go to a job interview, you can't talk about your degree because everyone has a degree... Unless you have your Master's and PhD, you can't stand out from the crowd. I think just an undergrad degree doesn't really get you that far anymore.
>
> (Lola, Nigerian, 22, London)

Other informants made similar remarks. For example, 'I guess nowadays, a degree is not even to get a good job because it's just hard to get a job nowadays. Even if you'd graduate and get a degree, it's hard to get a job' (Asma, Asian mixed, 22, London). These comments reflect a belief that the popularisation of university education in Britain over the last two decades has caused 'degree inflation' leading to a drop in its relative value. Accordingly, the statement that 'a degree has no value' means, in fact, that 'a degree is essential'.

In their narratives, it is important to note that an academic qualification was roughly equivalent to a career path in the labour market. Some informants emphasised that women's access to better jobs supplemented male income and contributed to maintaining a household. 'These days, one

234

person earning money is not enough. You need both persons to even survive. So I think now having a job is kind of a necessity for women' (Yasmin, Bangladeshi, 22, London). This economic need is an issue widely shared among the informants. These Muslim women believed that a sole breadwinner could not support a household in London where globalisation and a neoliberal economy prevail and where rising land and house prices are social problems (BBC 2014a).

Nevertheless, the value of education for the informants cannot be reduced to a career or money alone. It had symbolic meaning involving a more fundamental part of their lives:

> For someone who's got a degree, it will become like gold. 'You've got a degree, wow!'. It's very important, I think, definitely for the future. It is definitely very important to have a degree backing you up.
>
> (Rehana, Bangladeshi, 26, London)

Rehana described education as 'gold', a resource allowing her to take control of her own life, signified by the phrase 'backing you up'. Zeheda (Bangladeshi, 25, London), who was working after completing postgraduate studies, also stated: 'Where you are going in life, but when you have got a degree and when you are educating yourself, that's a backup plan'. These remarks indicate that the informants perceived education as a resource for securing 'autonomy' in an unstable economic environment.

The idea of autonomy was clearly expressed in their narratives of 'breaking away from dependency':

> I agree education is crucial. If I simplify everything, just knowing how to read something enlightens you and empowers you so that you are less dependent on someone else. For me, education is about standing on my own two feet.
>
> (Rukshana, Bangladeshi, 25, London)

> I'd like to have my own financial independence after marriage, so I don't want to be dependent financially on my husband. If I want to buy anything, I have to get money from him.
>
> (Yasmin, Bangladeshi, 22, London)

Rukshana and Yasmin were single, working women of Bangladeshi descent. Rukshana declared that having knowledge through education would allow her to design her own life without being controlled by or dependent on others.

Chapter 9

Yasmin thought that financial independence achieved through education would ensure her freedom from her husband's control.

These comments suggest that they were conscious of gender roles in their Asian families. As discussed in Chapters 2 and 3, some Asian cultures treat women as the faces of their families and associate women's behaviours with family honour. From this perspective, women's bodies belong to their families and must be tightly controlled (Gilliat-Ray 2010). This thinking was particularly relevant to the marriage question discussed in Chapter 7:

> My dad and brother literally said to me, 'Get your GCSEs, and then we'll let you go to the college you want. Or you stay home, and then we'll get you married at 16'. So, I was like, 'Oh my God, my life gets over!' So I studied and I passed.
>
> (Tasrin, Bangladeshi, 31, London)

Tasrin's family confronted her with a choice between 'college' and 'marriage' when she was considering her post-16 education. Women seek access to education to reduce or postpone marriage pressure from their family and relatives (Bhopal 2010: 92–4).[3] However, the fact that there was a 'choice' between marriage and college indicates that her family were positive toward their daughters' education.

Marriage pressure was a much heavier burden on the generation who completed compulsory education before the expansion of higher education in the 2000s. For informants over the age of thirty, marriage loomed as a realistic choice at the end of compulsory education, and some of them chose to marry. However, this did not mean that there was no room for them to negotiate. For example, Shirina, who had a 'conservative family', spoke of the marriage proposed by her family:

> I'm the oldest child in my family. I was going to get married young, very young. I was surprised that I got married at 16… The only reason I got married to the person was that he agreed for me to finish college.
>
> (Shirina, Bangladeshi, 31, London)

Shirina accepted marriage at the young of 16 because her partner agreed she could go to college. She quit the college before completion, but after further negotiations with her husband and his family, she studied at university in her twenties and went on to develop a career as a community manager.

For the informants, education was a requirement for their labour force participation and career path, as well as a shield against marriage and other gender roles imposed by the family.

Family's involvement in education

The previous section revealed that the informants placed great value on education. What influences did their families have on their education consciousness and access to higher education? This section examines the family's involvement in the informants' decisions about further education (Hussain and Bagguley 2007).

Many informants described their decision about further education as 'personal'. They stressed that their decision was independent of parental influence:

> I didn't talk to my family about going to university. It was a very independent decision. My parents don't really relate to education because they're not from this country. I didn't think that they could help me in making that decision because I don't think they fully understand. They know the meaning of education, but I don't think they fully understand what options there are for people.
>
> (Asma, Asian mixed, 22, London)

> I mean, my parents really didn't have any influence on me. They don't really know what I do.
>
> (Nasira, Bangladeshi, 18, London)

> I wouldn't say there is anything that directly influenced my decision... It's simply because I have enjoyed it. There is no one that actually directly influenced me and said, 'You should do this, you should do that'. It's just something that I have always enjoyed. So, I decided to take it up and just study in further detail for my degree.
>
> (Yasmin, Bangladeshi, 22, London)

These informants claimed that their parents did not influence their academic choice. As seen in Chapter 4, many of the informants' parents grew up overseas and had no experience of university in Britain. They lacked an understanding of the British tertiary education system and did not know the options available to their children. This situation diminished parental influence over children's education choices. As a result, most informants made

Chapter 9

decisions about their academic path and future occupation with the help of their schools and the media.

This does not mean, though, that their parents were uninterested in their children's education or discouraged their learning. Most of the informants felt that their parents understood the value of education and encouraged their learning.[4] They just supported their children in an indirect manner:

> I think my parents helped mainly by introducing people who could help me. They teach maybe basic things. But when it becomes more complex, and they don't get it, they might ask someone else who might have the knowledge, like an older cousin of mine or an uncle or aunty, anyone who has the knowledge.
>
> (Lola, Nigerian, 22, London)

> There was a private tutor, where my parents couldn't help me with certain bits of homework. Obviously, primary school was easy. They were able to do that. But as I got older and started to do my GCSE, it got more advanced level. They didn't really know. So they got tutors for me to cover that gap.
>
> (Yasmin, Bangladeshi, 22, London)

Many of the informants' parents had low education and English literacy and could not directly help their children with schoolwork once they advanced to the intermediate level. Instead, they tried to help their children's education through their community or personal networks, including asking relatives or neighbours, hiring private tutors and utilising supplementary schools. This indicates that the Asian community has the 'middle-class values' to hope for higher academic achievements for their children even though the community remains in a lower social stratum (Hussain and Bagguley 2007: 71).[5]

For informants who attended compulsory education in the 1990s, these supplementary education resources or infrastructure were not readily accessible:[6]

> My parents were very keen and supported us in every way. I was the first one in my family to go through the education system, so I didn't really have anyone to ask or get help with my studies in terms of academics, and no one could help me with my homework. I couldn't do work at

Women and Education

home and get support from extended families. So I did that just through friends and group work and my own independent work and study.

(Syeda, Bangladeshi, 40, London)

We have parents who are keen and supportive, but actually, they couldn't help us with our homework. They didn't know the system well enough to help whether to get tutors or whether there was some supplementary support out there... We found a supplementary school, and we found it through friends. It was not because our parents told us about it.

(Jakera, Bangladeshi, 40, London)

Forty-year-old professionals, Syeda and Jakera, reported that their parents wanted to give them education but could not offer any direct support. They found and accessed educational resources through their friends and other personal networks.

Many of the informants' parents were unable to give their children direct or specific support. Yet, the informants understood their parents' hardships and efforts and maintained their enthusiasm for study. This attitude stems from the 'aspirational culture' found among minority groups (Hutchings and Archer 2001: 88). Syeda, quoted above, said that her father was highly capable and enjoyed learning in his youth. Being the only son, however, he dropped out of college to support his family and migrated to the UK in the 1960s. He had to work as a manual labourer under harsh conditions due to a lack of qualifications and appropriate training. Knowing her father's experience, Syeda felt that 'the parents simply wanted their children to have something better' and aspired to go to university when the attendance rate among women was still low.

Asma, a 'second-generation' immigrant, made a similar comment:

Because my parents themselves didn't have any good educational life, they ended up not having a very good life. It was because they had to work very hard in their life to provide for the family. So they didn't want the same life for me. They wanted me to become something when I came out. I have an education, and I want to have something for myself.

(Asma, Asian mixed, 22, London)

Most of the informants' parents were first- or 'second-generation' immigrants with low educational qualifications and social strata. Many informants referred to their parents' hardships and the tough lives they had witnessed first-hand.

239

Chapter 9

Of course, not all parents were keen on their children's education. One informant (Nazma, Bangladeshi, 36, London) reported getting 'mixed messages' from her parents who had different opinions. Nazma, who 'grew up in a very conservative family', said her father pushed her to have a professional career, such as a doctor, but her mother wanted her to stay at home to help with the household. In many cases, the mother was reluctant to let her daughters go and opposed their leaving home to go to university. Nasira (Bangladeshi, 18, London) said, 'my dad was very easy to let me go to London, but my mom was not. She found it extremely hard'. In other families, the opposite was the case. Nafisah (Asian mixed, 22, London) reported that her late mother wanted to send her to university, but her father required her to get a job after finishing secondary education as he did not find university education important. Spurred by her late mother's wishes and expectations, Nafisah fought her father and won his approval to study at university. It is noteworthy that, although some parents had different opinions from those stated above, none of the informants had both parents strongly opposing their further education. The informants' families were generally supportive of their access to further education, so many informants could decide to go to university.

Islam, career and marriage

I have so far described the female informants' education consciousness and their families' influences on it. What was their perception of the relationship between Islam and education or career? This question is significant for discussing Muslim women's social integration. While many Muslims today recognise Islam as the most important element of their identities, there are concerns that this hinders their integration into Western society (Adachi 2013b). It is argued that Islam's patriarchal norms, symbolised by the headscarf and the veil, force women to be segregated from the public sphere.

The informants have constructed various counterarguments to the mainstream discourse of 'a religion preventing women's autonomy'. For example, one informant made the following comment about her Bangladeshi community's reluctance to support women entering the workforce:

> A lot of women in our community have been told that 'You should study, but then you should get married, and that's it. You do not need

to work anymore'. But my faith teaches me that women should push themselves and they should develop their own skills and talents.

(Banan, Bangladeshi, 24, London)

Banan noted that her ethnic community tended to confine women to domestic roles and did not expect women to go out to work. She stressed, in contrast, that Islam positively valued women participating and exercising their talents and skills in society.

Although data from the Coventry cohort are not included in this analysis, I quote Tabassum's and Saba's remarks about Islam's significance:

> Tabassum (Indian, 26, Coventry): I don't think Islam has prevented us from doing anything that we want to do.
>
> Saba (Pakistani, 25, Coventry): I think Islam lets us pursue our purpose rather than stopping us from doing anything.
>
> Tabassum: Islam has actually helped us. Because at the time when something doesn't turn out as you expect it or if it goes horribly wrong, then we have our religion and fall back on our religion… So, Islam helps us to get over quite a lot of things. It helps you to cope.

Tabassum and Saba presented Islam as 'helping' them to achieve what they wanted rather than 'restricting' women's freedom and autonomy (Hussain and Bagguley 2007: 142). As opposed to the prevailing social discourse of 'women's oppression' in the media, these women defined Islam as a positive religion that expanded women's autonomy and possibility.

They used a wide range of anecdotal evidence to present Islam as 'a religion promoting women's autonomy'. The most frequently mentioned topic was marriage. I discussed in Chapter 3 that women represented family honour, and their actions had significant implications for their families in the Asian community. A daughter's marriage at an appropriate age is a matter of concern for the whole family. Most informants up to the age of around thirty-five married or preferred to marry just after graduating from university. Many of them married or hoped to marry by their mid-twenties, or thirty at the latest. Poppy, though, a career woman of Bangladeshi descent in her late twenties, spoke of marriage pressure as follows:

Culture and religion are completely different. The culture expects you to get married a long time ago. Now I am 28. The culture just looks upon me and thinks, 'Oh my god, this girl is old!' That's what culture says. My culture, so my community, the Bangladeshi community, says, 'You are old, so no one wants you because you are this age. Why are you not married?' And people start commenting, your family starts worrying… Islam doesn't say, 'Oh no, she is 28. God, let's just kill her because she is not married'. Islam doesn't say that. Islam doesn't look at it as a negative, you know, because that happens, doesn't it? But it's the culture that makes you think I should be married.

(Poppy, Bangladeshi, 28, London)

Differentiating between culture and religion, as discussed in Chapter 7, again plays an important part here. Some roles and expectations imposed on women are cultural and do not come from Islam; thus, they are not things that women have to follow (Hoque 2015: 142–3).

Similarly, Toslima spoke of her experience of being told by some family members that university education was meaningless for women as they were raising children in the future:

When I was thinking about going to university, some of my family members said: 'Oh, it'll be a waste of money', 'When you're older, you're going to be looking after your kids. So what's the point of having a degree?' … Generally, Muslim families, I would say, do not have that women shouldn't have education now. Maybe years ago, my parent's generation may have had a different view. But we have a different perception because we grew up here, and we want to be part of the society.

(Toslima, Bangladeshi, 18, London)

Like Poppy, Toslima rejected the idea that women did not need education and attributed it to the older generation and the family's cultures. She stated that Islam did not conflict with 'the society', that is, the way of life in Britain.

The informants referred to the Islamic tradition of knowledge (*ilm*) discussed in Chapter 8, in negotiating their education and career:

Our Prophet said, 'Go to as far as China to study'… If a girl wants to go to university and study, let her go because our Prophet said, 'Go and study', because it's said, 'Everyday increase your knowledge'.

(Habibah, Asian mixed, 20, Coventry)

Habibah invoked the well-known 'China' *hadith* (The Prophet's saying) to emphasise that women have a religious duty to acquire knowledge.[7] She used it to justify women's access to higher education and the labour market.

Banan also referred to the knowledge tradition in her effort to deal with marriage pressure:

> My parents have been quite open-minded about marriage. My sister did not get married till she was 25, and that was three years after she graduated. She still teaches now. My parents would be very keen for me to settle down before I am 30. But I think the pressure does start mounting when you go past the age of 25, or you are starting to reach your 30s. And I guess that is something that is not in our control. But my faith teaches me that it is more important for you to develop yourself spiritually than to just rush into marriage for the sake of it. So I think I am learning a lot about that as well.
>
> (Banan, Bangladeshi, 24, London)

Banan felt that marriage was 'not in control' because of pressure from her community and relatives. She was trying to resist the pressure by referring to Islam. When she rejected 'marriage for the sake of it', she meant marriage based on cultural norms. She asserted that it was more important for her to acquire diverse knowledge and experience through education and social participation and develop herself spiritually as Islam teaches than to conform to cultural norms.

In some cases, knowledge of Islam was utilised in family negotiations after marriage. Middle school teacher Tasrin lived with her husband's family, took on much housework and cared for his parents and family. She was unhappy about her position in the household and wanted to move out. She used religious knowledge to that end:

> I love my husband. I want to be with him. Therefore, I have to be with his family. But I don't like his sisters. I don't like his extended family. But I get on with them because I want to be with my husband... Over the last 6 years, especially since my son's birth, I've now thought, 'Well, what does Islam say about looking after in-laws?' There is nothing in Islam that tells you to look after your parents-in-law. I do not have to do anything for my husband's parents. There is nowhere in Islam that says like that, whereas Islam says that the root of getting to heaven lies under my mother's feet and what I do for my parents.
>
> (Tasrin, Bangladeshi, 31, London)

Chapter 9

Tasrin tried to resist her in-laws' demands by arguing that Islam invokes an obligation to look after one's parents but nothing about an obligation to one's in-laws. Again, Islam was invoked to secure women's autonomy. Some of the career women among the informants had adopted this approach to resisting obligations to their husband's families.

Notably, many of the informants understood and presented Islam as a 'system of egalitarianism':

> To be honest, times have changed so much. A lot of families don't mind the girl going out working. I mean, it was so different before. You have to be in such a strict family, and I don't even think it's Islamic strictness. I think it's the family who just does not understand that women can go out and work. As I explained to you before, I look back at *Rasulullah*'s time, and so many women were working and making money.
>
> (Poppy, Bangladeshi, 28, London)

By differentiating between culture and religion, Poppy could present Islam as a religion embodying gender equality and women's liberation. However, this did not mean simply denying ethnic culture and pandering to Western values. Rather, she and other women emphasised Islam's superiority over Western society by attributing the origin of egalitarianism to Islamic history – i.e., to 'the time of *Rasulullah*' (the Messenger of Allah) (Parker-Jenkins and Haw 1996; Bhimji 2009).

For example, Parveen commented:

> I mean, women had rights in Islam 1,400 years ago. If you look in British history, women only got the right to vote; I think it was 1930 or so.[8] You just need to see where things have gone. We have maintained that 1,400 years ago and 1930, there's a very, very big difference.
>
> (Parveen, Pakistani, 31, London)

She emphasised Islam's progressiveness with the claim that Islam recognised gender equality from the start, whereas Britain did not introduce women's suffrage until the first half of the twentieth century. This narrative of Islam's superiority over Western society on gender equality was common among the self-presentation strategies adopted by the informants. As discussed in Chapter 7, it gave them room to negotiate their community's traditional gender norms in order to pursue education and careers. They also used it to rebut mainstream representations of Islam and Muslim women and to promote their positive identification with Islam (Adachi 2016).

Women and Education

They also positively linked the knowledge tradition to their careers. As discussed in Chapter 8, knowledge in Islam encompasses not only religious knowledge in the narrow sense but also much broader knowledge about the world, treating social engagement and contribution as important duties:

> If people get bigger and more independent, obviously no one can just stay at home cooking and cleaning all day. That'll drive me nuts. I want to take up classes, work part-time, do something, pursue some of my hobbies, and things like that. I would like to do things like that. Even in Islam, it never says that women should sit at home and cook and clean. It says that women should go out and seek knowledge, be busy, and be occupied in beneficial things that will benefit you. You should always try to seek knowledge.
>
> (Yasmin, Bangladeshi, 22, London)

> Yes. I would say one of the reasons why I decided to study is because Islam says seeking knowledge is obligatory for every Muslim. And a lot of people choose to study subjects that might just lead to a certain career. But I wanted to study a subject that was to give me a broader understanding of society and then use that perhaps to enter a career that would make a difference. So, I feel I get the best of both worlds. If I get the chance to educate myself, that will be a lifelong experience. Islam doesn't stop it.
>
> (Banan, Bangladeshi, 24, London)

Yasmin, working for a charity organisation, insisted that Islam required women to develop their ambitions, skills and careers and participate in and contribute to broader society, referring to the tradition of seeking knowledge. Banan, also employed at a charity organisation, referred to the Islamic knowledge tradition to explain that she chose to study a 'speciality' that would satisfy her religious interests and benefit her career. She also stated that knowledge acquisition includes various experiences through lifelong education and work and therefore pursuing a career conformed with rather than contravened Islam.

Other informants justified their education and career orientations by citing socially active women in the Muslim community:

Chapter 9

> Halimah (Pakistani, 19, London): Knowledge is very important definitely, even especially for girls. If you look through Islamic traditions in terms of education, females were prominent figures in education.
>
> Harir (Pakistani, 27, London): And business!
>
> Halimah: Yes, trade and stuff like that. So there are definitely role models within our religion to inspire us.
>
> Harir: Yes, that is cultural barriers more than religious when it comes to education. Definitely.

Halimah and Herir pointed to 'prominent' female Muslim leaders to counter the common perception that women in the Muslim community were oppressed and could not succeed in the public sphere. They attributed the fact that women in some Muslim families were not allowed to access education to ethnic cultures rather than religion.

The informants often mentioned Khadija and Aisha as role models. Khadija was the Prophet Muhammad's first spouse. The fact that she was his employer and older than him is important. This is why many female informants mentioned her as an embodiment of the 'autonomous' Muslim woman:

> Parveen (Pakistani, 31, London): When Khadija got married, she was 40.
>
> Nasira (Bangladeshi, 18, London): Yeah, so there is nothing wrong with Islam. It's not about age, but culturally it is bad.
>
> Parveen: She was also a widow. She was married before… She was actually a very successful businesswoman, which a lot of men forget… She gave Mohammed – peace be upon him – a job and subsequently proposed to him. It was totally accepted then.

> She was richer than he was. She said to him, 'Would you like to marry me?' He didn't go and say that to her. Her husband essentially worked for her. She was able to do that; such a strong figure. I think that's something that drives me as well. She was able to do that. Why can't I?
>
> (Rehana, Bangladeshi, 26, London)

Khadija is known as the woman who pursued her business and career to make money as well as became the Prophet's first follower, and thus led his family and community as the 'first Muslim'. She was a prominent 'businesswoman' who employed Muhammad and an independent woman who proposed to Muhammad (Haylamaz 2007). The informants invoked Khadija to justify their pursuit of careers and to refute the image of Muslim women as being submissive to their husbands and tethered to the family.

Aisha was the youngest of Muhammad's wives. She came to be called the 'repository of Islamic knowledge' and used her abundant knowledge in striving to promote Islam after Muhammad's passing (Khan 2016: 341). In fact, Aisha was the 'first female scholar' (Rukshana, Bangladeshi, 25, London) in the Islamic community, who reportedly recorded 2,210 *sunnahs* (the Prophet's actions). Primary school teacher Rehana referred to Aisha in the following comment:

> People find it a bit of a taboo that men go to learn from women. They find it very difficult. Especially in business, you find it very difficult. Is it right for a woman to be in charge? They find it very difficult, but Islam, from the early stages, has proved that that is something normal. It's allowed. It's permissible. Women, yeah, they can go and do that. People used to go to Aisha – peace be upon her – and ask her about religion.
>
> (Rehana, Bangladeshi, 26, London)

Rehana stressed that women such as Aisha were leaders in the early Islamic community although today men tend to see deference to women as a 'taboo'. By arguing that Islam allows women's social participation, Rehana pointed out the importance of acquiring knowledge and social participation for both herself and other contemporary Muslim women.[9]

Another function of education

Why is the labour participation rate of Muslim women low despite their high educational aspirations and enthusiasm for active social participation? Why is Muslim women's level of economic activity lower than other women despite their knowledge tradition?

While various factors such as parents' low education, economic deprivation, structural discrimination and Islamophobia are very likely responsible for this, Islamic knowledge also appears to be part of it:

> I don't agree with the idea Islam prevents women from education. I think, in general, as Muslim families, we want our daughters to be educated because our daughters are going to be the future mothers of children. In Islam, it is very encouraged that girls and women are educated because when young children are brought up, you know, they

Chapter 9

will be taught by their mom. The mother plays such a crucial role if the girls are educated. That is education for the future of Muslims when women are educated. It is very encouraged in Islam.

(Nazma, Bangladeshi, 36, London)

Nazma countered the argument that Islam did not value women's education, arguing that Muslim women needed education to play the central role in educating children, that is, reproducing Muslims.

Many informants expressed a desire to participate in the labour force and choose a career over marriage at some stage in their lives. Nevertheless, they recognised marriage and child-rearing as important women's roles:

Women should educate their children on what's right and wrong and about the world. So they need to be educated. Because the mother will be around the kids the most in normal regular life while the father goes out to work. So, the mother should be educated to teach the children.

(Harir, Pakistani, 27, London)

Khadija and Mohammad made sure that their daughters had a level of education, and they encouraged girls just as much as boys to be educated. If you do educate a woman, you are actually educating the family because the women bear the children and they bring the children up, so to speak. They spend more time with their children, so it's really critical that women are educated and they feel a sense of accomplishment and feel confident growing up. I would say it's really naive attitude that woman shouldn't be educated, and it's completely against what Islam says, anyway. And most Muslim families that I know are actively encouraging that.

(Jakera, Bangladeshi, 40, London)

Harir claimed that women had a profound effect on their children due to a special connection between them. She stated that the role of passing on knowledge to children largely fell on women; therefore it was important for mothers to have an education. Similarly, Jakera declared that education was vital for Muslim women to be able to perform their role of educating children (Hussain and Bagguley 2007: 73). This expectation surrounding complementary gender roles in Islam was one reason for strong support for girl's education. However, this may also be one of the factors diminishing women's employment opportunities, motivating women to leave work and accept mother roles in the family.[10]

248

Thus, education was regarded as a means to expand women's autonomy and liberation from subordination at a certain life stage while performing a gender role (e.g. child raising) at another life stage. In either case, women's education was justified from an Islamic perspective and served to promote their participation in the British education system.

Conclusion

My analysis of British Muslim women's education consciousness in this chapter found the following points. First, many informants recognised great value in education and had strong aspirations for higher education. Education was valued for providing access to the labour market, independence from the family and children's education, all of which motivated them to pursue educational qualifications. Second, the informants had such educational aspirations despite their parents' low academic qualifications or social strata. Many of their parents had difficulty directly supporting the informants' academic aspirations because of their immigrant backgrounds. Nevertheless, these parents were generally encouraging of their children's education and provided moral or indirect support. Third, support from parents, relatives and community was not readily available to those who received compulsory education before the 2000s. Those informants had to find resources through their own efforts and limited information networks to participate in the education system. Fourth, education resources were more readily accessible for the younger informants and it gave them an upper hand in negotiating their future with their families. Fifth, the informants used Islam to justify women's education. They defined Islam as liberal and egalitarian by attributing oppressive gender norms to culture. They also found grounds in Islam to reject traditional gender norms about marriage (or married life) and to justify their access to education and the labour market. Sixth, they associated the importance of women's education with 'child raising'. They perceived that child raising was important for transmitting knowledge to their children and reproducing the Muslim community and that women were centrally responsible for it. This attitude may partly explain the continuing low employment rate among Muslim women despite their rising academic achievements. These findings indicate that Muslim women support Islam's complementary gender relationship principle of 'different but equal' even when they are more highly-educated (Al-Ati 1977: 59; Khan 2008: 6–12).

These informants' attitudes reflect the influence of Islamic feminism, which has been developing in recent years (Stowasser 1994; Wadud 1999; Barlas 2002; Jeenah 2006). Islamic feminism aims to take the interpretation

Chapter 9

of religious texts back from male scholars – that is, they seek Islamic interpretations by women for women. This is precisely the practice of *ijtihad* discussed in Chapter 8. Islamic feminists emphasise *ijtihad* for the following reason:

> Doors of *ijtihad* (independent reasoning) are to be open in order to facilitate to them producing an Islamic knowledge that revives and emphasises gender justice, equality, and partnership – a knowledge alternative to the processes of exclusion and sense of male superiority we find in most traditional discourses.[11] Despite the scholarly efficiency of the classical *'ulama* (male religious scholars) and their efforts in adhering to the *shari'ah* (God's revealed Way) in deducing laws and rulings, they were products of their own eras and cultures, naturally not aware of or interested in establishing equal status for men and women. (Abou-Bakr 2013: 4)

The understanding that Islamic interpretations are always influenced by 'eras and cultures' is important here. Islamic feminism aims to utilise Islam for realising women's rights and gender equality by returning the right to interpretation to women from under the control of traditions and men (Wadud 1999; Abou-Bakr ed. 2013; Basarudin 2016). It promotes an understanding of Islam that is adaptable to the contemporary social context by criticising textual interpretations premised on outdated patriarchal cultural traditions and providing a more humanistic interpretation of the Quran (Basarudin 2016). After learning about this new perspective, many second-generation Muslim women have been attributing community practices that inhibit women's social participation to 'culture' and highlighting the absence of religious foundations for such practices, as discussed in Chapter 7 (Parekh 2008: 111).

Consequently, the Islamic tradition of knowledge has enjoyed renewed attention, generating strong interest among women. For example, the East London Mosque (ELM) established the Maryam Centre complex for Muslim women in 2013 with women's prayer facilities, a library (shared with the ELM) and a ladies gym. It has provided a wide range of services for women, including prayer, religious advice, education for girls, fitness, and counseling. In Coventry, by contrast, spaces for women to use and pray regularly were limited, although there were many mosques in the city. Nonetheless, the informants studied Islam through university and private groups or on the Internet to deepen their knowledge on subjects relevant to their own lives, as reported in Chapter 8. The efforts of interpretation based on religious

250

knowledge (i.e., *ijtihad*) has played a significant role in securing women's rights and social participation (Hoque 2015: 20).

These findings contradict the prevalent discourse that Muslim women have failed to integrate into Western liberal space. Islamic feminist Fatima Mernissi makes the following argument about Islamic knowledge and women's rights:

> We Muslim women can walk into the modern world with pride, knowing that the quest for dignity, democracy, and human rights, for full participation in the political and social affairs of our country, stems from no imported Western values, but is a true part of the Muslim tradition. (Mernissi 1991: viii)

She states that for Muslim women to be treated equally and participate actively as legitimate members of society, they should refer to the Islamic tradition rather than relying on Western social values. To realise gender equality, it is vital for Muslim women to study the Quran and other Islamic texts directly.

Education, be it religious or public, is a key resource for making such discoveries possible. By acquiring broader knowledge, women endeavour to contribute to society both as Muslims and members of civic society and to lead their lives meaningfully. This image of a second-generation Muslim woman can be described as an 'agent' participating in society and community through deep commitment to her religious duties (Adachi 2022).

Chapter 9

Notes

1 'Agency' here refers to 'one's will and ability to develop a flexible identity in response to various issues in a complex environment by adapting and drawing on different sources of identity depending on the situation while recognising that one's identity is embedded in multiple cultural communities' (Adachi 2012: 281). For a more detailed discussion on the relations between Muslim women and agency, see Sehlikoglu (2018) and Adachi (2022).

2 This does not mean that the 'ethnic penalties' Muslim students face have been re-solved. In trying to enter university, students of Pakistani and Bangladeshi descent suffer various disadvantages compared to white students. For example, while the impact of ethnicity on academic grades is largely explained by social hierarchy, it explains the considerable difficulties experienced by Pakistani and Bangladeshi groups, a large proportion of whom are in lower social strata (Rothon 2006). There is evidence that in addition to social strata, institutional discrimination in schools and further education reproduce the minority's disadvantages (Noden et al. 2014). As mentioned in Chapter 2, there is a tendency for minority students to enrol in newer education institutions because they are discriminated against by more prestigious universities such as Oxbridge (Modood and Berthoud eds. 1997; Malik and Wykes 2018: 16).

3 In fact, parent-arranged marriages feature prominently in groups with low education qualifications (Modood and Berthoud eds. 1997). One informant in a study on young women of Pakistani descent in the UK stated that 'if they [girls] screw up [getting into uni], they will not get a chance to do it again' (Dwyer and Shah 2009: 62). The pressure from their community and family increases their motivation to get higher education.

4 Previous studies have found that Britain's Muslim families highly value education qualifications (Dale et al. 2002; Tyrer and Ahmad 2006). While the informants in my research found the importance of general education in Islam, they attributed their parents' expectations for their children's educational achievements and qualifications (e.g., doctors and lawyers) to 'Asian' cultures.

5 Asian children, including Muslims, have achieved good results despite their low social strata. For example, the difference in the ratios of five or more GCSE passes between the students receiving the Free School Meals benefit and the students not receiving it was over 30 points in both the white female and male cohorts in 2006. In other words, white students from low-income families were markedly disadvantaged compared with other white students. In contrast, the difference was 8.1 points in girls and 11.1 points in boys among Pakistanis and only 4.7 points in girls and 4.6 points in boys among Bangladeshis. These values are the lowest among the major ethnic groups (DfES 2007: 66). The data demonstrate that Muslim families, even in lower social strata, have the 'middle-class values' of high educational expectations for their children and are willing to support them.

6 Besides the growth of supplementary schools/classes, the presence of aspiring parents who 'not only understand the system but are shaping it' has contributed to improving academic performance in recent years for Muslim girls and boys

Women and Education

(Economist 2013). Many of the young Muslims' parents were born or educated in the UK and are familiar with its system. They understand the importance and means of improving their children's ability and performance and are able to create an environment for that purpose. This situation has benefitted the younger generation.

7   The said *hadith* is: 'Seek knowledge even as far as China' (Multaqa Ahl al-Hadeeth). 'Knowledge' here is generally understood as referring to 'scientific knowledge' as China was an advanced civilisation in the seventh century. This suggests that Islam encourages Muslims to go to many places in pursuit of broader knowledge (Khan 2016: 341). While the authenticity of this *hadith* is disputed, Muslims I met often quoted it to explain the importance of seeking knowledge in Islam.

8   Universal suffrage with equal voting rights for women and men in the UK was legislated in 1928. The following year, the general election was the first in which women voted (Clarke 1996: 143).

9   There are conflicting views on Khadija and Aisha. According to Leila Ahmed, widely known for her study of Arab Muslim women's history, the ideal image of an 'independent woman' attributed to Khadija reflects the age of ignorance (*jahiliyyah*), i.e., the pre-Islamic Arab culture. Ahmed also describes Aisha, who married Muhammad at the age of nine, as a figure foreshadowing the fate of women under Islam. Her temporary ascendancy to political leadership was also influenced by the pre-Islamic Arab culture (Ahmed 1992: 42–3). Ahmed interprets the Quranic descriptions of Muhammad's wives as 'the steps by which Islam closed women's arenas of action' (Ahmed 1992: 53). The issue here, however, is not whether these points are historically true or not, but rather the fact that the informants (selectively) refer to Khadija and Aisha as evidence of Islam's respect for women's rights.

10   According to a study on Pakistani Muslim women in Britain, having children was the primary factor inhibiting their participation in the labour force (Dale et al. 2002: 22).

11   The 'doors of *ijtihad*' refers to the practice of interpretation in Islamic law. That it is 'closed' means that the practice is either no longer required or forbidden (Izutsu 1991: 162–3). This idea emerged in the ninth or tenth century and is still widely supported by scholars (Hallaq 1984). However, the term is primarily used to indicate the finalisation of various schools' theological principles, and *ijtihad* is still practised in different ways depending on various real-life situations and social changes (Nihon Isuramu Kyokai et al. eds. 2002: 91; Lamrabet 2016: 164).

Chapter

10 The Hijab

We cover our hair, not our brains.

Printed on the T-shirts of a Muslim women's' college organisation
(Haddad et al. 2006: 10)

Assume man to be man and his relationship to the world to be a human one: then you can exchange love only for love, trust for trust, etc. If you want to enjoy art, you must be an artistically cultivated person; if you want to exercise influence over other people, you must be a person with a stimulating and encouraging effect on other people. Every one of your relations to man and to nature must be a specific expression, corresponding to the object of your will, of your real individual life. If you love without evoking love in return – that is, if your loving as loving does not produce reciprocal love; if through a living expression of yourself as a loving person you do not make yourself a loved person, then your love is impotent – a misfortune.

The Economic and Philosophic Manuscripts of 1844
by Karl Marx (1964: 169)

Issues in question: Hijab

One of the most urgent challenges for globalised societies today is the integration of their increasingly multicultural and multi-ethnic members. The central question here is how host societies respond and accept growing ethnic minorities produced by influxes of migrants and refugees combined with escalating religious and cultural demands. The 'headscarf/veil debate' that has been brewing in the West since the late 1980s is the very embodiment of that challenge. The debate generally involves arguments for and against Muslim girls wearing headscarves or veils in public schools. The debate focuses on the question of whether the headscarf or veil of Muslim women infringes on the European secularisation principle of religious neutrality in public arenas or not, i.e., the conflict between the headscarf as a religious symbol and the doctrine of the separation of state and church (Naito 2007; Bowen 2008; Joppke 2009).

The headscarf serves as a touchstone for social integration because it is widely recognised as a religious 'symbol'. Clothing is one of the most visible markers of identity traits and attributes. Religions have valued and maintained such markers because they – e.g., crucifix, kippah, turban and sword – not only signify the wearer's affiliation with a religion, a sect or a community clearly to others but also heighten the wearer's awareness of their own identity. Islam is no exception. Its religious markers include the beard, loose-fitting clothes and hijabs (some form of head covering, sometimes combined with a long, loose-fitting robe) (Moriyama 2014: 3). The hijab in particular serves the symbolic function of signalling to (i.e., identifying) both the wearer and others that she is Muslim.

The word 'hijab' means 'something that conceals or separates a person or a thing from others' eyes', or more specifically a 'curtain', 'partition' and 'screen', which derives from the Arabic word *hajaba* which means 'to hide', 'to cover' and 'to separate' (Sardar 2011: 329; Goto 2014: 61; Moriyama 2014: 4–5). In the Quran, the hijab does not always refer to a head or face covering as it is commonly understood today. The term appears eight times in the Quran and is used in different contexts.[1] For example, hijab means the 'separation' between 'the inmates of Paradise' and 'the denizens of Hell' in one context while referring to 'something' which excludes sinful transgressors from God's mercy on the Day of Judgment in another context (Sardar 2011: 329–30).

The use of hijab in relation to women is found in only two verses: when Maryam (Maria) secluded herself from her family (19:17) and God's command to speak to the Prophet's wives 'from behind a screen' (33:53).[2]

Chapter 10

The latter is the textual basis for the spatial demarcation of women and men in Islam. While the word 'hijab' is not used, Verse 24:31 tells women to hide their private parts from any man outside a specified group of men:

> And tell believing women that they should lower their eyes, guard their private parts, and not display their charms beyond what [it is acceptable] to reveal; they should draw their coverings over necklines and not reveal their charms except to their husbands, their fathers, their sons, their husbands' sons, their brothers, their brothers' sons, their sisters' sons, their womenfolk, their slaves, such men as attend them who have no desire, no children who are not yet aware of women's nakedness... (24:31; words in square brackets are original)

Although scholars have different opinions over what exactly 'charms' refers to – ranging from 'adornments' to 'attractive parts of a woman' – there is an agreement that charms are 'what appears on the outside'. It is widely understood that the body parts that women are permitted to others include their 'clothes' and 'face and hands' (Goto 2014: 74–7; Nakata ed. 2014: 1315–6).[3]

Thus, the word hijab is ambiguously defined in Islam, giving rise to a wide variety of head and body coverings linked to diverse indigenous and ethnic cultures. For example, it is generally used to mean a headscarf covering the head and the neck. By comparison, a 'niqab' is commonly translated as a veil, which covers the head and face except for the eyes. An 'abaya' is a long robe covering the body from the neck down, commonly found in the Middle East. A 'burqa' conceals the entire body, including the face and the eyes. A 'chador' is a long cloak covering from head to toes often found in Iraq and other countries. In South Asia, where many of the informants' families originated, women commonly wear a 'shalwar kameez' and a 'dupatta', with some covering their hair completely while others allow their fringe to show. In Malaysia, a combination of a colourful long dress and a scarf called 'baju kurung' is customarily worn (Contractor 2012: 83–4; Fashionhance 2018). In this chapter, I refer to all of these head-covering garments collectively as 'hijab'.

The hijab arises in Muslim-related discourses because of its 'visibility' and the 'otherness' it signals. In Western societies, the headscarf and veil are recognised to function as identity markers separating 'them' (Muslims living in religious space) from 'us' (the West living in secular space) and serve as a 'partition' literally separating 'their' identity from 'ours'. Destroying this boundary by unveiling supposedly uncivilised Muslim women has long been

256

an important objective for the moral crusaders of the Christian world (Abu-Lughod 2013: 201).

Rema Hammami calls the worldwide Muslim women's movement to wear a hijab 'hijabisation' (Hammami 1990). The hijab spread as a sign of Islamist resistance to the secular and authoritarian post-colonial regimes in Iran and elsewhere since the 1970s. The hijab had been regarded under colonial rules as evidence of women's subordination and backwardness. However, the Islamist movements redefined it as a symbol of 'liberation from oppression', 'political agency' and 'autonomy' through the late twentieth century.

Muslim women's headscarves/veils continue to be a fraught subject in the Western public space. In France, wearing headscarves in schools has been on the public agenda since the 1980s and was legally banned in 2004 following three major debates (Hayashi 2001; Thomas 2006; Bowen 2008; Joppke 2009; Adachi 2011a; 2011b; 2013b: 303–23). Some German states have prohibited schoolteachers from wearing headscarves, while exempting Christian emblems (Hori 2008). France legally banned face-covering veils such as 'burqa' and 'niqab' in all public places in 2011. The veil ban was also introduced in parts or all of Belgium, Bulgaria, Switzerland, the Netherlands and Italy, followed by some German states (Tan 2018; BBC 2018).

In Britain, with its localism and non-secular tradition of modern state formation, Muslim women's headscarves did not become a serious issue. Although wearing a veil has been a topic of heated public discussions, it has not been legally ban (Adachi 2011a; 2011b).[4] During the 2000s, teachers and students wearing a jilbab and a niqab led to social and political controversies. For instance, a teaching assistant began wearing a niqab at Headfield Church of England Junior School in Dewsbury in 2006, and the school eventually suspended her. This incident became a touchstone in the post-7/7 political debates on social integration. Then Prime Minister Tony Blair invoked the case when arguing about the failure of integrating the Muslim community into British society. On the question of whether veil-wearing women could contribute to society, he answered, 'That's a very difficult question'; then explained that 'It is a mark of separation and that is why it makes other people from outside the community feel uncomfortable'. Blair went on to express his full support for the authority's handling of the case (BBC 2006).

Then Minister for Parliamentary Affairs Jack Straw presented a similar argument in a *Lancashire Evening Telegraph* column in 2006. He described feeling uncomfortable talking 'face-to-face' with veil-wearing women he met in his constituency and declared that he would ask them to remove their veils next time. He continued that the veil separated the British and Muslim

Chapter 10

communities and was 'a visible statement of separation and of difference' (Straw 2006). While this article sparked a major debate and drew much criticism, many mainstream politicians expressed support for his position. They thought that women's veils made non-Muslim citizens feel uneasy and could provoke anti-Islamist views, as Muslims were seen to prioritise their own religious identity and duties over British values and way of life (Finney and Simpson 2009: 164–6; Uberoi et al. 2011: 217–18).

In this context, how did the informants understand the hijab? What connections did they make between wearing a hijab or not and an individual's identity or participation in British society? To answer these questions, this chapter provides a detailed analysis of the meanings they attributed to the hijab. In this chapter, I use interview data from female informants only and indicate whether they were a hijab-wearer (*hijabi*) or not (non-*hijabi*) in citation.

The meaning of hijab (1): Modesty and self-respect

As mentioned above, there are many types of hijab, which Muslim women wear depending on an individual's cultural tradition and personal preference. Among the hijab-wearing informants, some wore a headscarf with Western-style jeans or a loose-fit long-sleeve dress, while others wore 'ethnic clothes' such as a shalwar kameez or a chador. Many wore black headscarves, but others preferred colourful ones such as purple, pink, blue, yellow and polka-dot. As Emma Tarlo explains, there is a wide range of hijabs in the world which women wear by tactfully combining one with other garments in a way meaningful to themselves (e.g., faith and fashion) (Tarlo 2010a; 2010b).

Specifically, approximately three-quarters of my female informants (41 persons or 72 per cent) answered that they regularly wore a hijab (including a headscarf, veil and other items). Only one person wore a so-called 'veil' covering everything except the eyes. The rest of the hijabis wore hair coverings such as chador and shalwar kameez. The remaining 16 informants (approx. 28 per cent) did not wear a hijab on a daily basis. The average age was 24.2 for wearers and 21.3 for non-wearers.

Most of my informants, including men and non-wearers, believed that wearing a hijab was important for Muslim women. While their reasons varied, many understood the hijab as an Islamic symbol or identity marker (Stowasser 1994):

The Hijab

Woman solely represents a religion because there's nothing you can see [that she is a Muslim] except a hijab.

(Zahra, Asian mixed, 22, Coventry, non-*hijabi*)

A scarf is a symbol that you're a Muslim by covering yourself up.

(Zaheda, Bangladeshi, 25, London, *hijabi*)

For me now, a scarf is like my identity, and it makes me a Muslim. It's a dress code, and it's an identification.

(Nafisah, Asian mixed, 22, London, *hijabi*)

These informants call the hijab a 'representation', 'symbol', 'identity' and 'identification' of Islam. All of these words indicate that they recognised the headscarf as a 'visible symbol' that identifies Muslims as a distinct group. Note that this view was shared by non-wearers such as Zahra as well as wearers.

However, a more important question is what part of Islam or a Muslim woman the hijab represents. The informants expressed a shared understanding here as well, speaking of the hijab as representing women's 'modesty':

Karam (Pakistani, 23, Coventry, non-*hijabi*): I mean, in terms of the way women are perceived, I would say that possibly it is a type of symbol because obviously, Islam has a different way of looking at women completely.

Uzma (Indian, 19, Coventry, non-*hijabi*): Yeah, modesty.

Karam: Yeah, it's all about modesty. I think the scarf could represent, it could represent modesty, it could represent so many different things. But, yeah, I guess it's a kind of, type of symbol.

Uzma: It shows that she is a Muslim. So I guess, in a way, it does represent Muslims.

I know if I wear a headscarf, it will be better for me. If it covers me, I will be more modest. It is that kind of protection and is a symbol of Islam. You know, in other religions, they might wear; Jews wear a little hat; Sikhs might wear a bracelet. These are just symbols of their religions.

(Majdah, Pakistani, 21, Coventry, non-*hijabi*)

Chapter 10

Karam and Uzma described the hijab as an Islamic symbol representing Muslim women's 'modesty'. Similarly, Majdah said that the hijab embodied (an ideal of) Islam as wearing it makes women 'more modest'.

So, what does modesty mean in Islam? The concept of *'haya'* is important in examining its meaning. According to Emi Goto, who researched the wearing of headscarves by Muslim women in contemporary Egypt, *haya* expresses 'bashfulness', but it is different from 'mere embarrassment' (*khajal/kusuf*). The latter is 'a feeling arising from one's insecurity about her own ability or quality' whereas the former is 'a feeling welling up from a high regard for oneself' (i.e., self-respect) (Goto 2014: 183–4). Accordingly, when *haya* is translated as 'shyness', it means 'to shy away from' damaging one's self-respect rather than being 'reserved' or 'bashful'. From this perspective, 'hijab wearing' serves to protect one's 'self-respect', which is an act of 'modesty'. In other words, the hijab is a concrete expression of one's modest attitude.

Many informants supported this understanding:

> Harir (Pakistani, 27, London, *hijabi*): Yes, modestly in terms of concealing your body, and sort of leaving less to be shown.

> Halimah (Pakistani, 19, London, *hijabi*): Wearing a scarf is almost like elevating yourself. I don't feel like I'm wearing it for other people even though it is this concept of modesty. It's like, I don't know, it's like quite a sacred thing.

> I believe the scarf is a symbol of Islam because of modesty. I've noticed it as a teenager, as a young woman, and as a young adult. When I went out without a hijab, I would be perceived differently. There'd be a lot of different kinds of attitudes towards me from men, even women, not just men. Now, there's a certain kind of respect, a certain kind of space that I'm allowed to have, which gives me security, like personal space. I get personal space enough. Not having the hijab made me feel as though anyone thought, in their head, they thought, 'Oh, she doesn't need to have personal space. It's fine if I interact to that level, to that proximity'.
>
> (Salimah, Bangladeshi, 33, London, *hijabi*)

Harir and Halimah indicated that the hijab was an expression of 'modesty' in the sense that the body was not exposed to others, and wearing it was 'elevating' oneself, i.e., protecting one's self-respect. Salimah felt that people had shown 'different kinds of attitudes' toward her before she started wearing a hijab. Unnecessary 'levels' of 'proximity' in personal interaction troubled her self-respect. When she wore a hijab, though, she felt that she was given a kind of 'privacy': the social distance or 'personal space' to protect her self-respect.

Similar arguments to Salimah's frequently mentioned a form of resistance to gender-discriminatory society:

> Yasmin (Bangladeshi, 22, London, *hijabi*): It [not wearing a scarf] just makes you feel very cheap.
>
> Lola (Nigerian, 22, London, *hijabi*): Yes, very cheap. You feel like you are nothing, you feel like you are worthless.
>
> Yasmin: You just feel like, you are just a walking piece of meat.
>
> Lola: Yes, like you are just a thing, like an object. So like you are non-existent or something. But when you are covered up, people actually consider you a human being. You are like, you are somebody or something. People speak to you with respect, whoever it is; your teachers, lecturers, colleagues, anyone, random people on the street, in public, wherever. You just have this respect from people and it's just because of the way you are dressed. Because you are dressed modestly, so people would treat you modestly as well.

Yasmin and Lola explained that in a society where looks were everything, people were deprived of their self-esteem as a 'piece of meat'. They felt that wearing a headscarf liberated them from looks-based alienation and enabled them to be treated as a person with self-respect and to communicate with civility.

As discussed in Chapter 5, the sexist diminution of women's self-respect and privacy is closely associated with 'commercialism' in Western society. In contrast, informants discussed the importance of the headscarf as the antithesis to contemporary culture, where sex is bought and sold as a commodity:

> Women are always at the forefront of criticism for the wrong reason. They are exposing themselves, they are exposing their private parts or behaving or talking towards men... Women are very sexualised to get to certain things... Trying to sell chocolate, you see, there's a naked woman somewhere. If she wasn't there, some people cannot sell their products. They use women as an instrument to get what they want. It's very sad. It's really sad.
>
> (Rehana, Bangladeshi, 26, London, *hijabi*)

Chapter 10

> Femininity is all about our beauty and the aspects that God has given us, and not for exposing it. By exposing, we will be putting ourselves in danger. We were created for one reason only. That was to worship God, and that can be done in many different ways. Covering ourselves is a form of worshipping God as well because that's what God commanded of us. When people meet us, they are not attracted to us because of the way we look. They won't judge us on the way we look but rather on how we think and how we behave.
>
> (Rukshana, Bangladeshi, 25, London, hijabi)

Rehana criticised the exploitation of women's bodies to sell products, reduced to a sales promotion tool. Conversely, she argued that the hijab safeguarded women's 'precious' self-respect by protecting women against commercial exploitation as sexualised objects. As Rukshana put it, the headscarf encourages people to judge based on 'how we think and how we behave' rather than 'how we look'.

Their criticism is not reserved solely for sexism and commercial exploitation in Western society, but is often levelled at Muslim communities as well:

> People still do talk to you, in really Muslim areas, and they will try and chat you up and stuff like that. But for me scarf really saves you from a lot of hassle – when it comes to abuse, from sexual abuse.
>
> (Harir, Pakistani, 27, London, hijabi)

> Hijab protects you from certain things; men don't talk to you. Well, sometimes they do, but you get less negative attention. And it marks you out as something else. If Muslim women do not wear a scarf, someone talks to you on the street and calls 'Hey, sister!' and stuff like that.
>
> (Inam, Pakistani, 17, London, hijabi)

They believed that by wearing a scarf or hijab, they could avoid the risk of being spoken to casually by men on the street or in their communities, which might damage their self-esteem. In other words, women felt that they could reduce problems such as harassment in their own communities by signifying through the hijab that their bodies do not belong to anyone but God.

Moreover, they understood the hijab in ways that were quite different from the Western interpretation of the negation of women's beauty. By equating 'femininity' with 'precious things', Muslim women seek to hide it from others' eyes, i.e., behaving modestly:

The Hijab

Hair is her beauty which is why we're taught to cover it… You can style your hair. You can do what you want to do. It's up to you how you look after your hair. When I wear a scarf on my head, it doesn't mean I don't style my hair or colour it. It's not against our religion… Religiously, we are meant to cover our hair because we were taught to cover our hair. A woman is a pearl; she's a jewel. And the reason why she guards her modesty is because she covers herself to protect her jewel. And her hair is one of the precious things as well.

(Zahra, Asian mixed, 22, Coventry, non-*hijabi*)

If you are married, your hair is for the eyes of your husband. If you open your scarf, it makes a woman more beautiful. If I open my scarf, I look prettier than when I am wearing it. It's actually covering in that way from other men from seeing.

(Rafima, Bangladeshi, 30, London, *hijabi*)

Zahra explained that the headscarf protected women's beauty, not denied it. Muslim women are permitted to seek beauty by styling and colouring their hair. However, because their beauty is as precious as jewels, they have no need to show it to unnecessary or inappropriate people. Rafima described the hair inside the headscarf as beautiful, asserting that women could protect their self-respect by not showing it to anyone other than their husbands. These informants expressed a belief that 'modesty' was important for these reasons.

The meaning of hijab (2): Faith and autonomy

Yasmin explained that liberation from men's eyes enhanced her own autonomy. Before she began wearing a headscarf, she had been buying more clothes than she could ever wear and spending much money on fashion:

'Oh, there is a new fashion now. That looks nice and I'll wear this'. It's all like. It's just to impress people. You can say, 'I dress to please myself and someone'. But really, you have been conditioned to think that way… I feel, before wearing a hijab, like, girls used to have a weird tension with me. It's always like some indirect underlined competition. It's very strange. For example, I would be walking, and some girls would just be looking at what I am wearing, and think, 'I can do better than her' or 'Why does she have that? I want to get that!' It's a very weird

263

Chapter 10

> competition… After I covered up, those girls who used to look at me in
> that way wouldn't even look twice. They'll think there's no competition
> there. 'She is just covered up'. Guys as well, they wouldn't look either
> because they just think, 'Oh, she is a covered-up girl'. I just felt I didn't
> have to live up to people's expectations. I felt I could just do what I want.
>
> (Yasmin, Bangladeshi, 22, London, *hijabi*)

Yasmin noted that women in modern society tended to be embroiled in commercialised competition over looks and fashion. She had convinced herself that she was dressing for herself but came to realise that she was being influenced by people and society around her. She was in constant 'competition' with friends and other girls over how she looked. Adopting the headscarf enabled her to drop out of that futile contest and subsequently live as she wanted rather than according to other people's expectations.

The hijab in this context is more an issue of the politics over women's bodies rather than a symbol of conflict between the West and Islam. As discussed in Chapter 1, these informants understood the hijab to be a key weapon for women in their political struggle for control over their own bodies rather than a tool used by men to control women.

This is an important aspect of Goto's discussion of *haya* mentioned in the previous section (Goto 2014). Goto distinguishes two major arguments about hijab-wearing in Islam. One relates to the concept of '*fitna*' and the other to '*haya*'. While the word *fitna* generally means trial or affliction, it typically refers particularly to 'female *fitna*' – social unrest and distress caused by women's charms or temptation. Many religious leaders view women as a potential threat to social order and teach their communities that families should solve this problem by using the hijab to conceal women's attractions. From the perspective of *haya*, however, the hijab is a means for women to avoid embarrassment, maintain modesty, and consequently protect their self-respect. Goto observes that the former prescribes women's hijab-wearing as 'men's' responsibility, whereas the latter puts the onus on 'women' themselves, a significant difference in the 'subject' of hijab-wearing (Goto 2014: 167–208). In other words, the latter theory 'brings to the fore the idea of God directly commanding women to wear a hijab' (Goto 2014: 203), thus giving women the responsibility for controlling their own bodies.

The informants talked about the hijab exclusively from the latter viewpoint. Most of my informants clearly denied that wearing a headscarf or veil was imposed upon them by others (e.g., father and husband) both normatively and empirically. They instead invoked the modesty that the hijab represented from the perspectives of autonomy, self-respect, and self-responsibility:

The Hijab

Wearing a scarf is almost like elevating yourself. I don't feel like I'm wearing it for other people even though it is this concept of modesty. It's like, I don't know, it's like quite a sacred thing.

(Halimah, Pakistani, 19, London, *hijabi*)

I face discrimination at work because of my hijab. When I started first wearing it at work – my main manager, who has been really nice to me all this time when I didn't wear a hijab – when I started wearing it, on the day I started wearing it, she said to me, 'Why are you wearing that? You've got lovely hair. Show it'. I said, 'No'. I know I have lovely hair, but I like to keep it covered. Only my God knows that is nice. I don't need to show it to people. I did face a bit of discrimination and people were not happy about my wearing it. But I didn't care because I am not pleasing you. I am pleasing the person who created me.

(Fahima, Bangladeshi, 28, London, *hijabi*)

What is interesting about these comments is that they emphasised 'wearing a hijab for God' (Goto 2014) rather than for their fathers, husbands, or the social order. For example, Halimah described the headscarf as 'a sacred thing' that she wore in her relationship with God, not for 'other people'. Fahima suggested the right to control her own body, describing hijab-wearing as 'living up to God's expectations' rather than pleasing 'others'.

Rehana (Bangladeshi, 26, London, *hijabi*) made a similar point, declaring that 'our creator has not asked us to, but rather told us to cover ourselves because we are precious'. Similarly, Rukshana (Bangladeshi, 25, London, *hijabi*) stated that 'covering ourselves is a form of worshipping God as well because that's what God commanded of us'. In other words, they understood hijab-wearing to be their duty to God. As Fahima put it, she wore a hijab because it was important for her to please the 'Creator', not anyone else. These informants stressed that it was Muslim women's 'sacred' duty to wear a hijab and that they hold the right to control their own bodies in their hands through this act of faith.

Not wearing a hijab (1): Outer veil and inner veil

Despite this strong support for the hijab, approximately 28 per cent (16 informants) responded that they did not wear it except on special occasions such as family gatherings and mosque visits. How did informants perceive not

Chapter 10

wearing the hijab? This question has important implications for women because in Muslim communities, wearing the hijab or not is often seen as a criterion for measuring people's religious beliefs and is potentially stigmatising for those who do not wear it.[5]

A concern about stigmatisation was expressed by Nasha and Rabab in Coventry who did not clearly distinguish between culture and religion, as discussed in Chapter 7:

> Probably other Muslims are looking down on you just because you don't wear a scarf and don't dress properly.
>
> (Nasha, Bangladeshi, 17, Coventry, non-*hijabi*)

> That [peer pressure to wear a hijab] makes us feel guilty because you see other girls wearing headscarves, and they are looking down on you; like 'Why are you not wearing one?', 'Are you not Muslim?', 'Don't you follow your religion?', and 'Don't you follow Islam?'
>
> (Rabab, Bangladeshi, 17, Coventry, non-*hijabi*)

Having assimilated into British youth culture and dressed in Western-style clothes, makeup and accessories, they reported experiencing strong pressure about their clothing from their own community.

Nasha and Rabab were not the only non-wearers. Unlike these two girls, though, the majority of the non-wearing informants did not regard it as a serious problem. While most acknowledged wearing hijab as a duty, they also offered similar reasoning to justify or accept their non-fulfilment.

The most common view was expressed by Khansa, who was not a regular hijab wearer:

> The scarf does represent Islam. It's a part of Islam. But Allah gave us free will. We can wear it or not wear it. But at the end of the day, we still have to follow Islam. So it doesn't mean if you wear a headscarf, you are not following religion well. It's a part of your good deeds that will take you.
>
> (Khansa, other mixed, 19, Coventry, non-*hijabi*)

There are two important points in this statement. First, while the hijab is an important 'part' of Islam, one cannot judge the 'whole' person by it alone. Second, Allah told people to wear a hijab but did not force it – he gave people 'free will'. We will analyse the first point in this section and return to the second one in the next section.

As discussed, the hijab is an important tool representing being Muslim for many women. However, the informants believed that it was only one of many Islamic duties and should not be used as the overriding criteria for evaluating a person. For example, Uzma and Rahmah, who preferred a contemporary style to a hijab, offered the following observations:

> I saw that a lot in my school. There was one girl; she even wore a headscarf. And then we went to Italy on a school trip, and she was drinking. And I was in some shock. I was like, 'Why?' She was the one that was wearing a headscarf, but she started drinking.
>
> (Uzma, Indian, 19, Coventry, non-*hijabi*)

> I've got a couple of friends who wear scarves. And when I heard what they do on the weekends. They've gone for a couple of days or something and not come back home. So I was thinking, 'I don't wear a scarf, but I do not go to clubs or drink, or meet with different men like every other day', and I'm saying to myself, 'I think I'm a better Muslim than you'. Then just you're wearing a scarf, but it doesn't mean you are any different. You can't judge a person by what she is wearing.
>
> (Rahmah, Indian, 18, Coventry, non-*hijabi*)

Their view was shared by a large majority of the informants, including hijab-wearers. While they recognised wearing a hijab as important for Muslims, they explained that the act by itself had no meaning. In other words, if it is not accompanied by the modesty it represents, 'it takes off the whole purpose of wearing a scarf' (Uzma). Conversely, 'people that actually don't wear scarf may be better than me' (Wardah, Indian, 27, Coventry, *hijabi*).

Beneath these comments was an understanding that no one can become a 'perfect' Muslim. When asked what is important in Islam, many informants named the 'six articles of faith' (or *aqidah*) and the 'five pillars of Islam' (or *ibadah*) almost automatically.[6] These duties – praying five times daily, Friday prayer, fulfilling family obligations, wearing a veil or hijab and so on – were not always practicable for young Muslims pursuing careers or educational qualifications and enjoying a wide circle of friends. Nevertheless, the informants expressed a strong desire to self-identify as Muslim.[7] The conflict between their aspirations and reality demands some sort of moratorium or leniency towards the non-observance of some Islamic practices, such as hijab-wearing.

Chapter 10

Faced with the difficulty of practising Islam, the informants differentiated between 'outward' and 'inward' faiths to justify themselves as Muslims:

A scarf is just an outward. This is what you see. But you don't know about anything else, and Islam is a vast religion which has so many dimensions. So who knows what these people are doing during the day and who can get so many rewards?

(Malikah, Bangladeshi, 26, London, *hijabi*)

It says, 'Don't judge the book by its cover'. It's the same with people. You don't judge a person by the way they look or how they dress.

(Zahra, Asian mixed, 22, Coventry, non-*hijabi*)

People may think, 'You're more religious than me because you wear a scarf'. Everything is like that.

(Uzma, Indian, 19, Coventry, non-*hijabi*)

Malikah said that people should not 'judge' if a person's religiosity by her or his 'outward' appearance, such as wearing a hijab or not. Zahara explained that judging how good a Muslim was based on whether or not she wore a hijab was as meaningless as judging a book by its 'cover'. On the same basis, Uzma declared that the perception that the equation 'hijab=religious' was superficial. All three expressed a belief that Muslim identity was not solely represented by hijab-wearing (Davids 2013: 58).

Some informants referred to the superficial wearing of a hijab as a 'fashion':

But I think for a lot of people who live in heavily Asian areas, wearing a scarf has now become a cultural obligation, rather than just religious, almost like a fashion thing... That's why I think a lot of people wear it, and they think it's like a symbol. It's just something that you just do now, but you don't question it. Everybody does it. It doesn't make them think about what they want in life.

(Halimah, Pakistani, 19, London, *hijabi*)

Even if you do not wear a scarf, it doesn't mean you're not religious. It's just a fashion thing.

(Ulfah, Indian, 21, Coventry, *hijabi*)

The Hijab

It's become a fashion statement. It's not anything to do with Islam. It's starting to become a fashion thing.

(Wardah, Indian, 27, Coventry, *hijabi*)

The informants used the term 'fashion' as synonymous with 'cultural thing' and 'outward faith' in its meaning, presenting it as the opposite of 'religious reason' and 'inward faith'. They implied that culture/fashion was introduced from outside whereas religion sprang from within or was voluntarily chosen by individuals. They connected fashion with culture to highlight the negative connotations and irrelevance to good intentions and faith – 'what they want in life'.

In sum, almost all informants regarded hijab-wearing as a good deed, but it is not a reliable indicator of a good Muslim. Instead, they emphasised the importance of 'inward' and 'good intentions':

I tried it for a couple of years personally... I found wearing a scarf very difficult. Initially, it was really easy, but then I felt judged a lot and I felt very restricted. People that I knew really well started judging me because of what I looked like. It upset me and I lost myself, I lost who I was... I felt when I was talking to people, they were least interested in what I was saying as opposed to what I was wearing. That bothered me. And I think also it affected my confidence a bit as well because I felt a bit isolated, because I like having friends from all sorts of backgrounds... I just wanted to be who I was and be confident in myself. But then I found there was a saying in religion that 'scarf is not just an outer veil, there's an inner veil in your manners', in the way you carry yourself.

(Parveen, Pakistani, 31, London, non-*hijabi*)

Parveen, a non-*hijabi* lawyer in London, was in many respects the most assimilated to British society among the female informants. She expressed a conscious commitment to Western social values and called herself 'feminist'. At the same time, she declared Islam to be the most important element in her identity. She, therefore, tried to wear a hijab as a Muslim duty for a brief period. However, when her hijab attracted too much attention, she felt she was being judged and experienced confusion about her identity. Discovering an Islamic saying about 'outer and inner veils' amid this inner conflict helped her to realise that the inner attitude of modesty was more important than the outer act of wearing a hijab.

Chapter 10

Similarly, a great majority of the informants declared that the outward act of wearing a hijab was meaningless unless it had inner quality:

> If you're not a Muslim, then I think you would see the scarf as a symbol; you would see it, 'Okay, that person is a Muslim'. For Muslims, there is a way of saying: 'You're more religious than me because you wear a scarf'. Maybe white persons, they maybe think, 'Okay, she is more religious than this girl because she is covering her head in a scarf'. Then, at the end of the day, I'd pray five times a day even though not wearing a scarf.
>
> (Karam, Pakistani, 23, Coventry, non-*hijabi*)

> I think a scarf is fundamentally about modesty, and that's also shown largely through your character as opposed to the actual garment itself. So that's why I don't like to differentiate between people who wear it and people who don't.
>
> (Harir, Pakistani, 27, London, *hijabi*)

According to non-wearer Karam, people tend to treat the hijab as a 'symbol' for Muslim women, but although it may be useful to identify them, it is not appropriate to judge if a person is a 'good Muslim' or not. Zaheda (Bangladeshi, 25, London, *hijabi*) clarified that 'it is important that we are wearing a scarf for the right reasons' while explaining the meaning of wearing a hijab.

Their emphasis on 'intentions' also informs their criticism of the hijab imposed by the community or the family. A few informants were forced to wear a hijab by family, and many had experienced people in their community who judged others by their appearance. Salimah, who described her mother as 'strict' in a quote in Chapter 7, commented on this issue:

> When I was 11, my mum forced me to wear a scarf. I would sneak it out and take it off as soon as I got to the school gates… I didn't wear it for Islam at all… She doesn't understand why she needs to wear the hijab. All she knows is that: 'You have to wear it. You have to wear it'. Force isn't the right way to teach somebody religion.
>
> (Salimah, Bangladeshi, 33, London, *hijabi*)

Salimah criticised her mother's insistence on wearing a hijab as being devoid of both the meaning of hijab and the idea of modesty (Sahin 2013: 116). I will return to this point in a later section.

270

Thus, the informants tended to emphasise inner values, including 'good intention' (Uzma, Indian, 19, Coventry, non-*hijabi*), 'being your personality right' (Selikah, Indian, 17, Coventry, *hijabi*), 'being polite to one another' and 'being respectful to one another' (Tabassum, Indian, 26, Coventry, *hijabi*). They were firm in the view that the hijab and prayers are simply some of the ways to express these inner qualities required by Islam:

> I have met so many people who do pray five times a day and then do really silly things… I just feel that being polite to one another and being respectful to one another are more important.
>
> (Tabassum)

> I think if your heart is clean – although we shouldn't be judging anyone – if their heart is clean and they have clean intentions, I don't believe to say that 'You don't wear a scarf, so you are not Islamic or anything'.
>
> (Labibah, Pakistani, 22, Coventry, *hijabi*)

> Saying to dress modestly, it means to be modest actually. It is not just how you dress, but how you conduct yourself. I don't think there's a striction definitely like: 'If you're Muslim, you have to wear this'. I don't think that at all.
>
> (Jannah, Bangladeshi, 18, London, non-*hijabi*)

These comments indicate that what is important about being Muslim is not wearing an 'outer veil' but an 'inner veil' associated with 'modesty' as discussed in Section 2, including attitudes such as right intentions and politeness.

The informants' emphasis on intention and interiority underpins another important attitude: 'reserving judgment', which is elaborated on in the next section.

Not wearing a hijab (2): Predestination, test and readiness

Now, let us examine the second argument, as announced at the outset of the previous section, that 'individuals decide to wear or not wear a hijab based on their free will'.

'Free will' has a special meaning in Islam, relating to one of the central creeds (the six articles of faith), '*qadar*', which is usually translated as 'predes-

Chapter 10

tination/destiny'. It refers to the concept that Allah has predestined all the occurrences in the world:

> Say, 'Only what God has decreed will happen to us, He is our Master: let the believers put their trust in God'. (9:51)

As mentioned above and in many other verses in the Quran (e.g., 25:2, 10:61), Allah created everything, and the fate of his creations is already in his hands.[8] For this reason, those who are to be created or protected are required to entrust their destinies to God.

In Islam, as in Christianity, there has been much debate about predestination. One question is whether having faith is a God-given 'destiny' or dependent on an individual's 'will'. If Allah has predetermined all happenings in the world, there is no room for human intervention. Then, no responsibility or freedom arises on the part of people, and faith – the potential for voluntary surrender (i.e., Islam) – becomes unnecessary (Tosun 2012: 209).

How does Islam overcome this paradox? Ghulam Sarwar of the Muslim Education Trust explained this in a textbook widely used in Britain's Muslim community:

> We believe that Allāh has created the universe and He is its Absolute Controller and Regulator. Allāh has fixed a set course for everything in the universe; this is called *al-Qadr*. Nothing can happen without the will and the knowledge of Allāh. The destiny of every creature is already known to Allāh. But this does not mean that man has no freedom of will. We know that man is the *Khalīfah* (agent) of Allāh on this earth. We also know that Allāh does not force us to do anything. It is up to us to obey or disobey Him. Whether we will obey or disobey is known to Him. But the fact that Allāh knows what we are going to do does not affect our freedom of choice. Man does not know what his destiny is. He has the free will to choose the course he will take. (Sarwar 2006: 22)

On one hand, God is the creator and controller of all. On the other hand, He gave people the ability to judge things and left it to each individual's will whether they accept their destiny and fulfil their obligations or not (Mawdudi 1996: 2). In other words, 'God does not change the condition of a people [for the worse] unless they change what is in themselves' (13:11, words in square brackets are original). This is called the 'doctrine of the acquisition' (*kasb*)

272

The Hijab

(Kosugi 1994: 182–9); people acquire their destiny through their own effort. The choice of not performing one's religious duties is available to all.

Islamic educator Sahin explains:

> According to the Qur'ān Islam is the central human quality signifying the human psychosocial and spiritual need to develop meaningful commitments in life. The Qur'ān... insists that the act of submission should not be confused with the phenomenon of involuntary surrender... What the Qur'ān demands from humanity is a personally constructed conviction and meaning that brings about a voluntary recognition of God and a self-conscious life of gratitude towards God's favours. (Sahin 2013: 76)

This 'voluntarism' was clearly expressed by Janan (Sudanese, 20, Coventry, *hijabi*). When her work colleague asked her why she was wearing a hijab, she answered as follows: 'Because it's my choice, I want to cover up my head'. This remark warrants an explanation. It is self-evident to her – and her colleague – that hijab-wearing is associated with Islam. However, Janan did not use 'religion' to justify her choice. That would have reinforced her colleague's image of Islam as 'absolute surrender to God' (Islam) and hence lacking autonomy, which might have invited the follow-up question: 'Why surrender to God?' Janan chose to speak about her hijab-wearing as a matter of personal choice, which is highly valued in British society. In her mind, faith was Allah-given duty, but whether she performed it or not and to what extent was a matter of personal choice.

Islamic duties and the choice to perform or not perform them have been often discussed in terms of a 'test':

> [I]n the Garden, and on earth, humankind share the same test: the choice between obedience and disobedience. Allah warns Adam and Eve against approaching one of the trees in the Garden. The Qur'an does not give special attributes to the tree itself: it is merely a symbol of the test. (Wadud 1999: 23)

This description indicates that, in Islam, God's commands are tests for the followers, who are ultimately responsible for their choice of whether to perform such duties or not.[9] Rabab commented on this point:

> We have to be prepared for the test. And obviously, God is going to ask this question, 'How much do you have faith in me?', 'Have you prayed

Chapter 10

five times a day?', 'Have you respected your parents?' It's all down to you really. To be a good Muslim, you have to show you are the one.

(Rabab, Bangladeshi, 17, Coventry, non-*hijabi*)

Rabab explained that God put people to the test and they must respond. There is a clear path 'to be a good Muslim' and people are required to get 'ready' for it.

The word 'ready' here connotes that the fulfilment of obligations was perceived not only from a synchronic but also a diachronic perspective. In other words, people choose when and how much they practice their Islamic faith depending on their life stage. The commonly uttered phrase 'when I am/you are ready' invokes this notion in response to the question of when and how much they accept Islamic practices, especially in discussions about the hijab:

You only wear a scarf when you're ready. It's like *hajj*, the pilgrimage. You do it when you're ready. It's compulsory. Once in your lifetime, you should do it. But it is when you're ready, not because it's compulsory.

(Banan, Bangladeshi, 24, London, *hijabi*)

I don't think I'm ready yet to wear a headscarf. I don't want to keep taking it. I want to be committed to it. When I do feel it's time, then I'm going to start wearing it.

(Toslima, Bangladeshi, 18, London, non-*hijabi*)

When you feel comfortable wearing a scarf, it's the right time for you. I actually can't wait for the day that I am comfortable in it. I feel like 'I'm going to wear the scarf and I'm going to wear it for the rest of the life'. That's nice.

(Karam, Pakistani, 23, Coventry, non-*hijabi*)

Banan compared wearing a hijab to the '*hajj*', one of the most important obligations in Islam, as discussed in the next section.[10] It is commonly believed that people should perform this duty only when they 'can afford' or 'when they are ready' to do so because it requires considerable time, as well financial and physical commitment.[11] Banan applied the same reasoning to hijab-wearing: it should be worn 'when you are ready'. By implication, one does not have to wear it until she is ready. Toslima expressed a desire to commit to wearing a hijab sometime in the future but was not 'ready yet'. Karam also expressed a desire to wear a hijab 'when it's the right time for'

274

The Hijab

her, adding that she could hardly wait for that day. These comments illustrate that the phrase 'when I am/you are ready' serves to justify a moratorium on some religious duties.[12]

A corollary to this idea about when duties should be performed is an attitude of 'not judging others'. As the 'right time' to fulfil a particular obligation will eventually arrive, people should not judge another's devotion to Islam just because she does not wear a hijab 'right now'.

The attitude of 'not judging others' is grounded in the Islamic belief that 'God only knows':

> Whether We let you [Prophet] see part of what We threaten them with, or cause you to die [before that], your duty is only to deliver the message: the Reckoning is Ours.
>
> (13:40; words in square brackets are original)

This verse indicates that only God can appraise and judge ('reckon') people. Even Muhammad is not authorised to do so. As the word 'prophet' suggests, Muhammad was merely entrusted with God's words; his role (i.e., *nadhir*, a warner) was to spread them to many people.[13] Whether people obey God's words or not and how they interpret them is up to each individual's free will. Appraising the extent to which people perform their obligations is Allah's sole prerogative.

This point informs the distinction between 'inward' and 'outward' discussed above. People judge others' faith by their outward signs because they cannot see their inner beliefs. God, however, can look below the surface to judge their deeper faith. Assigning 'outward judgment' to people and 'inward judgment' to God leads people to assume a non-judgmental attitude toward others. Salimah clearly expressed this point:

> At one point, my sister came in and she didn't wear a hijab at all. But there was no judging... I read one of the books of *hadith* that the prophet wrote. He said, 'Don't judge somebody. Don't think you're more pious and you're more righteous than somebody just because they're not covering or their sin is more obvious than yours. Your sin might be hidden from people, but Allah sees your sin'. So I might be well-covered, but I might go home and have some drugs. I might invite strange men to my house... You might think, 'Well, she's very bold and wild, but she might be, during the five daily prayers, she might be very spiritual'.
>
> (Salimah, Bangladeshi, 33, London, *hijabi*)

Chapter 10

Salimah did not think she was more religious than her sister just because she wore a headscarf and her sister did not. Salimah recognised that despite the headscarf, she could be more sinful because of her bad behaviour hidden from others' eyes, and her sister might be more faithful to God's teachings even though she did not wear a headscarf. The 'truth' of one's faith is invisible to others and only God can judge it. Hence it is meaningless for people to judge others by the headscarf.

The informants thought that this reservation of judgment was an Islamic tradition, which was conducive to the individualisation of faith. This is clear in the following exchange between Selikah and Karam:

> Selikah (Indian, 17, Coventry, *hijabi*): It's based on the interpretation. Because the headscarf is not mentioned in the Quran, some people will take different interpretations. So, some people might just see a requirement as just to cover themselves in their body but not their hair. And some people might go the other way. It's meaning to cover everything. So you're talking about covering your face, the entire body and your eyes. It depends on what interpretation you take as well.

> Karam (Pakistani, 23, Coventry, non-*hijabi*): Yeah, I think it's kind of based on your own idea of religion too, because you may not be religious and not follow a religious tradition; for example covering your hair, covering your body anything like that. But at the end of the day, it's on your intention, inside. If you're not doing something or if you're doing something wrong, I mean, God knows that. Anyway, God sees.

Hijab-wearer Selikah explained that the hijab meant different things (what to cover, with what, how much or when) depending on the individual interpretation. Meanwhile, non-wearer Karam pointed out that one's 'intention' could not be seen from the outward act of wearing a hijab, and it was meaningless for anyone other than God to judge it.

As we have seen, many informants understood that not wearing a hijab did not necessarily indicate a lack of faith in Islam and that one was free to choose to wear it when the time came. They typically shared the view that the purity of one's interior and intentions were more important than external appearances.

276

The Hijab

When will they be ready?

'School' as a catalyst: Creating desire through acquiring knowledge

What motivated informants to wear the hijab?; in other words, when did they get 'ready'?

In the 29 cases where the timing of hijab-wearing is known, the average age was 15.3 years. Five had started wearing a hijab by the end of their primary education at age ten. Fifteen started while they were middle school/ pre-university students (up to age 17) and nine people started when they were 18 or older.

The most common age for starting hijab-wearing was eleven (five informants). This coincided with their admission to secondary schools. Many children in their community started wearing a hijab around this age, which helped them to make a smooth transition:

> I saw some kids in London wearing it, and I said, 'Mum, I want to wear that'… I didn't know why.
>
> (Harir, Pakistani, 27, London, *hijabi*)

> When I started to wear, I was 11 years old. My family is quite religious and my mom wears the hijab. My sister used to wear the hijab. She never wore it all the time, but she was wearing. When I started wearing it, she was wearing it full-time. I guess I just followed suit, but I didn't know why I was wearing it.
>
> (Tabassum, Indian, 26, Coventry, *hijabi*)

Harir started wearing a hijab at age eleven because children around her did so. Tabassum also started wearing a hijab at eleven for no more reason than because her mother and sister wore them. Neither reported positive reasons for their hijab-wearing.

Many of the informants started wearing a hijab in their late teens and at university (ten informants). The number increases to twelve if we include those who started in their early teens, stopped at some stage and restarted. Many of the mid-teen and later starters described their decisions as part of the process of coming to grips with their faith:

> I just finished secondary education. I literally finished. After the day I finished, I put it on. My parents never sort of forced me to do… My

277

Chapter 10

sister, she is about three years older than me, she put it on slightly before me. She was doing a lot of research about wearing a scarf then. I started doing a lot of research around it as well.

(Rehana, Bangladeshi, 26, London, *hijabi*)

I started wearing a scarf when I was five years old. But it was really on-off, on-off. Then I went to school. I was the only Muslim there, and it was very difficult. So I just took it off because I was getting bullied as well. So I just took it off. Then in Year 10, I was studying Islam in RE and I read up on it. I had such a bare understanding of why we wear it and are to be modest. And I thought these people were not going to be with me forever. My god is going to be with me forever. He is there. He is going to help. And since then I have been wearing it. And He has given me confidence in that sense.

(Labibah, Pakistani, 22, Coventry, *hijabi*)

Rehana chose to wear a hijab at the age of 15 after researching the meaning of hijab-wearing and convincing herself, while influenced by her elder sister. Labibah explained that her parents made her wear a hijab from the age of five, but she stopped wearing it at age ten because she was being bullied at school for wearing it. In religious education classes in Year 10 (aged 14), she was inspired to research the hijab, and upon learning its meaning, she decided to wear it. Yasmin (Bangladeshi, 22, London, *hijabi*) and Salimah (Bangladeshi, 33, London, *hijabi*) reported similar experiences. Importantly, in each case, that they made a conscious effort to research the meaning of wearing a hijab and internalised this knowledge in deciding to don a hijab.

Those who began wearing a hijab in university similarly reported the importance of acquiring religious knowledge and understanding its meaning in their decisions, but they tended to mention an additional reason:

I started wearing it when I was at uni. And it was only because I went through like such a stressful time. I wasn't really following Islam and I wasn't a practising Muslim. Everything was just going wrong for me. That's why I thought. So I just thought, if I took a step back and focused on my purpose and often my faith. Maybe things would start improving for me. So that's when I started to really gain more knowledge in Islam and become a better Muslim. That's when I started wearing.

(Saba, Pakistani, 25, Coventry, *hijabi*)

> I only started to know the significance of wearing a hijab when I actually went to university. And that's when I started to wear it with the long dresses just covering myself because I was going to start living away from home. At university, everything happened, everything went, and I realized what my surroundings were. And I just thought that I didn't want to get distracted and get pulled into something, I didn't want to be part of it. So I guess I had to make that change. So I and my other friend who started wearing at the same time decided to cover fully and we started to read about why we do it.
>
> (Tabassum, Indian, 26, Coventry, *hijabi*)

Saba and Tabassum lost control of themselves in their hectic new campus lives away from their parents. Having acquired freedom among a new circle of friends in an urban environment, they plunged into a kind of anomie. They described how experiencing an identity crisis prompted them to grapple with their own faith. They sought knowledge with friends and learned more about Islam and why women wear a hijab. Finding the reasoning satisfactory, they started wearing a hijab.

I call their path to hijab-wearing the 'creating of desire through acquiring knowledge'. Many informants chose to face Islam at some point in life, but they were not necessarily committed to wearing a hijab at that point. Commitment to wearing the hijab appears to be conditional on their understanding and acceptance of its meaning in the process of acquiring knowledge about Islam. Once they understood and accepted the meaning, it turned into an essential desire.[14]

This process was clearly described by Asma (Asian mixed, 22, London, *hijabi*), who started wearing a hijab at the age of ten. According to Asma, her mother did not force it, but encouraged her to wear it. She was also required to wear a hijab at an Islamic *madrasa*, where she attended in the afternoon, and abided by it because she wanted to be a good Muslim. Nevertheless, she did not know why she had to wear a hijab. Eventually, she felt 'I didn't really care about this [wearing a hijab]… I didn't have that passion', and she stopped wearing it. However, her attitude changed when she studied Islam at university. She explained this change succinctly: 'When you actually realise the meaning of the headscarf, then you understand why you want to wear it'.

Fahima (Bangladeshi, 28, London, *hijabi*), like Asma and others, had a mother who encouraged her to wear a hijab without providing a reason. When Fahima went to university, she joined an Islamic student group, attended lectures about Islam and read books about religion under her friends' influence. Along the way, she came to realise that she was 'actually

Chapter 10

a Muslim' and feel a strong desire to have 'a proper identity' rather than being 'a Muslim… just by name'. As part of that process, she decided to wear a hijab.

Some non-*hijabi* informants also mentioned the possible desire created through acquiring knowledge:

> I'm not against the idea [of Islam]. Maybe if I study more and see why, I will wear a scarf. I don't feel safe right now doing it, wearing a scarf.
>
> (Jannah, Bangladeshi, 18, London, non-*hijabi*)

Jannah, a university student, speculated that she might choose to wear a hijab after studying Islam and understanding the reason. However, she denied wearing it at the time. She seemed to keep a lid on that desire by deferring the acquisition of such knowledge. She had chosen instead to immerse herself in her studies and enjoyed socialising with non-Muslim friends at university.

'Marriage' as a catalyst: Customs

Hijab-wearing following the acquisition of knowledge was also observed among the relatively young informants. By contrast, only a small number of informants aged thirty or older reported that process. The older group showed a tendency to attribute the catalyst for wearing a hijab to external factors. For example, Shirina began wearing a hijab following her marriage:

> My mum always made us go out in a scarf, but we didn't wear it in school. It was not necessary. So we had to wear it from our house to school. But we could take it off, and then we wore it from the school back to the house… When I went to college – that was the same time I got married – I started putting it on properly. So at 16, I started putting it properly, wearing it everywhere… I got married, and it was something, I thought, married women did. I thought it was what married women did. Also, I knew Islamically you were supposed to cover yourself. So you were supposed to cover your head.
>
> (Shirina, Bangladeshi, 31, London, *hijabi*)

Shirina's mother made her wear a hijab from a young age, but she removed it behind her mother's back because it was meaningless to her. Then she started wearing a hijab when she married at the age of 16. Her motivation, however, was different from those discussed above. The younger group (in their twenties) also chose to wear a hijab following a life event (e.g., schooling), but they attributed their choice to having acquired knowledge and internalised the creed as their own desire. In contrast, Shirina attributed her choice to external factors, including community expectations such as 'it was what married women did' and 'you were supposed to cover your head'.

Other informants in her age group expressed a similar attitude. Tasrin, who started wearing a hijab at the age of thirty, the latest among the hijab wearers, described being motivated by an external factor rather than an internal connection with her faith:

> My son is a reason why I've started wearing a headscarf because I thought I wanted to raise him as a Muslim. One day he turned around and said, 'Well, Mum, why don't you cover your head'. And that's what Islam says, you should dress modestly and certain parts of your body should be covered. I am not sure what I then said to my son. But I thought I got to learn about my religion.
>
> (Tasrin, Bangladeshi, 31, London, *hijabi*)

As Tasrin's child was growing up and started asking her about Islam and her clothing, she felt uncertain and a need to study Islam to answer his questions. She decided to don a hijab in that process. Thirty-year-old Rafima (Bangladeshi, 30, London, *hijabi*) also explained that her child's growth motivated her to enhance her knowledge of Islam and she started to 'cover up properly' with her husband's encouragement.

In contrast to Shirina and Tasrin, forty-year-old Jakera began wearing a hijab when she graduated from middle school, like many of the informants in their twenties. Although neither her marriage nor child raising appears to be a factor in her decision, her motivation was nevertheless more similar to her contemporaries than to the younger group who started wearing a hijab at a similar age:

> Jakera (Bangladeshi, 40, London, *hijabi*): I started wearing it when I was 16. Yeah, so that was quite a while, as soon as I finished school and went on to college.
>
> Author: What was the reason?
>
> Jakera: There was no trigger. My parents didn't tell me; my oldest sister didn't wear it. I just felt actually it was time that I did start wearing it. I wanted to identify myself as a Muslim woman. It was important to me for my religion, and I covered my hair. I just decided.

Chapter 10

Author: Why at 16 years old?

Jakera: Why 16? I don't know why 16. I just thought, well, you were finishing one stage of your life and starting anew. And that's as good a time as any.

While the younger informants who started wearing a hijab at the same life stage discussed the hijab in terms of their commitment to Islam, Jakera did not attach any special meaning to it. In fact, she denied any change before and after putting on a hijab, declaring that she 'was the same person with the same attitude'.

It seems likely that the changing environment surrounding Islamic knowledge discussed in Chapter 8 has a bearing on this difference between the twenties or less and over-thirties groups. The informants in their teens and twenties grew up in an environment where they could acquire knowledge unmediated by traditional authorities thanks to rapidly advancing information technology. It offered them direct access to Islam when they faced a decision about wearing a hijab. In comparison, those older than thirty had been more significantly influenced by their cultures and customs because they lacked such an environment.

'Pilgrimage' as a catalyst: Collective experience

Some informants said their first motivation to wear a hijab was a pilgrimage, one of the five pillars of Islam. As discussed, every Muslim is duty-bound to visit Mecca at least once – when they can. Pilgrimage has a special meaning to Muslims because it is not a daily routine, unlike the other five acts (i.e. prayer, alms and fasting) except for *shahada* or the confession of faith.

Some informants had decided that they would wear a hijab when they went on a pilgrimage or perhaps in preparations to do so:

> You do wear a scarf when you're ready, when you think, 'This is the time I'm changing'. To make myself a better person, I'm going to do my pilgrimage. I haven't been able to do mine yet. I've been saying it for the last 5 years: 'Yeah, when I'm ready, when I'm ready', but *insha'Allah* that one day is going to come. When I go on pilgrimage, that's the time, *insha'Allah*, to start changing in a good way.
>
> (Zahra, Asian mixed, 22, Coventry, non-*hijabi*)

> I just feel like I have a good *iman*. I have a good heart. I need to practice more, maybe attending courses. If I visit Saudi Arabia, maybe my

The Hijab

practice would be wider, and maybe I will start wearing a scarf. It's not that I don't want to, but I have to. This is part of my religion. *Insha'Allah*, I will.

(Shamina, Bangladeshi, 25, London, non-*hijabi*)

Zahra and Shamina were non-wearers when we spoke, but they both expressed an intention to start wearing a hijab when they eventually make a pilgrimage. However, they stated that the pilgrimage was merely a catalyst to put more effort into their faith and believed that wearing a hijab would be part of that process. They also implied that the decision was not merely an obligation but belonged to them. From this perspective, not (yet) being ready for pilgrimage was seen as a sufficient reason for not wearing a hijab (yet).

By contrast, those who had travelled to Mecca tended to emphasise the impact of the pilgrimage itself:

We were probably the only Muslims there. And then, as you get older, you start going to other areas, don't you? For example, you go to university, you mix with other cultures, and then you meet more Muslims. So then they influence your decision... But it didn't really make us think about the hijab. We just wanted to enjoy life, study, see friends, and show off our hair. We wanted to do all those kinds of things that girls generally want to do. But, when you go to Saudi, everyone is one, and it melted my heart.

(Poppy, Bangladeshi, 28, London, *hijabi*)

Poppy grew up in a white neighbourhood, enjoyed the British lifestyle and did not give serious thought to the hijab. However, she went to Saudi Arabia for a pilgrimage, where she joined Muslims gathered from around the world, all engaged in the same ritual and helping one another, and experienced a sense of belonging to a global religious community. The experience increased her awareness and led her to discover her 'Muslim' identity. She continued wearing the hijab she wore for her pilgrimage after returning home. Zeheda (Bangladeshi, 25, London, *hijabi*) described a similar experience: 'It [*hajj*] just changed my whole perspective'. Although there were only a few, the informants who had done their pilgrimage attributed their hijab-wearing to their collective experience in Mecca.

Chapter 10

Conclusion

Many of the informants perceived the hijab as both a symbol of Islam and an important part of their identity as Muslims. It represented both the value of 'modesty' and a means to achieve it (Mahmood 2005: 23; Mishra and Shirazi 2010: 204).

Commercialism is in many respects antithetical to 'modesty'. Women's bodies are sexualised and commercially exploited in contemporary society. Women are often judged and categorised according to superficial metrics such as looks and age and are evaluated, treated and exploited according to parameters unrelated to the operation of modern social systems (Parsons 1951).

In his criticism of capitalism, Karl Marx describes how the problematic combination of commercialism and sexism stems from the diabolical power of money:

> As money is not exchanged for any one specific quality, for any one specific thing, or for any particular human essential power, but for the entire objective world of man and nature, ... it therefore serves to exchange every property for every other, even contradictory, property and object: it is the fraternization of impossibilities. It makes contradictions embrace. (Marx 1964: 169)

Marx contends that money distorts relations between people by making things that should not be exchanged changeable.

Marx suggests that people can achieve an ideal 'human relationship' by eliminating the diabolical power of money and the capitalist relationships it symbolises. As he states in the beautiful passage from *Economic and Philosophic Manuscripts of 1844* quoted at the beginning of this chapter, an ideal 'human relationship' is a limited and equal relationship based on 'a specific expression... of your real individual life' and involving exchanging things such as 'love only for love, trust for trust'. This thought expresses a certain ideal type in modern society. Modern social relations are based on 'social roles' in each functional system rather than 'a total person', and people are expected to be deployed according to their 'abilities' corresponding to such roles (Parsons 1951). In reality, however, people are evaluated and deployed according to various criteria and attributes that have nothing to do with abilities. 'Sex' is one such attribute.

Marx hoped that commercialism and capitalism could be abolished to restore true human connections. This hope was an expression of an idealistic

284

The Hijab

view that human qualities and abilities uncorrupted by the market value of outward appearance should be the basis for human relationships. In a sense, the informants for this study attempt to embody a similar ideal through the hijab. Marx sought a solution for the issues in capitalist society by eliminating money – i.e., turning to communism; my informants appear to be trying to deal with some of the problems of modern life mixed with commercialism and sexism through the hijab – i.e., returning to religion.

Although the informants generally accepted that hijab-wearing was a God-given duty, they also recognised that wearing it or not was an individual's decision. They also perceived it as something to be chosen at various turns in life, which was signified by the phrase 'when I am ready'. This type of 'moratorium' on religious duties serves to enhance second-generation Muslims' adaptability to British society. They participate in British society through schooling and employment and develop their careers there. Some informants reported finding it difficult to fulfil particular religious obligations, such as the hijab, posing the kind of dilemma posited by the 'in-betrween-two-cultures' theory. However, they were adeptly managing to avoid a serious dilemma or conflict and performed their duties and roles required by the two cultures. Importantly, they did so within the Islamic frame or through reference to religious knowledge. As mentioned in Chapter 7, they brought the Islamic tradition of 'leniency' to the fore by ascribing strict and restrictive practices to ethnic cultures; by using this logic, they managed diverse expectations from society, their community and the family, and achieved their participation in and integration with British society.

The above attitudes concerning the hijab may be analogous to the message imbued in 'My body is not your battleground', a poem by Syrian-American poet Mohja Kahf. To achieve Muslim women's true liberation, Kahf expresses resistance against stereotyping gazes cast on them as well as discourses glorifying physical control of women:

> My Body is not your battleground
>
> My hair is neither sacred nor cheap,
>
> Neither the cause of your disarray,
>
> Nor the path to your liberation

(Amer 2014: 180)

This passage articulates the strong message that what to do with a Muslim woman's body is a matter for her to decide and not something to be judged

Chapter 10

by someone else or politically exploited (by the right or the left). Just as Kahf's poem asserts, the informants claimed jurisdiction over their own bodies by emphasising that it is up to individuals whether they wear a hijab. They achieved or justified their autonomy and jurisdiction by reference to 'deference to God' or 'wearing a hijab for God' (Goto 2014), whereas in Western society, autonomy and control of self are usually claimed by reference to human rights.

Notes

1   They are 7:46, 17:45, 19:17, 33:53, 38:32, 41:5, 42:51 and 83:15 in the Quran (Sardar 2011: 329; Amer 2014: 23).

2   The Quran Verse 33:53 says:

> Believers, do not enter the Prophet's apartments for a meal unless you are given permission to do so; do not linger until [a meal] is ready. When you are invited, go in; then, when you have taken your meal, leave. Do not stay on and talk, for that would offend the Prophet, though he would shrink from asking you to leave. God does not shrink from the truth. When you ask his wives for something, do so from behind a screen: this is purer both for your hearts and for theirs. (words in square brackets are original)

3   This is just one of many interpretations. Some of my informants and various media commentators maintain that Islam does not command women to cover their 'hair' or 'skin' (BBC 2014b).

4   The first headscarf controversy in Britain's public schools coincided with France's first headscarf debate in 1989, when the headmaster of a Manchester grammar school suspended two sisters for wearing headscarves, which were not approved at the time. The family consulted the Commission for Racial Equality, which concluded that the school's decision 'could' constitute unlawful discrimination. The school attempted to defend the decision from a health and safety perspective, as well as arguing that it complied with the local Muslim council's guidance, although the guidance did not mention the headscarf. Despite conflicting positions, however, the issue did not result in court action. The decision forbidding the headscarf was replaced by a moderate negotiation (Kiliç 2008: 443–4). School governors overturned the headmaster's decision and allowed the girls to wear scarves provided that they matched the school colour (navy blue) (Joppke 2009: 81). Headscarves did not become a major issue again until 2002 when a 15-year-old schoolgirl brought a lawsuit for permission to wear a jilbab at her high school in Luton, London. The school already allowed students to wear various items

of traditional South Asian or Muslim clothing, including headscarves, as 80 per cent of its students were of Muslim background. In fact, the plaintiff wore a school-approved shalwar kameez until September 2002. When the new school term started, however, she sought permission to wear a school-coloured jilbab on the grounds that the shalwar kameez did not cover her arms and ankles completely. When the school rejected her request, she filed a complaint with the court. Finally, the House of Lords overturned her appeal (Guardian 2006). In 2007, a conflict arose in a Buckinghamshire grammar school over a niqab. At this school, 120 of approximately 1,300 students were Muslim and 60 per cent of them wore school-approved hijabs. A twelve-year-old student sued for permission to wear a niqab, but the High Court rejected her appeal (Kiliç 2008: 445–6). Unlike France, however, Britain did not institute legislation concerning the jilbab or niqab despite these controversies and did not treat any of the court judgments as binding on later cases because they were individual rulings. In other words, Britain dealt with the hijab on a case-by-case basis (Kiliç 2008: 448). See Joppke (2009) and Adachi (2011b; 2013b: 303–23) for further discussions on the scarf/veil debates in France and Britain.

5   This was a point of debate in Europe's scarf/veil controversies. For example, a student in Luton, London, brought a lawsuit in 2002 over wearing a jilbab to school. In the end, the House of Lords supported the school's decision not to permit a jilbab on the campus. One of the reasons provided for the ruling was that a jilbab was an excessive representation of religious faith, which could put undue pressure on other students who did not wear it (House of Loads 2006: 6; Adachi 2013b: 318–9).

6   The six articles of faith are to believe in the Oneness of God, the Angels, the Holy Books, the Prophets, Judgment Day and Divine Predestination, and the five pillars of Islam refer to the profession of faith, prayer, alms, fasting and pilgrimage, both of which are considered to be obligatory for all Muslims.

7   As discussed in Chapter 4, previous studies focusing on religious identification among European Muslims found that no respondents denied being 'Muslim' regardless of their identity types (Sahin 2005; Phalet et al. 2012). This was also the case for my informants, but this book is attempting to explain how they identify themselves as 'Muslim' despite discrepancies between Islamic teachings and their practices.

8   These two passages in the Quran state:

It is He who has control over the heavens and earth and has no offspring – no one shares control with Him – and who created all things and made them to an exact measure. (25:2)

Not even the weight of a speck of dust in the earth or sky escape your Lord, nor anything lesser or greater: it is all written in a clear record. (10:61)

9   The Quran 67:2 states: 'to test you and reveal which of you does best'. Here, Allah is depicted as someone who tests people to judge if they perform their Islamic duties.

Chapter 10

10 *Surah* (Chapter) 22 of the Quran is called 'The Pilgrimage', detailing its steps.

11 The Quran 3:97 states: 'Pilgrimage to the House is a duty owed to God by people who are able to undertake it'. Here, 'people who are able to undertake it' has been interpreted as meaning 'people who can afford it' (Nihon Isuramu Kyokai et al. 2002: 279).

12 The expression '(not) ready' is found fragmentally in previous studies. For example, an informant in an Australian study on young Muslim women says that 'I know I should do it [wear a headscarf] but I'm not ready yet' (Poynting 2009: 378). Similarly, an informant in Hoque's research on 'third-generation' Muslim teens in East London commented that 'I do not wear it anymore. I will again, *inshallah*, when I am ready' (Hoque 2015: 152). Hence, the expression 'not ready' can be regarded as an excuse used by women to postpone their performance of an Islamic duty, such as wearing a headscarf – especially when dealing with conflict in Western society.

13 The Quran 25:1 states: 'Exalted is He who has sent the Differentiator down to His servant so that he may give warning to all people'.

14 This point is homologous with Mahmood's argument cited in Chapter 3 about Egyptian Muslim women's 'agency':

> I realized that al-ḥayā' was among the good deeds [*huwwa min al-aʿmāl al-ṣaliḥa*], and given my natural lack of shyness [al-ḥayā'], I had to make or create it first. I realized that making [*sanaʿ*] it in yourself is not hypocrisy, and that eventually your inside learns to have al-ḥayā' too. (Mahmood 2005: 156, words in square brackets are original)

Remarks like this signify the 'creation of desire through knowledge acquisition'. In other words, they 'acquire knowledge to create desire' rather than 'seeking knowledge out of desire'.

The Hijab

Conclusion

Towards a New Understanding of Islam

> My aim is general, and modest: to create a better understanding of the problem by highlighting the historical perspective and providing some previously unknown information and fresh insight. If at the end of the book the reader feels that [s]he is able to see the wood instead of the trees, the purpose of the book will have been amply served.
>
> *Black British, White British*
> by Dilip Hiro (1973: viii)

> Researching and writing on Islam and Muslim identities has become an unavoidably political enterprise. Superficially of course, this observation is (or should be) nothing more than a professional commonplace – all research processes are inherently political, as any reflexive researcher knows. Skewed relations of power between researcher and researched are a constant of most social research situations, further complicated by cross-cutting considerations such as whether the researcher is an insider or outsider of the research participants' social network, and whether or not there are gendered, generational, ethnic or class differences... Moreover, these considerations do not simply evaporate on the completion of fieldwork, but carry over into the writing process, taking on new dynamics as existing codes and conventions of writing are adapted to the task of articulating particular (read selected) cultural representations.
>
> *Muslims in Britain*
> by Richard Gale and Peter Hopkins (2009: 1)

Identity management and social integration of second-generation Muslims in reflexive modernity

This book set out to discover how second-generation Muslims were integrating into British society as they found themselves at the centre of post-9/11 Western political and social discourses on Islam. I adopted reflexive modernisation theory to tackle a theoretical issue concerning identity in a super-diverse society: how to explain the relationship between closedness and openness of identity. One position assumes the closedness of identity and culture; the other emphasises the openness of identity, which presumes identity is selectively constructed by crossing cultural borders. As discussed in Chapter 3, this attempt at understanding Muslims in contemporary Western society required a framework that could simultaneously explain both its closedness (obedience to Islam) and openness (adaptation to Western society). I adopted the theory of reflexive modernisation to understand these two aspects of the identities of second-generation British Muslims.

The first thing to emerge from my interview data analysis was that the informants were constantly aware of social discourses surrounding second-generation Muslims in discussing 'what Islam is' and 'how to live as a Muslim'. As shown in Chapter 5, they were questioned about Islam and being Muslim in their interactions with friends and colleagues as well as by the media and felt required to respond to these questions daily in the post-9/11 context. They were forced to face up to their own identity in this Islamophobic social space (Contractor 2012: 88–9). At the same time, however, the informants saw themselves as British and were content with living in British society – even if they were subjected to racism – as discussed in Chapter 6. This is because they recognised Britain as a 'multicultural space' and the tolerant character of 'Britishness'. They understood Britishness as a tolerant or bland national identity that could coexist and overlap with diverse cultures rather than as an exclusionary identity. They believed that this character constructed Britain as a multicultural space providing more structured interstices in which they could join as Muslims.

The informants' principal strategy for balancing the tensions between being British and being Muslim was to differentiate between culture and religion (Ryan 2012; Modood 2013; Sahin 2013). As discussed in Chapter 7, this refers to distinguishing religion from the traditional customs of ethnic communities, thereby removing Islam from a particular context and redefining it as purer but also more flexible (i.e., more adaptable to diverse contexts). By separating religion from culture, young second-generation

Conclusion

Muslims present Islam as compatible with social values and lifestyles in the West by ascribing to culture various practices that are regarded negatively by British society. They have strategically used Islamic knowledge, such as the history and figures of Islam, to emphasise that Islam shares democratic values (e.g. equality and tolerance) with Western society.

This differentiation, however, did not necessarily entail a radical departure from their ethnic communities. The informants justified their family ties and cultural traditions in Islamic terms – as they did in the case of their relationship with British society. For instance, although it is popular for Asian families to arrange a marriage between their child and a partner from the parents' hometown, Western society rejects this custom as undermining democratic values, such as individual liberty. The informants responded to this criticism by distinguishing arranged marriage from 'forced marriage', arguing that the former did not conflict with Islamic principles of autonomy and equality as the parties ultimately made their own decisions. Importantly, whether it is integration into British society or reverence for the practices of the Asian community, both are assessed and supported or rejected from an Islamic perspective. In other words, they drew their ultimate decision rule from their religion in any case.

The differentiation between culture and religion was made possible by Islamic knowledge, as discussed in Chapter 8 (Jones 2012). Giddens argues that people in reflexive modernity organise their lives with diverse knowledge and information that is individually and selectively acquired rather than according to inherited traditions (i.e., predetermined behavioural patterns). Similarly, young second-generation Muslims – unlike first-generation immigrants – enjoyed the benefits of today's highly informationalised society to rely on knowledge of Islam instead of their ethnic tradition in managing their lives. In the not-too-distant past, a small section of the religious elite and community traditions could retain monopoly control over Islamic interpretation. Today, though, individuals can acquire a broad range of knowledge and interpret religious teachings for themselves (i.e., *ijtihad*) due to enhanced religious facilities, improved literacy and the Internet and information technology (Larsson 2011). Young people reject those practices that are incongruous with their way of life by ascribing them to culture, thereby facilitating their participation 'as Muslims' in Western society.

As emphasised in Chapter 8, the ideas that enable their flexible relationships with society and religion – the traditional pursuit of knowledge and *ijtihad* – are immanent in Islam (Saeed 2006; Sahin 2013). More importantly, though, the reflexive, rather than axiomatic, nature of these Islamic ideas and traditions were brought to the fore by the informants themselves in the post-9/11 environment.

As discussed in Chapters 9 and 10, women have strategically mobilised the reflexively unearthed tradition of knowledge in Islam to enhance their social participation. Many of the female informants argued that the Quran required both women and men to acquire knowledge about the world, making academic learning and social engagement religious duties. Some justified their pursuit of education and career, and the resulting delay of marriage with reference to female leaders in Islamic history, such as Khadija and Aisha. In this way, they negotiated their education and careers with family and community by actively utilising knowledge of Islam (Adachi 2016).

Knowledge is also important in the context of a multicultural society. Communication with people from diverse backgrounds motivated informants to research 'what Islam is' (and 'what culture is' at the same time), which in turn compelled them to construct a personal Islam ('my Islam') (Bokhari 2013: 62) based on their own interpretations, as discussed in Chapter 8. The individualisation of faith, along with the Islamic idea that 'judging' people's performance of their religious duties is a prerogative reserved for God, contributed to strengthening their tolerance of faith practices. The idea that no one can know if one has fulfilled God-given obligations until the last judgment reinforces the individual responsibility for faith practice and serves to inhibit judgment of others' faith and practices. In fact, the informants tended to avoid judging others' faith, arguing that Islam was 'a relationship between me and God' after all (Jeldtoft 2013: 86).

Muslims can connect with Western social institutions and values more easily through individualising their faith. This is the logic some of the female informants used to justify devoting themselves to studying or a career. They justified delaying the performance of various Islamic duties (e.g., hijab, prayer and pilgrimage) with phrases such as 'when I am ready' and 'when the time is right'. These phrases express the Islamic idea that faith is a personal responsibility. Emphasising this religious principle has helped women to deepen their involvement in Western society as Muslims while resisting the role expectations imposed by Asian communities and families and rejecting the negative representations and discourses about Islam disseminated by broader society (Adachi 2016).

Multiculturalism and Muslims

Another key finding in our analysis is that young Muslims' perception of Britain as a multicultural society contributes to their commitment to British society. As illustrated in Chapter 6, the informants had a favourable view of Britain as a 'multicultural space', where different cultures, ethnicities

Conclusion

and religions gathered and recognised one another. This condition not only allowed them to be Muslims in British society but also gave them a reason to commit to that society.

This highlights the significance of the multicultural model to social integration. For minorities to actively accept laws and civic cultures in host societies, the cultures must be sufficiently inclusive and tolerant. Numerous attempts at assimilation as an integration principle for increasingly diverse societies have failed because they did not offer minority groups any motivation to accept the mainstream societal cultures and values (Kymlicka 1995; Modood 2013). On the contrary, tolerance and recognition of minority group cultures may motivate them to integrate into the host societies (Modood 2007; 2013), because 'only when people are secure in their own cultural identity will they be able to accept those who differ from themselves' (Berry 2001: 623). Multiculturalism highlights this correlation between 'being accepted' and 'accepting' (Kymlicka 1995; 2002; Miller 1995; Modood 2007).

This 'reciprocal acceptance' broadens the possibility of creating respect for one another's cultural norms. The informants were able to recognise non-Islamic lifestyles – drinking and intersexual socialising – as a 'way of life' because they felt that their own religious rituals and rules could be more or less accepted as another 'way of life' as well in Britain. Such reciprocal acceptance appears to be a necessary condition for social cohesion and integration, strengthening the spirit of inter-community tolerance as well as validating one's citizen status (Modood 2013). In fact, the informants expressed a strong sense of attachment to and pride in Britain as a multicultural space, contrasting it with France. While being Muslim was their primary identity, they perceived Britain as their 'home'.

Their attitudes may be a peculiar kind of paradox of British society, as Modood states:

> The imperial legacy has, paradoxically, both been a source of racism and constituted a set of opportunity structures for an easy acquisition and exercise of citizenship (for ex-imperial subjects), for political opposition to racism and for an ethnic minority assertiveness... (Modood 2013: 46)

As discussed in Chapter 5, 'being British' may be 'still not easy' for second-generation Muslims if they experience Britain as a racist society (Modood 2010). However, Britain's history of social integration – the British Empire, multi-nations and the unique relationship between church-state (Favell 2001; Fetzer and Soper 2005) – provides cultural interstices in which diverse communities can co-exist, as we saw in Chapter 2 (see also Adachi 2013b).

Towards a New Understanding of Islam

The multicultural space and the lenient British identity enable minorities to incrementally deepen their inclusion in broader society as well as keep their own spaces. Multiculturalism works as an ideology to provide a framework for forming this multicultural space (Parekh 2007: 131).

We should note, however, different kinds of multiculturalism. According to British political philosopher Bhikhu Parekh, there are two types of multiculturalism: one is a commitment to a plurality of self-contained cultures, while the other supports intercultural interaction and internally diverse cultures. Parekh calls the former 'multi-culturalism' and the latter 'multicultural-ism'. While many political discourses have assumed the former, the latter has been practised in Britain – in association with 'antiracism'. It means that British Muslims' high degree of identification with Britishness (see Chapter 2) and their perception of British society as their 'home' (as discussed in Chapter 6) must be understood as the product of multicultural-ism (Parekh 2007: 130–1; Meer and Modood 2012; Modood: 2013).

Given these findings, my analysis suggests that both advocates and critics of multiculturalism might have overestimated the gap between Islam and Western society (Haddad et al. 2006: 17). On one hand, young Muslims in the West are strongly committed to Islam. On the other hand, they live in a developed society, where they receive advanced education, use state-of-the-art electronic devices daily and have become accustomed to its lifestyle and values. Islamic teachings and Western lifestyles are equally facts of life for second-generation Muslims and are the conditions for their identity formation. Accordingly, the challenge for young Muslims in the West is not 'how to integrate themselves into Western social institutions and values' but 'how to justify their integration into Western society from an Islamic point of view'.

They utilise knowledge in Islam to that end. Second-generation Muslims in the West use discursive (religious) knowledge to reflexively re-examine those traditions considered self-evident by the first generation (i.e., customs of mixed Islamic and cultural origin). They dis-embed Islam from traditional cultural contexts (e.g., Arabic and Asian societies), add their own interpretations to it, and re-embed it in new contexts (i.e., European societies). They need not forsake Islam to form relationships with non-Islamic societies or ensure diversity in the Muslim community (Bokhari 2013: 63–4). Rather, they build bridges between Islamic teachings and citizenship in Western society through a form of 'elastic orthodoxy' (DeHanas 2013), which results from their reflexive engagement with their faith (Modood 2013: 129–35). In the language of social systems theory (Luhmann 1984: 64), second-generation Muslims achieve selective 'openness' (i.e., social

295

Conclusion

engagement and participation) toward Western civic society through their identity's 'closedness' (i.e., self-referencing to Islam).

If this holds true, recognition through multiculturalism can allow young Muslims to have a positive identity and to share in democratic citizenship in the post-9/11 era. Conversely, a lack of knowledge of Islam or an inability to find a connection between Western lifestyles and one's faith appears to be significant factors behind young people's anomie and attraction to extremism (Lewis 2007; Parekh 2008: 123–9). Although not extreme, we saw the situation in the cases of Rabab and Nasha in Chapter 7. Their underdeveloped knowledge of Islam led to insufficient differentiation between culture and religion, which fostered ambivalence toward Islam and its practices. Consequently, they had not (yet) found a way to be British with maintaining confidence in being Muslim (Ameli 2002). A 'lack of religious literacy and education' and the resultant failing to connect 'two cultures' seem to be 'a common feature among those that are drawn to extremist groups'. 'Religious novices exploring their faith for the first time' may be 'the most vulnerable' group (Choudhury 2007: 6).

Against this background, mosques and madrassas in the West have recently been organising regular meetings, lectures and seminars to improve young Muslims' knowledge of Islam and provide specific information on how to practise Islam in Western society; these efforts aim to reduce the risk of radicalisation by contributing to greater social integration (Sahin 2013). By translating the democratic citizenship principle into the language of Islam, they have encouraged young people to participate in Western society as Muslims (Modood 2013: 131). These initiatives have helped make it possible for young people to live as 'European Muslims' (Ramadan 2005) and 'British Muslims' (Modood 2013) – 'becoming British by becoming Muslim' makes sense to them (Kurien 1998).

These findings are significant for understanding second-generation Muslims' identity and social integration:

> There are signs of a 'British Muslim' identity forming in reaction to violent radicalism, which is proposing a 'receptive, integrationist and dynamic' Islam. It is receptive because it is open to Western influences; it is integrationist because it believes Muslims ought to take full part in British society and political processes; and it is dynamic because it acknowledges that as contexts change, so will the ways Muslims conceive of and practise their religion. (Choudhury 2007: 6)

And,

Towards a New Understanding of Islam

> [T]he discourse of 'European/British-Islam' is emerging as a powerful response to 'radical Islam'. Thus, whilst the politics of identity plays a [*sic*] in the radicalisation process, it remains an important tool for de-radicalisation. (Choudhury 2007: 22)

Accordingly, the second-generation's identification with Islam should not automatically be regarded as disengagement from Western society but rather as a representation of their desire to seek a deeper engagement in it:

> This religious mobilization is the result of the desire to produce an identity that would assist social integration, particularly among members of the younger European generation... (Dassetto et al. 2007: 7)

From this perspective, integrationist declarations of Muslims' failure to identify with Western society and vociferous demands for a shared national identity are counterproductive (Uberoi et al. 2011: 210–9). What is needed now is a new multiculturalism-based 'post-integrationist approach', which properly evaluates Islam's 'contribution' to democratic citizenship on the recognition that Islam is the second-largest religion in Europe (Parekh 2002; Bradley 2007; Ramadan 2010: 67–73; PRC 2011).

Academic contributions and challenges

As mentioned in Chapter 2, this book's uniqueness lies in its depiction of identity formation in Britain's second-generation Muslims exclusively from the perspective of reflexive modernisation theory. Some of its findings echo previous studies. For example, many studies since the late 1990s have acknowledged the differentiation between culture and religion, while research about Muslim women has explored their strategies for faith-based negotiation with their communities (Werbner 1996; Bagguley and Hussain 2005; Poynting 2009; Bhimji 2009). However, many of these studies adopt an open identity model, which holds that identities change depending on space and place (Mir 2014). They typically emphasise 'space' and 'intersectionality' but lack an understanding of 'agency' in the sense of ethical self-governance of the body and its mechanism (Mahmood 2005). Using the idea of reflexivity, however, this book has been able to describe young Muslims' practices of agency in managing identity. Focusing on organic relations between Islam and Western ways of life, this book approached the agency of young Muslims in ways that postcolonial feminist research has not recognised. As a result, it has examined

297

Conclusion

that second-generation Muslims mobilise Islamic knowledge to construct posirive religious identities and become active citizens in Western society.

The present study makes an important contribution to the field of research on second-generation Muslims in the West by explicating both a deepening religious commitment among young Muslims and Islam's high degree of openness. The book also has elucidated how 'identification with Islam' serves second-generation Muslims' resistance to the double consciousness imposed by mainstream discourse in the West, thus creating more optimistic possibilities for relations between the West and Islam.

This study also contributes to the development of the 'reflexive modernisation theory', which Anthony Giddens and Ulrich Beck advocate. The ways in which the second-generation immigrants in this book manage their identities can be understood from the perspective of reflexive modernisation theory. As discussed in Chapter 3, this theory provides a useful framework for understanding the experiences of second generation Muslims and their social environments in Britain. The cultural and religious practices brought in by the first generation have little meaning for the second generations who live in different environments than the ones in which the practices were originally embedded. Thus, by using expert knowledge about Islam, available both offline and online, they have re-embedded Islam in a new context to make it meaningful for their lives and identities. Religious knowledge both strengthens their religious identity and allows them to distance themselves from religious tradition by promoting the individualisation of faith. Thus, this book can be positioned as a sociological work based on reflexive modernisation theory, rather than simply a case study of Muslim youth in the West.

In Japan, this book fills a gap in the understanding of Western Muslims. Muslim research in Japan is underdeveloped because the country has a short history of contact with Islam (Komura 2015: 42–3). Japan's Islam research started as a national policy (the Islamic Policy in Wartime) at the beginning of the twentieth century. After WWII, the oil crises and the Israeli-Arab wars piqued economic interest in the Arab world and led more people to study Arabic and Islam (Higuchi 2007; Komura 2015). However, academic popularity and the scope of research remained limited.[1] Only since 9/11, has Japanese interest in Islam grown, evidenced by the release of numerous general-interest and academic books. Many publications discuss Islam in association with its doctrine, rituals, law, history, social life or political systems in Islamic states (Katakura et al. eds. 2004; Kamada 2015; Nakata 2015; Matsuyama ed. 2018). They tend to offer an 'idealised' (Bagguley and Hussain 2005: 218) understanding of Islam. By comparison, very few

298

Japanese academic works systematically discuss how everyday Muslims understand Islam and incorporate it into their lives in contemporary society.

Discussion on that theme finally started in the past decade. For example, Kamogawa (2008) studied Malaysian women's life course formulation from an ethnicity perspective; Adachi (2020b) reported on the family and work roles of female academics in Malaysia caught between Islamisation and modernisation; Minesaki (2015) analysed Egyptian women's *fatwas* via study meetings and telephone; Kudo (2008) examined Japanese female Muslim converts and how their participation in study groups impacted on their agencies; and Adachi (2017) explored the daily negotiations of Japanese female converts in non-Islamic society or with their Muslim husbands based on life history interviews. These studies are important in depicting the lived experience of how young Muslims, especially women, accept and use in contemporary society (Bagguley and Hussain 2005; Dessing et al. eds. 2013).

In Japan, however, there have been studies of second-generation Muslims in Western societies but not from the 'lived religion' perspective. For example, although Masanori Naito and his research groups have been publishing their research on European Muslims since the 2000s (Naito 2004; 2009; Naito and Sakaguchi eds. 2007; Nakano et al. eds. 2015), these studies generally adopt the approach of political sociology, which focuses on the social and political climate around Islam. Thus they tend to treat Muslims as a collective political force reacting to these conditions but do not delve into individual Muslims and their relations to European society (Mihara 2009; Mori 2016). Many studies of European Muslims, meanwhile, discuss Islam, where the separation of religion and state is difficult, under the 'secular' civic-democratic space typified by France's *laïcité*. Hence, the headscarf/veil controversy has been a common research theme (Naito and Sakaguchi eds 2007; Kondo 2007; Iwashita 2011). This approach could reinforce certain views such as the 'clash of civilizations' (Huntington 1996) and the 'in-between-two-cultures' theory because it focuses on conflicts whichever way the cause is placed. Such a view risks being absorbed into a part of the mainstream discourse that emphasises the incompatibility of Islam and Western societies (Miura ed 2001; Naito 2004). Very few studies have illuminated the lived experience of ordinary European Muslims based on interview research (Yamashita 2018; 2022).[2]

This book provides a new perspective and insight on previous European Muslim research inside and outside of Japan. I believe that this study provides a – reasonably stable and durable – 'springboard' (i.e. a critical point of reference) for advancing research on the relationship between Islam and the modern world and the engagement of second-generation Muslims in both religious and secular spaces.

Conclusion

Challenges and outlook

This research has some limitations and contentious points. In this closing section, I would like to discuss these challenges and my views on them.

The first is a theoretical issue. The present book develops its argument along with Giddens' identity theory of reflexive modernity. Scott Lash and others have criticised Giddens' theory as being overly individualised as well as for being biased towards the cognitive aspects of identity (Lash 1994; Lash and Urry 1994). According to Lash and others, Giddens' reflexivity is based on a highly individualistic idea of self-monitoring and self-objectifying through language. This approach, they argue, fails to account for the effects of collectively exercised reflexive practices which are culture-specific and not necessarily verbalised (i.e., aesthetic reflexivity). This criticism may apply to the present research as well. This book depicts second-generation Muslims as agents continuously monitoring their faith in the face of mainstream discourses on Islam in the West. It does not, though, explore enough the impact of their mental, spiritual and collective experiences – e.g., group prayers at a mosque, reciting the Quran, personal dialogues with the Quran, and collective experience of pilgrimage – on their identity formation as Muslim or British.

While this criticism is valuable, this book's approach is defensible in the light of the challenges confronting today's second-generation Muslims. As mentioned, the problem of Islam in Western society has too often been debated within the frame of 'the clash of civilizations' (Huntington 1996), which deems the supposed 'incommensurability' (Elshtain 1993) between the two civilisations to be axiomatic. It presupposes that Western society and Islam have no shared values or common denominators for dialogues and cohabitation. Faced with this mainstream post-9/11 discourse, young Western Muslims have been transforming their relationship with Islam from '*an sich*' to '*für sich*'. In other words, they reassess Islam from others' perspectives and reflexively and selectively take it as a necessary part of their identity. Recognition from others is essential in this process; therefore, the ability to translate religious concepts and practices into the language of civil society is indispensable. Hence, this book adopted a 'cognitive reflexivity' approach, following Giddens, emphasising the importance of discursive knowledge rather than an aesthetic reflexivity which operates in the background and repeats/intensifies differences.

The second is a methodological issue. As mentioned in Chapter 4, this book employs an interpretive objectivism approach to highlight 'cognitive' activities such as identity-formation and interpretation. Thus, while it was possible to identify common interpretive frameworks and meaning structures within the informants' narratives, it could not examine their actual behaviour in relation to society and family nor the extent to which the interview format influenced their narratives. With regard to the latter, the fact that the findings in this book are contiguous with some previous studies that took an insider approach lends a certain degree of validity to its procedures and objectivity (Bullock 2007; Kabir 2010; Bhimji 2012; Contractor 2012; Hoque 2015).[3] The former, however, warrants further investigation through research employing different types of data, methodologies and approaches.

The third is a normativity issue concerning the book's approach. Britain's second-generation Muslims have developed a reflexive relationship with Islam. However, it might be argued that such reflexive consciousness has been imposed rather than spontaneously generated. As discussed in Chapter 5, against Western society's pervasive racism, Islamophobia and exclusionary discourses, second-generation Muslims have had to redefine their faith and identity as meaningful within Western social values and culture (Ramadan 2010). As Michael Keith and Steve Pile argue, 'space is not an innocent backdrop to position, it is itself filled with politics and ideology' (Keith and Pile 1993: 4). Second-generation Muslims have had to reflexively examine their religion to adapt to this racialised space (Lyon 2005: 84–7). Does this imply that their reflexive consciousness is a desire created under pressure in the post-9/11 environment (Hoque 2015: 17)? Are they pressured to choose from limited options offered by the state between 'good Muslims' obedient to government ideologies and policies and 'bad Muslims' who object to them (Blick et al. 2006: 31; Mouffe 2005)? Although Tariq Ramadan urged Muslims in Western society to accept the current situation as 'fact', one might ask whether this is a reasonable request for the Muslims concerned (Ramadan 2010).

These issues warrant attention. In fact, many studies criticise Britain's political discourses of social integration from a normative perspective (McGhee 2005; 2010; Pitcher 2009). While assuming the dominant effects of such discourses, this book portrays second-generation Muslims' resistance to them by focusing on the paradoxical consequences of discourse and the agency of informants. Part II of this book has revealed that informants challenged representations of Muslims' non-integration while justifying their participation in British society as Muslims by using Islamic knowledge and exploiting the dominant discourses that sought integration through shared Britishness and democratic values. Together with 'the dialectic of control' (Giddens 1991: 138) mentioned in Chapter 3, the strategies that they used illustrate the agency exercised by second-generation Muslims.

Conclusion

In this light, it would be mistaken to conclude that second-generation Muslims have simply been forced by their environment to engage reflexively with Islam. As noted in Chapter 6, the UK and the rest of Western society are now 'home' for tens of millions of Muslims; thus, the Islam that has developed in Europe should also be seen as part of the long history and tradition of Islam (Sardar and Ahmad 2012: 7). As Rageh Omaar observes, Western cities where many second-generation Muslims live form 'a part of the modern story of Islam in the world' (Omaar 2007: 37).[4] This is inseparable from the massive currents of globalisation and modernisation. Islamisation since the second half of the twentieth century has taken place where the global flows of economy, politics, information and culture collide with the structural frameworks of modernity, such as tradition, secularisation and nation-state, which have historically contained the Islamic world. Islamisation is a reformist movement for the survival of Islam in the midst of these upheavals and hence has been reflexive since its inception (Roy 2004). Islamisation is, therefore, a phenomenon linked with broader economic, political and cultural modernisation and globalisation, which is not only characterised by 9/11 but also the development of the knowledge and information economy, improved educational standards, women's social advancement and demands for democracy (Ameli 2002). This context is the background to today's Islamisation, in which religious knowledge produced and supplied in response to people's needs should also be seen as part of the long Islamic tradition (Parekh 2008: 123).[5]

Fourth, this book might be criticised for the shortage of insights into young second-generation Muslims who are leaning toward extremism. Although this is certainly a blind spot in this study, requiring further enquiry socially and academically, it was also this book's starting point. As stated in Introduction, I chose as research subjects the group of second-generation who participated in the wider society and might represent a large proportion of the Muslims living in Britain, rather than the radicalised group who represented only a tiny part of the Muslim community. Most of the informants in this book were low socio-economic status, lived in economically deprived areas and suffered racism and Islamophobia; they also expressed dissatisfaction with and criticism of both British society and their own communities. Yet, I found no evidence that these conditions and experiences had led to a radical indictment of British social values and rules or generated any extremist fervour. On the contrary, they lived as citizens of British society, breathing its multicultural atmosphere, learning its manners and values, and making individual efforts to interpret Islam reflexively. An undue focus on extremism distorts Western perceptions of Muslims and Islam and increases the risk of double consciousness among young second-generation Muslims.

To achieve better social integration in Britain, it is necessary to develop a clearer picture of how Muslims live there and better understand the diverse ways they participate in it. Moreover, Western society needs to trust the potential of multiculturalism and accept Muslims as unique and equal citizens. This book set out to explore this positive potential in the relationship between Western society and Islam.

Notes

1   Toshihiko Izutsu deserves special mention for his tremendous contribution to Japan's understanding of Islam. Izutsu was the first to translate the Quran in its entirety from Arabic to Japanese, presenting it as a 'human documentary' rather than a 'religious scripture' in order to vividly convey its contents to the Japanese people who were new to Islam (Izutsu trans [1958] 1964). He developed a unique understanding of Islam informed by eastern and mystical philosophies while introducing Islamic ideas and culture to a broader readership without compromising its intellectual integrity (Izutsu 1980; 1991). His works laid the foundation for the development of Islamic studies in Japan.

2   One of the few studies – besides my own (Adachi 2013a; 2013b; 2015a; 2016; 2018; 2020c) – was Yasuyuki Yamashita's work on young Muslims in France. While the present book views the relationship between Western society and Islam as 'reflexive', Yamashita understands it as 'hybrid'. Yamashita proposes the concept of 'adaptive Islam' under which young Muslims seek to integrate into French society by limiting conspicuous religious practices (Yamashita 2018). Although his findings contrast sharply with what I have found from the British Muslim cases, these differences reflect differences in our theoretical approaches, the political systems of the two countries, and the historical and cultural backgrounds of British Asian Muslims and French Arab Muslims.

3   In her research on young British Muslim women, Deborah Phillips organised focus group interviews in several areas of Northern England. The actual interviews were conducted in separate areas by her, a non-Muslim white woman, and another researcher of Muslim origin. Although there were some differences in the way the two facilitators interacted with the participants, their different backgrounds did not produce any marked differences in the themes that emerged from each group discussion (Phillips 2009: 26). In this respect, the difference between insiders and outsiders may not need to be emphasised.

4   Islamic theologian Yohei Matsuyama comments on the new connection between Islam and Western society with reference to the recent 'Islamic pop' phenomenon (contemporary pop songs combined with English lyrics about Islamic values and teachings):

Conclusion

> This 'religious practice' [Islamic pop] may suggest that Muslims in Europe have simultaneously become the subject and the object of 'takeover'... Even if Muslims acquire a dominant status in Europe, how can we say that the outcome will be an Islamised Europe rather than Europeanised Islam? Muslims may be taking over Europe, but they are simultaneously being taken over by Europe. (Matsuyama 2019: 284–5)

Perhaps this relationship between the West and Islam is not so much a 'takeover' as a process by which both parties become part of one another's 'tradition'.

5   Islamic civilisations have been 'diasporic' since inception. The Prophet Muhammad started a diaspora when he migrated from Mecca to Medina. The earliest Islamic civilisations blossomed in Central Asia, the Indian sub-continent and Africa rather than Arabia (Sardar and Ahmad 2012: 7). Now, Islam has taken root in European soil and begun to create a new civilisation from its dialogue with many cultures and values.

Towards a New Understanding of Islam

Appendix A. Attributes of informants (Female)

Site	Research Round	Number	Name	Ethnicity*	Age	Country of Origin (Mother-side)	Country of Origin (Father-side)	Immigration Generation	Educational Qualification	Status	Mode of Employment
Coventry	1st	1	Hibah	Somali	17	Somalia	Somalia	2	College	Studying	
		2	Arub	Bangladeshi	18	Bangladesh	Bangladesh	2	Sixth Form	Studying	
		3	Yusra	Asian Mixed	17	Pakistan	England	2	Sixth Form	Studying	
		4	Rahil	Asian Mixed	18	Pakistan	England	2	Sixth Form	Studying	
		5	Daliya	Sudanese	17	Sudan	Sudan	2	Sixth Form	Studying	
	2nd	6	Atiyah	Pakistani	20	Pakistan	Pakistan	3	University	Studying	
		7	Bakarah	Indian	39	India	Pakistan	2	University	Graduated	Part-time
		8	Duha	Asian Mixed	19	Pakistan	England	2	University	Studying	
		9	Farwah	Asian Mixed	20	Pakistan	England	2	University	Studying	
		10	Habibah	Asian Mixed	20	Pakistan	England	2	University	Studying	
		11	Ibtisam	Bangladeshi	21	Bangladesh	Bangladesh	2	University	Dropout	Full-time
		12	Janan	Sudanese	20	Sudan	Sudan	2	University	Studying	
		13	Khansa	Other mixed	19	Africa	Arab	2	University	Studying	
		14	Labibah	Pakistani	22	Pakistan	Pakistan	3	University	Graduated	Full-time
		15	Majdah	Pakistani	21	Pakistan	Pakistan	2	University	Studying	
		16	Nasha	Bangladeshi	17	Bangladesh	Bangladesh	2	Sixth Form	Studying	
		17	Rabab	Bangladeshi	17	Bangladesh	Bangladesh	3	Sixth Form	Studying	
		18	Saba	Pakistani	25	Pakistan	Pakistan	2	University	Graduated	housewife
		19	Tabassum	Indian	26	India	India	2	University	Graduated	Part-time
		20	Ulfah	Indian	21	India	India	2	College	Graduated	Part-time
		21	Wardah	Indian	27	India	India	4	Secondary	Graduated	housewife
		22	Zahra	Asian Mixed	22	India	Fiji	3	Secondary	Graduated	LOA
		23	Karam	Pakistani	23	Pakistan	Pakistan	3	College	Graduated	Full-time
		24	Selikah	Indian	17	India	India	3	Sixth Form	Studying	
		25	Rahmah	Indian	18	India	India	3	University	Studying	
		26	Uzma	Indian	19	India	India	4	University	Studying	Part-time
London	3rd	27	Nazma	Bangladeshi	36	Bangladesh	Bangladesh	2	Postgraduate	Studying	Full-time
		28	Tazmin	Asian Mixed	19	Bangladesh	Mixed Background	3	Sixth Form	Studying	Part-time
		29	Ambreen	Asian Mixed	16	Bangladesh	Mixed Background	3	Secondary	Studying	
		30	Thahera	Bangladeshi	18	Bangladesh	Bangladesh	2	College	Studying	
		31	Toslima	Bangladeshi	18	Bangladesh	Bangladesh	2	College	Studying	Part-time
		32	Asma	Asian Mixed	22	Mauritius	Madagascar	2	University	Graduated	Full-time
		33	Nafisah	Asian Mixed	22	India	Mozambique	3	University	Graduated	Full-time
		34	Rafima	Bangladeshi	30	Bangladesh	Bangladesh	2	College	Graduated	Full-time
		35	Fahima	Bangladeshi	28	Bangladesh	Bangladesh	2	University	Graduated	LOA
		36	Shamina	Bangladeshi	25	Bangladesh	Bangladesh	2	University	Graduated	Full-time
		37	Rehana	Bangladeshi	26	Bangladesh	Bangladesh	1.5	University	Graduated	Full-time
		38	Rukshana	Bangladeshi	25	Bangladesh	Bangladesh	1.5	Postgraduate	Studying	Part-time
		39	Poppy	Bangladeshi	28	Bangladesh	Bangladesh	1.5	Postgraduate	Graduated	Full-time
		40	Zaheda	Bangladeshi	25	Bangladesh	Bangladesh	2	University	Studying	Full-time
		41	Nasira	Bangladeshi	18	Bangladesh	Bangladesh	2	University	Studying	
		42	Parveen	Pakistani	31	Pakistan	Pakistan	2	Postgraduate	Graduated	Full-time
		43	Shirina	Bangladeshi	31	Bangladesh	Bangladesh	2	University	Graduated	Full-time
		44	Tasrin	Bangladeshi	31	Bangladesh	Bangladesh	2	Postgraduate	Graduated	Full-time
		45	Jakera	Bangladeshi	40	Bangladesh	Bangladesh	1.5	Postgraduate	Graduated	Full-time
		46	Syeda	Bangladeshi	40	Bangladesh	Bangladesh	1.5	Postgraduate	Graduated	Full-time
		47	Lola	Nigerian	22	Nigeria	Nigeria	2	University	Studying	
		48	Yasmin	Bangladeshi	22	Bangladesh	Bangladesh	2	University	Graduated	Full-time
	4th	49	Banan	Bangladeshi	24	Bangladesh	Bangladesh	2	University	Graduated	Full-time
		50	Durrah	Indian	39	India	India	2	University	Graduated	Full-time
		51	Harir	Pakistani	27	Pakistan	Pakistan	2	University	Graduated	Full-time
		52	Inam	Pakistani	17	Pakistan	Pakistan	2	Sixth Form	Studying	
		53	Halimah	Pakistani	19	Pakistan	Pakistan	2	University	Studying	
		54	Jannah	Bangladeshi	18	Bangladesh	Bangladesh	2	University	Studying	
		55	Malikah	Bangladeshi	26	Bangladesh	Bangladesh	2	University	Graduated	Full-time
		56	Raniyah	Bangladeshi	19	Bangladesh	Bangladesh	2	Sixth Form	Studying	
		57	Salimah	Bangladeshi	33	Bangladesh	Bangladesh	2	University	Graduated	Full-time

* "Asian Mixed" means only one of the parents is Asian.
** "O" denotes "married", "×" denotes "unmarried", and "△" denotes "unmarried after divorce".
*** The number following "→" means the age at which the informant resumed wearing a hijab after stopping for a period.

Occupation	Educational Qualification (Mother)	Educational Qualification (Father)	Marriage**	Marriage Age	Marriage Type	Expecting Type of Marriage	Hijab	Hijab Wearing Age***
			×			Non-arranged	×	
			×			Non-arranged	○	Unknown
			×			Either	○	Unknown
			×			Either	○	Unknown
			×			Non-arranged	×	
			×			Arranged	○	Unknown
Community Worker			○	21	Non-arranged		○	Unknown
			○	18	Non-arranged		○	Unknown
			×			Non-arranged	×	
Store Employee			×			Non-arranged	○	Unknown
			×			Arranged	○	Unknown
			×			Arranged	○	Unknown
			×			Arranged	×	
IT Assistant			×			Arranged	○	5→14
			×			Non-arranged	×	
			×			Non-arranged	×	
			×			Non-arranged	×	
			×			Arranged	○	Unknown
English Lecturer			○	22	Non-arranged		○	11
Store Employee			×			Either	○	Unknown
			○	19	Arranged		○	22
			○	22	Arranged		×	
Unknown			×			Non-arranged	×	
			×			Non-arranged	○	7
			×			Non-arranged	×	
Medical Officer			×			Either	×	
Community Worker	No Qualification	University	○	16	Non-arranged		○	15
Project Manager	Secondary and Below	Secondary and Below	×			Either	○	13
	Secondary and Below	Secondary and Below	×			Either	○	12
	Secondary and Below	Secondary and Below	×			Non-arranged	○	10
Store Employee	Secondary and Below	Secondary and Below	×			Either	×	
Charity Staff (Islam)	Secondary and Below	Secondary and Below	○	21	Non-arranged		○	10
Charity Staff (Islam)	Secondary and Below	Secondary and Below	○	21	Non-arranged		○	18
Dental Hygienist	Unknown	Secondary and Below	○	24	Arranged		○	29
Civil Servant	Secondary and Below	Secondary and Below	○	23	Arranged		○	20
Teaching Assistant (Primary School)	Secondary and Below	Unknown	×			Arranged	×	
Teacher (Primary School)	College	University	○	23	Arranged		○	15
Midwife	Secondary and Below	University	×			Arranged	○	12
Nursery Nurse	Secondary and Below	Secondary and Below	×			Arranged	○	27
Nursery Nurse	Secondary and Below	Secondary and Below	×			Arranged	○	24
	Secondary and Below	Secondary and Below	×			Arranged	○	Unknown
Lawyer	Unknown	Unknown	○	29	Non-arranged		×	
Community Manager	Unknown	Unknown	○	16	Arranged		○	16
Teacher (Secondary School)	Secondary and Below	Secondary and Below	○	20	Arranged		○	30
NHS Staff	Secondary and Below	Secondary and Below	○	24	Arranged		○	16
Teacher (Primary School)	Secondary and Below	Secondary and Below	△	25	Arranged		○	16
	Secondary and Below	Secondary and Below	×			Arranged	○	19
Charity Staff (Islam)	Secondary and Below	Secondary and Below	×			Arranged	○	12→18
Charity Staff (Islam)	Secondary and Below	Secondary and Below	×			Non-arranged	○	15
Event Staff	Secondary and Below	Secondary and Below	×			Non-arranged	×	
Newspaper Reporter	Secondary and Below	Secondary and Below	×			Non-arranged	○	11
	Unknown	Unknown	×			Non-arranged	○	11
	University	Secondary and Below	×			Arranged	○	9
	Secondary and Below	Secondary and Below	×			Non-arranged	×	
Office Worker	Unknown	Unknown	×			Non-arranged	○	18
	Secondary and Below	Unknown	×			Arranged	○	11
Teacher (Primary School)	Unknown	Unknown	×			Non-arranged	○	11→16

Appendix B. Attributes of informants (Male)

Site	Research Round	Number	Name	Ethnicity*	Age	Country of Origin (Mother-side)	Country of Origin (Father-side)	Immigration Generation	Educational Qualification	Status	Mode of Employ-ment
Coventry	1st	1	Arham	Pakistani	24	Pakistan	Pakistan	2	Postgraduate	Studying	
		2	Huzaifa	Pakistani	18	Pakistan	Pakistan	2	Sixth Form	Graduated	Part-time
		3	Maaz	Pakistani	21	Pakistan	Pakistan	2	University	Studying	
	2nd	4	Waqas	Pakistani	24	Pakistan	Pakistan	2	University	Studying	
		5	Husnain	Bangladeshi	21	Bangladesh	Bangladesh	2	University	Studying	
		6	Imran	Pakistani	24	Pakistan	Pakistan	2	University	Graduated	Full-time
		7	Sufian	Pakistani	25	Pakistan	Pakistan	2	University	Graduated	Full-time
		8	Fahad	Indian	26	India	India	2	University	Graduated	Full-time
		9	Zubair	Barbadian	20	Barbados	Barbados	2	College	Graduated	Full-time
		10	Noman	Indian	18	India	India	3	University	Studying	
		11	Owais	Indian	18	India	India	2	University	Studying	
		12	Rizwan	Asian mixed	19	India	Kenya	4	University	Studying	
		13	Usama	Bangladeshi	21	Bangladesh	Bangladesh	2	University	Studying	
		14	Ahmed	Pakistani	21	Pakistan	Pakistan	3	University	Studying	
London	3rd										
	4th	15	Jacob	Bangladeshi	19	Bangladesh	Bangladesh	2	University	Studying	
		16	Hannan	Bangladeshi	32	Bangladesh	Bangladesh	3	Postgraduate	Studying	Full-time
		17	Yasir	Bangladeshi	19	Bangladesh	Bangladesh	2	College	Studying	
		18	Umair	Bangladeshi	21	Bangladesh	Bangladesh	2	University	Studying	
		19	Taimoor	Pakistani	27	Pakistan	Pakistan	2	Postgraduate	Graduated	Full-time
		20	Abaan	Bangladeshi	25	Bangladesh	Bangladesh	2	Postgraduate	Graduated	Job Seeking
		21	Hamdan	Bangladeshi	34	Bangladesh	Bangladesh	2	College	Graduated	Full-time
		22	Haris	Bangladeshi	27	Bangladesh	Bangladesh	2	College	Dropout	Part-time
		23	Farhan	Bangladeshi	23	Bangladesh	Bangladesh	3	University	Graduated	Part-time
		24	Sohail	Bangladeshi	28	Bangladesh	Bangladesh	2	University	Graduated	Full-time
		25	Bilal	Bangladeshi	27	Bangladesh	Bangladesh	2	College	Dropout	Full-time
		26	Shoaib	Bangladeshi	29	Bangladesh	Bangladesh	2	University	Graduated	Full-time
		27	Kashif	Bangladeshi	22	Bangladesh	Bangladesh	2	University	Graduated	Full-time
		28	Aflan	Pakistani	35	Pakistan	Pakistan	2	Postgraduate	Graduated	Full-time
		29	Daniyal	Bangladeshi	27	Bangladesh	Bangladesh	2	Postgraduate	Graduated	Full-time
		30	Talha	Pakistani	27	Pakistan	Pakistan	2	Postgraduate	Graduated	Job Seeking
		31	Faisal	Bangladeshi	18	Bangladesh	Bangladesh	2	College	Studying	
		32	Umar	Bangladeshi	26	Bangladesh	Bangladesh	2	College	Dropout	Part-time

* "Asian Mixed" means only one of the parents is Asian.
** "○" denotes "married", "×" denotes "unmarried".

Occupation	Educational Qualification (Mother)	Educational Qualification (Father)	Marriage**	Marriage Age	Marriage Type	Expecting Type of Marriage
Salesperson			×			Non-arranged
			×			Non-arranged
			×			Either
Salesperson			×			Arranged
			×			Non-arranged
Staff in Water Company			×			Arranged
Staff in Education Company			×			Arranged
Unknown			×			Arranged
			O	19	Non-arranged	
			×			Arranged
			×			Arranged
			×			Arranged
			×			Non-arranged
			O	20	Arranged	
	Unknown	Unknown	×			Arranged
Community Worker	Secondary and Below	College	O	19	Non-arranged	
	Unknown	Secondary and Below	×			Arranged
	No Qualification	Secondary and Below	O	21	Non-arranged	
Consultant	Secondary and Below	College	×			Either
	Postgraduate School	University	×			Either
Adviser	Secondary and Below	College	O	34	Non-arranged	
Staff in Printing Company	Unknown	Unknown	×			Arranged
Sales Assistant	Secondary and Below	Unknown	×			Arranged
Staff in Performance Company	Secondary and Below	College	O	28	Arranged	
Distribution Coordinator	Secondary and Below	Secondary and Below	×			Either
Staff in Education Company	No Qualification	Unknown	O	27	Arranged	
Facility Manager	Secondary and Below	Secondary and Below	×			Arranged
Partner	Secondary and Below	Secondary and Below	O	27	Arranged	
Office Worker	Secondary and Below	Secondary and Below	×			Arranged
	Postgraduate School	Postgraduate School	×			Arranged
	College	College	×			Non-arranged
Security Staff	Secondary and Below	Secondary and Below	×			Either

Bibliography

Abbas, Tahir, 2005, 'British South Asian Muslims: State and Multicultural Society', in Tahir Abbas ed., *Muslim Britain: Communities under Pressure*, London: Zed Books.

————, 2011, *Islamic Radicalism and Multicultural Politics: The British Experience*, Oxon: Routledge.

Abou-Bakr, Omaima, 2013, 'Introduction: Why Do We Need an Islamic-Feminism?', in Omaima Abou-Bakr ed., *Feminist and Islamic Perspectives: New Horizons of Knowledge and Reform*, Mohandeseen: Promotion Team.

Abou-Bakr, Omaima ed., 2013, *Feminist and Islamic Perspectives: New Horizons of Knowledge and Reform*, Mohandeseen: Promotion Team.

Abu-Lughod, Lila, 2002, 'Do Muslim Women Really Need Saving? Anthropological Reflections on Cultural Relativism and Its Others', *American Anthropologist*, 104(3): 783–90.

————, 2013, *Do Muslim Women Need Saving?*, Cambridge: Harvard University Press.

Adachi, Satoshi, 2007, 'Shakai Bungyoron Saiko: Nashonarizumuron no Shikaku kara' [Rethinking the Division of Labor in Society: On the Perspective of Nationalism Theory], *Shakaigaku Nenpo* [The Tohoku Sociological Society], 36: 105–125.

————, 2008a, 'Igirisu no Jinshu Kankei Seisaku wo Meguru Ronso to sono Moten: Posuto Tabunka Shugi ni okeru Shakai teki Kessoku to Bunka teki Tayosei ni tsuite' [The Controversy regarding Race Relations Policy in Britain and Its Blind Spot: Social Cohesion and Cultural Diversity in Post-Multiculturalism], *Foramu Gendai Shakaigaku* [Kansai Sociological Review], 7: 87–99.

————, 2008b, 'Shinrai to Kanyo no Shakaigaku: Tabunka Shugi no Genkai to Riberaru Nashonarizumuron' [Sociology of Trust and Toleration: The Limit of Multiculturalism and Liberal Nationalism Theory], *Shakaigaku Kenkyu* [The Study of Sociology], 84: 15–44.

————, 2008c, 'On the Function of Britishness on Social Cohesion and Cultural Diversity: A Perspective for the Appreciation of the Social Integration Policy in Britain', *Multicultural Relations*, 5: 49–63.

————, 2009, 'Posuto Tabunka Shugi ni okeru Shakai Togo ni tsuite: Sengo Igirisu ni okeru Seisaku no Hensen tono Kakawari no nakade' [Social Integration in Post-Multiculturalism: An Analysis of Social Integration Policy in Postwar Britain], *Shakaigaku Hyoron* [Japanese Sociological Review], 60(3): 433–48.

————, 2011a, 'Furansu to Igirisu ni okeru Shakai Togo no Hikaku: Dento Seiji Jissen ni Chakumoku Shite' [Comparative Studies on Social Integration between France and the UK: Tradition, Politics and Practice], *Korokiumu* [Colloquium: the new horizon of contemporary sociological theory], 6: 74–92.

――――, 2011b, 'Gurobaruka Jidai ni okeru Shakai Togo Seisaku ni tsuite: Furansu to Igirisu no Sukafu Ronso no Hikaku wo toshite' [Social Integration in the Era of Globalization: Comparative Analysis on Scarf Affairs between France and the UK], *Shakaigaku Kenkyu* [The Study of Sociology], 89: 85–109.

――――, 2011c, 'Reflexive Modernity and Young Muslims: Identity Management in a Diverse Area in the UK', in Kunihiro Kimura ed., *Minorities and Diversity*, Melbourne: Trans Pacific Press.

――――, 2011d, 'Social Integration in Post-Multiculturalism: An Analysis of Social Integration Policy in Post-war Britain', *International Journal of Japanese Sociology*, 20(1): 107–20.

――――, 2012, 'Riberaru na Tabunka Shugi ni okeru Bunka to Aidentithi: Saikisei, Ejenshi Moderu, Jiritsusei' [Culture and Identity in Liberal Multiculturalism: Reflexivity, Agency Model of Identity, and Autonomy], *Shakaigaku Hyoron* [Japanese Sociological Review], 63(2): 274–89.

――――, 2013a, '"Cho" Tayoka Shakai ni okeru Shinko to Shakai Togo: Igirisu ni okeru Wakamono Musurimu no Tekio Senryaku to sono Shigen' [Faith and Social Integration in Super-Diverse Society: Young British Muslims' Strategy and Resources for Adaptation to Secular Society], *Soshioroji* [Sociology], 177: 35–51.

――――, 2013b, *Riberaru Nashonarizumu to Tabunka Shugi: Igirisu no Shakai Togo to Musurimu* (Liberal Nationalism and Multiculturalism: Social Integration Policy and Muslims in Britain), Tokyo: Keisoshobo.

――――, 2015a, 'Tabunka Shakai ni okeru Josei Wakamono Musurimu no Aidenthithi to Shakai Togo: Isuramu, Bunka, Igirisu' [Identity and Social Integration of Young Muslim Women in a Multicultural Society: Islam, Culture and British Society], *Shakaigaku Kenkyu* [The Study of Sociology], 96: 139–64.

――――, 2015b, 'Johoka Jidai ni okeru Wakamono Musurimu no Shakai Togo: Isuramu no "Chishiki" ni Chakumoku shite' [Social Integration of Young British Muslims in the Information Age: Focusing on 'Knowledge' of Islam], *Shakaigaku Hyoron* [Japanese Sociological Review], 66(3): 346–63.

――――, 2016, 'Isuto Rondon no Josei Musurimu no Kyoiku Ishiki: Kazoku, Shutaisei, Shinko' [Educational Attitudes of Muslim Women in East London: Family, Agency and Faith], *Hakusan Jinruigaku* [Hakusan Review of Anthropology], 19: 33–55.

――――, 2017, '"Hibi Ikirareru Shukyo" to shite no Isuramu: Nihonjin Musurimu Josei no Jirei kara' [Islam as 'everyday lived religion' : A Case of Japanese Muslim Women], *Shakaigaku Kenkyu* [The Study of Sociology], 100: 181–205.

――――, 2018, 'Tabunka Shugi to Seio Musurimu: "Heisasei" to "Kaihosei" no Aidenthithiron' [Multiculturalism and European Muslims: Identity Theory of 'Closedness' and 'Openness'], *Gendai Shakaigaku Riron Kenkyu* [The Journal of Studies in Contemporary Sociological Theory], 12: 103–15.

————, 2020a, '"Zonbi Gainen" to shite no Tabunka Shugi?: Posuto 7/7 Jidai no Igirisu ni okeru Shakai Togo wo meguru Riron Gensetsu Seisaku' [Multiculturalism as a 'Zombie Concept'?: Theories, Discourses and Policies on Social Integration Post-7/7 in Britain], Machiko Nakanishi and Shingo Torigoe eds., *Gurobaru Shakai no Henyo: Sukotto Rasshu Rainichi Koen wo hete* [The Transformation of Global Society: After Scott Lasch's Lecture in Japan], Kyoto: Koyoshobo.

————, 2020b, 'Shin Chusan Kaikyu Musurimu Josei no Rodo to Kaji Yakuwari wo meguru Ishiki: Mareshia no Shiritsu Daigaku no Kyoin wo Jirei ni' [New Middle-Class Muslim Women's Social Attitudes on Working and Family Roles: A Case Study of Lecturers at a Private University in Malaysia], *Shakaigaku Kenkyu* [The Study of Sociology], 104: 175–99.

————, 2020c, 'Isuramu wo Ningenka suru: Tabunka Shakai Igirish ni okeru Musrimu Joosei to Hizyabu' [Humanising the Sacret: Muslim Women and the Hijab in Britain as a Multicultural Society], *Gendai Shakaigaku Riron Kenkyu* [The Journal of Studies in Contemporary Sociological Theory], 14: 6–18.

————, 2022, 'Isuramu to Josei no Ejenshi: Posuto Kozo Shugi, Jiko Kiritsu Ron, Posuto Dento Shakai' [Agency of Islam and Women: Post-Structuralism, Self-Discipline Theory, Post-Traditional Society], Shakaigaku Hyoron [Japanese Sociological Review] 73(3): 246-61.

Afshar, Haleh, 1989, 'Education: Hopes, Expectations, and Achievements of Muslim Women in West Yorkshire', *Gender and Education*, 1(3): 261–72.

Ahmad, Fauzia, 2006, 'The Scandal of "Arranged Marriages" and the Pathologisation of BrAsian Families', in Nasreen Ali, Virinder S. Kalra and Salman Sayyid eds., *A Postcolonial People: South Asians in Britain*, New York: Columbia University Press.

Ahmad, Fauzia and Mohammad Seddon eds., 2012, *Muslim Youth: Challenges, Opportunities and Expectations*, London: Continuum.

Ahmad, Waqar, 2012, '"Creating a Society of Sheep"? British Muslim Elite on Mosques and Imams', in Waqar Ahmad and Ziauddin Sardar, eds., *Muslims in Britain: Making Social and Political Space*, New York: Routledge.

Ahmed, Leila, 1992, *Women and Gender in Islam: Historical Roots of a Modern Debate*, London: Yale University Press.

Ahmed, Sara, 2005, 'The Skin of the Community: Affect and Boundary Formation', in Tina Chanter and Ewa Ziarek eds., *Revolt, Affect, Collectivity: The Unstable Boundaries of Kristeva's Polis*, New York: State University of New York Press.

Akedo, Takahiro, 2010, 'The Reconstruction of Taylor's "The Politics of Recognition": Recognition in the Intimate Sphere and the "Fusion of Horizon" in the Public Sphere', *The Journal of Studies in Contemporary Sociological Theory*, 4: 3–15.

Akhtar, Parveen, 2014, '"We Were Muslims but We Didn't Know Islam": Migration, Pakistani Muslim Women and Changing Religious Practices in the UK', *Women's Studies International Forum*, 47: 232–38.

Akhtar, Sayyid, 1997, 'The Islamic Concept of Knowledge', *Al-Tawhid: A Quarterly Journal of Islamic Thought and Culture*, 12(3): 101–8.

Alam, M. Y., 2006, *Made in Bradford*, Pontefract: Route.

Al-Ati, Hammudah Abd, 1977, *The Family Structure in Islam*, Indianapolis: American Trust Publication.

Alexander, Claire, 2004, 'Imagining the Asian Gang: Ethnicity, Masculinity and Youth After "the Riots"', *Critical Social Policy*, 24(4): 526–49.

Ali, Rahielah and Peter Hopkins, 2012, 'Everyday Making and Civic Engagement among Muslim Women in Scotland', in Waqar Ahmad and Ziauddin Sardar eds., *Muslims in Britain: Making Social and Political Space*, New York: Routledge.

Ali, Yasmin, 1992, 'Muslim Women and the Politics of Ethnicity and Culture in Northern England', in Gita Sahgal and Nira Yuval-Davis eds., *Refusing Holy Orders*, London: Virago.

Al Jazeera, 2022, 'King Charles: What Are His Views on Islam?', *Aljazeera, 11 September 2022*. https://www.aljazeera.com/news/2022/9/11/king-charles-what-are-his-views-on-islam (accessed 27 September 2022).

Allen, Chris, 2005, 'From Race to Religion: The New Face of Discrimination', in Tahir Abbas ed., *Muslim Britain: Communities under Pressure*, London: Zed Books.

————, 2015, 'A Critical Analysis of Britain's Living Dead and Zombie Multiculturalism: From 7/7 to the London 2012 Olympic Games', *Social Sciences*, 4(1): 18–33.

Allen, Christopher and Jørgen Nielsen, 2002, *Summary Report on Islamophobia in the EU after 11 September 2001*, Vienna: European Monitoring Centre on Racism and Xenophobia.

Allport, Gordon, 1954, *The Nature of Prejudice*, Cambridge: Addison-Wesley.

Amed, Sameera T., 2003, *Young British Muslims: Social Space and Active Identity*, Doctoral Thesis, University of Leicester.

Ameli, Saied, 2002, *Globalization, Americanization and British Muslim Identity*, London: Islamic College for Advanced Studies Press.

Ameli, Saied and Arzu Merali, 2004, *British Muslims' Expectations of the Government: Dual Citizenship – British, Islamic or Both? Obligation, Recognition, Respect and Belonging*, Wembley: Islamic Human Rights Commission.

Amer, Sahar, 2014, *What Is Veiling?*, North Carolina: University of North Carolina Press.

Amos, Valerie and Pratibha Parmar, 1981, 'Resistances and Responses: The Experiences of Black Girls in Britain', in Angela McRobbie and Trisha McCabe eds., *Feminism for Girls: An Adventure Story*, London: Routledge and Kegan Paul.

Ansari, Humayun, 2004, *The Infidel Within: Muslims in Britain since 1800*, London: Hurst & Company.

Anwar, Muhammad, 1976, *Between Two Cultures: A Study of Relationships between the Generations in the Asian Community in Britain*, London: Community Relations Commission Pamphlets.

Muslim and British post-9/11

————, 1994, *Race and Elections*, Coventry: Centre for Research in Ethnic Relations.

————, 1996, *British Pakistanis: Demographic, Social and Economic Position*, Coventry: Centre for Research in Ethnic Relations.

————, 1998, *Between Cultures: Continuity and Change in the Lives of Young Asians*, London: Routledge.

Appadurai, Arjun, 1996, *Modernity at Large: Cultural Dimensions of Globalization*, Minneapolis: University of Minnesota Press.

Appiah, Anthony, 1994, 'Identity, Authenticity, Survival: Multicultural Societies and Social Reproduction', in Amy Gutmann ed., *Multiculturalism: Examining the Politics of Recognition*, 2nd edition, Princeton: Princeton University Press.

Appleyard, Reginald, 1991, *International Migration: Challenge for the Nineties*, Geneva: IOM.

Archer, Louise, 2001, 'Muslim Brothers, Black Lads, Traditional Asians: British Muslim Young Men's Constructions of Race, Religion and Masculinity', *Feminism and Psychology*, 11(1): 79–105.

————, 2002, 'Change, Culture and Tradition: British Muslim Pupils Talk about Muslim Girls' Post-16 "Choices"', *Race Ethnicity and Education*, 5(4): 359–76.

————, 2005, 'Muslim Adolescents in Europe', in Márta Fülöp and Alistair Ross eds., *Growing up in Europe Today: Developing Identities among Adolescents*, Stoke-on-Trent: Trentham Books.

Asad, Talal, 1993, *Genealogies of Religion: Discipline and Reasons of Power in Christianity and Islam*, London: Johns Hopkins University Press.

Aslan, Reza, 2005, *No god but God: The Origins, Evolution, and Future of Islam*, New York: Random House.

Azram, Mohammad, 2011, 'Epistemology: An Islam Perspective', *IIUM Engineering Journal*, 12(5): 179–87.

Badran, Margot, 2009, *Feminism in Islam: Secular and Religious Convergences*, Oxford: Oneworld Publications.

Bagguley, Paul and Yasmin Hussain, 2005, 'Flying the Flag for England? Citizenship, Religion and Cultural Identity among British Pakistani Muslims', in Tahir Abbas ed., *Muslim Britain: Communities under Pressure*, London: Zed Books.

————, 2008, *Riotous Citizens: Ethnic Conflict in Multicultural Britain*, Aldershot: Ashgate Publishing.

Ballard, Catherine, 1978, 'Arranged Marriages in the British Context', *New Community*, 6(3): 181–96.

————, 1979, 'Conflict, Continuity and Change: Second Generation South Asian', in Verity Saifullah Khan ed., *Minority Families in Britain: Support and Stress*, London: Macmillan.

Ballard, Roger, 1982, 'South Asian Families', in Robert N. Rapoport, Michael Fogarty and Rhona Rapoport eds., *Families in Britain*, London: Routledge and Kegan Paul.

Bibliography

————, 1994, 'Introduction: The Emergence of Desh Pardesh', in Roger Ballard ed., *Desh Pardesh: The South Asian Presence in Britain*, London: Hurst & Company.

Ballard, Roger and Catherine Ballard, 1977, 'The Sikhs: The Development of South Asian Settlement in Britain', in James L. Watson ed., *Between Two Cultures: Migrants and Minorities in Britain*, Oxford: Basil Blackwell.

Banerjee, Pallavi, 2018, 'Muslim Immigrant Bangladeshi Women and the Politics of Gender, Class and Religion', Paper presented at XIX ISA World Congress of Sociology, Metro Toronto Convention Center, Toronto, 17 July.

Banton, Michael, 1967, *Race Relations*, London: Basic Books.

————, 1977, *The Idea of Race*, London: Tavistock.

Baringhorst, Sigrid, 1992, 'Cultural Pluralism and Anti-Discrimination Policy: The Case of the City of Bradford', in Dietrich Thränhardt ed., *Europe – A New Immigration Continent: Policies and Politics in Comparative Perspective*, Münster: Lit Verlag.

Barlas, Asma, 2002, *Believing Women in Islam: Unreading Patriarchal Interpretations of the Qur'an*, Austin: University of Texas Press.

Barry, Brian, 2001, *Culture and Equality: An Egalitarian Critique of Multiculturalism*, Cambridge: Polity Press.

Barth, Fredrik, 1969, 'Introduction', in Fredrik Barth ed., *Ethnic Groups and Boundaries: The Social Organization of Cultural Difference*, London: Allen & Unwin.

Basarudin, Azza, 2016, *Humanizing the Sacred: Sisters in Islam and the Struggle for Gender Justice in Malaysia*, London: University of Washington Press.

Basit, Tehmina N., 1997, '"I Want More Freedom, But Not Too Much": British Muslim Girls and the Dynamism of Family Values', *Gender and Education*, 9(4): 425–40.

Baubérot, Jean, 2007, *Histoire de la laïcité en France*, Paris: Presses Universitaires de France.

Beck, Ulrich, 1986, *Risikogesellschaft auf dem Weg in eine andere Moderne*, Frankfurt am Main: Suhrkamp.

————, 2010, *A God of One's Own: Religion's Capacity for Peace and Potential for Violence*, Cambridge: Polity Press.

Bendix, Reinhard, 1977, *Nation-building and Citizenship: Studies of Our Changing Social Order*, new enlarged edition, Berkley: University of California Press.

Berg, Bruce, 1989, *Qualitative Research Methods for the Social Sciences*, Boston: Allyn and Bacon.

Berger, Peter, 1967, *The Sacred Canopy: Elements of a Sociological Theory of Religion*, New York: Doubleday.

Berger, Peter and Thomas Luckmann, 1966, *Social Construction of Reality*, New York: Anchor Books.

Berman, Paul, 1996, 'The Gay Awakening', in Paul Berman ed., *A Tale of Two Utopias: The Political Journey of the Generation of 1968*, New York: W.W. Norton and Company.

Berry, John, 2001, 'A Psychology of Immigration', *Journal of Social Issues*, 57(3): 615–31.

Bhabha, Homi, 1994, *The Location of Culture*, London: Routledge.

————, 1996, 'Culture's In-between', in Stuart Hall and Paul du Gay eds., *Questions of Cultural Identity?*, London: Sage.

Bhaskar, Roy, 2008, *A Realist Theory of Science: With a New Introduction*, London: Routledge.

Bhimji, Fazila, 2009, 'Identities and Agency in Religious Spheres: A Study of British Muslim Women's Experience', *Gender, Place and Culture*, 16(4): 365–80.

————, 2012, *British Asian Muslim Women, Multiple Spatialities and Cosmopolitanism*, Hampshire: Palgrave Macmillan.

Bhopal, Kalwant, 2010, *Asian Women in Higher Education: Shared Communities*, Stoke on Trent: Trentham Books.

Birt, Jonathan, 2005, 'Lobbying and Marching: British Muslims and the State', in Tahir Abbas ed., *Muslim Britain: Communities under Pressure*, London: Zed Books.

Blackstone, Tessa, Bhikhu Parekh and Peter Sanders eds., 1998, *Race Relations in Britain: A Developing Agenda*, London: Routledge.

Blair, Tony, 2006, *The Duty to Integrate: Shared British Values*. http://www.number10.gov.uk/Page10563 (accessed 01 August 2009).

Bleich, Erik, 2003, *Race Politics in Britain and France: Ideas and Policymaking Since the 1960s*, Cambridge: Cambridge University Press.

Blick, Andrew, Tufyal Choudhury and Stuart Weir, 2006, *The Rules of the Game: Terrorism, Community and Human Rights*, York: Joseph Rowntree Reform Trust.

Bloom, Allan, 1987, *The Closing of the American Mind: How Higher Education Has Failed Democracy and Impoverished the Souls of Today's Students*, New York: Simon and Schuster.

Blunkett, David, 2002, 'What Does Citizenship Mean Today?', *The Guardian*, 15 September 2002. http://www.guardian.co.uk/world/2002/sep/15/race.thinktanks (accessed 22 September 2008).

————, 2016, 'David Blunkett – 2003 Speech on Multi-Faith Britain', *UKPOL*. http://www.ukpol.co.uk/david-blunkett-2003-speech-on-multi-faith-britain/ (accessed 12 July 2017).

Bokhari, Raana, 2013, 'Bihishti Zewar: Islam, Text, and the Daily Lives of Gujarati Women in Leicester', in Nathal Dessing, Nadia Jeldtoft, Jørgen Nielsen, and Linda Woodhead eds., *Everyday Lived Islam in Europe*, Farnham: Ashgate Publishing.

Bouchard, Gérard, 2012, *L'interculturalisme. un point de vue québécois*, Montréal: Boréal.

Bouchard, Gérard and Charles Taylor, 2008, *Building the Future: A Time for Reconciliation*, Quebec: Gouvernement du Québec.

Bibliography

Bourdieu, Peter, 1977, *Outline of a Theory of Practice*, Cambridge: Cambridge University Press.

Bourdieu, Pierre, 1979, *La Distinction: Critique sociale du jugement*, Paris: Les Editions de Minuit.

Bowen, John, 2008, *Why the French Don't Like Headscarves: Islam, the State, and Public Space*, Princeton: Princeton University Press.

Bowlby, Sophie and Sally Lloyd-Evans, 2009, '"You Seem very Westernised to Me": Place, Identity and Othering of Muslim Workers in the UK Labour Market', in Peter Hopkins and Richard Gale eds., *Muslims in Britain: Race, Place and Identities*, Edinburgh: Edinburgh University Press.

Bozorgmehr, Medhi and Philip Kasinitz eds., 2018, *Growing Up Muslim in Europe and the United States*, New York: Routledge.

Bozorgmehr, Medhi and Philip Kasinitz, 2018, 'Introduction: Second-generation Muslims in Europe and the United States', in Medhi Bozorgmehr and Philip Kasinitz eds., *Growing Up Muslim in Europe and the United States*, New York: Routledge.

Bradley, Ian, 2007, *Believing in Britain: The Spiritual Identity of Britishness*, New York: I.B. Tauris.

Brah, Avtar, 1996, *Cartographies of Diaspora: Contesting Identities*, New York: Routledge.

————, 2006, 'The "Asian" in Britain', in Nasreen Ali, Virinder S. Kalra, Salman Sayyid eds., *A Postcolonial People: South Asians in Britain*, New York: Columbia University Press.

Brah, Avtar and Rehana Minhas, 1985, 'Structural Racism or Cultural Difference? Schooling for Asian Girls', in Gaby Weiner ed., *Just a Bunch of Girls: Feminist Approaches to Schooling*, Milton Keynes: Open University Press.

Brah, Avtar and Sobia Shaw, 1992, *Working Choices: South Asian Muslim Women and the Labour Market*, Sheffield: Department of Employment.

Braun, Virginia, and Victoria Clarke, 2006, 'Using Thematic Analysis in Psychology', *Qualitative Research in Psychology*, 3(2): 77–101.

Brice, Kevin, 2014, 'Counting the Converts: Investigating Change of Religion in Scotland and Estimating Change of Religion in England and Wales Using Data from Scotland's Census 2001', *Diskus*, 16(2): 45–59.

British Broadcasting Corporation (BBC), 2001, 'Prince Joins Ramadan Ceremony', *BBC News*, 23 November 2001. http://news.bbc.co.uk/2/hi/uk_news/england/1671797.stm (accessed 27 September 2022).

————, 2002, 'Forced Marriage Annulled', *BBC News*, 23 April 2002. http://news.bbc.co.uk/2/hi/uk_news/scotland/1946135.stm (accessed 5 November 2019).

————, 2005, 'London Bomber: Text in Full', *BBC News*, 1 September 2005 http://news.bbc.co.uk/1/hi/uk/4206800.stm (accessed 15 September 2008).

————, 2006, 'Blair's Concerns over Face Veils', *BBC News*, 17 October 2006. http://news.bbc.co.uk/2/hi/6058672.stm (accessed 28 May 2016).

————, 2011, 'Profile: Mohammad Sidique Khan', *BBC News*, 2 March 2011. https://www.bbc.com/news/uk-12621381 (accessed 8 February 2022).

————, 2014a, 'London Drives House Price Increase, Says ONS', *BBC News*, 19 August 2014. http://www.bbc.co.uk/news/business-28850292 (accessed 23 June 2018).

————, 2014b, 'Women Equality, Islam', *Woman's Hour Daily Podcast*, BBC Radio 4.

————, 2018, 'The Islamic Veil across Europe', *BBC News*, 31 May 2018. https://www.bbc.com/news/world-europe-13038095 (accessed 24 April 2019).

Brown, Gordon, 1999, 'Speech to the Smith Institute Conference on Britishness', 15 April.

————, 2006, 'Speech by the Rt Hon Gordon Brown MP, Chancellor of the Exchequer, at the Fabian New Year Conference', *London 03/06*. http://www.hm-treasury.gov.uk/1864.htm (accessed 30 July 2008).

Bryman, Alan, 2012, *Social Research Methods, 4th edition*, New York: Oxford University Press.

Bullock, Katherine, 2007, *Rethinking Muslim Women and the Veil: Challenging Historical and Modern Stereotypes*, 2nd edition, London: International Institute of Islamic Thought.

Bunt, Gary R., 2003, *Islam in the Digital Age: E-jihad, Online Fatwas and Cyber Islamic Environments*, London: Pluto Press.

Bush, Laura, 2001, 'Radio Address by Mrs. Bush', *White House Washington DC*. http://georgewbushwhitehouse.archives.gov/news/releases/2001/11/20011117.htm (accessed 01 November 2014).

Butler, Judith, 1993, 'Critically Queer', in Judith Butler ed., *Bodies That Matter: On the Discursive Limits of "Sex"*, New York: Routledge.

————, 1997, *The Psychic Life of Power: Theories in Subjection*, California: Stanford University Press.

Caeiro, Alexandre, 2011, 'Transnational Ulama, European Fatwas, and Islamic Authority: A Case Study of the European Council for Fatwa and Research', in Martin van Bruinessen and Stefano Allievi eds., *Producing Islamic Knowledge: Transmission and Dissemination in Western Europe*, London: Routledge.

Cameron, David, 2011, 'PM's Speech at Munich Security Conference', *The National Archives*, 5 February 2011. http://webarchive.nationalarchives.gov.uk/20130109092234/, http://number10.gov.uk/news/pms-speech-at-munich-security-conference (accessed 13 April 2013).

Cantle, Ted, 2001, *Community Cohesion: A Report of the Independent Review Team*, London: Home Office.

————, 2008, *Community Cohesion: A New Framework for Race and Diversity, revised and update edition*, Basingstoke: Palgrave Macmillan.

————, 2015, 'Interculturalism: "Learning to Live in Diversity"', *Ethnicities*, 16(3): 471–9.

Castles, Stephen and Godula Kosack, 1973, *Immigrant Workers and Class Structure in Western Europe*, London: Oxford University Press.

Castles, Stephen and Mark Miller, 1993, *The Age of Migration: International Population Movements in the Modern World*, Basingstoke: Palgrave Macmillan.

Caws, Peter, 1994, 'Identity: Cultural, Transnational, and Multicultural', in David Theo Goldberg ed., *Multiculturalism: A Critical Reader*, Oxford: Blackwell.

Chambers, Claire and Caroline Herbert eds., 2015, *Imagining Muslims in South Asia and the Diaspora: Secularism, Religion, Representations*, New York: Routledge.

Channel 4, 2010, 'Britain's Islamic Republic', *Dispatches*, 1 March 2010.

Choudhury, Tufyal, 2002, *Monitoring Minority Protection in the EU: The Situation of Muslims in the UK*, Budapest: Open Society Institute.

———, 2007, *The Role of Muslim Identity Politics in Radicalisation (A Study in Progress)*, London: Department for Communities and Local Government.

Choudhury, Tufyal and Helen Fenwick, 2011, *The Impact of Counter-terrorism Measures on Muslim Communities*, London: Equality and Human Rights Commission.

Clarke, Peter, 1996, *Hope and Glory: Britain 1900–1990*, London: Penguin Press.

Cohen, Abner, 1974, *Two-dimensional Man: An Essay on the Anthropology of Power and Symbolism in Complex Society*, London: Routledge and Kegan Paul.

———, 1979, 'Political Symbolism', *Annual Review of Anthropology*, 8: 87–113.

Cohen, Joshua, Matthew Howard and Martha C. Nussbaum eds., 1999, *Is Multiculturalism Bad for Women?*, Princeton: Princeton University Press.

Cohen, Phil, 1999, 'Through a Glass Darkly: Intellectuals on Race', in Phil Cohen ed., *New Ethnicities. Old Racisms?*, London: Zed Books.

Cohen, Stanley, 2011, *Folk Devils and Moral Panics: The Creation of the Mods and Rockers*, 3rd edition, London: Routledge.

Colley, Linda, 1992, *Britons: Forging the Nation 1707–1837*, New Haven: Yale University Press.

Commission for Racial Equality (CRE), 1988, 'Ethnic Classification System Recommended by CRE', Press Statement, 7 December 1988.

Commission on Integration and Cohesion (CIC), 2007, *Our Shared Future*, London: CIC.

Community Cohesion Panel (CCP), 2004, *The End of Parallel Lives? The Report of the Community Cohesion*, London: Home Office.

Condor, Susan, 2011, 'Rebranding Britain? Ideological Dilemmas in Political Appeals to "British Multiculturalism"', in Martyn Barrett, Chris Flood and John Eade eds., *Nationalism, Ethnicity, Citizenship: Multidisciplinary Perspectives*, Newcastle upon Tyne: Cambridge Scholars Publishing.

Contractor, Sariya, 2012, *Muslim Women in Britain: De-mystifying the Muslimah*, Oxfordshire: Routledge.

Corman, Crystal, 2014, 'Praying for All the Single Ladies', 22 May. https://berkleycenter.georgetown.edu/posts/praying-for-all-the-single-ladies (accessed 02 April 2018).

Costa-Lascoux, Jacqueline, 1996, *Les trois âges de la laïcité*, Paris: Hachett.

Council of Europe, 2008, *White Paper on Intercultural Dialogue: "Living Together as Equals in Dignity"*, Strasbourg: Council of Europe.

Cox, Oliver, 1948, *Caste, Class and Race*, New York: Monthly Review.

Crenshaw, Kimberlé, 1989, 'Demarginalizing the Intersection of Race and Sex: A Black Feminist Critique of Antidiscrimination Doctrine, Feminist Theory and Antiracist Politics', *University of Chicago Legal Forum*, 140: 139–68.

————, 1991, 'Mapping the Margins: Intersectionality, Identity Politics, and Violence against Women of Color', *Stanford Law Review*, 43(6): 1241–99.

Crick, Bernard, 1998, *Education for Citizenship and the Teaching of Democracy in Schools: Final Report of the Advisory Group on Citizenship*, London: Qualifications and Curriculum Authority.

————, 2000, *Essay on Citizenship*, London: Continuum.

————, 2003, *The New and the Old: The Report of the 'Life in the United Kingdom' Advisory Group*, London: Home Office.

Crouch, Gregory, 2006, 'Dutch Immigration Kit Offers a Revealing View', *New York Times*, 16 March 2006. https://www.nytimes.com/2006/03/16/world/europe/16iht-dutch-5852942.html (accessed 16 September 2018).

Dale, Angela, Nusrat Shaheen, Virinder Kalra and Edward Fieldhouse, 2002, 'Routes into Education and Employment for Young Pakistani and Bangladeshi Women in the UK', *Ethnic and Racial Studies*, 25(6): 942–68.

Dassetto, Felice, Silvio Ferrari and Brigitte Maréchal, 2007, *Islam in the European Union: What's at Stake in the Future?*, Brussels: European Parliament.

Davids, Nuraan, 2013, *Women, Cosmopolitanism and Islamic Education: On the Virtues of Engagement and Belonging*, Hochfeldstrasse: Peter Lang.

Debord, Guy, 2009, *The Society of the Spectacle*, The Anarchist Library. https://theanarchistlibrary.org/library/guy-debord-the-society-of-the-spectacle (accessed 19 April 2018).

de Certeau, Michel, 1984, *The Practice of Everyday Life*, London: University of California Press.

DeHanas, Daniel, 2013, 'Elastic Orthodoxy: The Tactics of Young Muslim Identity in the East End of London', in Nathal Dessing, Nadia Jeldtoft, Jørgen Nielsen and Linda Woodhead eds., *Everyday Lived Islam in Europe*, Farnham: Ashgate Publishing.

Delanty, Gerard, 2003, *Community*, London: Routledge.

Dench, Geoff, Kate Gavron and Michael Young, 2006, *The New East End: Kinship, Race and Conflict*, London: Profile Books.

Denham, John, 2001, *Building Cohesive Communities: A Report of the Ministerial Group on Public Order and Community Cohesion*, London: Home Office.

Department for Education and Skills (DfES), 2007, *Gender and Education: The Evidence on Pupils in England*, Nottingham: DfES.

Déroche, François, 2005, *Le Coran*, Paris: Presses Universitaires de France.

Dessing, Nathal, Nadia Jeldtoft, Jørgen Nielsen and Linda Woodhead eds., 2013, *Everyday Lived Islam in Europe*, Farnham: Ashgate Publishing.

de Vries, Hent and Lawrence Sullivan eds., 2006, *Political Theologies: Public Religions in a Post-secular World*, New York: Fordham University Press.

Donaldson, Laura and Kwok Pui-Lan eds., 2002, *Postcolonialism, Feminism and Religious Discourse*, New York: Routledge.

Du Bois, William Edward Burghardt, 2020, *The Souls of Black Folk*, Independently Published.

Durkheim, Emile, 1893, *De la division du travail social: Etude sur l'organisation des sociétés supérieures (DTS)*, Paris: Preses Universitaires de France.

—————, 1912, *Les formes élémentaires de la vie religieuse*, Paris: Félix Alcan.

Dwyer, Claire, 1998, 'Contested Identities: Challenging Dominant Representations of Young British Muslim Women', in Tracey Skelton and Gill Valentine eds., *Cool Places: Geographies of Youth Culture*, London: Routledge.

—————, 1999, 'Veiled Meanings: Young British Muslim Women and the Negotiation of Difference', *Gender, Place and Culture*, 6(1): 5–26.

—————, 2000, 'Negotiating Diasporic Identities: Young British South Asian Muslim Women', *Women's Studies International Forum*, 23(4): 475–86.

Dwyer, Claire and Bindi Shah, 2009, 'Rethinking the Identities of Young British Pakistani Muslim Women: Educational Experiences and Aspirations', in Peter Hopkins and Richard Gale eds., *Muslims in Britain: Race, Place and Identities*, Edinburgh: Edinburgh University Press.

Dyke, Anya, 2009, *Mosques Made in Britain*, London: Quilliam Foundation.

Economist, 2013, 'On the Road: Ethnic-Minority Pupils Are Storming ahead, Thanks partly to Tutors', *The Economist*, 16 November 2013. https://www-economist-com.libproxy.smu.edu.sg/britain/2013/11/16/on-the-road (accessed 13 May 2019).

—————, 2014, 'No One to Talk to: A Muslim Group Falls from Favour', *The Economist*, 18 October 2014. https://www.economist.com/britain/2014/10/18/no-one-to-talk-to (accessed 02 February 2019).

—————, 2018, 'Europe's Anti-immigrant Parties Are Becoming more Gay-friendly: Partly as a Way to Bash Muslim Immigrants', *The Economist*, 5 July, 2018. https://www.economist.com/europe/2018/07/05/europes-anti-immigrant-parties-are-becoming-more-gay-friendly (accessed 09 September 2018).

Eickelman, Dale and James Piscatori, 2004, *Muslim Politics*, 2nd edition, Princeton: Princeton University Press.

El-Wafi, Layla, 2006, *British Arab Muslims and the "War on Terror": Perceptions of Citizenship, Identity and Human Rights*, unpublished manuscript. http://www.naba.org.uk/content/articles/2006/BrArabs/61010_BrArMus_AlWafiL.pdf (accessed 12 November 2012).

Eller, Jack David, 1999, *From Culture to Ethnicity to Conflict: An Anthropological Perspective on International Ethnic Conflict*, Ann Arbor: University of Michigan Press.

Ellinas, Antonis, 2010, *The Media and the Far Right in Western Europe: Playing the Nationalist Card*, New York: Cambridge University Press.

el Saadawi, Nawal, 1980, *The Hidden Face of Eve: Women in the Arab World*, Boston: Beacon Press.

Elshtain, Jean, 1993, *Democracy on Trial*, New York: Basic Books.

English, Leona, 2003, 'Identity, Hybridity, and Third Space: Complicating the Lives of International Adult Educators', *Convergence*, 36(2): 67–80.

————, 2004, 'Feminist Identities: Negotiations in the Third Space', *Feminist Theology*, 3: 97–125.

Erikson, Erik, 1956, 'The Problem of Ego Identity', *Journal of the American Psychoanalytic Association*, 4: 56–121.

————, 1994, *Identity: Youth and Crisis*, New York: W. W. Norton & Company.

Esposito, John, 2003, *The Oxford Dictionary of Islam*, New York: Oxford University Press.

ETHNOS, 2005, *Citizenship and Belonging: What is Britishness?*, London: Commission for Racial Equality.

Fahrmeier, Andreas, 2000, *Citizens and Aliens: Foreigners and the Law in Britain and the German States, 1789–1870*, New York: Berghahn Books.

Fairclough, Norman, 1992, *Discourse and Social Change*, Cambridge: Polity.

Fanon, Frantz, 2004, *The Wretched of the Earth*, New York: Grove Press.

Farley, Harry, 2018, 'Sajid Javid: What Has the New Home Secretary Said about Faith?', *Christian Today*, 30 April 2018. https://www.christiantoday.com/article/sajid-javid-what-has-the-new-home-secretary-said-about-faith/128840.htm (accessed 01 May 2019).

Fashionhance, 2018, '14 Different Types of Head Coverings Worn by Muslim Women', *Fashionhance*, 27 February 2018. https://fashionhance.com/different-types-of-head-coverings-worn-by-muslim-women (accessed 21 July 2018).

Faux, Andrew, 2017, 'Michael Gove's "Brain Flip" Poisoned Schools Extremism Debate', *The Guardian*, 4 July 2017. https://www.theguardian.com/education/2017/jul/04/michael-gove-extremism-trojan-horse-schools (accessed 02 May 2019).

Featherstone, Mike, 1995, *Undoing Culture: Globalization, Postmodernism and Identity*, London: Sage.

Fetzer, Joel and Christopher Soper, 2005, *Muslims and the State in Britain, France, and Germany*, Cambridge: Cambridge University Press.

Finney, Nissa and Ludi Simpson, 2009, *'Sleepwalking to Segregation'? Challenging Myths about Race and Migration*, Bristol: Policy Press.

Fisher, Mitchel Herbert, 2006, 'Working across the Seas: Indian Maritime Labourers in India, Britain, and in Between, 1600–1857', *International Review of Social History*, 51: 21–45.

Bibliography

Fish, Michael Steven, 2011, *Are Muslims Distinctive? A Look at the Evidence*, New York: Oxford University Press.

FitzGerald, Marian, 1998, '"Race" and the Criminal Justice System', in Tessa Blackstone, Bhikhu Parekh and Peter Sanders eds., *Race Relations in Britain: A Developing Agenda*, London: Routledge.

5 Pillars, 2013, 'Citizen Khan Is a Mockery of Islam and Muslims', *5 Pillars*, 07 October 2013. https://5pillarsuk.com/2013/10/07/citizen-khan-a-mockery-of-islam-and-muslims (accessed 14 February, 2019).

————, 2022, 'God Save the King: Pro-establishment Muslim Leaders Have Let the Mask Slip', *5 Pillars*. https://5pillarsuk.com/2022/09/17/god-save-the-king-pro-establishment-muslim-leaders-have-let-the-mask-slip/ (accessed 27 September 2022).

Fletcher, Denise, 2007, 'Social Constructionist Thinking: Some Implications for Entrepreneurship Research and Education', in Alain Fayolle ed., *Handbook of Research in Entrepreneurship Education, Volume 1*, Cheltenham: Edward Elgar.

Flick, Uwe, 2009, *An Introduction to Qualitative Research*, 4th edition, London: Sage.

Foucault, Michel, 1997, *Ethics: Subjectivity and Truth (Essential Works of Foucault 1954–1984), Volume 1*, New York: The New Press.

Freeman, Gary, 1979, *Immigrant Labor and Racial Conflict in Industrial Societies: The French and British Experience 1945–1975*, Princeton: Princeton University Press.

French, Megan, 2010, 'English Defence League's Planned March on Mosque is "Pointless"', *The Guardian*, 9 July 2010. https://www.theguardian.com/world/2010/jul/09/english-defence-league-super-mosque (accessed 13 July 2019).

Freud, Sigmund, 2001, *The Complete Psychological Works of Sigmund Freud Vol.20*, London: Vintage.

Frisk, Sylva, 2009, *Submitting to God: Women and Islam in Urban Malaysia*, Seattle: University of Washington Press.

Fujiwara, Satoko, 2017, *Posuto Tabunka Shugi Kyoiku ga Egaku Shukyo: Igirisu 'Kyodotai no Kessoku' Seisaku no Kozai* [Religion in Post-Multiculturalist Education: The Merits and Demerits of the British 'Community Cohesion' Policy], Tokyo: Iwanamishoten.

Gale, Richard and Peter Hopkins, 2009, 'Introduction: Muslims in Britain – Race, Place and the Spatiality of Identities', in Peter Hopkins and Richard Gale eds., *Muslims in Britain: Race, Place and Identities*, Edinburgh: Edinburgh University Press.

Gardham, Duncan, 2010, 'Mainstream Islamic Organisations "Share Al-Qaeda Ideology"', *The Telegraph*, 05 Aug 2010. https://www.telegraph.co.uk/news/uknews/7928377/Mainstream-Islamic-organisations-share-al-Qaeda-ideology.html (accessed 22 May 2019).

Gavron, Kate, 2005, 'Migrants to Citizens: Bangladeshi Women in Tower Hamlets, London', *Revue Européenne des Migrations Internationales*, 21(3): 69–81.

Geaves, Ron, 2005, 'Negotiating British Citizenship and Muslim Identity', in Tahir Abbas ed., *Muslim Britain: Communities under Pressure*, London: Zed Books.

Geertz, Clifford, 1973, *The Interpretation of Cultures: Selected Essays*, New York: Basic Books.

————, 1988, *Works and Lives: The Anthropologist as Author*, Stanford: Stanford University Press.

Giddens, Anthony, 1990, *The Consequences of Modernity*, Cambridge: Polity Press.

————, 1991, *Modernity and Self-identity: Self and Society in the Late Modern Age*, Cambridge: Polity Press.

————, 1992, *The Transformation of Intimacy: Sexuality, Love and Eroticism in Modern Societies*, Cambridge: Polity Press.

————, 1994, 'Living in a Post-Traditional Society', in Ulrich Beck, Anthony Giddens and Scott Lash eds., *Reflexive Modernization: Politics, Tradition and Aesthetics in the Modern Social Order*, Cambridge: Polity Press.

Giddens, Anthony and Christopher Pierson, 1998, *Conversation with Anthony Giddens: Making Sense of Modernity*, Cambridge: Polity Press.

Gillespie, Marie, 2006, 'Transnational Television Audiences after September 11', *Journal of Ethnic and Migration Studies*, 32(6): 903–21.

Gilliat-Ray, Sophie, 2010, *Muslims in Britain: An Introduction*, Cambridge: Cambridge University Press.

Gilroy, Paul, 1993, *The Black Atlantic: Modernity and Double Consciousness*, London: Verso.

————, 2004, *After Empire: Melancholia or Convivial Culture*, Abingdon: Routledge.

Gitlin, Todd, 1995, *The Twilight of Common Dreams: Why America Is Wracked by Culture Wars*, New York: Metropolitan Books.

Glynn, Sarah, 2009, 'Liberalizing Islam: Creating Brits of the Islamic Persuasion', in Richard Phillips ed., *Muslim Spaces of Hope*, London: Zed Books.

Goffman, Erving, 1959, *The Presentation of Self in Everyday Life*, New York: Doubleday.

————, 1963, *Stigma: Notes on the Management of Spoiled Identity*, New Jersey: Prentice Hall.

Goldberg, Ellis, 1991, 'Smashing Idols and the State: The Protestant Ethic and Egyptian Sunni Radicalism', *Comparative Studies in Society and History*, 33(1): 3–35.

Göle, Nilüfer, 2003, 'The Voluntary Adoption of Islamic Stigma Symbols', *Social Research*, 70(3): 809–28.

Gomm, Roger, 2004, *Social Research Methodology: A Critical Introduction*, Basingstoke: Palgrave Macmillan.

Goodhart, David, 2004, 'Too Diverse?', *Prospect*, 20 February 2004. https://www.prospectmagazine.co.uk/magazine/too-diverse-david-goodhart-multiculturalism-britain-immigration-globalisation (accessed 10 November 2019).

Gordon, Matthew, 2001, *Islam: World Religions*, revised edition, New York: Facts on File.

Goto, Emi, 2014, *Kami no tame ni Matou Veru: Gendai Ejiputo no Josei to Isuramu* [Wearing the Veil for God: Women and Islam in Modern Egypt], Tokyo: Chuokoron Shinsha.

Goulbourne, Harry, 1998, *Race Relations in Britain Since 1945*, Basingstoke: Macmillan Press.

Gove, Michael, 2006, *Celsius 7/7*, London: Weidenfeld & Nicolson.

Grosby, Steven, 2005, 'The Primordial, Kinship and Nationality', in Atsuko Ichijo and Gordana Uzelac eds., *When Is the Nation: Towards an Understand of Theories of Nationalism*, London: Routledge.

Guardian, 2005, 'What the Papers Say: How Today's Newspapers Reported the Bomb Attacks on London', *The Guardian*, 8 July 2005. https://www.theguardian.com/media/2005/jul/08/pressandpublishing.terrorism (accessed 15 January 2013).

————, 2006, 'Kelly Calls for "Honest Debate" on Multiculturalism', *The Guardian*, 24 August 2006. https://www.theguardian.com/politics/2006/aug/24/uksecurity.terrorism

————, 2018, 'Muslim Couple Denied Swiss Citizenship over Handshake Refusal', *The Guardian*, 18 August 2018. https://www.theguardian.com/world/2018/aug/18/muslim-couple-denied-swiss-citizenship-over-handshake-refusal (accessed 15 August 2018).

Guest, Greg, Kathleen MacQueen, and Emily Namey, 2012, *Applied Thematic Analysis*, California: Sage.

Gurr, Ted Robert, 1986, 'The Political Origins of State Violence and Terror: A Theoretical Analysis', in Michael Stohl and George Lopez eds., *Government Violence and Repression: An Agenda for Research*, New York: Greenwood Press.

Habermas, Jürgen, 2011, '"The Political": The Rational Meaning of a Questionable Inheritance of Political Theology', in Eduardo Mendieta and Jonathan Vanantwerpen eds., *The Power of Religion in the Public Sphere*, New York: Columbia University Press.

Habermas, Jürgen, Charles Taylor, Judith Butler and Cornel West, 2011, 'Concluding Discussion: Butler, Habermas, Taylor, West', in Eduardo Mendieta and Jonathan Vanantwerpen eds., *The Power of Religion in the Public Sphere*, New York: Columbia University Press.

Haddad, Yvonne Yazbeck, Jane I. Smith and Kathleen M. Moore, 2006, *Muslim Women in America: The Challenge of Islamic Identity Today*, Oxford: Oxford University Press.

Hadjetian, Sylvia, 2008, *Multiculturalism and Magic Realism? Between Fiction and Reality*, Norderstedt: Grin Publishing.

Haleem, M. A. S. Adel, 2016, *The Qur'an: English Translation and Parallel Arabic Text*, New York: Oxford University Press.

Hallaq, Wael, 1984, 'Was the Gate of Ijtihad Closed?', *International Journal of Middle East Studies*, 16(1): 3–41.

Hall, Stuart, 1987, 'Minimal Selves', *ICA Documents 6: Identity*, London: ICA.

————, 1989, 'The Meaning of New Times', in David Morley and Kuan-Hsing Chen eds., *Stuart Hall: Critical Dialogues in Cultural Studies*, London: Routledge.

————, 1991, 'Old and New Identities, Old and New Ethnicities', in Anthony King ed., *Culture, Globalization and the World-System: Contemporary Conditions for the Representation of Identity*, Binghamton: State University of New York.

————, 1996 [1989], 'New Ethnicities', in David Morley and Kuan-Hsing Chen eds., *Stuart Hall: Critical Dialogues in Cultural Studies*, London: Routledge.

————, 1997, 'Culture and Power', *Radical Philosophy*, 86: 24–41.

Hamid, Sadek ed., 2018, *Young British Muslims: Between Rhetoric and Realities*, New York: Routledge.

Hammami, Rema, 1990, 'Women, the Hijab and the Intifada', *Middle East Report*, 164/165: 24–8, 71, 78.

Hanisch, Carol, 2006 [1969], 'The Personal is Political', http://www.carolhanisch. org/CHwritings/PersonalIsPol.pdf (accessed 30 September 2018)

Harada, Momoko, 2015, 'Hisu Hoshuto Naikaku ni okeru Imin Mondai: 1971 nen Iminho no Setsuritsu wo megutte (Immigration Problem within the Heath Conservative Government: Concerning the Immigration Act, 1971)', *Yoroppa Bunkashi Kenkyu* [The study of the history of European culture] 16: 27–56.

Harris, Clive, 1988, 'Images of Blacks in Britain: 1930–60', in Sheila Allen and Marie Macey eds., *Race and Social Policy*, London: Economic and Social Research Council.

Hashimoto, Kazuya, 2005, *Dhiasupora to Senjyumin: Minshu Shugi Tabunka Shugi to Nashonarizumu* [Diaspora and Indigenous Peoples: Democracy, Multiculturalism and Nationalism], Kyoto: Sekaishisosha.

Haw, Kaya, 1998, *Educating Muslim Girls: Shifting Discourses*, Buckingham: Open University Press.

Hayashida, Shinichi, 2001, 'Kinsei no Furansu' [Early Modern Era in France], Norihiko Fukui ed., *Furansu shi* [History of France], Tokyo: Yamakawa Shuppansha.

Hayashi, Mizue, 2001, 'Isuramu Sukafu Jiken to Hishukyosei' [The Islamic Scarf Incident and Non-Religiousness], in Nobutaka Miura ed., *Fuhensei ka Sai ka: Kyowa Shugi no Rinkai, Fransu* [Universality or Difference: The Criticality of Republicanism, France], Tokyo: Fujiwara Shoten.

Haylamaz, Reşit, 2007, *Khadija: The First Muslim and Wife of Prophet Muhammad*, New Jersey: Tughra Books.

Heidegger, Martin, 1927, *Sein und Zeit*, Tübingen: Max Niemeyer Verlag.

Hellyer, H. A., 2014, 'To Be a "Happy British Muslim" or Not: That Is the Question', *Al Arabiya*, 21 April 2014. http://english.alarabiya.net/en/views/news/ world/2014/04/21/To-be-a-Happy-British-Muslim-or-not-that-is-the-question.html (accessed 29 May 2019).

Her Majesty's Government (HMG), 2008, *The Prevent Strategy: A Guide for Local Partner in England*, London: Stationary Office.

Hermansen, Marcia and Mahruq Khan, 2009, 'South Asian Muslim American Girl Power: Structures and Symbols of Control and Self-expression', *Journal of International Women's Studies*, 11(1): 86–105.

Hessini, Leila, 1994, 'Wearing the Hijab in Contemporary Morocco: Choice and Identity', in Fatma Müge Göçek and Shiva Balaghi eds., *Reconstructing Gender in the Middle East: Tradition, Identity, and Power*, New York: Columbia University Press.

Higuchi, Mimasaka, 2007, *Nihonjin Musurimu to shite Ikiru* [Living as a Japanese Muslim], Tokyo: Koseishuppansha.

Hirano, Takahiro, 2018a, 'Shia ha towa Nani ka' [What is Shia?], Yohei Matsuyama ed., *Kuruan Nyumon* [Introduction to the Quran], Tokyo: Sakuhinsha.

————, 2018b, 'Shia ha no Tafusuiru' [*Shiite Tafsir*], Yohei Matsuyama ed., *Kuruan Nyumon* [Introduction to the Quran], Tokyo: Sakuhinsha.

Hiro, Dilip, 1973, *Black British, White British*, London: Monthly Review Press.

Hobsbawm, Eric, 1994, *The Age of Extremes*, London: Michel Joseph.

Hopf, Christel, 1978, 'Die Pseudo-Exploration: Überlegungen zur Technik qualitativer Interviews in der Sozialforschung', *Zeitschrift für Soziologie*, 7: 97–115.

Hopkins, Peter and Richard Gale eds., 2009, *Muslims in Britain: Race, Place and Identities*, Edinburgh: Edinburgh University Press.

Hoque, Aminul, 2015, *British-Islamic Identity: Third-generation Bangladeshis from East London*, London: Institute of Education Press.

Hori, Ayako, 2008, 'Doitsu ni okeru Sukafu Ronso' [Controversy about a Scarf in Germany], in Masanori Naito ed., *Gekido no Toruko: 9.11 igo no Isuramu to Yoroppa* [Turkey undergoing Major Changes: Islam and Europe after 9/11], Tokyo: Akashishoten.

Houellebecq, Michel, 2015, *Soumission*, Paris: French and European Publications Inc.

House of Loads, 2006, 'Judgments - R (on the application of Begum (by her litigation friend, Rahman)) (Respondent) v. Headteacher and Governors of Denbigh High School (Appellants)'. https://publications.parliament.uk/pa/ld200506/ldjudgmt/jd060322/begum.pdf (accessed 15 November 2010)

Howe, Melissa, 2007, 'Shifting Muslim Gender and Family Norms in East London', Paper presented at the American Sociological Association, New York, 11 August.

Hummon, David, 1992, 'Community Attachment: Local Sentiment and Sense of Place', in Irwin Altman and Setha Low eds., *Place Attachment*, New York: Plenum.

Huntington, Samuel, 1996, *The Clash of Civilizations and the Remaking of World Order*, New York: Touchstone.

Husain, Ed, 2007, *The Islamist: Why I Joined Radical Islam in Britain, What I Saw Inside and Why I Left*, London: Penguin Books.

Hussain, Mahtab, 2018, 'Mahtab Hussain on the Multiple Identities of Young British Muslim Men', *Financial Times*, 5 January 2018. https://www.ft.com/content/f04a5904-f015-11e7-ac08-07c3086a2625 (accessed 01 March 2019).

Hussain, Yasmin and Paul Bagguley, 2007, *Moving on up: South Asian Women and Higher Education*, Stoke-on-Trent: Trentham Books.

Hussein, Jamil, 2022, 'Muslim Tributes Pour in for Queen Elizabeth II', *Islam Channel*, 9 September 2022. https://www.aljazeera.com/features/2022/9/12/british-muslims-reflect-on-late-queen-elizabeth-ii-uks-monarchy (accessed 27 September 2022).

Hutchings, Merryn and Louise Archer, 2001, 'Higher than Einstein: Constructions of Going to University among Working Class Non-participants', *Research Papers in Education*, 16(1): 69–91.

Hutnik, Nimmi, 1985, 'Aspects of Identity in Multi-ethnic Society', *New Community*, 12(1): 298–309.

Imai, Hiroshi, 1993, *Igirisu: Hisutorikaru Gaido* [United Kingdom-Historical Guide], Tokyo: Yamakawa Shuppansha.

Isaka, Riho, 2013, 'Kingendai Indo no Seiji Shakai Henyo to Suiku Aidenthithi' [Sikh Identity and Social and Political Changes in Modern India], *Gendai Indo Kenkyu* [Contemporary India], 3: 171–89.

Ishida, Reiko, 1975a, 'Eikoku ni okeru Jinshu Kankeiho no Rippo Katei (1)' [The Legislative Process of the Race Relations Act in the United Kingdom (1)], *Chosen Kenkyu* [Korean Studies], 151: 34–53.

————, 1975b, 'Eikoku ni okeru Jinshu Kankeiho no Rippo Katei (2)' [The Legislative Process of the Race Relations Act in the United Kingdom (2)], *Chosen Kenkyu* [Korean Studies], 152: 4–23.

Iwashita, Yoko, 2011, '"Shukyo Shinboru Kinshiho" to Danjo Byodo no Keisoka e no Ichikosatsu: Isuramu no Sukafu wa "Josei e no Yokuatsu ka"' [A Study on the Dispute over the 'Religious Symbols Law' and Gender Equality: Does the Islamic Scarf present 'Oppression of Women'?], *Tagen Bunka* [Multicultural Studies], 11: 133–43.

Izutsu, Toshihiko, 1980, *Isuramu Tetsugaku no Genzo* [The Original Image of Islamic Philosophy], Tokyo: Iwanamishoten.

————, 1991, *Isuramu Bunka: Sono Kontei ni aru mono* [Islamic Culture: Its Roots], Tokyo: Iwanamishoten.

Izutsu, Toshihiko translated., 1964 [1958], *Koran (Jo/ Chu / Ge)* [Quran 1, 2, 3], Tokyo: Iwanamishoten.

Jacobson, Jessica, 1998, *Islam in Transition: Religion and Identity among British Pakistani Youth*, London: Routledge.

James, Malcolm, 2008, *Interculturalism: Theory and Policy*, London: Baring Foundation.

Jeenah, Na'eem, 2006, 'The National Liberation Struggle and Islamic Feminism in South Africa', *Women's Studies International Forum*, 29: 27–41.

Jeldtoft, Nadia, 2011, 'Lived Islam: Religious Identity with "Non-Organized" Muslim Minorities', *Ethnic and Racial Studies*, 34(7): 1134–51.

————, 2013, 'Spirituality and Emotions: Making a Room of One's Own', in Nathal Dessing, Nadia Jeldtoft, Jørgen Nielsen and Linda Woodhead eds., *Everyday Lived Islam in Europe*, Farnham: Ashgate Publishing.

John of Damascus, n.d., *Fount of Knowledge*. http://orthodoxinfo.com/general/stjohn_islam.asp (accessed 26 May 2018).

John, Tara, 2019, 'Shamima Begum to be Stripped of British Nationality and will not be Allowed into Bangladesh, government says', *CNN*, 22 February 2019. https://edition.cnn.com/2019/02/20/uk/shamima-begum-uk-citizenship-stripped-gbr-intl/index.html (accessed 01 May 2019).

Joly, Danièle, 1995, *Britannia's Crescent: Making a Place for Muslims in British Society*, Aldershot: Ashgate Publishing.

Jones, Stephen, 2012, 'Knowledge, Tradition and Authority in British Islamic Theology', in Mathew Guest and Elisabeth Arweck eds., *Religion and Knowledge: Sociological Perspectives*, Farnham: Ashgate Publishing.

Joppke, Christian, 2009, *Veil: Mirror of Identity*, Cambridge: Polity Press.

Kabeer, Naila, 2000, *The Power to Choose: Bangladeshi Women and Labour Market Decisions in London and Dhaka*, London: Verso.

Kabir, Nahid, 2010, *Young British Muslims: Identity, Culture, Politics and the Media*, Edinburgh: Edinburgh University Press.

Kahf, Mohja, 1999, *Western Representations of the Muslim Woman: From Termagant to Odalisque*, Austin: University of Texas Press.

Kalra, Virinder, 2000, *From Textile Mills to Taxi Ranks: Experiences of Migration, Labour and Social Change*, Aldershot: Ashgate Publishing.

Kamada, Shigeru, 2000, 'Isuramu ni okeru Gaku no Rinen' [The Philosophy of Learning in Islam], *Kotengaku no Saikochiku* [Reconstruction of Classical Studies], 5: 16–7.

————, 2015, *Isuramu no Shinso: 'Henzai suru Kami' towa* [The Depths of Islam: What is the Ubiquitous God?] Tokyo: NHK Publishing.

Kamogawa, Akiko, 2008, *Mareshia Seinenki Josei no Shinro Keisei* [Shaping the career paths of adolescent Malaysian women], Tokyo: Toshindo.

Karatani, Rieko, 2003, *Defining British Citizenship: Empire, Commonwealth and Modern Britain*, London: Frank Cass Publishers.

Katakura, Motoko, Hiroshi Umemura and Yoshimi Shimizu eds., 2004, *Isuramu Sekai* [Islamic world], Tokyo: Iwanamishoten.

Kawash, Samira, 1997, 'Good Ethnics, Bad Aliens: Imagining the Global Village', *Macalester International*, 4: 175–97.

Kaya, Ayhan, 2009, *Islam, Migration and Integration: The Age of Securitization*, Hampshire: Palgrave Macmillan.

Kayanoki, Seigo, 2013, 'Namiuchigiwa no "Eikoku Shinmin": Daiei Teikokunai no Imin Kanri ni kansuru Rekishi Shakaigaku teki Kosatsu' ['British Subject' at Bay: A Historical Sociological Study on Migration Controls in the British Empire], *Kokusai Bunkagaku* [Intercultural Studies Review], 26: 1–21.

Keith, Michael and Steve Pile, 1993, *Place and the Politics of Identity*, London: Routledge.

Kelly, Ruth and Liam Byrne, 2007, *A Common Place*, London: Fabian Society.

Kepel, Gilles, 2005, 'Europe's Answer to Londonistan', *openDemocracy*, 24 August 2005. http://www.opendemocracy.net/conflict-terrorism/londonistan_2775.jsp (accessed 15 August 2012).

Kershen, Anne J., 2005, *Strangers, Aliens and Asians: Huguenots, Jews and Bangladeshis in Spitalfields 1666–2000*, Oxon: Routledge.

Kesvani, Hussein, 2019, *Follow Me, Akhi: The Online World of British Muslims*, London: Hurst & Company.

Keval, Harshad, 2009, 'Negotiating Constructions of "Insider" / "Outsider" Status and Exploring the Significance of Dis/Connections', *Enquire*, 4: 51–72.

Khan, Muhammad Zafrulla, 2008, *Women in Islam*, Islamabad: Islam International Publications.

Khan, Saira, 2012, 'Offensive? Racist? No, just funny – and oh so true! ', *Mail Online*, 23 September 2019. https://www.dailymail.co.uk/debate/article-2195459/Citizen-Khan-Offensive-Racist-No-just-funny--oh-true.html?ito=feeds-newsxml

Khan, Shahnaz, 1995 'The Veil as a Site of Struggle: The "Hijab" in Quebec', *Canadian Women Studies*, 15(2/3): 146–52.

Khan, Sumaira T., 2016, 'Islam and Girls' Education: Obligatory or Forbidden', *Cultural and Religious Studies*, 4(6): 339–45

Khattab, Huda, 1994, *The Muslim Woman's Handbook, 2nd edition*, London: TA-HA Publishers.

Kiliç, Sevgi, 2008, 'The British Veil Wars', *Social Politics*, 15 (4): 433–54.

King, Russell, 2002, 'Towards a New Map of European Migration', *International Journal of Population Geography*, 8(2): 89–106.

King's College London for European Commission (KCLEC), 2007, *Recruitment and Mobilisation for the Islamist Militant Movement in Europe*, London: International Centre for the Study of Radicalisation and Political Violence.

Kinnvall, Catarina and Paul Nesbitt-Larking, 2009, 'Security, Subjectivity and Space in Postcolonial Europe: Muslims in the Diaspora', *European Security*, 18(3): 305–25.

Kinoshita, Yasuhito, 2007, 'Shuseiban Guraundeddo Seori Apurochi (M-GTA) no Bunseki Giho' [Analytical Techniques of the Modified Grounded Theory Approach (M-GTA)], *Toyama Daigaku Kango Gakkaishi* [The journal of the Nursing Society of University of Toyama], 6(2): 1–10.

———, 2016, 'M-GTA no Kihon Tokusei to Bunseki Hoho——: Shitsuteki Kenkyu no Kanousei wo Kakunin suru' [Basic Characteristics of M-GTA and Its Analytical Process: Renewing Possibilities of Qualitative Research], *Iryo Kango Kenkyu* [Journal of Health Care and Nursing], 13(1): 1–11.

Knott, Kim and Sajda Khokher, 1993, 'Religious and Ethnic Identity among Young Muslim Women in Bradford', *New Community*, 19(4): 593–610.

Komura, Akiko, 2015, *Nihon to Isuramu ga Deau toki: Sono Rekishi to Kanousei* [When Japan Meets Islam: Its History and Possibilities], Tokyo: Gendaishokan.

Kondo, Junzo, 2007, *Iminkoku to shiteno Doitsu: Shakai Togo to Heiko Shakai no Yukue* [Germany as a Nation of Immigrants: Social Integration and the Future of Parallel Societies], Tokyo: Bokutakusha.

Kosugi, Yasushi, 1994, *Isuramu to wa Nani ka: Sono Shukyo Shakai Bunka* [What is Islam?: Its Religion, Society, and Culture], Tokyo: Kodansha.

Kotani, Hiroyuki, 2004, 'Mugaru Teikoku to Marata no Jidai' [The Mughal Empire and the Age of the Marathas], Noboru Karashima ed., *Minami Ajia shi* [South Asian History], Tokyo: Yamakawa Shuppansha.

Kotani, Hiroyuki and Noboru Karashima, 2004, 'Isuramu Sekai no Kakudai to Indo Atairiku' [The Expansion of the Islamic World and the Indian Sub-continent], Noboru Karashima ed., *Minami Ajia shi* [South Asian History], Tokyo: Yamakawa Shuppansha.

Kudo, Masako, 2008, *Ekkyo no Jinruigaku: Zainichi Pakisutanjin Musurimu Imin no Tsuma tachi* [The Anthropology of Crossing Borders: Wives of Pakistani Muslim Immigrants in Japan], Tokyo: University of Tokyo Press.

Kundnani, Arun, 2009, *Spooked! How Not to Prevent Extremism*, London, Institute of Race Relations.

Kurien, Prema, 1998, 'Becoming American by Becoming Hindu: Indian Americans Take Their Place at the Multicultural Table' in Stephen Warner and Judith Wittner eds., *Gatherings in Diaspora: Religious Communities and the New Immigration*, Philadelphia: Temple University Press.

Kymlicka, Will, 1995, *Multicultural Citizenship: A Liberal Theory of Minority Rights*, Oxford: Oxford University Press.

———, 2001, *Politics in the Vernacular: Nationalism, Multiculturalism, and Citizenship*, New York: Oxford University Press.

———, 2002, *Contemporary Political Philosophy: An Introduction, 2nd edition*, Oxford: Oxford University Press.

———, 2007, *Multicultural Odysseys: Navigating the New International Politics of Diversity*, Oxford: Oxford University Press.

———, 2012, 'Comment on Meer and Modood', *Journal of Intercultural Studies*, 33(2): 211–16.

Lamrabet, Asma, 2016, *Women in the Qur'an: An Emancipatory Reading*, Leicestershire: Square View.

Larsson, Göran, 2011, *Muslims and the New Media: Historical and Contemporary Debates*, Farnham: Ashgate Publishing.

Lash, Scott, 1994, 'Reflexivity and Its Doubles: Structure, Aesthetics, Community', in Ulrich Beck, Anthony Giddens and Scott Lash eds., *Reflexive Modernization: Politics, Tradition and Aesthetics in the Modern Social Order*, Cambridge: Polity Press.

Lash, Scott and John Urry, 1994, *Economies of Signs and Space*, London: Sage.

Laurence, James and Anthony Heath, 2008, *Predictors of Community Cohesion: Multi-level Modelling the 2005 Citizenship Survey*, London: Department for Communities and Local Government.

Lawler, Steph, 2008, *Identity: Sociological Perspectives*, Cambridge: Polity.

Layton-Henry, Zig, 1984, *The Politics of Race in Britain*, London: Allen & Unwin.

Lea, John and Jock Young, 1982, 'The Riots in Britain in 1981: Urban Violence and Political Marginalisation', in David Cowell, Trevor Jones and Jock Young eds., *Policing the Riots*, London: Junction Books.

Lee, Simon, 2006, 'Gordon Brown and the "British Way"', *The Political Quarterly*, 77(3): 369–78.

Leiken, Robert, 2012, *Europe's Angry Muslims: The Revolt of the Second Generation*, New York: Oxford University Press.

Levitas, Ruth, 2005, *The Inclusive Society?: Social Exclusion and New Labour, 2nd edition*, New York: Palgrave Macmillan.

Lewis, Philip, 1994, *Islamic Britain: Religion, Politics and Identity among British Muslims: Bradford in the 1990s*, London: I.B. Tauris & Co.

———, 2007, *Young, British and Muslim*, London: Continuum International Publishing Group.

Lichter, Ida, 2009, *Muslim Women Reformers: Inspiring Voices against Oppression*, New York: Prometheus Books.

Liddle, Joanna and Rama Joshi, 1985, 'Gender and Imperialism in British India', *South Asia Research*, 5(2): 147–64.

Lindley, Jonne, Angela Dale and Shirley Dex, 2006, 'Ethnic Differences in Women's Employment: The Changing Role of Qualifications', *Oxford Economic Papers*, 58: 351–78.

London 2012 Olympic, 2005, 'Singapore Presentation – 6 July 2005'. singapore-presentation-speeches-2.pdf (accessed 23 July 2012).

Loyd, Anthony, 2019, 'Shamima Begum: Bring Me Home, Says Bethnal Green Girl Who Left to Join Isis', *The Sunday Times*, 13 February 2019. https://www.thetimes.co.uk/article/shamima-begum-bring-me-home-says-bethnal-green-girl-who-fled-to-join-isis-hgvqw765d (accessed 01 May 2019).

Luhmann, Niklas, 1984, *Soziale Systeme: Grundriß einer allgemeinen Theorie*, Frankfurt am Main: Suhrkamp.

Lyon, Stephen, 2005, 'In the Shadow of September 11: Multiculturalism and Identity Politics', in Tahir Abbas ed., *Muslim Britain: Communities under Pressure*, London: Zed Books.

Macfie, Alexander Lyon, 2002, *Orientalism*, London: Longman.

Macpherson, William, 1999, *The Stephen Lawrence Inquiry: Report of an Inquiry by Sir William Macpherson of Cluny, CM 4262-I*, London: Stationery Office.

Mactaggart, Fiona, 2004, *Strength in Diversity: Towards a Community Cohesion and Race Equality Strategy*, London: Home Office.

Mahmood, Saba, 2005, *The Politics of Piety*, Princeton: Princeton University Press.

Mail Online, 2006, 'Whatever Happened to Free Speech Britain?', *Mail Online*, 07 October 2006. http://www.dailymail.co.uk/news/article-409135/Whatever-happened-free-speech-Britain.html (accessed 15 June 2018).

————, 2011, 'Nicolas Sarkozy Joins David Cameron and Angela Merkel View that Multiculturalism Has Failed', *Mail Online*, 11 February 2011. http://www.dailymail.co.uk/news/article-1355961/Nicolas-Sarkozy-joins-David-Cameron-Angela-Merkel-view-multiculturalism-failed.htmll (accessed 24 July 2018).

Malešević., Siniša, 2004, *The Sociology of Ethnicity*, London: Sage.

Malik, Abida and Emily Wykes, 2018, *British Muslims in UK Higher Education: Socio-political, Religious and Policy Considerations*, London: Bridge Institute.

Malik, Shiv, 2011, 'Watchdog Recommends Tory U-turn on Banning Hizb ut-Tahrir', *The Guardian*, 18 July 2011. https://www.theguardian.com/politics/2011/jul/18/watchdog-tory-uturn-hizb-ut-tahrir-ban (accessed 02 May 2019).

Mandaville, Peter, 2001, 'Reimaging Islam in Diaspora: The Politics of Mediated Community', *Gazette*, 63(2/3): 169–86.

————, 2002, 'Reimagining the Ummah? Information Technology and the Changing Boundaries of Political Islam', in Ali Mohammadi ed., *Islam Encountering Globalization*, London: Routledge.

Mariani, Ermete, 2011, 'Cyber-fatwas, Sermons, and Media Campaigns: Amr Khaled and Omar Bakri Muhammad in Search of New Audiences', in Martin van Bruinessen and Stefano Allievi eds., *Producing Islamic Knowledge: Transmission and Dissemination in Western Europe*, London: Routledge.

Marquand, David, 1988, *The Unprincipled Society*, London: Fontana Press.

Marx, Karl, 1964, *The Economic and Philosophic Manuscripts of 1844*, New York: International Publishes.

Mason, David, 2000, *Race and Ethnicity in Modern Britain, 2nd edition.*, Oxford: Oxford University Press.

Massey, Doreen, 1994, *Space, Place and Gender*, Cambridge: Polity Press.

Matsuyama, Yohei, 2017, *Isuramu Shiso wo Yomitoku* [Reading and Understanding Islamic Thought], Tokyo: Chikumashobo.

————, 2018a, 'Kuruan towa Nanika' [What is the Quran?], Yohei Matsuyama ed,. *Kuruan Nyumon* [Introduction to the Quran], Tokyo: Sakuhinsha.

————, 2018b, 'Koramu 6 Sunnaha towa Nani ka' [Column 6: What is Sunna?] Yohei Matsuyama ed., *Kuruan Nyumon* [Introduction to the Quran], Tokyo: Sakuhinsha.

————, 2018c, 'Sunnaha no Tafusuiru', Yohei Matsuyama ed,. *Kuruan Nyumon* [Introduction to the Quran], Tokyo: Sakuhinsha.

————, 2019, 'Isuramu Nanameyomi: #1 Isuramikku Poppu to Yoroppa' [Islam at a Glance: #1 Islamic Pop and Europe], *Genron 10*, Tokyo: Genron.

Matsuyama, Yohei ed., 2018, *Kuruan Nyumon* [Introduction to the Quran], Tokyo: Sakuhinsha.

Mawdudi, Syed, 1996, *Islamic Way of Life*, Batha: Co-operative Office for Call and Guidance.

Maxwell, Rahsaan, 2006, 'Muslims, South Asians and the British Mainstream: A National Identity Crisis?', *West European Politics*, 29(4): 736–56.

May, Tim, 1999, 'Reflexivity in Social Life and Sociological Practice: A Rejoinder to Roger Slack', *Sociological Research Online*, 5(1). http://www.socresonline.org.uk/4/3/may.html (accessed 20 July 2018).

McCarthy, E. Doyle, 1996, *Knowledge as Culture: The New Sociology of Knowledge*, London: Routledge.

McGhee, Derek, 2005, *Intolerant Britain? Hate, Citizenship and Difference*, Maidenhead, Open University Press.

————, 2010, *Security, Citizenship and Human Rights: Shared Values in Uncertain Times*, New York: Palgrave Macmillan.

McLoughlin, Seán, 2005, 'Mosques and the Public Space: Conflicts and Cooperation in Bradford', *Journal of Ethnic and Migration Studies*, 31(6): 1045–66.

McNay, Lois, 2000, *Gender and Agency: Reconfiguring the Subject in Feminist and Social Theory*, Malden: Blackwell Publishers.

Mead, George Herbert, 1934, *Mind, Self and Society: From the Standpoint of a Social Behaviorist*, Chicago: University of Chicago Press.

Meer, Nasar, 2010, *Citizenship, Identity and the Politics of Multiculturalism: The Rise of Muslim Consciousness*, Hampshire: Palgrave Macmillan.

Meer, Nasar and Tariq Modood, 2012, 'How Does Interculturalism Contrast with Multiculturalism?', *Journal of Intercultural Studies*, 33(2): 175–96.

Mernissi, Fatima, 1991, *The Veil and the Male Elite: A Feminist Interpretation of Women's Rights in Islam*, Massachusetts: Perseus Books.

Merriam, Sharan, Juanita Johnson-Bailey, Ming-Yeh Lee, Youngwha Kee, Gabo Ntseane and Mazanah Muhamad, 2001, 'Power and Positionality: Negotiating Insider/Outsider Status within and across Cultures', *International Journal of Lifelong Education*, 20(5): 405–16.

Merrick, Rob, 2017, 'Michael Gove Has Same "Crazy" anti-Muslim Policies as Donald Trump, Former Tory Chairwoman Says', *Independent*, 25 March 2017. https://www.independent.co.uk/news/uk/politics/michael-gove-donald-trump-baroness-warsi-anti-muslim-crazy-tory-chairwoman-a7649411.html (accessed 16 August 2018).

Mihara, Reiko, 2009, *Oranda to Berugi no Isuramu Kyoiku: Kokyoiku ni okeru Shukyo no Tagensei to Taiwa* [Islamic Education in the Netherlands and Belgium: Religious Pluralism and Dialogue in Public Education], Tokyo: Akashishoten.

Miles, Robert, 1989, *Racism*, London: Routledge.

——————, 1993, *Racism after 'Race Relations'*, London: Routledge.

Miles, Robert and Paula Cleary, 1992, 'Britain: Post-Colonial Immigration in Context', in Dietrich Thränhardt ed., *Europe – A New Immigration Continent: Policies and Politics in Comparative Perspective*, Münster: Lit Verlag.

Miller, David, 1995, *On Nationality*, New York: Oxford University Press.

Minamikawa, Fuminori, 2021, *Mikan no Tabunka Shugi: Amerika ni okeru Jinshu, Kokka, Tayosei* [Multiculturalism as an Unfinished Project: Race, State, and Diversity in the United States], Tokyo: University of Tokyo Press.

Minesaki, Hiroko, 2015, *Isuramu Fukko to Jenda: Gendai Ejiputo Shakai wo Ikiru Josei tachi* [Islamic Revival and Gender: Women in Contemporary Egyptian Society], Kyoto: Showado.

Ministry of Justice, 2007, *The Governance of Britain*, London: Stationery Office.

Mir, Shabana, 2014, *Muslim American Women on Campus: Undergraduate Social Life and Identity*, Chapel Hill: The University of North Carolina Press.

Mirza, Munira, Abi Senthilkumaran and Ja'far Zein, 2007, *Living Apart Together: British Muslims and the Paradox of Multiculturalism, Policy Exchange*, London: Policy Exchange.

Misgar, Umar, 2022, 'British Muslims reflect on late Queen Elizabeth II, UK's monarchy', *Aljazeera*, 12 September 2022. https://www.aljazeera.com/features/2022/9/12/british-muslims-reflect-on-late-queen-elizabeth-ii-uks-monarchy (accessed 27 September 2022).

Mishra, Smeeta and Faegheh Shirazi, 2010, 'Hybrid Identities: American Muslim Women Speak', *Gender, Place and Culture*, 17(2): 191–209.

Miura, Nobutaka ed., 2001, *Fuhensei ka Sai ka: Kyowa Shugi no Rinkai, Furansu* [Universality or Difference: The Criticality of Republicanism, France], Tokyo: Fujiwara Shoten.

Modood, Tariq, 1988, '"Black", Racial Equality and Asian Identity', *New Community*, 14: 397–404.

——————, 1994, 'Political Blackness and British Asians', *Sociology*, 28(4): 859–76.

——————, 1997, 'Culture and Identity', in Tariq Modood and Richard Berthoud eds., *Ethnic Minorities in Britain: Diversity and Disadvantage – Fourth National Survey of Ethnic Minorities*, London: Policy Studies Institute.

————, 2006a, 'British Muslims and the Politics of Multiculturalism', in Tariq Modood, Anna Triandafyllidou and Ricard Zapata-Barrero eds., *Multiculturalism, Muslim and Citizenship: A European Approach*, Oxon: Routledge.

————, 2006b, 'Politics of Blackness and Asian Identity', in Nasreen Ali, Virinder S. Kalra and Salman Sayyid eds., *A Postcolonial People: South Asians in Britain*, New York: Columbia University Press.

————, 2007, 'Multiculturalism, Citizenship and National Identity', *openDemocracy*, 16 May 2007. http://www.opendemocracy.net/faith-europe_islam/multiculturalism_4627.jsp (accessed 01 October 2012).

————, 2010, *Still Not Easy Being British: Struggle for a Multicultural Citizenship*, Stoke on Trent: Trentham Books.

————, 2013, *Multiculturalism, 2nd edition*, Cambridge: Polity Press.

————, 2015, 'What Is Multiculturalism and What Can It Learn from Interculturalism?', *Ethnicities*, 16(3): 480–89.

Modood, Tariq and Richard Berthoud eds., 1997, *Ethnic Minorities in Britain: Diversity and Disadvantage – Fourth National Survey of Ethnic Minorities*, London: Policy Studies Institute.

Mohammed, Robina, 2004, 'British Pakistani Muslim Women: Marking the Body, Marking the Nation', in Lise Nelson and Joni Seager eds., *A Companion to Feminist Geography*, Oxford: Blackwell.

Mohanty, Chandra, 1984, 'Under Western Eyes: Feminist Scholarship and Colonial Discourses', *Boundary 2*, 12(3): 333–58.

————, 2003, *Feminism without Borders: Decolonizing Theory, Practicing Solidarity*, Durham: Duke University Press.

Moore, Henrietta, 1988, *Feminism and Anthropology*, Minneapolis: University of Minnesota Press.

————, 1994, *A Passion for Difference: Essays of Anthropology and Gender*, Cambridge: Polity Press.

Morey, Peter and Amina Yaqin, 2011, *Framing Muslims: Stereotyping and Representation after 9/11*, Cambridge: Harvard University Press.

Mori, Chikako, 2016, *Haijo to Teiko no Kogai: Furansu 'Imin' Shujyu Chiiki no Keisei to Henyo* [Exclusion and Resistance in the Suburbs: The Formation and Transformation of Immigrant Settlements in France], Tokyo: University of Tokyo Press.

Mori, Hiroshi, 2001, *Ima wa Mo Inai* [Switch Back], Tokyo: Kodansha.

Mori, Koichi ed., 2006, *Iyu to Isuramu no Shukyo Dento wa Kyozon dekiruka* [Can the EU and Islamic Religious Traditions Coexist?], Tokyo: Akashishoten.

Moriyama, Takuya, 2014, 'Hijyabu Fasshon ga Arawasu Mono: Yosooi kara Miru Musurimu Shakai no Henka' [What Does Hijab-fashion Convey?: Changing Style of Hijab and Muslim Society], *Doshisha Gurobaru Sutadhizu* [Journal of Global Studies], 5: 3–24.

Mouffe, Chantal, 2005, *On the Political*, London: Routledge.

Murakami, Haruki, 2014, *Colorless Tsukuru Tazaki and His Years of Pilgrimage*, London: Harvill Secker.

Murphy, Neil, 2022, 'Muslim community leaders come together to sing "God Save the King"', *The National*, 16 September 2022. https://www.thenationalnews.com/world/uk-news/2022/09/15/muslim-community-leaders-come-together-to-sing-god-save-the-king/ (accessed 27 September 2022).

Muslim Council of Britain's Research and Documentation Committee (MCB), 2015, *British Muslims in Numbers: A Demographic, Socio-economic and Health Profile of Muslims in Britain Drawing on the 2011 Census*, London: Muslim Council of Britain.

Nabe, Keiichi, 2018, 'Kozoka Riron Saiko: Modanithiron tono Renzokusei/Danzetsu' [Rethinking Structuration Theory: On Its Continuity/Discontinuity with Modernity Theory], *Shakaigaku Ronshu* (St. Andrew's University Sociological Review), 51: 269–80.

Nadel, George and Perry Curtis, 1964, *Imperialism and Colonialism*, New York: Macmillan.

Nagasaki, Nobuko, 2004, 'Eiryo Indo no Seiritsu to Indo Minzoku Undo no Hajimari', Noboru Karashima ed., *Minami Ajia shi* [South Asian History], Tokyo: Yamakawa Shuppansha.

Nagel, Caroline, 2005, 'Introduction', in Ghazi-Walid Falah and Caroline Nagel eds., *Geographies of Muslim Women: Gender, Religion and, Space*, New York: Guilford Press.

Naik, Zakir, 2014, 'What Does It Mean When One Says, Islam is a "Way of Life"', *YouTube*, 21 October 2014. https://www.ft.com/content/ff41a586-197f-11da-804e-00000e2511c8 (accessed 28 April 2019).

Naito, Masanori, 2004, *Yoroppa to Isuramu: Kyosei wa Kanou ka* [Europe and Islam: Is coexistence possible?], Tokyo: Iwanamishoten.

———, 2007, 'Sukafu Ronso towa Nani ka' [What is the Scarf Controversy?], Masanori Naito and Shojiro Sakaguchi eds., *Kami no Ho vs Hito no Ho: Sukafu Ronso kara miru Seio to Isuramu no Danso* [The Law of God vs. the Law of Man: The Fault Lines between the West and Islam in the Scarf Controversy], Tokyo: Nippon Hyoron Sha.

———, 2009, *Isuramu no Ikari* [The Wrath of Islam], Tokyo: Shueisha.

Naito, Masanori and Shojiro Sakaguchi eds., 2007, *Kami no Ho vs Hito no Ho: Sukafu Ronso kara miru Seio to Isuramu no Danso* [The Law of God vs. the Law of Man: The Fault Lines between the West and Islam in the Scarf Controversy], Tokyo: Nippon Hyoron Sha.

Nakanishi, Mikinori, 2013, 'Retorikku Hihyo ni okeru Metonimi no Kanousei: Misheru do Seruto to Poru do Man wo Yomu' [A Consideration of the Possibility of Metonymy in Rhetorical Criticism: Reading the Texts of Michel de Certeau and Paul de Man], *Gifu Shiritsu Joshi Tanki Daigaku Kenkyu Kiyo* [Bulletin of Gifu City Women's College], 63: 1–8.

Nakano, Yuji, Chikako Mori, Hélène Le Bail, Shintaro Namioka, Daisuke Sonoyama eds., 2015, *Haigai Shugi wo Toinaosu: Furansu ni okeru Haijo Sabetsu Sanka* [Reconsidering Exclusionism: Exclusion, Discrimination, and Participation in France], Tokyo: Keisoshobo.

Nakata, Ko ed., 2014, *Nichia Taiyaku Kuruan* [Japanese-Arabic Translation Qur'an], Tokyo: Sakuhinsha.

Nakata, Ko, 2015, *Isuramu Ho to wa Nani ka?* [What is Islamic Law?], Tokyo: Sakuhinsha.

Nawaz, Maajid, 2012, *Radical: My Journey from Islamist Extremism to a Democratic Awakening*, London: W. H. Allen.

Newman, Cathy, 2009, 'BNP's Griffin: Islam Is a Cancer', *Channel 4 News*, 09 July 2009. http://www.channel4.com/news/articles/politics/domestic_politics/bnpaposs+griffin+islam+is+a+cancer/3257872.html (accessed 30 October 2018).

NewSphere, 2013, 'Igirisu Heishi Satsugai "Tero" Jiken no Eikyo to wa?' [What is the Impact of the 'Terrorist' Attack that Killed a British Soldier?], *NewSphere*, 5 May 2013. https://newsphere.jp/world-report/20130525-1/ (accessed 05 May 2019).

Nielsen, Jørgen, 1992, *Muslims in Western Europe*, Edinburgh: Edinburgh University Press.

Nihon Isuramu Kyokai, Johei Shimada, Yuzo Itagaki, Tsugitaka Sato, eds., 2002, *Shin Isuramu Jiten* [New Islamic Encyclopedia], Tokyo: Heibonsha.

Noble, Molley, 2018, 'Religiosity and Feminism: Navigation Gender Constructions and Ideologies', Thesis: Master of Arts in Sociology, Humboldt State University.

Noden, Philip, Michael Shiner and Tariq Modood, 2014, 'University Offer Rates for Candidates from Different Ethnic Categories', *Oxford Review of Education* 40(3): 349–69.

Okahisa, Kei, 2009, 'Eikoku no Tai Kokusai Terorizumu Senryaku: CONTEST' [The United Kingdom's Strategy against International Terrorism: CONTEST], *Gaikoku no Rippo* [Foreign Legislation], 241: 198–226.

Okin, Susan, 1999, 'Is Multiculturalism Bad for Women?', in Joshua Cohen, Matthew Howard and Martha Nussbaum eds., *Is Multiculturalism Bad for Women?* Princeton: Princeton University Press.

Omaar, Rageh, 2007, *Only Half of Me: British and Muslim – The Conflict Within*, London: Penguin Books.

Ong, Aihwa, 1995, 'State versus Islam: Malay Families, Women's Bodies, and the Body Politics in Malaysia', in Aihwa Ong and Michael Gates Peletz eds., *Bewitching Women, Pious Men: Gender and Body Politics in Southeast Asia*, London: University of California Press.

Osman, Zuraini Jamil, 2013, *Malay Muslim Academic Women in Dual-Career Families: Negotiating Religious and Cultural Identities and Practices*, PhD thesis, York: University of York.

Ouseley, Herman, 2001, *Community Pride Not Prejudice*, Bradford: Bradford Vision.

Panayi, Panikos, 2010, *An Immigration History of Britain: Multicultural Racism since 1800*, Harlow: Person Education.

Parekh, Bhikhu, 2002, *The Future of Multi-Ethnic Britain*, reprinted with corrections, London: Profile Books.

————, 2006, *Rethinking Multiculturalism: Cultural Diversity and Political Theory*, 2nd *edition*, Hampshire: Palgrave Macmillan.

————, 2007, 'Reasoned Identities: A Committed Relationship', in Margaret Wetherell, Michelynn Laflèche and Robert Berkeley eds., *Identity, Ethnic Diversity and Community Cohesion*, London: Sage.

————, 2008, *A New Politics of Identity: Political Principles for an Independent World*, Hampshire: Palgrave Macmillan.

————, 2009, 'Being British', in Andrew Gamble and Tony Wright eds., *Britishness: Perspectives on the British Question*, Oxford: Wiley-Blackwell.

Parker-Jenkins, Marie and Kaye F. Haw, 1996, 'Equality within Islam, Not without It: The Perspectives of Muslim Girls in a Muslim School in Britain', *Muslim Education Quarterly* 3(3): 17–34.

Parmar, Pratibha, 1988, 'Gender, Race and Power: The Challenge to Youth Work Practice', in Philip Cohen and Harwant S. Bains eds. *Multi-Racist Britain*, London: MacMillan Education.

Parsons, Talcott, 1951, *The Social System*, Illinois: Free Press.

Peach, Ceri, 1968, *West Indian Migration to Britain: A Social Geography*, London: Oxford University Press.

————, 1997, 'Estimates of the 1991 Muslim Population of Great Britain', in Oxford Plural Societies and Multicultural Cities Research Group eds., *Working paper I*, Oxford: Oxford School of Geography.

————, 2005, 'Muslims in the UK', in Tahir Abbas ed., *Muslim Britain: Communities under Pressure*, London: Zed Books.

Pennycook, Alastair, 1994, 'Incommensurable Discourses?', *Applied Linguistics*, 15(2): 115–38.

Perozzo, Cristina, Roxane de la Sablonnière, Emilie Auger and Mathieu Caron-Diotte, 2016, 'Social Identity Change in Response to Discrimination', *British Journal of Social Psychology*, 55(3): 438–56.

Pew Research Center, 2006 (PRC), *The Great Divide: How Westerners and Muslims View Each Other*, Washington D. C.: Pew Research Center.

————, 2011, *The Future of the Global Muslim Population: Projections for 2010–2030*, Washington D. C: Pew Research Center.

Pfaff, William, 2005, 'A Monster of Our Own Making', *Observer*, 21 August 2005. http://www.guardian.co.uk/uk/2005/aug/21/july7.terrorism (accessed 15 August 2012).

Phalet, Karen, Fenella Fleischmann and Snežana Stojčić, 2012, 'Ways of "Being Muslim": Religious Identities of Second-generation Turks', in Maurice Crul, Jens Schneider and Frans Lelie eds., *The European Second Generation Compared: Does the Integration Context Matter?*, Amsterdam: Amsterdam University Press.

Phillips, Anne, 2007, *Multiculturalism without Culture*, Princeton: Princeton University Press.

Phillips, Deborah, 2009, 'Creating Home Spaces: Young British Muslim Women's Identity and Conceptualisations of Home', in Peter Hopkins and Richard Gale eds., *Muslims in Britain: Race, Place and Identities*, Edinburgh: Edinburgh University Press.

Phillips, Trevor, 2005, 'After 7/7: Sleepwalking to Segregation', 22 September 2005. http://www.humanities.manchester.ac.uk/socialchange/research/social-change/summer-workshops/documents/sleepwalking.pdf (accessed 2 January 2010).

Phoenix, Ann, 1994, 'Practicing Feminist Research: The Intersection of Gender and "Race" in the Research Process', in Mary Maynard and June Purvis eds., *Researching Women's Lives from a Feminist Perspective*, London: Taylor & Francis.

Piela, Anna, 2013, *Muslim Women Online: Faith and Identity in Virtual Space*, London: Routledge.

Pitcher, Ben, 2009, *The Politics of Multiculturalism: Race and Racism in Contemporary Britain*, Basingstoke: Palgrave Macmillan.

Portlock, Sarah, 2016, 'Coventry: Is the UK's "Motor City" Still Driving Forwards?', *BBC News*, 12 December 2016. https://www.bbc.com/news/uk-england-coventry-warwickshire-38212517 (accessed 19 June 2018).

Poynting, Scott, 2009, 'The "Lost" Girls: Muslim Young Women in Australia', *Journal of Intercultural Studies*, 30(4): 373–86.

Puar, Jasbir, 1996, 'Resituating Discourses of "Whiteness" and "Asianness" in Northern England: Second-generation Sikh Women and Constructions of Identity', in Mary Maynard and June Purvis eds., *New Frontiers in Women's Studies: Knowledge, Identity and Nationalism*, London: Taylor & Francis.

Pugh, R., 1991, 'Culture Clash on Their Plate', *Times Educational Supplement*, 8 March 1991.

Rabe, Marlize, 2003, 'Revisiting "Insiders" and "Outsiders" as Social Researchers', *African Sociological Review*, 7(2): 149–61.

Ramadan, Tariq, 2005, *Western Muslims and the Future of Islam*, New York: Oxford University Press.

————, 2010, *What I Believe*, New York: Oxford University Press.

Ramírez, Ángeles, 2014, 'Control over Female "Muslim" Bodies: Culture, Politics and Dress Code Laws in some Muslim and Non-Muslim Countries', *Global Studies in Culture and Power*, 22(6): 671–86.

Rampton, Anthony, 1981, *West Indian Children in Our Schools*, London: Her Majesty's Stationery Office.

Rashid, Naaz, 2014, 'Giving the Silent Majority a Stronger Voice?: Initiatives to Empower Muslim Women as Part of the UK's "War on Terror"', *Ethnic and Racial Studies*, 37(4): 589–604.

————, 2017, '"Everyone is a Feminist when It Comes to Muslim Women": Gender and Islamophobia', in Farah Elahi and Omar Khan eds, *Islamophobia: Still a Challenge for Us All*, London: Runnymede Trust.

Rayaprol, Aparna, 1997, *Negotiating Identities: Women in the Indian Diaspora*, Delhi: Oxford University Press.

Relph, Edward, 1976, *Place and Placelessness*, London: Pion.

Revell, Lynn, 2012, *Islam and Education: The Manipulation and Misrepresentation of a Religion*, Stoke-on-Trent: Trentham Books.

Rex, John and Robert Moore, 1967, *Race, Community and Conflict: A Study of Sparkbrook*, Oxford: Oxford University Press.

Richardson, Robin, 2010, 'Foreword', in Tariq Modood ed., *Still Not Easy Being British: Struggle for a Multicultural Citizenship*, Stoke on Trent: Trentham Books.

Roald, Anne Sofie, 2001, *Women in Islam: The Western Experience*, London: Routledge.

Robert, Na'ima, 2005, *From My Sisters' Lips*, London: Bantam Books.

Robertson, Roland, 1992, *Globalization: Social Theory and Global Culture*, London: Sage.

Robinson-Dunn, Diane, 2006, *The Harem, Slavery and British Imperial Culture: Anglo-Muslim Relations in the Late Nineteenth Century*, Manchester: Manchester University Press.

Rohloff, Amanda and Sarah Wright, 2010, 'Moral Panic and Social Theory: Beyond the Heuristic', *Current Sociology*, 58(3): 403–19.

Rorty, Richard, 1998, *Achieving Our Country: Leftist Thought in Twentieth-century America*, Cambridge: Harvard University Press.

Rose, Nikolas, 1999, *Powers of Freedom: Reframing Political Thought*, Cambridge: Cambridge University Press.

————, 2001, 'The Politics of Life Itself', *Theory, Culture and Society*, 18(6): 1–30.

Rothon, Catherine, 2006, 'The Importance of Social Class in Explaining the Educational Attainments of Minority Ethnic Pupils in Britain: Evidence from the Youth Cohort Study', *Sociology Working Papers, Paper Number 2006–02*, Oxford: Department of Sociology, University of Oxford.

Poulter, Sebastian, 1997, 'Muslim Headscarves in School: Contrasting Legal Approaches in England and France', *Oxford Journal of Legal Studies*, 17(1): 43–74.

Roy, Olivier, 2004, *Globalised Islam: The Search for a New Ummah*, London: Hurst & Company.

Runnymede Trust, 1997, *Islamophobia: A Challenge for Us All*, London: Runnymede Trust.

————, 2004, *Islamophobia: Issues, Challenges and Action*, London: Runnymede Trust.

Ryan, Louise, 2012, 'Young Muslims in London: Gendered Negotiations of Local, National and Transnational Places', in Waqar Ahmad and Ziauddin Sardar, eds., *Muslims in Britain: Making Social and Political Space*, New York: Routledge.

Saeed, Abdullah, 2006, *Interpreting the Qur'an: Towards a Contemporary Approach*, New York: Routledge.

Sahin, Abdullah, 2005, 'Exploring the Religious Life-world and Attitudes toward Islam among British Muslim Adolescents', in Leslie John Francis, Mandy Robbins and Jeff Astley eds., *Religion, Education and Adolescents: International Empirical Perspectives*, Cardiff: University of Wales Press.

——————, 2013, *New Directions in Islamic Education: Pedagogy and Identity Formation*, Leicestershire: Kube Publishing.

Said, Edward, 1978, *Orientalism*, New York: Georges Borchardt.

——————, 1981, *Covering Islam: How the Media and the Experts Determine How We See the Rest of the World*, New York: Pantheon Books.

Sakuma, Kousei, 1998, *Henbo suru Taminzoku Kokka Igirisu: 'Tabunka' to 'Tabunka' ni Yureru Kyoiku* [The Changing Multi-Ethnic Britain: Education in the Conflict between 'Multiculturalism' and 'Multi-Diversification'], Tokyo: Akashishoten.

Sakurai, Atsushi, 2002, *Intabyu no Shakaigaku: Raifu Sutori no Kikikata* [The Sociology of Interviews: How to Listen to Life Stories], Tokyo: Sericashobo.

Sales, Rosemary, 2012, 'Britain and Britishness', in Waqar Ahmad and Ziauddin Sardar, eds., *Muslims in Britain: Making Social and Political Space*, New York: Routledge.

Sanghera, Gurchathen and Suruchi Thapar-Björkert, 2007, '"Because I'm Pakistani... and I'm Muslim... and I Am Political" – Gendering Political Radicalism: Young Femininities in Bradford', in Tahir Abbas ed., *Islamic Political Radicalism: A European Perspective*, Edinburgh: Edinburgh University Press.

Sardar, Ziauddin, 2011, *Reading the Qur'an: The Contemporary Relevance of the Sacred Text of Islam*, New York: Oxford University Press.

Sardar, Ziauddin and Waqar Ahmad, 2012, 'Introduction', in Waqar Ahmad and Ziauddin Sardar eds., *Muslims in Britain: Making Social and Political Space*, New York: Routledge.

Sartre, Jean-Paul, 1961, 'Préface', in Frantz Fanon ed., *Les damnés de la terre*, Paris: Maspero.

——————, 1976, *Anti-Semite and Jew*, with new preface by Michael Walzer, New York: Schocken Books.

Sarwar, Ghulam, 2006, *Islam: Beliefs and Teachings, 8th revised edition*, London: The Muslim Educational Trust.

Sayyid, Bobby S., 1997, *A Fundamental Fear: Eurocentrism and the Emergence of Islamism*, London: Zed Books.

Schneppel, Matthias, 2014, *Understanding Skills and Qualification Levels in Tower Hamlets*, London: HMSO.

Schütz, Alfred, 1973, *Collected Papers I: The Problem of Social Reality*, The Hague: Martinus Nijhoff.

Scott, Joan Wallach, 2007, *The Politics of the Veil*, Princeton: Princeton University Press.

Sehlikoglu, Sertaç, 2018, 'Revisited: Muslim Women's Agency and Feminist Anthropology of the Middle East', *Contemporary Islam*, 12: 73-92.

Seida, Natsuyo, 2005, *Gendai Igirisu no Kyoiku Gyosei Kaikaku* [Educational Administrative Reform in Modern Britain], Tokyo: Keisoshobo.

Seldon, Anthony ed., 2007, *Blair's Britain: 1997–2007*, Cambridge: Cambridge University Press.

Sen, Amartya, 2006, *Identity and Violence: The Illusion of Destiny*, London: Penguin Books.

Sewell, Tony, 1998, *Keep on Moving: The Windrush Legacy – The Black Experience in Britain from 1948*, London: Voice Enterprises.

Shain, Farzana, 2003, *The Schooling and Identity of Asian Girls*, Stoke on Trent: Trentham Books.

————, 2011, *The New Folk Devils: Muslim Boys and Education in England*, Stoke on Trent: Trentham Books.

Shamsie, Kamila, 2009, 'A Dark Chapter in Pakistan's History', *Qauntara.de*, 23 October 2009. https://en.qantara.de/content/interview-with-kamila-shamsie-a-dark-chapter-in-pakistans-history (accessed 10 August 2018).

Shannahan, Chris, 2017, 'Zombie Multiculturalism Meets Liberative Difference: Searching for a New Discourse of Diversity', *Culture and Religion*, 17(4): 409–30.

Shaw, Alison, 1994, 'The Pakistan Community in Oxford', in Roger Ballard ed., *Desh Pardesh: The South Asian Presence in Britain*, London: Hurst & Company.

Shimomura, Kazuki, 2014, 'Jo' [Preface], Ko Nakatasa supervised., Kaori Nakata and Kazuki Shimomura translated., *Nichia Taiyaku Kuruan* [Japanese-Asian Bilingual Translation of the Quran], Tokyo: Sakuhinsha.

Siddiqui, Haroon, 2006, *Being Muslim*, Toronto: Groundwood Books.

Simpson, Alyson, 1997, '"It's Game!" The Construction of Gendered Subjectivity', in Ruth Wodak ed., *Gender and Discourse*, London: Sage.

Singh, Ramindar, 2002, *The Struggle for Racial Justice: From Community Relations to Community Cohesion*, Bradford: Print Plus UK.

Smith, Dorothy, 1987, *Everyday World as Problematic: A Feminist Sociology*, Toronto: University of Toronto Press.

Smith, Michael, 1986, 'Pluralism, Race and Ethnicity in Selected African Countries', in John Rex and David Mason eds., *Theories of Race and Ethnic Relations*, Cambridge: Cambridge University Press.

Solomos, John, 1989, *Race and Racism in Contemporary Britain*, Hampshire: Macmillan Education.

Spivak, Gayatri C., 1994, 'Can the Subaltern Speak?', in Patrick Williams and Laura Chrisman eds., *Colonial Discourse and Post-colonial Theory: A Reader*, Hemel Hempstead: Harvester Wheatsheaf.

Stephens, William B., 1969, 'The City of Coventry: Crafts and Industries, Modern Industry and Trade', in William B. Stephens ed., *A History of the County of Warwick: volume 8, the City of Coventry and Borough of Warwick*, London: Victoria County History. http://www.british-history.ac.uk/vch/warks/vol8/pp162-189 (accessed 01 September 2018).

Stevenson, Jacqueline, Sean Demack, Bernie Stiell, Muna Abdi, Lisa Clarkson, Farhana Ghaffar and Shaima Hassan, 2017, *The Social Mobility Challenges Faced by Young Muslims*, London: Social Mobility Commission.

Steyn, Mark, 2005, 'A Victory for Multiculti over Common Sense', *The Telegraph*, 19 July 2005. http://www.telegraph.co.uk/comment/personal-view/3618488/A-victory-for-multiculti-over-common-sense.html (accessed 23 March 2012).

Stivens, Malia, 2006, '"Family Values" and Islamic Revival: Gender, Rights and State Moral Projects in Malaysia', *Women's Studies International Forum*, 29(4): 354–67.

Stopes-Roe, Mary and Raymond Cochrane, 1991, *Citizens of This Country*, Clevedon: Multilingual Matters.

Stowasser, Barbara, 1994, *Women in the Qur'an, Traditions, and Interpretations*, New York: Oxford University Press.

Straw, Jack, 2006, '"I Felt Uneasy Talking to Someone I Couldn't See"', *The Guardian*, 06 October 2006. https://www.theguardian.com/commentisfree/2006/oct/06/politics.uk (accessed 26 May 2018).

Stuurman, Siep, 2004, 'How to Write a History of Equality', *Leidschrift*, 19(3): 23–38.

Sugino, Isamu, 2013, 'Shakai Chosa no Shurui: Shitsuteki Chosa to Ryoteki Chosa towa?' [Types of Social Research: What is Qualitative and Quantitative Research?], in Makoto Todoroki and Isamu Sugino eds., *Nyumon Shakai Chosaho: 2 Sttepu de Kiso kara Manabu (Dai 2 han)* [Introductory Social Research Methods: Learning from the Basics in Two Steps (2nd Edition)], Kyoto: Horitsubunkasha.

Tajfel, Henri, 1978, 'Interindividual Behaviour and Intergroup Behaviour', in Henri Tajfel ed., *Differentiation between Social Groups: Studies in the Social Psychology of Intergroup Relations*, London: Academic Press.

Takada, Hirofumi, 2011, *Sezoku to Shukyo no Aida: Charuzu Teira no Seiji Riron* [Between Secularity and Religion: Charles Taylor's Political Theory], Tokyo: Fukosha.

Tamir, Yael, 1993, *Liberal Nationalism*, Princeton: Princeton University Press.

Tanigawa, Minoru and Yutaka Uegaki, 2006, 'Furansu Kakumei to Naporeon Teisei' [French Revolution and Napoleonic Empire], in Minoru Tanigawa and Kazuyuki Watanabe eds., *Kindai Furansu no Rekishi: Kokumin Kokka Keisei no Kanata ni* [A History of Modern France: Beyond the Formation of the Nation-State], Kyoto: Minervashobo.

Tan, Rebecca, 2018, 'From France to Denmark, Bans on Full-face Muslim Veils Are Spreading across Europe', *The Washington Post*, 16 August 2018. https://www.washingtonpost.com/world/2018/08/16/france-denmark-bans-full-face-muslim-veils-are-spreading-across-europe/?utm_term=.119546d064a6 (accessed 24 April 2019).

Tarlo, Emma, 2010a, 'Hijab Online: The Fashioning of Cyber Islamic Commerce', *Interventions: International Journal of Postcolonial Studies*, 12(2): 209–25.

————, 2010b, *Visibly Muslim: Fashion, Politics, Faith*, New York: Berg Publishers.

Taylor, Charles, 1979, *Hegel and Modern Society*, Cambridge: Cambridge University Press,

————, 1985, *Philosophical Papers I: Human Agency and Language*, Cambridge: Cambridge University Press.

————, 1989, *Sources of the Self: The Making of the Modern Identity*, Cambridge: Harvard University Press.

————, 1994, 'The Politics of Recognition', in Amy Gutmann ed., *Multiculturalism and the 'Politics of Recognition'*, Princeton: Princeton University Press.

Templeman, Sasja, 1999, 'Constructions of Cultural Identity: Multiculturalism and Exclusion', *Political Studies*, 47(1): 17–31.

Thomas, Elaine, 2006, 'Keeping Identity at a Distance: Explaining France's New Legal Restrictions on the Islamic Headscarf', *Ethnic and Racial Studies*, 29(2): 237–59.

Thomas, Paul, 2011, *Youth, Multiculturalism and Community Cohesion*, Basingstoke: Palgrave Macmillan.

Thoms, David and Tom Donnelly, 2000, *The Coventry Motor Industry: Birth and Renaissance*, Aldershot: Ashgate Publishing.

Thornley, Edelweisse and Gerda Siann, 1991, 'The Career Aspirations of South Asian Girls in Glasgow', *Gender and Education*, 3(3): 237–48.

Tomioka, Jiro, 1998, *Igirisu ni okeru Jinshu to Kyoiku* [Race and Education in Britain], Tokyo: Akashishoten.

Tosun, Ender, 2012, *Guide to Understanding Islam*, Istanbul: Esen Ofset Matb.

Tsolidis, Georgina, 2017, 'Multiculturalism and Feminism: Women and the Burden of Representation', in Martina Boese and Vince Marotta eds., *Critical Reflections on Migration, 'Race' and Multiculturalism: Australia in a Global Context*, London: Routledge.

Turner, Bryan, 2012, 'Secularisation and the Politics of Religious Knowledge', in Fernando Rubio and Patrick Baert eds., *The Politics of Knowledge*, Oxon: Routledge.

Tyrer, David and Fauzia Ahmad, 2006, *Muslim Women and Higher Education: Identities, Experiences and Prospects*, Oxford: Oxuniprint.

Uberoi, Varun, Nasar Meer, Tariq Modood and Claire Dwyer, 2011, 'Feeling and Being Muslim and British', in Tariq Modood and John Salt eds., *Global Migration, Ethnicity and Britishness*, Hampshire: Palgrave Macmillan.

Umekawa, Masami, Tomokazu Sakano and Masayuki Rikihisa eds., 2006, *Gendai Igirisu Seiji* [Contemporary British Politics], Tokyo: Seibundoh.

van Dijk, Teun, 1993, *Elite Discourse and Racism*, London: Sage.

Vertovec, Steven, 2007, *New Complexities of Cohesion in Britain: Super-diversity, Transnationalism and Civil-integration*, West Yorkshire: Communities and Local Government Publications.

Vintges, Karen, 2012, 'Muslim Women in the Western Media: Foucault Agency, Governmentality and Ethics', *European Journal of Women's Studies*, 19(3): 283–98.

Virdee, Pippa, 2006, *Coming to Coventry: Stories from the South Asian Pioneers*, Coventry: Coventry Teaching PCT & The Herbert.

Visram, Rozina, 1986, *Ayahs, Lascars and Princes: Indians in Britain 1700–1947*, London: Pluto Press.

————, 2002, *Asians in Britain: 400 Years of History*, London: Pluto Press.

Voas, David and Alasdair Crockett, 2005, 'Religion in Britain: Neither Believing nor Belonging', *Sociology of Religion*, 39(1): 11–28.

Wadud, Amina, 1999, *Qur'an and Woman: Rereading the Sacred Text from a Woman's Perspective*, Oxford: Oxford University Press.

————, 2006, *Inside the Gender Jihad: Women's Reform in Islam*, Oxford: Oneworld.

Wahhab, Iqbal, 1989, *Muslims in Britain: Profile of a Community*, London: Runnymede Trust.

Walford, Geoffrey, 1998, 'Durkheim, Democracy and Diversity: Some Thoughts on Recent Changes in England and Wales', in Geoffrey Walford and W. S. F. Pickering eds., *Durkheim and Modern Education*, London: Routledge.

Walzer, Michael, 2004, *Politics and Passion: Toward a More Egalitarian Liberalism*, New Haven: Yale University Press.

Watson, James L. ed., 1977, *Between Two Cultures: Migrants and Minorities in Britain*, Oxford: Basil Blackwell.

Watson, Richard, 2017, 'Has al-Muhajiroun been underestimated?', *BBC News*, 27 June 2017. https://www.bbc.com/news/uk-40355491 (accessed 03 July 2022).

Watt, William Montgomery, 1991, *Muslim-Christian Encounters: Perceptions and Misperceptions*, London: Routledge.

Weber, Max, 1956, *Wirtschaft und Gesellschaft, 4 auflage*, Tübingen: J. C. B. Mohr.

————, 1968, *Economy and Society*, Berkeley: University of California Press.

Werbner, Pnina, 1988, 'Taking and Giving: Working Women and Female Bonds in a Pakistan Immigrant Neighbourhood', in Sallie Westwood and Parminder Bhachu eds., *Enterprising Women: Ethnicity, Economy and Gender Relations*, London: Routledge.

——, 1994, 'Islamic Radicalism and the Gulf War: Lay Preachers and Political Dissent among British Pakistanis', in Bernard Lewis and Dominique Schnapper eds., *Muslims in Europe*, London: Pinter.

——, 1996, 'Essentialising the Other: A Critical Response', in Terence Ranger, Yunas Samad and Ossie Stuart eds., *Culture, Identity and Politics: Ethnic Minorities in Britain*, Aldershot: Avebury.

——, 1997, 'Introduction: The Dialectics of Cultural Hybridity', in Pnina Werbner and Tariq Modood eds., *Debating Cultural Hybridity: Multicultural Identities and the Politics of Anti-racism*, London: Zed Books.

——, 2002, *Imagined Diasporas Among Manchester Muslims: The Public Performance of Pakistani Transnational Identity Politics*, Oxford: James Currey.

Wieviorka, Michel, 2005, *La différence – identités culturelles: enjeux, débats et politiques*, Paris: Éditions de l'Aube.

——, 2012, 'Multiculturalism: A Concept to be Redefined and Certainly Not Replaced by the Extremely Vague Term of Interculturalism', *Journal of Intercultural Studies*, 33(2): 225–31.

Willig, Carla, 2012, 'Perspectives on the Epistemological Bases for Qualitative Research', in Harris Cooper ed., *APA Handbook of Research Methods in Psychology, volume 1, Foundations, Planning, Measures, and Psychometrics*, Washington D.C.: American Psychological Association.

Wilson, Amrit, 1978, *Finding a Voice: Asian Women in Britain*, London: Virago.

Wolf, Martin, 2005, 'When Multiculturalism Is a Nonsense', *The Financial Times*, 31 August 2005. https://www.ft.com/content/ff41a586-197f-11da-804e-00000e2511c8 (accessed 03 January 2019).

Wolfers, Arnold, 1962, *Discord and Collaboration: Essays on International Politics*, Baltimore: Johns Hopkins University Press.

Woodhead, Linda, 2013, 'Tactical and Strategic Religion', in Nathal Dessing, Nadia Jeldtoft, Jørgen Nielsen and Linda Woodhead eds., *Everyday Lived Islam in Europe*, Farnham: Ashgate Publishing.

Woodward, Kath, 2004, 'Questions of Identity', in Kath Woodward ed., *Questioning Identity: Gender, Class, Ethnicity*, London: Routledge.

Yagi, Kumiko, 2010, 'Tayoka suru Isuramu no Katachi: "Zokujinka" no Motarasu Kanousei' [The Role of 'Lay' Muslims in Transforming Islam], *Sogo Bunka Kenkyu* [Trans-Cultural Studies], 13: 119-34.

——, 2011, *Gurobaruka to Isuramu: Ejiputo no 'Zokujin' Sekkyoshi tachi* [Globalization and Islam: Egypt's 'Philistine' Preachers], Kyoto: Sekaishisosha.

Yamada, Yoko, 2007, 'Raifu Hisutori Intabyu' [Life History Interview], in Yoko Yamada ed., *Shitsuteki Shinrigaku no Hoho: Katari wo Kiku* [Methods in Qualitative Psychology: Listening to Narratives], Tokyo: Shinyosha.

Yamashita, Yasuyuki, 2018, 'Haiburiddo Bunka to shite no Furansu no Atarashii Musurimu: Shinko Jissen wo Kaihi Suru Imin Daini Sedai no Musurimu no Katari kara' [A New Islam in France as a Hybrid Culture: Analysis of the Narrative of a Second-generation Muslim Evading Religious Practices], *Soshioroji* [Sociology], 63(1): 39–57.

————, 2022, 'Assimilation and Postcoloniality from a Micro Perspective: A Narrative of Laila, a Highly Educated French Muslim Woman', *Soshioroji* [Sociology], 67(1): 21-39.

Yuval-Davis, Nira, 1997, *Gender and Nation*, London: Sage.

Yuval-Davis, Nira and Floya Anthias eds., 1989, *Women-Nation-State*, London: Sage.

Zaman, Dina, 2007, *I Am Muslim*, Kuala Lumpur: Silverfish Books.

Zebiri, Kate, 2008, *British Muslim Converts: Choosing Alternative Lives*, Oxford: Oneworld.

Žižek, Slavoj, 2008, 'Tolerance as an Ideological Category', *Critical Inquiry*, 34(4): 660–82.

Index

Personal

Abase, Amira   xv
Abu Bakr   200
Ahmed, Leila   253
Aisha   246–7, 253, 293
Ali   33, 200
Ali, Muhammed   104
Ali, Yasmin   85
al-Nabhani, Taqi al-Din   70
Althusser, Louis   23, 92, 100
Al Za'ayr   178
Ameli, Saied   201
Appadurai, Arjun   27
Appiah, Anthony   99
Asad, Talal   178

Bagguley, Paul   232
Ballard, Roger   83
Banerjee, Pallavi   86
Basit, Tehmina   90, 200
Baubérot, Jean   228
Beck, Ulrich   100, 298
Begum, Shamima   xv, xviii, 30
Begum, Sharmeena   xv, xviii
Berman, Paul   27
Bhabha, Homi   83
Bhimji, Fazila   111–2
Bhopal, Kalwant   233
bin Laden, Osama   4, 135
Blair, Tony   29, 44, 47, 54–6, 257
Blunkett, David   48, 51
Bouchard, Gérard   29
Bourdieu, Pierre   95
Brah, Avtar   84
Braun, Virginia   115
Brown, Gordon   29, 55-6, 71, 179
Bullock, Katherine   20
Bush, George W.   4
Bush, Laura   21, 30
Butler, Judith   23, 100–1
Byrne, Liam   48

Cameron, David   14, 58, 70, 179
Cantle, Ted   108
Charles III   xii
Clarke, Victoria   115
Cohen, Abner   10
Contractor, Sariya   90
Cook, Robin   179
Corman, Crystal   100
Crenshaw, Kimberlé Williams   84

de Certeau, Michel   123
DeHanas, Daniel Nilsson   112, 123
Dehlawi, Waliullah   201
Derrida, Jacques   82
Du Bois, W. E. B.   3, 78, 146
Durkheim, Emile   71, 203

Elizabeth I   33
Elizabeth II   xi
Erikson, Erik   8

Fletcher, Denise   114
Fortuyn, Pim   31
Foucault, Michel   22, 90, 96, 100
Freud, Sigmund   8
Frisk, Sylva   100
Fujiwara, Satoko   28

Gadamer, Hans-Georg   100
Geertz, Clifford   77, 226
George VI   xi
Giddens, Anthony   ix–x, 9, 24, 93–4, 96, 292,
   298, 300
Gillespie, Marie   150
Gilligan, Andrew   107
Gilroy, Paul   24, 88
Goffman, Erving   ix, 112, 128
Goto, Emi   260, 264
Gove, Michael   48, 51, 70
Griffin, Nick   xvi

349

Habermas, Jürgen ix–x, 96, 101, 133
Hall, Stuart 81–3, 87 99
Hammami, Rema 257
Hattersley, Roy 69
Hegel, G. W. F. 78
Hessini, Leila 91
Hildbrand, Pierre-Antoine 30
Honeyford, Ray 69
Hopf, Christel 123
Hoque, Aminul 111, 288
Howard, John 14
Howe, Melissa 85
Hummon, David 127
Husain, Ed viii, 50–1, 70, 107
Hussain, Mahtab 32, 126
Hussain, Saddam 47
Hussain, Yasmin 232
Hutnik, Nimmi 8

Izutsu, Toshihiko 303

Jacobson, Jessica 111
Javid, Sajid xv, xviii,
Jenkins, Roy 69
John of Damascus 19
Jose, Maria Aznar 14

Kabeer, Naila 95
Kabir, Nahid 111
Kahf, Mohja 20, 285–6
Kalra, Virinder 41, 85
Keith, Michael 301
Kelly, Ruth 14, 48
Khadija 246–8, 253, 293
Khan, Sadiq 179
Khan, Saira 152
Khan, Sidique Mohammad 12
Khomeini, Ayatollah 45, 47

Lamont, Norman 51
Lash, Scott 300
Lawrence, Stephen 44
Lea, John 75
Lewis, Philip viii, 48–9, 80
Livingstone, Kenneth 54
Louis XIV 67

Loyd, Anthony xv
Luhmann, Niklas ix, xi

Macfie, Alexander 19
Mahmood, Saba 90–1, 288
Malik, Shahid 179
Mandaville, Peter 220, 225
Marquand, David 180
Marx, Karl 27, 284–5
Maryam (Maria) 255
Matsuyama, Yohei 303
McEwan, Lord 2
Mead, G. H. 78
Merkel, Angela 14
Mernissi, Fatima 251
Miles, Robert 68
Minhas, Rehana 84
Modood, Tariq 45, 88, 294
Mohammed, Zara xii,
Mu'awiya 33
Muhammad viii, 19, 29–30, 33, 45, 67, 101,
  152, 200, 228, 246–7, 253, 275, 304

Naik, Zakir 178
Naito, Masanori 299
Nawaz, Maajid 70, 107
Newman, Cathy 146–7

Okin, Susan 11
Omaar, Rageh 302

Panayi, Panikos 68
Parekh, Bhikhu 99, 295
Pennycook, Alastair 22
Phalet, Karen 117
Philippot, Florian 31
Phillips, Anne 10
Phillips, Deborah 303
Phillips, Trevor 14, 28, 180
Pickles, Eric 51
Pile, Steve 301
Powell, Enoch 42, 54

Quilliam, Abdullah (Quilliam, William Henry)
  67

Ramadan, Tariq   97–8, 100, 301
Rashid, Naaz   30
Raza, Ahmed   201
Relph, Edward   127
Rigby, Lee   151
Roald, Anne Sofie   111
Robert, Na'ima   7
Rushdie, Salman   45–7

Sahin, Abdullah   88, 117–8, 217, 273
Said, Edward   19, 143
Sakurai, Atsushi   114
Salmond, Alex   71
Sarkozy, Nicolas   14
Sartre, Jean-Paul   29
Sarwar, Ghulam   272
Schütz, Alfred   113
Shain, Farzana   84
Shamsie, Kamila   129, 150
Shaw, Alison   83
Smith, Dorothy   22
Smith, Michael   75
Spivak, Gayatri   21

Stivens, Malia   100
Straw, Jack   55, 257
Sultana, Kadiza   xv

Taylor, Charles   ix, 78–9, 82, 100–1
Thatcher, Margaret   43, 54, 85
Trump, Donald   70
Tynkkynen, Sebastian   31

Umar   200
Uthman   200

Warsi, Baroness   70, 179
Watt, William   29
Weber, Max   94, 99, 203
Werbner, Pnina   46
Wieviorka, Michel   226
Williams, Pharrell   200

Yamashita, Yasuyuki   303
Young, Jock   75

Zebiri, Kate   88

Subject

7/7   xvi, 6, 12, 14, 17, 47–8, 52, 54, 57–8, 70, 142, 179
  post-——   14, 16, 19, 51–2, 56–8, 79–80, 87, 257
9/11   xviii, 3–4, 6, 12, 16, 18, 21, 45, 47, 58, 74, 114, 117, 129–36, 144–5, 150, 152, 179, 183, 203, 205, 298, 302
  post-——   viii, xi–xii, xvii, 4–5, 19, 24, 26, 74, 97, 108, 113, 126–9, 134, 150, 205, 233, 291–2, 296, 300–1

agency   5, 7, 8, 26, 89–93, 95, 97, 116, 227, 231, 233, 252, 257, 288, 297, 301
alcohol   101, 161–2, 164–6   see also khamr
aqidah (creed or six articles of faith)   97, 267, 271, 287
aspirational culture   239
assimilationism   13
  postmodern ——   88

Barelvi   200–1

being British   xvii, 5, 25, 30, 48, 55–6, 146, 150, 155–60, 167–9, 171, 173, 176–7, 183, 187–8, 197, 291, 294
biradari (kinship network)   37, 40–1, 49, 65, 79, 86, 185, 195, 199, 216
  quasi-——   40, 41
BNP (British National Party)   xvi
British Empire   33–7, 56, 67, 105, 294
British Nationality Act
  —— 1948   38, 68
  —— 1981   43
Britishness   viii, 16–7, 44, 50, 53–8, 63, 68, 71, 73, 83, 88, 99, 154–181, 291, 295, 301

cartoon controversy   xviii
citizenship
  —— test   24
clash of civilizations   299–300
commercialism   143, 261, 284–5
Committee for Racial Equality   99

Commonwealth Immigrants Act
—— 1962   38, 68
—— 1968   39
community cohesion   viii, 16–7, 52–3, 56
   Institute of —— (ICoCo)   viii, xiii, xvi
constructs   113–4
contact hypothesis   52, 70
conveyor belt theory   70
Council of Europe   15, 29, 86–7
cultural studies   27, 81
culturalization of politics   91
culture
   cultural navigator   83–4
   cultural pathology   80, 232
   cultural relativism   92
   differentiation between —— and
      religion   25–6, 184–5, 187, 189, 192,
      197, 200, 205, 292, 296–7
   essentialist understanding of ——   10, 53
   —— of migration   37–8

democracy
   anti- ——   4
   democratic values   7, 15–7, 21, 55–6, 73,
      81, 87, 145, 155–6, 197, 231, 292, 301
   war for ——   6
Deobandi   200–1
Department for Communities and Local
   Government   14, 108
dialectic of control   x, 96, 301
diaspora   73, 85, 99, 150, 182, 185, 304
diasporic space   82–3, 105, 176, 199
différance   82
dilemma between efficiency and openness   123
din (way of life or religion)   178
   see also religious way of life
discourse   viii–ix, xvii, 4–7, 12–24
distinction   205–9
double consciousness   2–5, 10, 24, 78, 128,
   146, 298, 303
drinking   160–8, 173–6, 267, 294

e-Jihad   225
East London   xv, 67, 103, 105–6, 110–1,
   169–70, 200, 231, 233, 288
East London Mosque (ELM)   xii, 107, 109, 250
Education Reform Act 1988   43

elastic orthodoxy   295
embedment
   dis- ——   217, 295
   re- ——   x, 41, 98, 217, 295, 298
English Defense League   viii, 108
Englishness   17, 63, 83, 155
ethnicity
   new ethnicities   82–3, 87–9
   old ethnicities   81–2, 87–8
ethnoscape   54

faith
   democratisation of ——   26, 225
   individualisation of ——   200, 222–3, 226,
      276, 293, 298
family
   —— honour   79, 185, 199, 236, 241
   —— reunion   40–1, 43, 79
fatwa (legal ruling)   45, 51
   cyber ——   225
feminism
   feminist state   21
   black ——   85
   Islamic ——   249–50
   minority ——   85, 89, 92
   post-colonial ——   89
fitna (trial or affliction)   264
   female ——   264
Further and Higher Education Act 1992   65

gender apartheid   7
Government of India Act 1858   34
governmentality   24
hadith (collection of Muhammad's sayings and
      actions)   101, 208, 218–9, 221–2, 243,
      253, 275
hajj (pilgrimage)   148, 274, 282–3, 287–8, 293,
      300
halal (permissible or lawful)   117, 196
   —— food   13, 43, 171, 173–4, 222
Hanafi   122, 193, 200, 207
haram (forbidden)   196
haya (bashfulness or shyness)   91, 260, 264, 288
   see also shyness
headscarf / veil controversy   69, 286, 299

Index

hijab *see also* scarf and veil
  hijabisation 257
  wearing a —— for God 265, 286
Hizb al-Tahrir 70
home 158–60
home-grown terrorist 12–3, 54, 178
Huguenot 67, 106

ibadah (worship or five pillars of Islam) 97,
  205–6, 267, 282, 287
identity
  —— management 25, 97, 108, 112, 291–3
  —— politics 8–12, 23, 73
  collective —— 27, 82, 226–7
  closedness of —— 73–4, 78–9, 291
  fluid —— 52–6, 177
  hybrid —— 83, 88, 93
  hyphenated —— 11
  multiple —— 11, 32, 53, 82, 126, 160
  national —— 10, 16–7, 44, 54–6, 62, 83,
    155, 291, 297
  openness of —— 73–4, 86, 89, 291
  primordial —— 77–9, 81, 88, 92
  sub-national —— 63
ijma (consensus) 101, 228
ijtihad (independent reasoning) 98, 101, 213–4,
  220–5, 227–8, 250–1. 253, 292, 295
  doors of —— 250, 253
ilm (knowledge) 133, 208, 242 *see also* Islamic
  knowledge and religious knowledge
  —— *fiqh* (Islamic jurisprudence) 208
imam (prayer leader of a mosque) 49, 215–7,
  221–2, 225
iman (faith) 162, 178, 282
in-between-two-cultures theory 79–81, 89,
  92–3, 185, 299
incommensurability 300
information
  informationalised society 292
  —— Technology 282, 292
insider ix, 111, 290, 303
  —— approach ix, 111, 301
Institute of Community Cohesion (iCoCo)
  viii, xiii, xvi, 108
integration
  —— contract 24
  Commission on —— and Cohesion 52–3, 71

duty to —— 21, 54
integrationist 296–7
interactive constructionism 114
interculturalism 15–7, 24, 29, 52–3, 56, 71,
  81–4, 86, 88, 93
Internet xi, 26, 66, 123, 136, 204, 217–26,
  228, 250, 292
interpretive
  —— approach 113–4
  —— objectivism 114–5, 300
intersectionality 84–6, 139, 297
Islam
  adaptive ——
  —— as a system of egalitarianism 244
  Islamic knowledge x, 26, 66, 101, 201,
    203–29, 245, 247, 250–1, 282, 292, 298, 301
    see also ilm and religious knowledge
  Islamic law 46–7, 76, 100, 193, 247
    see also sharia
  my —— 222, 293
  protestantisation of —— 204
Islamophobia viii, xii, 18–22, 31, 51, 135,
  171, 247, 301–2
  gay-friendly —— 31

jahiliyyah (pre-Islamic period or 'unenlightened
  state) 208, 228, 253
Jamaat-e-Islami 107
judgment 148, 164, 214, 216, 271, 275–6, 293

kasb (doctrine of the acquisition) 272
khajal / kusuf (embarrassment) 260
khalifah (political leader or agent of God)
  33, 272
khamr (wine or alcohol) 101 *see also* alcohol
knowledge
  background —— 95–6, 226
  discursive —— 95–6, 226, 300
  religious —— x–xi, 26, 203–4, 206–8, 214,
    220, 222–8, 243, 245, 278, 285, 295, 298,
    302 *see also ilm* and Islamic knowledge
  power / —— 22, 95
  shopping around for religious —— 223
laïcité 172, 179–80, 228, 299
leniency 148, 188–92, 194, 267, 285, 295
liberal nationalism viii, xvii, 15–7, 24, 29,
  52–6, 71, 86

353

lived religion 299
Local Government Act 1966 42, 68
Local Government Grants Act 1969 42
London Olympics 54, 179

madrasa (school of Islamic instruction) 279
marriage
  arranged —— 4, 6, 46, 81, 186–7, 190, 195–7, 201, 252, 292
  forced ——
  love —— 186–7, 196–7
Maryam Centre 250
McCarran–Walter Act 36
middle-class values 238, 252
minority
  ethnic —— 13, 28, 42, 53, 59, 68–9, 76, 83, 155–6, 178, 180, 255, 294
  national —— 28, 156, 178
moral panic 4, 27
moratorium 267, 275, 285
mujtahadat (issues without explicit provisions) 228
mujtahid (one who exercises independent reasoning) 228
Multicultural space 25, 154–81, 183, 199, 213, 228, 291, 293–5
Multiculturalism xvi, 2–31, 33, 42–5, 47, 53, 57, 68–9, 73, 81–2, 86–8, 91–2, 108, 169, 293–7, 303
  failure of —— 12–5, 47, 58
  irony of —— 10
  post- —— viii, 16, 28
  state —— 14, 44
murder of Stephen Lawrence 44
muscular liberalism 21
Muslim
  —— Council of Britain (MCB) xii, 44–5, 58, 69
  —— tag 144–5
  being —— xvii, 5, 25, 48, 86, 97, 108, 129–30, 146, 155, 160, 166, 168–70, 176, 183, 188, 197, 211–2, 267, 271, 291, 294, 296
  British —— viii–ix, xviii, 5, 12, 25, 32–71, 74, 76–7, 80, 88, 112, 116–7, 119, 129, 150, 152, 175, 201, 215–6, 233, 249, 291, 295–6, 303
  diffused mode of —— 117–8, 201
  European —— 97–8, 287, 296, 299

  exploratory mode of —— 117–8
  foreclosed mode of —— 117–8
  London —— Centre xiii, 109, 179
  Muslimness 126, 129, 135, 138, 140
  private —— 117–8, 201
  selective —— 117–8
  strict —— 117–8
myth of return 41, 83–4

namaz (prayer) 205
nasiha (advice or counsel) 178
Navigation Act 1660 67
New Commonwealth 36, 38–40, 59, 99, 105
new folk devil 4
New Labour 14, 17, 29–30, 44–5, 47–8, 51, 54–5, 59, 71, 83, 177, 179
nur (light) 208

objectification 66, 128
ontological security 8–12
orientalism 18–22
other
  othering 5, 17–9, 22, 24, 45, 57, 61, 137
  otherness 58, 74, 256
  generalized —— 78
  significant —— 78–9
outsider ix, xi, 25, 110–4, 290, 303
  —— approach 110–4

parallel lives 47–52, 70, 81
positionality 81
positivist approach 113
post-secular ix–x, 101
post-structuralism 81
post-traditional society 93–4
preacher 57, 178, 218–9, 221, 223, 225
Public Order Act 1986 45

qadar (predestination) 271–2
qiyas (analogical reasoning) 101
Quran 41, 45, 71, 101, 160, 162, 178, 183, 188, 191, 194, 200, 204–5. 208, 210–1, 214–5, 217–22, 228, 250–1, 255, 272, 276, 286–8, 293, 300, 303

Index

Race Relations Act
  —— 1965   42, 69
  —— 1968   42, 69
  —— 1976   42, 45, 6–9
Race Relations (Amendment) Act 2000   44
racial dualism   75
racism
  anti- ——   6, 17, 58
  institutional ——   17, 25, 44, 58, 65, 68, 75, 137–42, 150–1
  overt ——   75
  street ——   25, 134–7, 142
rapport   110–2
  over- ——   110
Rasulullah (the Messenger of Allah)   244
recognition
  misrecognition   46, 78
  politics of ——   10, 78–9, 82
reflexive
  —— modernisation theory   ix–x, 92–8, 291, 297–8
  —— modernity   xi, 5, 25, 74, 93–4, 96, 291–3, 300
  —— project   24, 94
reflexivity
  aesthetic ——   300
  cognitive ——   300
relative deprivation   5, 75
Roman Catholic Relief Act 1829   68
Runnymede Trust   18–9
Rushdie Affair   ix, 45–7, 69, 76, 97, 129, 203

sahaba (companions of the Prophet)   101, 200
salaf (predecessors)   100
Salafi
  —— reformism   97, 100
  Salafism   100, 201
scarf   *see also* hijab and veil
  headscarf controversy   69, 286
secularisation   59, 203, 255, 302
self   *see also* hijab and veil
  —— -presentation   ix–x, 24–5, 112–4, 123, 184, 188, 244
  —— -segregation   47, 51, 81, 155
  cultured ——   24
  entrepreneurial ——   24

  technologies of the ——   90
sexism   262, 284–5
shahada (confession of faith)   282
sharia (Islamic law)   30, 57, 70, 100, 228
  see also Islamic law
sheikh   223–5, 229
  —— Google   218
Shia   193, 200–1
  Shiite   111
shyness   90–1, 260, 288   *see also haya*
social systems theory   xi, 295
spectacle   3, 27
stigma   ix, 10, 25, 110, 113, 127–9, 131, 146, 150, 266
Sufism (mysticism)   58, 229, 201, 224
sunnah (actions and saying of the Prophet)   98, 101, 200, 228, 247
Sunni   67, 100, 122, 193–4, 200–1
surah (chapter)   214, 219, 287

tactics   123
taqlid (imitation)   228
terrorism   xvii, 4, 14, 18, 21, 23, 28, 30, 51, 54, 56–8, 97, 131–2, 142–6, 151, 183
  counter- ——   30, 52, 57
Terrorism Act
  —— 2000   151
  —— 2006   30
test   178, 271–6, 287
thrownness   9
translation   ix–xi, 101, 133–4, 300
Trojan Horse Scandal   51
ulama (religious scholar)   101, 208, 220, 225, 228–9, 250
umma (Global Islamic community)   46–7, 76, 193, 283

veil   *see also* hijab and scarf
  inner ——   265–271
  outer ——   265–271
Wahhabism   201
way of life
  British ——   68, 163, 167, 169, 176, 198, 242, 258, 294
  Islamic ——   162–3, 167, 169, 176, 178, 184, 292   *see also din*

355

Printed in the USA
CPSIA information can be obtained
at www.ICGtesting.com
LVHW021824250524
780636LV00006B/1